MAINE

A Narrative History

Books by Neil Rolde

Maine: A Narrative History
Rio Grande Do Norte (1984)
So You Think You Know Maine (1984)
Sir William Pepperrell of Colonial New England (1982)
York is Living History (1975)

Maine

A Narrative History

Neil Rolde

TILBURY HOUSE, PUBLISHERS
Gardiner, Maine

Tilbury House, Publishers
The Boston Building
132 Water Street
Gardiner, Maine 04345

Third Printing
Copyright © 1990 by Neil Rolde

Designed on Crummett Mountain by Edith Allard
Layout by Nina Medina, Basil Hill Graphics, Somerville, Maine

Library of Congress Catalog Card Number 90-83499
ISBN 0-88448-069-0

CONTENTS

INTRODUCTION

Neil Rolde's *Maine: A Narrative History,* is the most recent in a
long tradition of publications which examine the state's rich past.
Beginning in the late eighteenth century when the first of these
works appeared, each successive analysis has contributed in its own
fashion to the study of Maine history. Likewise, this new volume
presents a fresh approach to the subject with a particular concentration on politics and political figures. This is best appreciated
when reviewed in the context of the earlier histories.

In 1795 James Sullivan's *The History of the District of Maine*
was published in Boston. Among the first of the state histories
written in this country, Sullivan's work was, as he described it, an
attempt to organize known information about the region into one
"distinct History." Sullivan's volume was followed a generation
later by William D. Williamson's *History of the State of Maine*
published in 1832. This work is noteworthy for its copious refer-
ences to primary documents and its lengthy description of the
coast, waterways, flora, and fauna, the latter of which reflect the
scientific curiosity of the early nineteenth century. More than a
half century passed before the appearance in 1875 of John S. C.
Abbott's *The History of Maine from the Earliest Discovery of the
Region by the Northmen Until the Present Time.* The state and nation
had changed dramatically during this period, and Abbott's opus
reflects this, particularly in its discussion of such topics as education and industry. Nonetheless, its romantic style, while highly
popular at the time, came at the expense of accurate history. It was
not until the publication in 1919 of Louis C. Hatch's *Maine: A
History* that the first highly readable scholarly text appeared.
Prepared on the eve of the centennial of Maine's statehood, this
work was, in the words of its author, "primarily a political his-

tory..." with a chief goal of "reviving the memory of half-forgotten leaders of former days...." The subsequent histories of Harrie B. Coe (1928) and Richard A. Hebert (1951) entitled, respectively, *Maine: Resources, Attractions, and Its People* and *Modern Maine: Its Historic Background, People and Resources*, have updated Hatch and included biographies of notable twentieth century individuals.

Neil Rolde brings to the present work a longstanding interest in Maine history combined with the insight of a seasoned politician and the pen of an experienced writer. These attributes provide the framework for *Maine: A Narrative History*. It is principally a study of the state's development as seen through the actions of its political figures, who have represented all aspects of society. However, this is by no means a rewriting of Hatch. While they naturally invite comparison, Neil Rolde highlights his narrative with skillfully crafted biographical vignettes of the individuals about whose activities he writes. Our understanding of the events which have effected the state's history is thereby much enhanced by our ability to more fully appreciate the lives of those who shaped it. Neil Rolde's book is the Maine history of our time, an engaging yet truthful account worthy of the independent and enterprising people whose story it tells.

Earle G. Shettleworth, Jr., Director
Maine Historic Preservation Commission

FOREWORD

There is a definite mystery about any particular body politic: how did it come into being, how did its boundaries form, how did it develop, what effect on its people does its natural landscape have, who are its people, what is special about them, what might have happened differently? The questions multiply, whether one is writing about a town, a county, a province, a state, a nation.

Maine is a singular jurisdiction, one of 50, within a powerful and unique country. To most Americans, it has several meanings. It is at once remote, rural, out of the way...yet it is not just a boondocks, peopled by quaint Yankees who say "Ayuh." The name comes trippingly to the tongue as one defines the national geographical limits of "from Maine to California." It is where the U.S.A. starts, so to speak. An anchor in the Northeast is another way of looking at it...Maine is pine trees beside a sylvan lake. Maine is a coastline of cubistic rocks splashed with lacy, salty spray. Maine is a lobster in calloused hands. Maine is lean, angular, spare and, well, sort of...full of old-fashioned virtue. It is also a place of pristine beauty where rich people from the cities (and now, even the President of the United States) go to vacation.

But Maine is also a long and often violent history, a place of conflict, a land fought over and only partly settled, even to this day. Half its land area still has no organized towns. In an area of 33,000 square miles, only about 1.2 million people live. Until very recently, the outflow of its population to other parts of America was considered a norm. Using today's vernacular, it has been called, a "kinder, gentler place," and perhaps subliminally, that special quality of neighborliness exhibited by Maine people derives from the fact that the most ambitious, the most driven, among their forebears went off somewhere else, leaving behind the most stable, the most adjusted, to the bareness of rock-bound lives.

If there is a continuity to Maine—a single thread to its history—it lies in this mystery of why it did become a separate place. The political currents that led to statehood were perhaps mere surface manifestations of an underlying social bedrock. "Scratch a Russian and you'll find a Tatar," the old saying goes. *Scratch a Mainer and you'll find a Jeffersonian,* is a statement that could be made. It was a long way to Federalist Massachusetts for those hard-scrabble Yankees up on the northeast frontiers and they pulled together a sense of distinct territoriality out of populist traditions that went back many years, and, as in the rest of the United States, gave it the flexibility to accept new generations, including large numbers of people of foreign origin. Such a State mini-melting pot now produces distilled types—like lobstermen with French or Lithuanian or Polish surnames, every bit as Maine in their oilskins and with their dry humor as those quintessential Anglo-Saxon coastal folks, the Looks and Alleys of downeast Jonesport. And so on, through the rest of Maine society, which has every so quietly built its own culture that it imparts to all of its denizens.

A problem for the writer of history is whether to try to impose a point of view on the mass of scattered documentation of events that have survived the ages. No one can ever know the true complete picture of every life lived, every deed carried out, within no matter how limited a geographical area. Perhaps someday exciting enough records will be found for an author to do the portrait of a single Maine community through the experiences of its common citizens in the same microcosmic, historico-sociological fashion in which the French writer Le Roy Ladurie immortalized Montaillou in medieval Provence. That is history in depth; what is attempted here is history in breadth—as much as possible through the ordinary people of whom we have a trace, but also focusing on those who have emerged from the ordinary ranks as players, particularly political players, of note.

On the land between the Piscataqua and St. John Rivers, this cast of historic characters has performed a drama that the historian, in retrospect, must shape into narrative form. The very word *history*, after all, contains the word *story*. So that is what I have tried to tell, a tale of sorts, focused on how Maine came to be. Volumes of material had to be sifted, and the selection, admittedly, can be seen as random and subjective, especially by those who might find their favorite parts or special interests left out.

Time and space are the writer's enemies. Maine should be a quick story—it's not a big or a populous place and nowhere near as old as any comparable site in Europe or Asia. But the historic flavor of this small corner of America needs room for its rich diversity to be explained, to be narrated, even to be sung in bits of poetry and scraps of fiction intermingled with the exposition of facts.

Maine, as it was, as it came to be, as it continues—updated— that is the living legend now once again told.

Maine

A Narrative History

CHAPTER One

PRE-HISTORY

The Stone Age

For centuries, under a sheet of ice a mile thick, Maine slowly,
unconsciously, was taking shape. The great glacier entombed much
more than the present outline of the State, extending eastward out
to sea well beyond today's rock-bound shore. Only to the southwest
did patches of drab tundra break the white monotony, as if
harbingers of the greenery to come. Then, about 14,000 years ago,
the vast frozen mass began to melt and retreat. The sea flooded in
as far from the coast as East Millinockett and Bingham, but withdrew when the land rose in most places, leaving a collection of gulf
islands that once were high points and a scoured landscape ready to
turn into lakes and forests.

Trees followed. Willows and alders came first, about 12,000
years ago, and then spruce and poplar. Not long afterward—
perhaps 11,500 years ago—humans appeared in Maine.

These were "Paleo Indians," to use the lingo of those who
study them—*paleo* meaning *old* in Greek. Digs in Oxford and
Piscataquis Counties have recently unearthed two of their ancient
encampments.

The former, the Vail Site, lies beneath Azicohos Lake, a
Central Maine Power Company impoundment at the headwaters of
the Androscoggin River. In 1980, when the water level dropped
low enough, a local fishing guide and amateur arrowhead collector
named Francis Vail Jr. was able to confirm that the Paleo Indians
had a "killing ground" here. It was a point along a narrow river

crossing where caribou herds were intercepted and slaughtered. This site, alone, yielded 10,000 specimens of flaked tools, weapons and other artifacts, dating back 11,200 years.

The second major Paleo Indian find was much farther north, around Munsungan and Chase Lakes, 40 miles above Baxter State Park. It was essentially a center for the production of tools and weapons, where *chert*, a highly pliable fine-grained rock, was mined, producing useful items in attractively colored red, grey, black, green and mottled hues until as late as only 5,000 years ago.

The Paleo Indians then disappear. Their place is taken by native inhabitants whom the specialists have dubbed as belonging to the "Archaic," with, typically, sub-classifications into *Early*, *Middle* and *Late* Archaic. In any event, it was a period when the pine forests had begun and, intermixed with birch and oak, were creating woods too thick for good deer hunting. Therefore, fish diets became important. Along the rivers, these people could catch anadromous species like salmon, shad and alewives when they came to spawn and from the lakes, they could pull brook trout, togue and whitefish. At the well-known Hirundo Site near Alton in Penobscot County, Middle Archaic Indians have left projectile points (arrowheads) 7,000 years old.

By 4,500 years ago, the Archaic Indians were also gone. They were replaced by the most famous of all Maine's prehistoric folks— the mysterious Red Paint People.

The discovery of Indian graves where quantities of red ochre were found along with sophisticatedly fashioned ceremonial objects led to the sensational myth of the *Lost Red Paint People*. On a more prosaic level, certain scientists have argued that there was no such "people," only a burial cult. Red Paint cemeteries, which have been located as far north as central Labrador and northern Newfoundland, abound in Maine, but always east of the Kennebec.

On North Haven Island, at the richly varied Turner Site, the Red Paint artifacts were discovered in conjunction with swordfish remains, indicating a sea-going tradition. Then once again, this particular ancient culture was supplanted and a new style intruded itself, typified by its beautifully wrought stone implements, including sculpted stone bowls. The savants labelled this particular way of life the *Susquehanna Tradition*, having traced its origins to Pennsylvania.

When clay pottery was finally made, we enter yet another era, appropriately called the "Ceramic." The best repository of its re-

2

mains in Maine turned out to be on land belonging to a Mr.
DeWitt Goddard at Naskeag Point in the town of Brooklin.
Diggings began there in 1956 and more than 30,000 items formed
the Goddard collection that was donated to the Maine State
Museum by two amateur archaeologists, Guy Mellgren and Ed
Runge, who did the preliminary work.

Among their findings was metal, bringing us beyond the
Ceramic Age and into almost historic times. They found native
copper—sheets, beads and nuggets of it—but most importantly,
they included in their findings a tiny scrap of metal, blackened and
nearly unrecognizable, which was tentatively identified as silver.

That is, it was thought to be a 12th century British penny.
But it wasn't. The entire scholarly world was eventually to be elec-
trified by the startling news that an authenticated Norse coin (for
that's what it was) had been found on the Maine coast. A new
dimension had been added to the pre-history of the Pine Tree
State.

Detail of the Norse Coin

Red Paint People artifacts

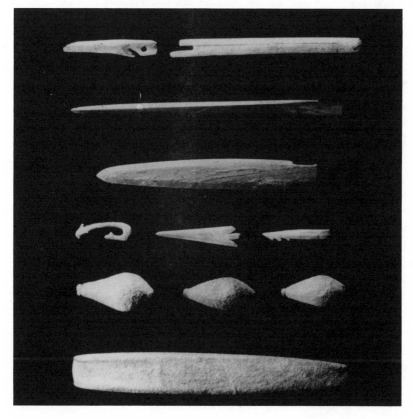

3

Focus

The Red Paint People

The phrase, the "Lost Red Paint People," was coined in the late 19th Century by Warren K. Moorehead, Director of the Peabody Museum at Phillips Academy, Andover. It seemed particularly apt for the romantic mood of the times. Then, again, Moorehead had a penchant for overdramatizing and also for conducting his archaeological digs with less than careful methods. "One of the last self-taught archaeologists in America," as he has been described, Moorehead was not the original discoverer of the Red Paints; he came to do his excavations in Maine only in 1898, abandoning his previous work of exhuming the "Lost Mound Builders of Ohio." But Moorehead is so identified with the term "Red Paint People" that scientists have now given his own name to them. In the official jargon, they are known as the *Moorehead Phase* of the *Laurentian Tradition*.

Actually, it was thirteen years earlier that the Red Paints first came to light, thanks to a Mayor of Bangor, Augustus Hamlin, who examined a batch of pits a farmer showed him near the Penobscot River. Inside were smooth polished stones of extraordinary workmanship covered with red ochre. A Harvard professor and his assistant were drawn to the subject through a paper Hamlin read to a scientific association.

The assistant, Charles Willoughby, then conducted a dig in Maine on the shores of Lake Alamoosook. A scale model he did of it for the Columbian Exposition in Chicago was what caught Warren K. Moorehead's attention and imagination. The popular press of the time fastened on Moorehead's titillating description. Who were these Lost Red Paints? One newspaper even declared that the shallow graves Moorehead was recklessly uncovering were the "lost tombs" of Irish chieftains.

Years later, more important and more scientific finds were made, such as that on North Haven, or at the Nevin Site in Blue Hill. And the emergence of similar sites in Labrador and Newfoundland has postulated a single uniform culture linking Maine and Canada. Those who argue, instead, that the Red Paints were merely a burial cult point to the fact that certain of today's Indian tribes, like the Ojibwa and the Athabascans, associate the color red with death.

Either way, it was a short-lived cultural trait, the existence of these ochre-filled burial grounds, lasting but a thousand years. Their indelible imprint is due mostly to the skill of a clever publicist who promoted the haunting sense of a lost civilization. But for Maine history, they have acquired the status of a living legend.

The Vikings

Another living legend, another lost civilization—with purported ties to Maine—is "Vinland the Good." The Viking sagas tell of the expedition by Leif Ericson, son of Eric the Red, westward from

4

Greenland to an unknown shore, where he planted a colony. Long before the sensational discovery of a Norse coin on the Maine coast, there had been speculation that Leif the Lucky's landfall had been somewhere Downeast.

Maine became directly involved through rune stones found at Spirit Pond and Popham Beach. Cryptograms chiseled into these rocks were given dates by certain scholars who examined them— May 27, 1123 and October 6, 1123 at Spirit Pond and November 29, 1114 at Popham Beach—all fitting the time scale of Leif's adventure. *Poppycock*, declare other savants, who reject all of the North American relics attributed to the Vikings, notwithstanding the extraordinary attention given to some like the Kensington Stone in Minnesota and the Viking Tower in Newport, Rhode Island.

The whole idea can be carried much too far, as it was at Hampton, New Hampshire, close to the Maine border, where local authorities determined that the strange markings on a large rock designated the gravesite of Thorvald Ericson, Leif's brother, who, according to the sagas, was killed by an arrow in a fight with the *Skraelings* ("wretches"), as the Norsemen called the Indians they encountered. EARLY NORSEMEN WERE FIRST VACATIONERS, an uninhibited press agent wrote in an article subsequently, claiming that Thorvald visited Hampton and Rye Beach in the year 1004 "with a party of nomadic brothers" and was buried in Hampton soon after. Given Thorvald's gory end, it seemed a bit much for this unembarrassed booster of the area to conclude that "Thorvald Ericson appreciated the value of a vacation along the Maine-New Hampshire coast."

Such silliness aside, the search for Vinland has long contin-ued to engross inquiring minds. In 1961, a real breakthrough was made, a discovery on the order, as one newspaper unblushingly put it, of Heinrich Schliemann's discovery of Troy. Thanks to a Norwegian lawyer, author and explorer named Helge Ingstad, Vinland appears to have been located on a wind-swept stretch of grassy lowland in northern Newfoundland at a place called L'Anse aux Meadows. Ruins of an unmistakable Viking settlement here were meticulously combed during a six year dig sponsored by the National Geographic Society and Ingstad was able to back his theory with hard scientific data.

What, then, of Vikings in Maine? Helge Ingstad, himself, feels Norsemen may have gone as far south as Maine, New Hampshire and Massachusetts; he simply does not believe "they

5

covered the immense distance from Greenland to New England in one stage. They must have had a more northerly headquarters."

Ingstad's argument seemed sensible enough at the time, prior to the surfacing of the Norse coin in Hancock County. Then, the old question was immediately revived. Had the Vikings, indeed, settled in Maine?

Focus

The Norse Penny

What was recovered of the coin, blackened and distorted as it appeared, measured out to be the size of a dime, or a tad smaller than the original. Over the thousand years since its minting, it had lost tiny bits of material. Little wonder it was mistaken for something else for at least 21 years.

When it was suspected by two experts from London that the silver penny might be Norse rather than British, the world's foremost authority on such coinage, Dr. Kolbjorn Skaare, was brought to Maine.

After intense inspection, he dramatically declared, "I believe the coin in the Maine State Museum is a genuine Norwegian penny struck in the period 1065-80." Several technical criteria, which he explained, had led him to assign it to the reign of King Olav Kyrre, who had ruled Norway from 1066 to 1093.

Next question, as posed by Dr. Skaare: "Is the find as genuine as the coin?"

In other words, had the site in Maine been "salted?" Was this simply a new and audacious case of "Scandiknavery?"

But what made fraud seem most unlikely was the coin's rarity. In 1957,

when the Norse penny was first found, common coins from the Leif Ericson era could have been bought in New York City for a few dollars. If someone had wanted to perpetrate a hoax, it's unlikely they would have tossed the rarest of Norse coins into the midst of an Indian midden, full of shells, animal bones and pottery pieces and hope it would be discovered and identified for what it was.

Because Guy Mellgren, the attending archaeologist, had a Norwegian-sounding name, there was some further skepticism. Yet Mellgren died two weeks before Dr. Skaare's pronouncement, never knowing the coin had been declared authentic.

The final mystery, of course, became how the coin had gotten to Brooklin, Maine.

Dr. Skaare's thesis was that it came during the pre-Columbian age, carried along traditional Viking sailing routes to the west, and because it was once pierced, worn as an ornament or brought as part of a Norse trader's wealth. A different hypothesis has been advanced by Dr. Bruce Bourque of the Maine State Museum. He sees it as having been an item of inter-Indian trade, acquired through the contact of Maine groups

6

with tribes farther north or even Eskimos.

No further Viking relics have been uncovered in Maine (the Spirit Pond rune stones revealed in 1971 are not considered genuine). We are thus no closer to establishing the presence of a Viking settlement in Maine. But the priceless Norse penny in the Maine State Museum, the oldest European object ever found in North America, is a joltingly real reminder that misty legends sometimes have a touch of truth.

The Indians of Maine

Thousands of years separate the caribou killers of Azicohos Lake from birchbark canoers paddling past evergreen forests on the eve of the Age of Discovery. Just as the landscape of Maine had been transformed from tundra and scrub brush into woodland, so, too, had the Paleo Indians evolved into the *Abnaki*, "the people of the dawn."

Their very name denotes an extremely ancient ancestry. Although Native Americans are supposed to have migrated across the Bering Strait from Siberia to this continent, a vital principle of Indian philosophy is that older forms of life dwell in the east, that the people of the sunrise are grandfathers to other tribes. Like the history of the United States, itself, the key Indian sense of direction is from east to west.

One legend says the precursors of the Abnaki, an Ojibwa band, settled on the upper Saco River. There, they formed the Pennacooks who moved toward the ocean and, in turn, created the Sokokis, plus ultimately the Androscoggins, the Wawenocs, the Kennebecs, the Penobscots and the Malecites.

No one knows the exact truth and this welter of tribal names is but an introduction to the confusion of ascertaining political and ethnic boundaries in a vast area of wilderness inhabited primarily by nomads. The Saco River was the only clear dividing line. Below it, the people practiced agriculture and were far more sedentary. These, the French called *Armouchiquois*, to differentiate them from the *Souriquois* and *Etchemins* above the line. All spoke variant tongues of the great Algonquian language family, but even from the Saco to the Penobscot, the differences could be as great as between Italian and French.

The English used a different method of naming the tribes, identifying them by the rivers they lived near—consequently, we have Penobscots, Kennebecs, Androscoggins and Sacos. The sub-tribes like the Pegwackets and Norridgewocks contributed an addi-

7

tional confusion of titles and to Frenchmen like Champlain the
Penobscots were Pentagoets and the Kennebecs the Quinnebequy
and also the Indians had their own names for themselves so that
the Malecites, who had been given that name by their enemies the
Micmacs (it meant "those who speak badly"), were in their own
eyes the *Wulastigwiak*, "the people of the beautiful river."

Despite the territorial differences and linguistic nuances, a
fairly uniform Indian culture prevailed throughout Maine. In the
summertime, like moderns, they went to the seashore and feasted
on lobsters and clams. Unlike today's tourists, they also caught
porpoises and seals. In September, they harvested, if they had
crops, and October found them upstream, hunting game. They,
too, in late fall, had Thanksgiving dinners, featuring turkey,
cranberries and Indian pudding. Winter was the season for moose
hunting and trapping in the deep woods. When the ice went out,
they could catch beaver and otter before heading back downstream
for spring planting—and after the Europeans came—bartering for
trade goods. They did extensive trading among themselves, as well,
and were seafarers.

Better diets and increased medical knowledge (they avoided
scurvy by making a tea out of hemlock needles to obtain vitamin
C) produced ever larger populations, requiring more elaborate
social and religious customs. The outcome was a complex matrix of
tribes as groups outgrew their space and separated.

This pre-European Woodland Period seems in retrospect an
halcyon age, an Arcadian idyll. The sole intruders may have been
those Vikings in their long boats who touched at parts of the coast
and fought with the *Skraelings*. Inter-tribal warfare also no doubt
existed for its hatreds were carried forward into historic times. One
nostalgically envies the Indians of Maine, a rather peaceable
people, living their difficult but attractive lives century after century, in tune with their environment, unaware of the challenges of
disease, cultural change and eventual invasion that would be coming from across the Atlantic.

It was not, however, a wholly benign world they inhabited.
At least, they populated it with ghosts of their own making, the
projections of tensed imaginations. Cannibal giants lurked in the
forests, the evil spirits of hunters who had died of starvation, and
were wont to pounce upon unsuspecting bands of men to suck
their blood while they slept or snatch out their livers. Ogres in the
north combed the brains of the dead, transforming them into gam-
boling white arctic hares, and the chief ogre was Pamola (pro-

8

nounced Bumohle), a terrible giant with stone eyebrows who lived on Mount Katahdin.

Also sporting stone eyebrows was a less forbidding god, in fact a near human, the Abnaki culture hero Gluskap. His name, in translation, means Liar. The story of he came by this unflattering title involves an evil brother of his who wanted to kill him and first asked, seemingly innocently, "Tell me, immortal Gluskap, what does it take to slay you?" Just as straightfaced, Gluskap responded that his only mortal weakness was to be hit over the head with a cat-o-nine tails—a lie, of course—which the Abnaki Cain discovered when he struck the sleeping Gluskap with one of those swamp plants. Awakening unscathed, Gluskap then shattered the would-be murderer's skull with a blow from his stone axe.

Truthful or not, Gluskap proved a boon to mankind. Endless stories are told of his beneficent adventures. He made beavers the size they are today by petting down a monster beaver whose dam had clogged the St. John River. Frogs have a broken-back look because Gluskap struck Oglebamu, the great frog, an axe blow to the spine for having sucked all the water from the land. After the world ceased to be covered with ice and snow (i.e., after the glacier left), it was Gluskap who created the four seasons. Even in historic times, this Native American Superman is pictured as active. One contemporary tale has him visiting the King of France, but being treated badly. Ordered shot from a cannon, he caused the gun to explode and kill hundreds of soldiers nearby. Disgusted, Gluskap sailed home on his boat, which was a wooded island crewed by squirrels, and he is allegedly holed up in a cave on Mt. Katahdin, making arrowheads for the day when the Indians will drive all the white men from the land.

In the mythology created around figures like Gluskap and Pamola and others, there are tantalizing glimpses of a human memory of the past ice age. Not only in the attribution to Gluskap of the creation of the seasons after the great glacial chill, but in statements like one credited to Snowy Owl, another of the Abnaki pantheon, who saw "great beasts that resembled huge brown haystacks" and had long, long teeth—tusks, no doubt—so it seems incontrovertible that mastodons and woolly mammoths are meant. Such pachydermic animals did roam Maine once upon a time. Snowy Owl, by the way, used an *ivory* bow and *ivory*-tipped arrows.

Or was the Indian acquaintance with ivory a reference to walrus ivory, known via the northern trade? Probably it's impossible ever to tell.

9

The Indian scheme of belief also included afterworlds—a paradise full of nature's bounty as well as an infernal region for the wicked. The priests who could commune with those other worlds were called *shamans* or medicine men; specifically to the Abnaki, each was a *m'teoulino*, literally a "drummer," a wizard with powers no ordinary clergyman would have.

A latter day *m'teoulino* is described by Fanny Hardy Eckstrom in her biography of the 19th century Penobscot Governor John Neptune. Among other things, he is involved in an epic battle with a Micmac chief at Boyden's Lake in Washington County. But this is no ordinary fistfight. Neptune transforms himself into an enormous eel and the Micmac becomes a 40 foot water snake. When the thrashing of the two monsters is over, the lake is muddy and foul and Neptune, reverted to human form, but smelling of fish, drags out the human body of his adversary. Then, there is Piel Susup, another of the real-life *m'teoulimak* and Eckstrom describes how he could take a beam of sunlight, full of dust motes, pull it

John Neptune

and double it like molasses candy, then hang it across two chairs and lay his axe on it. Differences of perception as deep as these also were reflected in Indian attitudes toward the animals their hunters killed. The *m'teoulimak* instructed:

> Teach them also never to abuse the spirit of animals. You may kill the animal and eat his flesh but never abuse the spirit of it, because if you do abuse the spirit of the animal he will never come to your calling.

How ludicrous the idea must seem to a non-Indian sportsman of owing a debt of gratitude to the animal one kills. How alien to our thinking is the example of the young Indian hunter-to-be who fasts and seeks a vision in dreams of an animal representing *manito*, his guardian spirit and personal totem. How foreign, too, for Europeans, was the Indian notion of land ownership where all land was held in common and each tenant had only the right of usage, not a property right. Another key difference between the two cultures lay in their sense of time. As the modern-day Passamaquoddy Governor John Stevens has put it, "To the non-Indian, time is of more value than life. For Indians, time is secondary; life is sacred." In a society like the Abnaki that honors a man primarily "for what he has done for his community, not for himself," government was by unanimous consensus rather than majority rule, a far more time-consuming process.

Within their own territories, whose boundaries in the wilderness had been defined by custom and language, the various tribal entities lived out their lives as if in an eternal rhythm of seasonal changes, measured by moons—*Ouglusamwessit* (January) "the moon in which it is hard to get a living," *Taquasknikizoos* (February) "the moon in which there is crust on the snow," *Muskoskikizoos* (June) "the moon in which we catch young seals," *Mantchewadokkikizoos* (September) "the moon in which there are herds of moose and bear"—a life spiced by occasional warfare against neighbors or interrupted by murderous raids of the Iroquoian Mohawks from the west, saddened by intermittent famine, touched with primitive cruelty in the treatment of prisoners, but a good life, well adapted to the Maine environment out of which it developed.

As the 15th century arrived, the Indians of Maine all unknowingly approached their entry into world history.

11

CHAPTER TWO

THE EUROPEANS ARRIVE

The Earliest Explorers

While Indian life went placidly on in the Americas, medieval Europe began sending out feelers toward the rest of the world.

For twelve frustrating years, Prince Henry the Navigator of Portugal dispatched ships along the west coast of Africa, urging his mariners to break the psychological barrier of passing beyond Cape Bojador to "shallow seas...so terrible...that no ship...will ever be able to return." Yet once intrepid Gil Eanes had crossed this fateful line in 1434, it would still be more than half a century before Columbus traversed the Atlantic and Vasco da Gama rounded the Cape of Good Hope to pioneer a sailing route from Lisbon to India.

In 1497, the same year da Gama left on his epic voyage, a citizen of Venice, born in Genoa, living in England, his name anglicized to John Cabot, sailed west from Bristol and struck the North American coast at either Cape Breton Island or Newfoundland. All subsequent British claims in North America were based on Cabot's singular feat (he disappeared the next year on another transatlantic attempt). As for New England proper, the first to reach it may have been a Portuguese Azorean, Gaspar Corte-Real, during his second trip (1501) in search of a "Northwest Passage" to India. Last sighted heading southwest from Newfoundland, Gaspar was sought the following year by his brother Miguel, who, in turn, was never seen again.

Before vanishing, Gaspar Corte-Real commenced a practice that was to bedevil European-native relations ever afterward. He

12

captured indigenous peoples and sold them as slaves in Europe. From Newfoundland, Gaspar shipped 57 Indian men, women and children to Portugal. The sensation they caused was recorded by several eye-witnesses. One of them, Alberto Cantino, wrote of long-haired men, tall of stature, with decorated faces, greenish eyes and darker skins than the women who "have small breasts and most beautiful bodies and rather pleasant faces...they all go quite naked except for their privy members, which they cover with the skin of a deer."

Following upon the heels of Cabot and Corte-Real were hosts of anonymous fisherman[1]—Portuguese, Basque, Breton, English, etc.—and increased European-native contact no doubt increased friction. So it was that the next important explorer, Giovanni Verrazano, also an Italian, but sailing for France, met outright hostility when he landed in Maine in 1524. He had made his land-fall in the Carolinas and everywhere, as he coasted north, the

Early map showing New England and New France

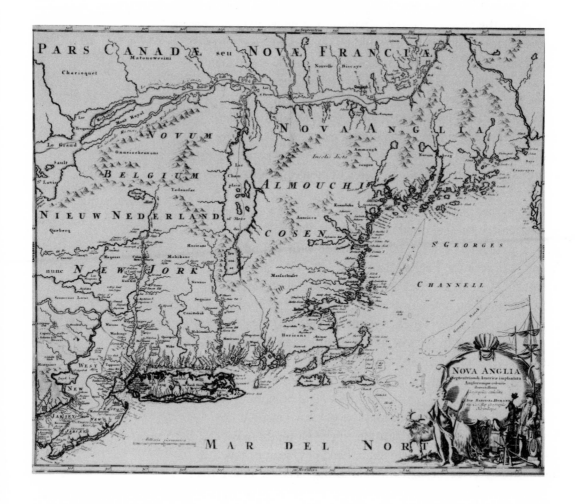

Indians he encountered were friendly and unsuspicious. The Maine natives, however, were at first aloof, then fiercely combative when Verrazano sent an armed party ashore. Understandably, the explorer's impressions of Maine were less than glowing.

A year later, Esteban Gomez reached the same Downeast shores, sent by the Hapsburg Emperor of Spain on yet another quixotic quest for the "Northwest Passage." Instead of finding the Great Khan, Gomez (in actuality a Portuguese who had once sailed with Magellan) explored the whole Atlantic coast from the Grand Banks to Florida. He left Spanish names for many of the northern sites he visited and some of them have stuck, like Casco Bay, so-called because Gomez thought it helmet (*casco*) shaped and the Bay of Fundy, transliterated from *Bahia Profundo* (Deep Bay).

Jacques Cartier of St. Malo in Brittany came next, in 1535, but he never got to Maine. His three voyages, likewise seeking the fabled "Northwest Passage," were exclusively to Canada.

Will-o-the-wisps aplenty, such as the Northwest Passage or El Dorado or the Seven Cities of Cibola or Norumbega enticed these early explorers. Gluskapian lies told by the Indians were often responsible as the natives spun stories of what the white men wanted to hear—that pots of gold lay just around the corner. Also, it was not a bad technique for getting intruders to move on. True, *real* gold had been found by the Spanish in Mexico and Peru, while slaves, fish and beaver fur did promise *real* profit. But in the 16th century, it was mainly the power of myth and the hope of instant fabulous wealth that fired men's imaginations and led nations to venture across the oceans.

David Ingram of Essex, England was a bit of a Gluskap, himself; at least, he embellished what seemed like an absolute whopper—that he had been put ashore in 1568 with 113 other seamen from the fleet of the English slaver, Sir John Hawkins, near Tampico, Mexico, and had walked north for eleven months to Cape Breton Island off Nova Scotia. Returned to England with two companions aboard a French ship, he and his pals regaled many a tavern audience with tales of their adventure. As Ingram told them, these included his seeing an elephant in North America, Indians using iron and a chief wearing a great ruby. And the centerpiece of Ingram's repertoire was the legend of Norumbega,[2] a walled, golden city full of furs and ivory that he insisted lay between 38° and 45° north latitude on the Norumbega River. Agents for Sir Francis Walsingham, head of Queen Elizabeth's intelligence service, brought Ingram to the palace to repeat his

14

stories to Crown officials. One of the most impressed was Sir Humphrey Gilbert, a Devonshire-born soldier who had been busy until then expanding England's imperial power in Ireland. Together with his half-brother Sir Walter Raleigh, Gilbert had already listened to similar testimony of America's riches from a French Huguenot, Jacques Le Moyne, an artist who had survived a massacre of Gallic Protestants by the Spanish in Florida.

The "Northwest Passage" bug, in particular, bit Gilbert deeply and he wrote a book about it. A man of action as well as letters, Gilbert did more than merely propagandize the elusive "New Passage to Cataia."; he inspired expeditions to the Arctic by Martin Frobisher and John Davis and, once the Queen had granted him a patent to plant colonies in America, he went himself.

One trip, planned with Raleigh in 1578, never got much beyond England due to storms and desertions. But in 1583, Gilbert arrived in Newfoundland, entered St. John's harbor and took possession of the island. Headed home, after a fruitless search for the Northwest Passage, he drowned when his ship foundered off the Azores. But Gilbert left an important legacy of interest in exploration and settlement, which soon directly affected Maine.

In fact, his son Bartholomew Gilbert was aboard the *Concord*, captained by Bartholomew Gosnold, when she touched Maine's shores in 1602. Landfall occurred in the Cape Elizabeth area and shortly afterward the English encountered seagoing Indians in a European-style "Biscay shallop with sail and oars" off *Savage Rock*, since identified as the Cape Neddick *Nubble* at York Beach. The lasting impression of natives in a non-native vessel was reinforced by the costume of the chief, "a waistcoat of black work, a pair of breeches, cloth stockings, shoes, hat and band." Although the natives asked him to stay, Gosnold sailed southwestward, reached Cape Cod and built a small fort on Cuttyhunk Island.[3] When those of his men slated to be colonists refused to remain, he returned to England, but not empty-handed. With him he took a valuable cargo of sassafras, cedar and furs, and more importantly, a positive report on the potential of the new land.

Two journals of Gosnold's experiences were published. Their effect was presently felt in Bristol, where the urging of a local clergyman, Richard Hakluyt, later to become the chronicler par excellence of English overseas activity, led Mayor John Whitson to raise £1000 for another voyage. A Devon sea captain, Martin Pring, was sent, landed in Penobscot Bay and reached Savage Rock, "where going upon the Mayne we found people with whom

15

we had no long conversation, because here also we could find no sassafras."

Sassafras root could fetch the extraordinary price of 20 shillings a pound in London, being considered a general cure-all medicine and above all, "a specific for the French poxe," the English name for syphilis. Pring's description of what he found in the New World was as glowing as Gosnold's. Here was an abundance of fish almost impossible to believe, lobsters 16 and 20 pounds, shellfish "exceeding good and very great." No wonder wealthy men like the Earl of Arundel, Sir Ferdinando Gorges, commander of Plymouth Fort and Sir John Popham, Chief Justice of England, began to show interest in the development possibilities of America.

Yet the honor of placing the first settlement outside of Florida in what is now the United States was to belong to the French.

The site was St. Croix Island, in the St. Croix River, in a part of Maine's Washington County.

Settlement Starts

One of the outstanding Kings of France was Henri IV, who has left a glowing heritage of his gallantry, good nature, tolerance and love for the common people. Born a Protestant, fighting as a youth for Huguenot causes, he finally converted to Catholicism with the cynical declaration that "Paris is worth a mass." Throughout his reign, a spirit of co-existence between Catholics and Protestants in France was tenuously maintained.

After Henri IV's assassination in 1610, it was not possible for a Protestant to partake in French overseas activities. But seven years earlier, the King had granted a large section of North America to his former companion-in-arms, Pierre de Gua (or de Guast), a prominent Protestant. The King's commission made de Monts the Lieutenant-Governor of La Cadie and ordered him to people it and cultivate it.

La Cadie? We know it as Acadia. It ran between 40° and 46° north latitude, roughly from Philadelphia to Nova Scotia, and included most of Maine. A 10 year monopoly of furs was granted de Monts and on this basis, he was able to borrow 90,000 *livres* from a number of provincial merchants.

He was no stranger to North America. He had already participated in an abortive attempt to establish a French colony at

Samuel de Champlain

mouth of the Saguenay River. To secure royal permission for
another try, de Monts had to overcome the opposition of the Duc
de Sully, the King's chief minister, who thought such expeditions a
waste of resources.

On February 4, 1604, de Monts formed his company and on
April 7, the flagship, the 120 ton La Bonne Renommée left Le
Havre, to be followed by two other vessels. Commanding the
flagship was de Monts with Samuel de Champlain as his navigator.
It didn't matter that Champlain was a staunch Catholic. The
group's ecumenical nature was underscored by the fact it included
both Catholic priests and a Protestant minister.

On May 1, La Bonne Renommée sighted land—Nova

17

Scotia—around which they sailed. At an anchorage, one of the Catholic clergy disappeared, but mercifully was found a few days later wandering in the wilderness. It had been feared the Protestant pastor with whom he habitually quarrelled would be accused of murdering him. On the north coast, they discovered a beautiful harbor, later to become Port Royal. They discovered the St. John River and once they had crossed Passamaquoddy Bay to what is now Maine, the St. Croix River. The Frenchmen decided to settle on an island in the St. Croix. It was late June, 1604.

Focus

The St. Croix Island Experience

In his diary, Champlain explains the choice of this particular island, whose circumference was 800-900 paces, with rocky sides 18-24 feet high.

Vessels could pass up the river only at the mercy of the cannon on this island, and we deemed the location the most advantageous, not only on account of its situation and good soil, but also on account of the intercourse which we proposed with the savages of these coasts and of the interior...

To begin with, the French built a "barricade" on a small islet a short distance from the main island and placed

St. Croix
Island

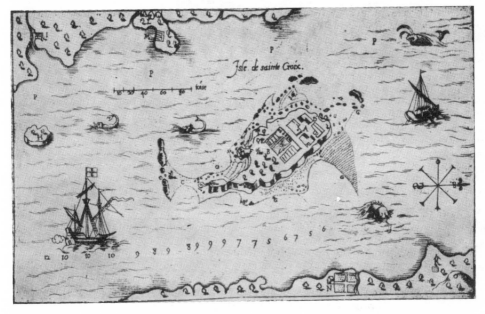

cannon there. Mosquitoes bothered them (or were they black flies?) and several men had faces swollen so badly they could barely see. Houses were erected on a pattern designed by Champlain and communal structures were raised. They planted gardens that unfortunately days of hot sun burned up, since the "good soil" turned out to be sandy. It was better on the nearby mainland, "where Sieur de Monts had some wheat sown, which flourished finely."

Early September saw the colony well enough established for Champlain to go exploring along the Maine coast. In sight of a dramatic, mountainous island, their craft hit a rock and tore a hole in the keel. Had the accident not impressed itself, the spectacle of those bare rock summits they saw would have been indelible. "I named it *Isle de Monts Deserts*," wrote Champlain.

The date was September 5, 1604. A day later, they came upon two canoe-loads of Indians who promptly fled. But eventually, these Indians returned and led the Frenchmen up the Penobscot River, reaching the Kenduskeag near present-day Bangor. Here, Champlain went hunting in "very pleasant country, where the oaks...appear as if they were planted for ornaments." On September 16, the great chief Besabes arrived to meet Champlain and another chief, Cabahis, also joined the pow-wow. The Indians were friendly, although the white men held their guns ready. Then, Champlain made a diplomatic speech, which he followed with gifts of hatchets, knives, caps and other "knicknacks." All night until dawn, the Indians danced and sang, but finally there was trading for beaver furs and the gathering broke up with all parties satisfied.

Back at St. Croix Island, winter began on October 6 when it snowed. By December 3, ice was floating down the river. But the worst danger was scurvy, *mal de terre*. The Indian remedy of drinking hemlock tea was known to the French but apparently ignored by de Monts men.

Champlain is horrifyingly graphic in describing the malady:

> There were produced in the mouths of those who had it great pieces of superfluous and drivelling flesh (causing extensive putrefaction)...Their teeth became very loose, and could be pulled out with the fingers...Afterwards, a violent pain seized their arms and legs, which remained swollen and very hard, all spotted as if with fleabites, and they could not walk on account of the contraction of the muscles...

Out of 79 men on the island, 35 died and 20 more nearly did.

It had been a truly ghastly winter. All their liquid froze, except their Spanish sherry. Cider was chopped in blocks. They drank melted snow and subsisted on salt meat and vegetables. When their fuel supplies ran low, they were unable to go to the mainland for wood because of drift ice. So, not surprisingly, de Monts decided to seek a better site. They travelled south, past Mount Desert, past the Penobscot, to the Kennebec, then the Saco and beyond, to the vicinity of Boston, where they named the Charles River the *Riviére du Guast*. Other Massachusetts areas were reached— Plymouth Harbor, Cape Cod. Yet inexplicably, none of these attractive locations suited the Sieur de Monts. For his permanent settlement, he chose Port Royal on the north shore of Nova Scotia.

A Fateful Kidnapping

An incident during yet another French expedition south was to
seal their choice of Port Royal. In the spring of 1606, the Baron St.
Just, Jean de Poutrincourt, who had been given possession of the
Nova Scotian harbor by de Monts, became disenchanted with the
area. He and Champlain then travelled to Maine and Massachusetts, seeking a better site. But at Nauset Beach, on Cape Cod, the
local Indians massacred four or five of their party who were sleeping on the sand. One body was found with a little dog on its back,
both transfixed by the same arrow. The natives taunted the intruders by casting "sand with their two hands betwixt their buttocks in
derision, howling like wolves." Such dire enmity drove the French
back to Port Royal.

Had they in 1605 or 1606 chosen any of a number of ideal
New England locations for a colony, perhaps we would be referring
to *Rocher du Port du Cap St. Louis* instead of Plymouth Rock. And
although the French gave Gallic equivalents to places like *Port du
Cap St. Louis* (Plymouth), *Mallebarre* (Nauset), *Cap aux Isles* (Cape
Anne), events were already in progress that would lead to an English occupation of Massachusetts and a goodly portion of Maine.

Champlain in a way learned of the most important of these
events during his first trip to New England in 1605. At the mouth
of the Kennebec, he met an Indian chief who told him that a
fishing vessel crew had killed five Indians. Champlain concluded
these Europeans were English and dubbed the island where this
happened *La Nef* (The Nave). Today, it is Monhegan.

What isn't know is whether Champlain ever found out the
truth. The five Indians weren't killed; they were kidnapped.

Much has been written about this Indian quintet. Four were
Maine locals, Wawenocs, most likely. The fifth, and most famous,
was a visitor from Cape Cod whose full name was Tisquantum,
better known to history as Squanto, the Pilgrims' friend and interpreter. That Squanto became so proficient in English and so useful
was hardly foreseen by the men who abducted him. Their motive
was intelligence gathering. Captain George Weymouth had been
sent over to investigate economic opportunities; if gold mines
existed, these Indians, once they knew English, would say where.

James Rosier, a crewman, who helped lure three of the Indians
to board their ship with bowls of peas, a dish they loved, and in
capturing the other two on shore, wrote, "And it was as much as
five or six of us could do to get them into the light horseman (a

small boat). For they were strong and so naked as our best hold was by their long hair on their heads." Two of their canoes and all of their bows and arrows were also carried back to England as further curiosities.

Kidnapped Indians in England weren't new. The significant fact here was this group's destination: three of them, including Squanto, were lodged with Sir Ferdinando Gorges in Plymouth; the other two went to London to Chief Justice Sir John Popham. Both Gorges and Popham had backed Weymouth's voyage. Their interest in America soon received added fuel from the detailed descriptions their guests provided of the far-off land.

Shortly thereafter, in 1606, Gorges, Popham and others persuaded King James I to issue charters for two colonizing joint stock companies: the London Company and the Plymouth Company. Since the entire New World coast had been named Virginia (at Queen Elizabeth's insistence), their respective jurisdictions became known as South Virginia and North Virginia. Gorges then had two of the Indians sent back with Captain Henry Challons to pick a site for settlement in the northern zone. However, they were all captured by Spaniards. Next, Popham had Martin Pring set off with two more of the Indians and Pring reached the mouth of the Kennebec and returned to report an ideal location for a colony. The fifth Indian was Squanto, who did not leave England until 1614 when he sailed with Captain John Smith.

The stage was now set, with the stories told by the Indians, the reconnaissance voyages, conditions of high unemployment at home and even the traditional memory of earlier failures by those half-brothers Humphrey Gilbert and Walter Raleigh, for that extraordinary year of colonizing, 1607. Those who were to populate South Virginia reached Jamestown in May. The same month, a slightly larger complement of "planters" left for Maine.

Focus

The Popham Colony

Certain names stand out in this first English settlement in North Virginia. Popham, of course—both the Chief Justice, who was sponsoring the expedi-tion with Gorges, and his nephew George Popham who went along as its "President." The "Admiral" of the operation was Raleigh Gilbert, son of Sir

Humphrey. And yet another person of note in the entourage was Skitwarroes, one of the five kidnapped Indians.

Two ships, the *Gift of God* and *Mary and John* departed Plymouth, England on May 31, 1607 and first anchored in Maine near the mouth of the St. George River. Skitwarroes, brought to New Harbor, then led the English on a three mile march across the Pemaquid peninsula to pay a call on his fellow captive in England, Chief Nahanada, who had gone home earlier. The visit was not an unqualified success due to lingering resentment over the kidnapping incident.

On August 19, the English chose a site for their colony, overlooking Atkins Bay in the town of Phippsburg. The location commanded an entrance to the "Sagadahoc River," i.e., the Kennebec. "All went to shore" and a religious service was held and work commenced on a fort, a large earthwork. Soon, timber was being cut for a vessel. When built, this pinnace of 30 tons, the *Virginia*, was the first boat constructed in America.

While "Fort St. George" was being completed, Popham went up to Merry-meeting Bay, that vast confluence of the Kennebec and Androscoggin Rivers, and he may have reached the falls at Brunswick. An outbreak of inter-Indian warfare had just occurred. The ferocious "Tarratines," identified by most historians as sea-going Micmacs from Nova Scotia, were raiding the Maine coast. Sasanoa, the prime chief in the Pemaquid area, was their target and in a violent battle, in which Skitwarroes and Nahanada took part, Sasanoa's son was shot dead by a Tarratine musket ball. The English

colonists were not involved except when Nahanada tried to trade them furs for guns. Raleigh Gilbert and Popham refused.

After Popham's return from upriver, Gilbert reconnoitered south, sailing about in Casco Bay where he was impressed by the "gallant and goodly islands...all over-grown with...oaks, pine trees and many other things growing as sarsaparilla (sic), hazle nuts (sic) and whorts (?)..."

October 8, 1607, the *Mary and John* left to return to England. The *Gift of God* went around the middle of December. Only 45 of the company remained to face the New England winter. Internal feuding had contributed to the exodus, but those who stayed were optimistic. Popham wrote to the King and his report was not only cheery but highly exaggerated: he claimed the land they had settled would furnish such exotic products as nutmegs, cinna-mon and Brazilian cochineal.

By February, George Popham was dead. Gorges described him as "an honest man, but old and of an unwieldy body." At the time of his death, he was 58; despite the severity of the winter, he was the only one to die.

Raleigh Gilbert succeeded him. Then, two more unexpected blows were dealt the little group of Englishmen. They learned that Sir John Popham, their patron, had died, followed by news of the death of Raleigh Gilbert's older brother, which meant he had to return home as heir to the family estate. Left leaderless, the Popham colonists, bringing the *Virginia* with them, abandoned their settlement. Sir Ferdinando Gorges commented gloomily, "...all our former hopes were frozen to death."

The French Again

Of Father Pierre Biard, the Jesuit, it was said in French: "*C'est un homme plutôt austere, incapable de transiger quand un principe est en jeu.*" ("He is a rather austere man, incapable of compromising when a principle is at stake.") He must also have been a patient man, for it took almost three years before he was able to depart for New France after he'd been chosen by his Order to cross the Atlantic. What had to be settled were the political and financial machinations of bringing the first in a long line of Jesuit priests to Acadia.

It was the Sieur de Poutrincourt, in charge now at Port Royal, who had left Father Biard cooling his heels at various Jesuit schools in France until 1611. Since Jesuits, the shock troops of the Catholic Counter-Reformation, did not sit well with French Protestants and since Poutrincourt was indebted to Huguenot ship's chandlers in Dieppe, the promoter of New France must have thought it wise not to bring over members of the Society of Jesus.

However, the era of relative religious tolerance in France was about to come to a sudden, tragic end. Henri IV was stabbed to death by a Catholic fanatic. His widow, the devout Catholic Marie de Medici, was left as regent for their nine year old son, Louis XIII.

At this point, a 40 year old lady-in-waiting to the Queen enters the Port Royal scene. She was Antoinette de Pons, Marquise de Guercheville, no less of a Catholic devotee than Marie, with strong ties to the Jesuits. In her youth, the lovely Antoinette had refused to become Henri IV's mistress, despite the ardent entreaties of that inveterate womanizer. Now, as the matronly wife of the Governor of Paris, she raised 4,000 *livres* for Poutrincourt and the Protestant merchants were bought off. Her stipulations: *two* Jesuits, Biard and her own confessor, Father Ènémond Massé, would go to Acadia and half the return cargo would belong to the "black robes."

Overseas at last, Biard wrote of his adventures in the first of the famous *Relations*, or Jesuit reports, and he and Father Massé travelled extensively. On several occasions, they were in Maine. During one trip, the Frenchmen reached the mouth of the Kennebec River and visited the ruins of the Popham colony. At St. Croix Island, they encountered a ship's captain from Normandy who complained that English fisherman had seized his shallop and all his furs. On the spot, Poutrincourt's son, the fiery 20-year-old known as Biencourt, swore revenge.

Left in charge at Port Royal by his father, this immature young man soon was embroiled not with the English but with the Jesuit fathers, who now included a third "black robe," Brother Gilbert du

Thet, sent over by the Marquise de Guercheville. The Jesuits and Biencourt quarrelled frequently, an extended spat that culminated in Biard's excommunication of the young hothead and the Jesuits' refusal to perform any religious rites.

Apprised by returning sailors of what had happened, Mme. de Guercheville was infuriated. She broke off relations with Poutrincourt and outfitted a new, wholly independent expedition to the New World. Its eventual destination was the coast of Maine. The idea was to pick up the Jesuits at Port Royal and then settle at Kadesquit (near Bangor). Instead, they landed at Lamoine Point, across from Mount Desert, where they established a short-lived but historically important colony named St. Sauveur.

FOCUS

St. Sauveur and its Aftermath

An omen of war had been experienced by Father Biard on one of his earlier trips, a blood-red sky over the St. Croix River, staining the waters crimson and bringing cries of *Gara, gara*—there will be fighting—from the Indians in the party.

When Biard and his compatriots came ashore in Maine in June 1613, conflict seemed remote from the peaceful scene. The commander of the ship *Jonas*—the "Mayflower of the French" to quote the Boston Brahmin historian Francis Parkman—was so lulled by the quietude that he ordered his men to plant gardens rather than build a fort. This man, René Le Coq de la Saussaie, a former hanger-on at the French court, acting as Mme. de Guercheville's agent, figured that the English were far away, but winter wasn't.

But unbeknownst to the French, the English were also off the Downeast coast. Captain Samuel Argall from Jamestown was less than a day's sail away

in a man-of-war.

It perhaps was a coincidence. The Jamestown settlement annually sent a ship to Maine to gather fish and other supplies. Orders were also given, though, to "dislodge" any Frenchmen they came upon, since the South Virginians laid claim to the whole coast.

Argall had been sailing to Maine since 1610. He was a young man of considerable cunning and nerve; indeed, it was Argall who had daringly kidnapped Pocahontas from under the nose of her father, the all-powerful Chief Powhattan, so she could be held for ransom.

When he met some Indians in Penobscot Bay, Argall cleverly pretended to be French. He listened with interest as they told him of the new settlement near Mount Desert and he even persuaded them to guide him there.

Father Biard has described what happened next: "*Le navire anglais venait plus vite qu'un dard, ayant vent à souhait,*

24

*tout pavis de rouge, les pavillons
d'Angleterre flottant, trois trompettes et
deux tambours faisant rage de sonner."*
("The English ship sped forward faster
than a dart, having wind to spare, all
decked out in red, the flags of England
flapping, three trumpets and two drums
joining in the racket.")

La Saussaie was in the nearby woods
with most of the colonists. Only 10
Frenchmen were available for defense.
The *red* Father Biard had noted on the
English ship proved to be scarlet screens
behind which musketeers crouched. A
volley was loosed by the attackers. The
skipper of the *Jonas*, Captain Charles
Fleury, ordered a return fire. Since the
cannoneer was absent, Brother Gilbert du
Thet ran to the sole artillery piece and
shot off a ball without aiming. Moments
later, he was cut down by musket fire.
Captain Fleury was wounded in the foot
and three other Frenchmen also hit. Two
of the defenders who jumped overboard
drowned. Within minutes, the fire fight
was over.

Shot in the chest, de Thet lay
mortally wounded and would die the next
day. The other three priests, ashore in
camp, were taken prisoner. They watched
mystified as Argall had La Saussaie's
trunk brought to him and out of it
removed his commission to establish a
colony in Acadia. but when La Saussaie
finally came out of the woods to surrender, the Englishman's slyness became
evident. Argall at once demanded to see
La Saussaie's papers. One can imagine
the ex-courtier's suave manner discom-
posed as he searched frantically for his
official documents. Not having them, he
could be accused, as he was by Argall, of
being a pirate. On these grounds, the
English captain allowed his men to
plunder the Frenchmen's possessions.

Argall proved more humane in
later dealings with his prisoners. Originally, he planned to ship all of them out
to sea in an open boat to find a fishing
vessel to take them back to France.
When it was pointed out the boat would
probably swamp and sink, he reduced the
number by half. The remaining 15,
including Father Biard, he carried back
to Jamestown.

There, the greatest danger was from
Governor Thomas Dale. Particularly
fond of hangings, he initially proposed
the gallows for these foreigners who had
intruded on English soil. Argall came to
their rescue by producing the commission
he had purloined out of La Saussaie's
trunk.

Thus, having established his
prisoners weren't pirates, Argall took
them back to Maine. He had orders to
demolish St. Sauveur, then St. Croix and
Port Royal. Biard risked Argall's displeas-
ure by refusing to act as a guide. But
some Indians did and the Virginian
totally destroyed these French centers.
Among his new prisoners was Biencourt
who maliciously told Argall that Biard
was really a Spaniard, a spy, and should
be hanged. Despite his annoyance with
the Jesuit, Argall paid no heed.

Yet Father Biard's adventures
continued. At Port Royal, the French
prisoners were put aboard the old *Jonas*,
now placed in service by the English
under a Lieutenant Turnell. Only 25
leagues from Jamestown, they were hit by
a hurricane and driven to find refuge in
the Azorean island of Fayal. Lt. Turnell
was terrified the Catholic Portuguese
might find his Jesuit captives. Things
grew tense when the *Jonas* bumped into a
Spanish vessel and the port officials
arrived to investigate. But the priests,
hidden below, never revealed themselves

25

and the *Jonas* at last departed for England. There, paradoxically, Lt. Turnell was arrested as a pirate for turning up in a French ship without papers. Father Biard actually had to vouch for his captor.

Conclusion

St. Sauveur's place in the history of Maine is a pivotal one. The entire incident, characterized by Biard[4] as *"fourmillant d'absurdités"* ("swarming with absurdities") pinpointed the essence of rival claims to the same land—claims that were, themselves, something of absurdities in the extent of their pretensions. For the French, *Acadia* stretched from northern Canada theoretically to Florida, and more immediately to the Kennebec River; for the English, *Virginia* encompassed the whole North American Atlantic coast, and by implication, went as far west as the Pacific. Francis Parkman has asked in one of his books on the Anglo-French conflict in North America: "What would have been the issue had the zeal of the pious lady of honor (Mme. de Guercheville) preoccupied New England with a Jesuit colony?" It was only seven years later that the Pilgrims were landing at Plymouth.

The next half-century after St. Sauveur saw decades of peace, but the seeds of war had been planted. To quote Parkman again, "...an obscure stroke of lawless violence started the whole strife between France and England."

CHAPTER Three

THE ENGLISH STAKE THEIR CLAIM

The Fishing Communities

In 1614, a year after St. Sauveur, the legendary Captain John Smith sailed from England on an expedition whose first stop was Maine. He landed at Monhegan Island, or *Monahiggan*, as he called it in his best seller book entitled "A Description of New England," which was the first to use the term *New England* in place of *North Virginia*.

The voyage was financed by four London merchants and its two ships were captained by Smith and Thomas Hunt. Their purpose, as Smith put it, was "there to take whales and trials of a mine of gold and copper...If those failed, fish and furs was then our refuge." As it turned out, the hoped-for mines proved illusory and while whales were sighted and chased, none were killed. Accordingly, Smith roamed the coast, trading for furs. For a few "trifles," he collected 1,100 beaver skins, 100 martens and as many otter.

New England was a fitting name for Smith to use, since he counterpoised it in his work to *New France, New Spain, New Granada* and *New Andalusia*. He described New England as "that part of America in the Ocean Sea opposite to Nova Albyon in the South Sea, discovered by the most memorable Sir Francis Drake..." Off Maine, Smith sailed as far north as the Penobscot and his portrait of the intervening "Sagadahoc" country would make a Chamber of Commerce booster proud:

> ...the coast is all mountainous and isles of huge rocks, but overgrown with all sorts of excellent good woods for building

houses, boats, barks or ships; with an incredible abundance of most sorts of fish, much fowl and sundry sorts of good fruits for man's use.

On board Smith's vessel was Squanto, who was landed at his home on Cape Cod. Then, incredibly, he was immediately kidnapped again—and by none other than Thomas Hunt, Smith's sidekick. This ruthless sea captain invited Squanto and 26 other Indians aboard his ship, clapped them in chains and spirited them to Spain, where they were sold as slaves. The resourceful Squanto escaped from a monastery, got to England and reached Cape Cod a year before the Pilgrims, to find an epidemic had wiped out his whole tribe.

As long as Smith was in the Gulf of Maine, he made Monhegan his headquarters. Although fishing was to be Monhegan's mainstay, Smith admitted his surprise that it was not good throughout the year. By the middle of June, "the fishing failed," he wrote.

Of the fish he did take back to England, 40,000 were "dry fish," cured ashore, as opposed to "wet fish" that were simply salted on board and transported straight to Europe. On islands like Monhegan, the fishermen erected *stages* and *flakes*, wooden structures used for processing. Here, too, bulky supplies, like salt, could be left and such practices led to year-round occupation of these

CAPTAIN JOHN SMITH
ADVENTURER IN MANY OLD WORLD COUNTRIES
A PIONEER IN THE NEW WORLD
GOVERNOR OF VIRGINIA
CAME HERE WITH TWO VESSELS IN 1614
ANCHORED IN THIS ISLAND HARBOR
AND EXPLORED THE COAST FROM PENOBSCOT BAY TO CAPE COD
DISCOVERING A LARGE OPPORTUNITY
FOR ADDING TO ENGLAND'S GLORY BY COLONIZATION
HE RETURNED HOME AND SPENT HIS REMAINING YEARS
IN ADVANCING AMERICAN ENTERPRISES
BECAUSE OF HIS GREAT INTEREST IN THE FUTURE OF AMERICA
AND TO COMMEMORATE HIS CONNECTION WITH THIS ISLAND
THIS TERCENTENARY TABLET IS PLACED
BY MONHEGAN RESIDENTS
1914

Captain John Smith plaque on Monhegan Island

28

off-shore sites. They had the added advantage of being relatively safe from Indian attacks.

It is therefore not surprising that two particular islands, Monhegan and Damariscove, both lying well out to sea, should boast the earliest regular settlements on Maine territory.

Monhegan was a busy place. Even in 1614, Smith came across another English ship, belonging to Sir Francis Popham, and two French vessels. The next year, he refers to "the success of six ships." The year 1616 found Sir Richard Hawkins, President of the Plymouth Council, arriving at Monhegan on the *Garland*. Also, the *Nachen*, the *Trial* and the *Judith* from London, and the *Blessing* and the *David* from Plymouth were recorded.

In 1618, Sir Ferdinando Gorges sent a fishing vessel to Monhegan. The captain, Edward Rocraft, disobeyed his instructions to wait for a rendezvous and impetuously headed south to Jamestown. Those who protested, like Richard Vines, a servant of Gorges's, were dropped off at Winter Harbor (Saco).

From "New Plymouth," the Pilgrims were soon sending emissaries to Monhegan for supplies. Edward Winslow came in 1622 and 1623. He brought Miles Standish. Through Monhegan, too, passed ships owned by Thomas Weston. This London merchant, an investor in the Pilgrims, had also sponsored a notorious non-Pilgrim colony at Wessaguscus (Weymouth, Massachusetts). Weston, himself, disguised as a blacksmith, touched at Damariscove in 1623. In the area then were seven English vessels, all fishing without a license.

This license question had caused a storm of controversy in England. On November 3, 1620, Sir Ferdinando Gorges and the Plymouth Company had secured a monopoly from the King to grant licenses to fish in North America. Each vessel would have to pay the equivalent of $100. Introduced in Parliament on April 7, 1621 was "An Act for the freer liberty of fishing and fishing voyages to be made and performed on the seacoasts and places of America."Sir Edwin Sandys, as treasurer of the Virginia Company whose Jamestown settlers wanted free fishing in the northern waters, moved the bill. However, on June 4, the King suspended Parliament until November and that same month, Sir Ferdinando's privileges were reconfirmed. A new bill was tried, but fell victim to the larger battles between James I and Parliament.

Gorges made various attempts to enforce his monopoly. His own son, Robert Gorges, was appointed Governor of New England and spent a year on the coast. After him, Captain Francis West was given titles of Admiral and Chief Naval Officer and ordered to seize Monhegan. West asserted his authority in vain. "...they were too strong for him and he found ye fishermen to be stubborn fellows," wrote the Pilgrims' William Bradford.

During the Parliamentary debates, the charge had been levelled against Gorges that his organization had not established a single settler. Stung by the accusation, the Plymouth Company soon reacted. It came up with a general plan of colonization wherein every ship it sent over would, ark-like, carry two pigs, two calves, two tame rabbits, two pairs of hens and a cock, etc. More directly, 13 fishermen were located on Damariscove year-round.

Today, Damariscove Island, in the Boothbay Region, is uninhabited. But in 1622, it, too, was a busy place. The 13 fishermen built a ten foot high spruce palisade, mounted a cannon and made use of "ten good dogs," which were either canines or slang for a type of small arm. Thirty vessels were in the harbor at Damerill's Cove, named for Humphrey Damerill, a master mariner. Edward Winslow stopped by and the Damariscove fishermen, in a generous mood because of good catches, gave him the supplies he wanted gratis. Since it was early May, they held celebrations around a maypole, a frivolity that may not have been to the sober Pilgrim's liking.

No doubt even less to the Pilgrims' liking was the capsizing of their pinnace, the *Little James*, at Damariscove in 1624. Slipping her moorings, she crashed on the rocks at Cape Newhagen. The locals refloated her with large barrels, patched her hull and relaunched her.

Thomas Weston's ships frequented Damariscove. The much-used *Swan*, coming from Virginia in 1625, sprang a leak there and her cargo of tobacco leaf was spoiled. The resulting lawsuit was among Weston's more minor troubles.

His colony at Wessaguscus consisted of 60 men hand-picked from the taverns of London. His addled theory of colonization was that single men would do better than family men in sticking to the only true goal of settlement—making money for the investors. This reflected Weston's deep disappointment with the lack of remunerative returns from New Plymouth.

But the London bar flies proved worse than useless in the wilderness. They mooched from the Pilgrims, consuming their scanty resources, and more dangerously still, they stole from the Indians. When Wessaguscus died, doomed by its own inner lassitude, Weston's people scattered, a number of them to

30

Monhegan, Damariscove and other points downeast, where they mostly disappeared from history.

One who didn't was Walter Bagnall, called "Great Walt" because of his huge size, who landed on Richmond's Island off Cape Elizabeth in 1628. Of Bagnall, it was said, "He was a wicked fellow and had much wronged the Indians." Supposedly Bagnall had amassed 1,000 gold pence from his sharp dealings in beaver furs. If so, the loot was never found.

Mistreatment of the natives was a problem at Damariscove, as well. Nicholas Frost, later a founder of the town of Eliot, was banished from Damerill's Cove for drunkenness, fornication and *theft from the Indians.*

Early in the 1620's, Gorges relinquished control of Monhegan to a fellow member of the Plymouth Company, the merchant Abraham Jennings. When Jennings later wanted to sell the island, the Pilgrims were interested. However, the eventual buyers were two worthies of the city of Bristol, the mayor's son, Robert Aldworth, and his partner, Giles Elbridge.

Their agent, Abraham Shurt, lived on Monhegan from 1626-29. He left to go to Pemaquid to manage the 12,000 acres his employers had bought on the mainland. This shift onshore was a major turning point in Maine's development. A plague in the years 1617-19 had decimated the Indians and it was claimed that from Penobscot Bay to Cape Anne, not more than 50 natives were left alive. So here and there on the coast, the English set tentative footholds—at Casco Bay, Saco, Pemaquid, Pejepscot, Kittery, York.

Today, none of the offshore islands where the early English fishermen encamped are centers of population. Monhegan is a summer colony, with a small year-round lobstering community. Damariscove is deserted. Richmond's Island is owned by a private family and sometimes let out to sheep. Hog Island in the Isles of Shoals, known now as Appledore, has only Cornell University's summer marine biology station.

Inevitably, "the Maine," the nearby fringe of continent, drew those hardy 17th century harvesters of the sea. From Appledore, they could spy the coast on a clear day. But even out of sight, the shore must have always been in their minds, framed by giant evergreens, promising a forest of vast dimension, cut by great rivers, inviting discovery and exploitation.

Focus

Sir Ferdinando Gorges

If Champlain is the "Father of New France," then Sir Ferdinando Gorges has to be the "Father of New England." But the old knight would have deplored his ultimate offspring. Instead of a feudal replica of Tudor-Stuart England, embodying large estates, tenant farmers, a centralized monarchy and church, his domains in America became democratic, levelling, non-Church of England and fiercely independent vis a vis authority. Worse, a despised, self-made merchant class, the antithesis of hereditary nobility, rose to positions of power.

Ferdinando derived his aristocratic lineage (and his unusual surname) from a petty nobleman in Normandy—a vassal of William the Conqueror who came to England during the epic invasion of 1066. His knighthood he won on his own, by feats of arms. He was made Sir Ferdinando on the battlefield of Noyon in France, fighting as an English Protestant volunteer with Henri IV's Huguenots, when his commander, the Earl of Essex conferred the honor upon him, which military leaders could do in those days.

Later, his connection with Essex, who was accused of treason by Queen Elizabeth, landed him in the Tower of London. But after James I was crowned, he was sent back to his old post in charge of Plymouth Fort.

His interest in North America began at this period of his life.

On April 10, 1606 James I issued a royal charter for two separate colonies in "Virginia." Gorges, as part of the ruling body, played a dominant role in "North Virginia." Many ships and men were dispatched by him; he liberally spent his own money and that of his four successive wives and ended up having precious little to show for it.

With the blind stubbornness of a Quixote, he tilted against powerful forces by his insistence on a fishing monopoly in northern waters. When the Plymouth Company evolved into the Council of New England in 1620, New England was expanded by royal decree to the mouth of the St. Lawrence and the Council directed to undertake "planting, ruling, ordering and governing."

The Council was designed to be self-perpetuating, with 40 members, almost all noblemen, and almost half from the West Country shires, Gorges's home territory, the prime breeding ground of most early English trans-Atlantic adventurers.

Ironically, one of the first sub-patents was to a group as different from the Council as possible. The Pilgrims—a body of dissenters from the established church, Calvinists, mostly plain people from the east of England—were given 100 acres per settler and 1,500 acres for public use.

Another grant was to prove even more momentous. The reverend John White of Dorchester, Dorsetshire, asked for and received land to set up a permanent fishing station on Cape Anne. From John White's initiative, the Massachusetts Bay Company was formed. This created the vehicle for the massive Puritan migration of the next decade; not only that, but because of a loophole in the King's charter, the Massachusetts Bay Company's "General Court," its governing body, was brought to America. Soon, the floodgates

32

of emigration opened under the systematic persecution of Puritans inspired by Archbishop William Laud of the Anglican Church. In 1630, alone, 17 ships carried 1,700 passengers to Massachusetts.

It was hardly the kind of success Sir Ferdinando had envisaged. Nor had his own affairs gone well. Not all of the 40 Council members anted up the money each had pledged. New investors had to be brought in, like Abraham Jennings. That Jennings had once sued Gorges was overlooked.

Before the Puritan occupation of Massachusetts Bay, Gorges had sent his son Robert to stake out the area. But Robert accomplished nothing beyond visiting deserted Wessaguscus. Furthermore, the Council's offer of lands on a tenant farmer basis found no takers. People wanted to own, not rent. A large ship, the *Great Neptune*, 534 tons and 40 cannon, was ordered built by Gorges to carry him to America. Legend has it— Puritan legend and wishful thinking— that God caused her to fall to pieces when she was launched. But the *Great Neptune* did go to sea eventually.

After his fourth and final marriage to Elizabeth Smyth in 1629, the old nobleman created the Laconia Company, a fur trading operation. Settlers were landed at the mouth of the Piscataqua River, the dividing line between New Hampshire and Maine. They were commanded by Walter Neale and he turned out to be a vigorous Governor. Pursuing the killers of "Great Walt" Bagnall, he hanged an Indian named Black Will on Richmond's Island and also sailed all the way to Majabagaduce (Castine) to arrest the company's agent who had gone native and was selling firearms and liquor to the Indians.

Destined to end in failure and bankruptcy, the Laconia Company, while it lasted, made numerous grants. Thomas Cammock, nephew of the Earl of Warwick, received 1,500 acres near Prout's Neck, Aldworth and Elbridge got Pemaquid and Colonel Walter Norton was allotted 12,000 acres on either side of the York River, then known as the Agamenticus. Here, Gorges's capital was later established.

In a political maneuver designed to help revoke the Puritans' Massachusetts Charter, Gorges dissolved the Council of New England in 1635. Advising him in these machinations was Thomas Morton, a rascally lawyer who had been with Weston at Wessaguscus and who, when he'd tried to revive the place as the infamous Merrymount, site of alleged orgies connected with maypole dancing, had been run out of the Bay Province.

When the Council of New England broke up, Gorges received a one-eighth share, which he called New Somersetshire, after his native county. Following a period of informal rule, this land grant, stretching from the Piscataqua to the Kennebec and also including the northern Isles of Shoals, Martha's Vineyard and Nantucket, was officially decreed by the King on April 3, 1639 to be the "Province of Maine". Under the royal patent, Gorges was to be the supreme feudal landholder—the Lord Proprietor, with extensive powers. To run his empire, Sir Ferdinando sent over his distant cousin, Thomas Gorges.

Thomas came from the Puritan side of the family and his appointment may have been aimed at conciliating Massachusetts. He proved to be a good choice. As mayor first of the incorporated *borough* of Agamenticus, then of the *city* of Gorgeanna when its name was changed,

33

he brought order to the province. He lived in a "manor" house at Point Christian on the York River that he had constructed for Sir Ferdinando. But when the English Civil War broke out, he went home to fight against the King (and Sir Ferdinando), leaving behind him a shaky but perhaps manageable governmental structure.

The old soldier, Sir Ferdinando Gorges, fought for his King in a losing cause. He died in 1647, at the age of 81, without seeing the final triumph of the Puritan Revolution. At the time of his death, Maine's future could best be deemed uncertain.

Maine Grows

Like Topsy, Maine grew without much direction from above. The proliferation of land grants had steadily spotted the southern and mid-coast shorelines with Englishmen. When Sir Ferdinando died in 1647, settlers were already living from Kittery to St. George.

Also, there were Pilgrim traders on the Kennebec. Depending which side of a current scholarly controversy one cares to take, they were either at Augusta or somewhere south of the first falls. The Pilgrims had outposts at Castine and Machias, too, until the French chased them away.

The Pilgrims' connection with Maine went back to 1625 when they sent Edward Winslow up the Kennebec with a boatload of corn that he traded for 700 pounds of beaver fur. Always pressed to pay back their creditors in England, the Plymouth Colony moved to take advantage of an economic "good thing." On January 13, 1629, a patent was issued to William Bradford for all land between "the utmost limits of Cobbosseecontee...and a place called the falls of Nequamkick..." Where Nequamkick may have been is the heart of the scholars' contention. Were the Pilgrims initially at Cushnoc (Augusta) or somewhere else? Some claim Nequamkick was north of Cobbosseecontee, perhaps at Vassalboro; others say it was to the south, around Swan Island, opposite Richmond.

Figuring in this clash of academic theories is the most dramatic event of the Pilgrims' stay in Maine—the double killings in 1634 of Moses Talbot and John Hocking.

It was Hocking, an agent for Lords Say and Brooke, who invaded Pilgrm territory, sailing up the Kennebec above their trading post in order to intercept the Indians canoeing downstream with their furs. John Howland, in charge of the Pilgrim "truck house," protested. When his words had no effect, he sent two men

34

to cut Hocking's cables. Once the interloper's vessel started to slip, he seized a musket and fatally shot one of the Pilgrims—Moses Talbot. The other man fired back and mortally wounded Hocking.

The scholars base their differing arguments on how far upriver Hocking might have gone. If the first falls are at Cushnoc, how could Hocking sail upriver past them? Thus, the Pilgrims had to be south of Cushnoc. A counter-argument is that at high water the Augusta falls are passable and the first real falls aren't until Taconic (Winslow).

Wherever the gun battle occurred, the incident had repercussions in England and Massachusetts. Lords Say and Brooke were furious. A reflection of their discontent reached the Massachusetts Bay Colony. When a Pilgrim vessel landed in Boston, John Alden, who had been present during the fracas but not a participant, found himself under arrest and in jail. Miles Standish was sent to secure his friend's release. The innocent Alden never went to trial and the Puritan authorities eventually did declare Hocking at fault.

Pilgrim trade on the Kennebec prospered. Between 1631 and 1636, the Pilgrims shipped more than 12,500 pounds of beaver to London. Yet price gouging by their creditors kept their obligations outpacing payments. Despite beaver exports worth £10,000, they still owed £1,200 and William Bradford declared they had been "hoodwincte."

As for the Puritans in Massachusetts, the years 1630-42 saw a massive influx of settlers of their persuasion—the Great Migration. While the inhabitants of Maine could be counted in the tens and the Pilgrims around Plymouth in the hundreds, the Puritans crossed the Atlantic by the thousands. The 1,700 who arrived in 1630 swelled to 24,000 within a dozen years.

That the Puritans differed from the pioneers in Maine was hardly surprising. The latter were mainly either adherents of the orthodox Anglican Church or mere ruffians and adventurers. These Puritans were God-fearing folk, intent on practicing their own form of non-hierarchical church government. So, too, were the Pilgrims, but the Puritans parted company from the Pilgrims on the question of separation from the established church. The Pilgrims openly proclaimed themselves Separatists. The Puritans insisted on staying within the Church of England to "purify" it.

This question of "Separation" indirectly led to the first *Puritan* movement north into Maine. The controversial religious views of Anne Hutchinson led not only to her banishment from Massachusetts, but also the expulsion of her brother-in-law and principal follower, the Reverend John Wheelwright. While she went south, he went north, first to Exeter, New Hampshire, then to Wells, Maine.

Governor Thomas Gorges, who had Puritan sympathies, gave Wheelwright and his followers 400 acres between Ogunquit and Kennebunk. This was in 1641 and three years later, a Maine government under Richard Vines confirmed the Planation of Wells,[1] named for Thomas Gorges's English hometown. The Wheelwright exiles included persons with surnames still prominent in the area—Edmund *Littlefield*, William *Cole*, William *Wentworth*—and one whose family appellation has long since vanished—Edward Rishworth.

Rishworth married Wheelwright's daughter and moved to York. He became well known as an indispensable bureaucrat and a nimble politician, too, able through talent to mollify both Puritans and Royalists, serving first one and then the other as they alternated in power.

The York to which Rishworth removed had been founded in 1630. Edward Godfrey, a prosperous London merchant who emigrated to America at the age of 45, was its first settler. Soon joining him were Colonel Walter Norton and Edward Johnson, both refugees from the stifling theological atmosphere of Massachusetts. In Rishworth's day, the original settlement of Agamenticus had become the city of Gorgeana. A city on paper, anyway, meant to have a mayor, 12 aldermen, 24 councilmen, two to four "sergeants of the white rod," two courts, etc. Not much of this ever reached fruition. A mayor, yes, one Roger Garde, who died in the 1640's, reputedly of a "broken heart" over the charge that he'd consorted with a Mrs. Richard Cornish, subsequently executed for the murder of her husband.

Early York mirrored the quintessence of Maine settlement under Sir Ferdinando Gorges. Aristocratic pretensions and bunch of tough, unruly backwoodsmen. The "armigerous gentry," to use the quaint phrase of York's historian Charles Banks—such men as Colonel Norton and Edward Godfrey at York, Arthur Champernowne and Alexander Shapleigh at Kittery, Captain Richard Bonython at Saco, Henry Josselyn at Black Point, Captain Thomas Cammock at Prout's Neck and Robert Trelawney at Cape Elizabeth—were "Loyal to their King and faithful to their church." They were mostly from the West Country, adventurous in spirit, liberal in their fondness for the good life (and loose customs) of

THE ENGLISH STAKE THEIR CLAIM

Merrie England, and staunchly opposed to the Puritanism that had seized Massachusetts. For two decades, a non-violent struggle ensued between these two types of Englishmen who had come to New England. Overseas in the home country, their military counterparts—cavaliers and Roundheads—fought a bloody Civil War.

Maine was not yet Maine but still New Somersetshire when the first court (and government) was organized within the province on March 21, 1636. Representation on it stretched from Agamenticus in the south to Pejepscot in the north. Captain Richard Bonython's house on the east bank of the Saco River provided the courtroom space. The good captain, himself, during the proceedings, brought a complaint against his scapegrace son John, who not only had insulted Richard Vines but more seriously had committed incontinency with Ann, his father's servant"—only the first in a long line of outrages perpetrated by the young Bonython.

Greater Saco was considered the oldest, most flourishing center of habitation in the province. The ubiquitous Richard Vines had set the pattern by wintering in the area in 1616. This was at Biddeford Pool, known then, not surprisingly, as Winter Harbor.

On one of his trips from England to visit his brother at Scarborough, John Josselyn described the region from Winter Harbor to Saco as "one scattering town of large extent, well-stored with cattle, arable land and marshes and a saw mill."

A vivid writer, and often cited as Maine's first naturalist, John Josselyn has left us many interesting descriptions of early Maine, some real, some frankly quite fanciful.

On August 10, 1638, as he relates it, he was out hunting near the seashore, about to pick some black currants, when a "great and grim over-grown she-wolf" appeared. He rushed for his gun, shot the creature, cut open her belly and found she had been feeding on his brother's goats, worth £5 per animal. About a year later, so he says, he killed four score snakes, "some as big as the small of my leg...three yards long...with a sharp horn on the tip of their tail..." If these are rattlesnakes (they existed in Maine until the 19th century), the number of them and the size seem a bit much. Next, he was on to *sea serpents,* a large one "quoiled up like a cable" on a rock at Cape Anne.

Human misadventures of a mystic nature were also tales that Josselyn related. Like the experience of Mr. Foxwell—most likely Richard Foxwell of Scarborough who had married Captain Bonython's daughter Winnifred—wherein ghostly figures of men

37

and women dancing about a fire on shore called "Foxwell, Foxwell," to him, then vanished after he brought his boat in for a closer look. But far more hallucinatory, and an enduring feature of Maine folklore, is Josselyn's story of what happened to Michael Mitton in Casco Bay. While out "fowling" (hunting seabirds), he was attacked by a "Merman" or "Triton." Two scaly hands grabbed a gunwale of his canoe and the terrified Mitton chopped them off with an axe, watching in horror as purple blood spurted everywhere and the hideous creature sank.

Yet like Richard Foxwell, Michael Mitton was an historical personage. In June, 1640, Mitton was made Constable of Casco when the "Province of Maine" held a general court session at Saco.

That session entertained 18 civil actions and 9 complaints and also allowed for lesser courts to be held at York, thus setting the precedent by which a courthouse would be established to the south and the political center of Maine would eventually shift from Saco.

Another focus of development was in and around Casco Bay. Michael Mitton lived on Peaks Island, which was known then as Mitton's Island and had been a gift from his father-in-law, George Cleeve. An interesting man was Cleeve, a gadfly, almost always in trouble. It started when he was evicted from his squatter's claim at the mouth of the Spurwink River by John Winter, agent for Robert Trelawney, the august Lord Mayor of Plymouth. Undaunted, Cleeve sailed to England, met with Sir Ferdinando Gorges and returned to Maine in 1637 as Deputy Governor (but not for long). With him, too, he had brought a patent from Gorges for a place the Indians called Machegonne—today, the "Peninsula," the heart of Portland. He had been given rights to the Casco Bay Islands, as well, and thus his gift of Peaks to Mitton.

Cleeve attended the various courts in Saco; as a defendant in 1636, where he paid a £5 fine for "rash speech" and as a plaintiff in 1640, when he won £80 in damages against Winter for his eviction from Spurwink.

The Cleeve-Winter feud represented a running picaresque theme of discord that would have been comic if it hadn't had unfortunate future consequences. Bound to triumph over the "grave and discreet" man who had humiliated him, Cleeve appealed to the Puritans for help and when turned down, went off to England to pursue his enmity and ambition.

Winter, meanwhile, kept to business on Richmond's Island, where he supervised more than 60 people, most of them engaged in

38

fishing. Six to eight women, including Winter's wife Joan, helped make the colony self-sustaining. John Josselyn wasn't very flattering to Maine fishermen, "roystering and gulling in Wine," and ready to fight "when Wine in their guts is at full tide." But there is evidence the hard-working young fellows on Richmond's Island were rather more sedate and even religious.

It is known they voluntarily chipped in from their wages to have an Anglican priest, Richard Gibson, minister to them and many became solid citizens after they left the island. They were loyal enough to Winter so that when government officials came to collect the £80 court assessment against him, they formed a mob to drive them away. A few, led by John Lander, deserted in a dispute over wages. One of these was John Bailey who saved his money, moved to Blue Point in Scarborough and became a wealthy farmer.[2] The women were a varied lot. Poor Maid Thompson was a good worker who drowned while fetching cows;then, there was Priscilla Beckford, described as filthy and grossly obese, and repugnant to the point where the men wouldn't have her boil a kettle for them, "she is so sluttish."

Winter was a tough boss. It is said he didn't care for ordinary people nor was he slow to find ways to dock his workers' wages—wages contracted for in England that were below prevailing rates in America. It wasn't hard for Cleeve to profit by the depth of feeling against him.

To be sure, Cleeve was no angel. Dropped by Sir Ferdinando Gorges as Deputy-Governor, he quickly gravitated to Colonel Alexander Rigby, a member of Parliament, whom he induced to buy an important tract of Maine land and put him, Cleeve, in charge. This was the Lygonia Patent[3] and stretched from Cape Porpoise to Cape Elizabeth. "The General Assembly of the Province of Lygonia," held by Cleeve and Henry Josselyn at Black Point was an example of the fracturing of governmental authority in early Maine. Indeed, the "Province of Maine" was soon to find itself with *four* separate governments.

The territory eventually split included sparse settlements north of Portland and areas farther down east, like Castine and Machias, that had come under the French. Closest to Casco Bay was the settlement started by Thomas Purchase at Brunswick. As a fur trader, he found the falls of the Androscoggin River the ideal site for intercepting Indian hunters and trappers en route to the coast. Here, too, was some of the best salmon and sturgeon fishing in New England.

39

The business Purchase carried on near Pejepscot Falls lasted more than 35 years. It was known he cheated the Indians. Not only did he sell them liquor but he watered it so much that one Indian is reported to have cried, waving a rum bottle, that he was drinking from "Mr. P., his well."

Colonists were slow to follow Purchase into the virgin wilderness. Huge grants had been given in England, like the Muscongus Patent to John Beauchamp and Thomas Leverett, but these were not immediately populated. A man named John Brown supposedly received the first deed ever granted by an Indian when he paid Samoset 50 beaver skins for a piece of land. A present-day pro-Indian historian[4] has questioned this transaction. Why would an Englishman give furs to an Indian? Yet it is recorded that a John Parker bought Sebascodegan Island for one beaver skin, plus corn and liquor.

Pemaquid was the next major locus of development going farther down east. The estuary of the Pemaquid River was occupied on both sides, the western side perhaps as early as 1623.

John Brown and his future son-in-law Richard Pearce may

Early map of Province of "Mayne"

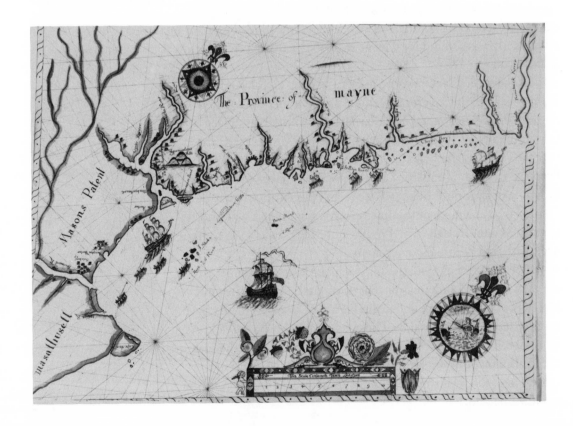

have been those 1623 settlers. By 1626, Abraham Shurt was on the scene. It was Shurt who acknowledge the famous Samoset deed to John Brown. A man of "great prudence and discretion," Shurt was the magistrate at Pemaquid for 30 years. In 1686, when he must have been over 80, he was still town clerk.

Unlike most of his colleagues, Shurt gained a reputation for fair dealing as a trader and this earned him the respect of both the Puritans and the Indians. The latter even allowed him to settle disputes among themselves, like that of 1631 when some Penobscots raided Agawam (Ipswich) in Massachusetts and carried off the wife of a local chief. Shurt diplomatically arranged for the squaw to be returned.

By 1640, Pemaquid was adjudged a prosperous community. John Winthrop's journal records that a Massachusetts merchant took aboard 20 cows and oxen at Pemaquid the same year, with a value of more than £500.

The arrival of the ship *Angel Gabriel* at Pemaquid was considered memorable. While anchored, she was caught in a hurricane and broke up; a seaman and three or four passengers were lost, as well as most of the cattle and goods. "From the character of the furniture which was saved, and is now greatly prized," wrote the noted Maine historian James Phinney Baxter, "the passengers must have been persons of some wealth and social importance."

Because of its strategic location, the proprietors ordered a fort built at Pemaquid. Its exact site is in dispute. But whether it was by the mouth of the harbor at Fish Point or elsewhere, one fact is clear: "Fort Pemaquid was the scene of the first pirate attack on the Maine coast."

Dixie Bull was the pirate. The possessor of this unforgettable name was a young man of good English family who had come over to York in 1631, with a deed to property from Sir Ferdinando Gorges, himself. He began fur trading down east and was ostensibly honest until robbed at Castine by a party of French interlopers. Soon, Bull and his crew of 15-20 men were roving the coast, seeking revenge. Unfortunately, in the absence of French targets, they chose English ones. Sailing boldly into Pemaquid in the fall of 1632, they plundered £500 worth of merchandise. On their way out, however, a lucky shot from the fort killed Bull's second-in-command.

A wild chase ensued. Hot on the pirates' trail were five vessels, including one from Massachusetts commanded by Samuel Maverick, a co-owner of Bull's land in York. The pursuit con-

tinued even after a letter was sent by the miscreants, promising not
to molest any more Englishmen. But by all accounts, Bull eluded
capture and somehow got back to England unscathed.

Like the wreck of the *Angel Gabriel*, the story of Dixie Bull
became a favorite fireside folk tale in Maine. It spawned an apocryphal ballad, in which the pirate is dispatched by plain old Daniel
Curtis, a fisherman of Bristol Bay. "The Slaying of Dixie Bull"
depicts the two men, stripped to the waist, fighting a Hollywood-
like sword duel on Beaver's Isle.

> Like a flash at him Dan went
> And through his breast his sword he sent,
> The blood rushed out warm, bright and red,
> The pirate staggered and fell dead.
> Then like a stream rushed Dixie's gore
> O'er Beaver's bleak and rocky shore.

Still farther down east, two English outposts existed, yet the
French persisted in their claims to the area. At Machias, where
Richard Vines had a trading house, the French struck in 1634 and
two of Vines's men were killed—accidentally, said the attackers.
The next year, the Pilgrims' fur swapping station at Castine was
seized.

Maine's biggest problem, on the other hand, remained internal dissension. As the decade of the 1650's began, the
settlers, themselves, had split into three governments. The
Province of Maine, the Gorges empire, had shrunk to a handful
of towns—Kittery, York, Wells—under the Royalist Edward
Godfrey. The next "province," that of pro-Parliament Lygonia,
was ruled by George Cleeve and stretched, at least theoretically,
from Kennebunk to the Kennebec. The third jurisdiction was
Sagadahoc, from the Kennebec to the Penobscot. Beyond were
the French, on territory deemed to be part of Maine.

Into this power vacuum, the mini-imperialism of Massachusetts was soon drawn, perhaps inevitably and certainly inexorably.

CHAPTER Four

A TIME OF CHANGE

The Massachusetts Takeover

The burgeoning Puritan colony in Massachusetts had a natural proclivity for expansion. This had been demonstrated during the Pequot War of 1636 when Massachusetts troops marched south in what was really a complicated land grab. As an excuse for the invasion, blame was laid on to the violent deaths, two years apart, of Englishmen who, coincidentally, had Maine ties.

The first incident involved Captain John Stone who went to York and took two local men with him on a return voyage to Connecticut. What Colonel Walter Norton and young John Godfrey, nephew of Edward Godfrey, were doing with Stone, a man of evil reputation, isn't known. On board his ship were kidnapped Indians and at the mouth of the Connecticut River, these rebelled, killed Stone, the crew and finally Norton, whom they overcame after his gunpowder blew up in his face and blinded him.

The other slain Englishman was John Oldham, originally from Biddeford and a one-time partner of Richard Vines. The Pequots were blamed for killing him, but the murder, which took place on Block Island was actually committed by their arch-rivals, the Narragansetts.

No such dramatic pretexts were necessary for the Massachu-setts thrust northward. It started when the General Court gave its permission for a house to be built at Winnicunnet, today's Hampton, New Hampshire, to shelter men sent to harvest the salt hay of the bountiful coastal marshes. Already, Massachusetts had inter-

preted its charter to allow it to creep into territory allotted to
Captain John Mason, since the Puritan leaders took the language
"three English miles northward" of the Merrimack River to mean
three miles north of the *source*, not the mouth. Subsequent surveying set the upper Massachusetts border in the vicinity of Lake
Winnipesaukee to the west and Casco Bay to the east.

So Hampton was fair game for settlement; in 1639, 56 Puritans were sent into the region. A year later, armed conflict nearly
broke out in Dover, N.H. between Puritans and Anglicans, and
Massachusetts was called upon for protection. Portsmouth fell not
long afterward and Exeter, the last of the quartet of towns that
made up New Hampshire, succumbed in 1643.

The totally suffocating theocracy of the parent body was not
forced upon the newcomers. They were allowed their own courts,
no taxes except for their own benefit and could send deputies who
were not church members to vote in the General Court—a privi-
lege denied to towns in Massachusetts. This was a pattern of semi-
tolerance later also accorded to Maine.

The year 1643 saw Massachusetts initiate an alliance—the
United Colonies of New England—linking Massachusetts Bay,
Plymouth, Connecticut and New Haven for defense and offensive
action (against the Indians). The exclusion of Maine was deliberate. John Winthrop explained why:

> Those of Sir Ferdinando Gorges, his province beyond
> Pascataquack were not received nor called into the confedera-
> tion, because they ran a different course from us both in their
> ministry and civil administration: for they had lately made
> Acomenticus (a poor village) a corporation, and had made a
> tailor their mayor, and had entertained one Hull, an excom-
> municated person and very contentious, for their minister.

The "one Hull," by the way, was the Reverend Joseph Hull, a
graduate of Cambridge University.

Edward Godfrey's "province" in the three southernmost
Maine towns began to feel the heat. It was proposed to seek confir-
mation of the government they had formed as a lawful substitute
for Gorges's rule. Word of their plan reached Boston. On October
23, 1651, the General Court sent a "loving letter and friendly" to
Maine to declare it lay within Massachusetts' jurisdiction. Godfrey
drew up his petition and shipped Richard Leader of Kittery home
to England with it. That Cromwell's Puritan regime would recog-

44

nize any Royalists overseas was a naive hope, at best.

Massachusetts moved again in June 1652, this time with Commissioners who went in person to Kittery. They received no submission, neither then, nor in October, when an ultimatum expired. A marshall and his deputies accompanied the next group of Commissioners who arrived on November 16, 1652. These four men, Simon Bradsteet, Samuel Symonds, Thomas Wiggins and Bryan Pendleton, bargained with the locals and finally induced 44 of them, a large majority, to sign an agreement to capitulate.

Once across the "Pascataquack," Massachusetts turned on York. Another "loving letter and friendly" summoned the people of "Acomenticus" to assemble at Nicholas Davis's tavern between 6:00-8:00 P.M. on November 22. This stormy town meeting ended with 50 signers, and they included Governor Godfrey, who'd led the vain opposition. Edward Rishworth was among those who submitted. In the newly formed County of Yorkshire, Rishworth secured the job of Recorder, plus magistrate of the court Maine was allowed to keep. Godfrey, too, was made a magistrate.

Next, Wells. More than half a year later, on July 5, 1653, it voted to join Massachusetts. The Bay Colony had moved its fron- tier up to that of the Province of Lygonia.

In point of fact, the border had already been crossed. The sub- mission of July 5, 1653 had included Saco (with Biddeford), Cape Porpoise and Kennebunk. George Cleeve came back from England in September and learned that Massachusetts had laid claim to a large portion of his "province". He then sent a series of diplomatic letters to Boston, asking for clarification and expressing doubts about the claim. Just as politely, he was told of the blessings that would accrue from a merger.

On May 15, 1657, two of Cleeve's fellow Lygonians, Henry Josselyn and Robert Jordan, received another of those "loving letters and friendly." They were asked to journey to York to settle the governmental future of "those parts beyond Saco to the utmost bounds of the Massachusetts charter." Neither appeared nor did they honor a request to present themselves in Boston five months later.

Once more, commissioners were sent north. Yet another meeting was held—this time at Robert Jordan's house in Spurwink. The inevitable again was accepted—29 signers from Black Point, Blue Point, Spurwink and Casco Bay, among them Cleeve, Jordan and Michael Mitton, bowed to Massachusetts. The date was July 13, 1658.

FOCUS

D'Aulnay and La Tour

In northeast Maine, meanwhile, a tale straight out of the fevered imagination of a fiction writer held center stage. The plot, involving two fiery Frenchmen and their wives, was as complicated as a Feydeau farce, but with overtones of violence and tragedy. Although one had Protestants antecedents and the other was pure Catholic, the two rivals were personal antagonists rather than political or religious foes. They fought for power.

It all began when the Treaty of St. Germain in 1632 restored Acadia to France. Sent to govern the land was Isaac de Razilly, cousin of Cardinal Richelieu. In separate sub-commands, Razilly assigned key lieutenants and they included, in Maine, Charles de Menou, Seigneur d'Aulnay de Charnissay, and, in Nova Scotia, Charles Éstienne de la Tour. As long as Razilly lived, there were no conflicts between his subordinates. But once he died in 1635, La Tour and D'Aulnay were at each other's throats.

La Tour had a Protestant background. But he had proved his loyalty to France by fighting off an English attack on Acadia headed by his own father, a Huguenot. Moreover, he was a patron of the Recollect Fathers and seemingly devoted to the Church of Rome. Yet when he needed help against D'Aulnay, he wasn't bashful about seeking it among the Puritans in Boston.

One fine June day in 1643, Governor John Winthrop was enjoying a picnic with his family on an island in Boston Harbor when a boatload of armed Frenchmen arrived. It was La Tour and since Boston's fort lay practically defenseless, its walls crumbling, Winthrop was relieved that his intentions were friendly. What La Tour wanted was to hire men and ships for an expedition against D'Aulnay. A month later, having added 70 men and four ships to his forces, he departed for the north country.

At first, La Tour harassed his enemy continually, driving him from St. John to Port Royal and at last to Castine (Pentagoët). A raid on a mill there left three of D'Aulnay's men dead and a year later, in another raid, an Englishman working for La Tour was shot and killed. The turning point of the war-feud came in 1647. Counterattacking, D'Aulnay stormed La Tour's fort at St. John. In the absence of La Tour, Mme. La Tour had to lead the defense. After the garrison surrendered, D'Aulnay broke his word to spare her men. He had them all hanged before the horrified eyes of his rival's wife who was forced to watch with her hands bound and a noose around her neck. The poor woman never recovered from the shock and died three weeks later.

However La Tour had the last laugh. D'Aulnay eventually drowned while swimming in the river at Port Royal. La Tour, a widower because of his enemy, married his enemy's widow, a denouement that no writer of fiction would ever dare attempt.

The North Country

"Aux yeux des Francais, la riviere Kennebec marquait la frontiere de la Nouvelle-France..." ("In the eyes of the French, the Kennebec River marked the frontier of New France...") So states a Canadian publication celebrating "350 years of Partnership" between New England and Quebec. *Contact* would be a better word than *Partnership*, for at the outset, religious and national differences between the two entities, as well as overlapping land claims, created a natural enmity over contested territory. After the trading post (at Castine) the English called Penobscot was captured by the French in 1635 and became Pentagoët, priests followed. As early as 1640, Capuchin monks were at Pentagoët, where they established a hospice and built a chapel in honor of Our Lady of Holy Hope. The most noted of the early clerics, Father Gabriel Druillettes, was a Jesuit, and he began his mission in 1646 at *Narantsouak*, or Norridgewock, on the Kennebec. A Christianized Indian, Charles Meiaskat, had paved the way by converting the Kennebecs—an unsung event of great importance in Maine history. Norridgewock's Catholic Indians were to play a major role for the next 80 years.

Father Druillettes stayed with them first for a year, then seven years. He consolidated firm, lasting ties between the Abenakis and the French. When a group of Maine Indians, captured by the English, were questioned as to what the French had taught them, they replied:

> We have learned that the Lord Jesus Christ was of the French nation, that his mother, the Virgin Mary, was a French lady, that the English murdered Jesus, that he rose from the dead and that all who would win his favor must avenge themselves on the English...

Yet it's doubtful such propaganda originated with Father Druillettes. He was not that anti-English or else he wouldn't have undertaken several trips into the heart of New England—to Boston and Connecticut—seeking allies against the rampaging Mohawks from the west.

The black-robed Jesuit seemed always on the go. No sooner had he arrived at Norridgewock than he was off again, visiting the Capuchins at Pentagoët, then taking a general tour of Maine, including Augusta, Damariscove, Pemaquid, New Harbor and St. George's. When the United Colonies of New England asked the

French to open trade relations, the good father was sent. Was this conscious irony? Massachusetts had a law on its books at the time, banning all priests and especially Jesuits.

Father Druillettes met open hostility at Damariscove, where the fishermen accounted him a spy. But in Boston, the General Court received him and prominent citizens invited him to dinner.

Unable to converse in English, his Latin came in handy. His special friend was John Winslow, who ran the Pilgrims' Augusta outpost. Thanks to Winslow, a merchant's house in Boston was made available where he had full freedom to say his prayers and exercise his religion. The two men even had pet nicknames for each other. Druillettes was *Xavier*, after the famed Jesuit St. Francis Xavier, and Winslow was *Pereira*, after a Portuguese merchant who'd accompanied the Saint to the Orient.

As a diplomat, Druillettes had been authorized to offer the English: "*plus amples avantages commerciaux et une grande compensation pour les depenses de guerre.*" ("Most ample commercial advantages and generous compensation for military expenses.") His appeal for troops to fight the Mohawks was based on defending "Canadian Christians," including the Abenakis of Maine. Druillettes asked the General Council of the United Colonies to unleash Plymouth, which already controlled parts of Maine.

But the Jesuit failed to persuade the Yankees. Some were tempted by the promised trade with Quebec, especially since commerce with Virginia and the West Indies seemed threatened by the English Civil War, but in the end they were afraid to incite the Iroquois confederation. Thus, an opportunity which might have avoided decades of conflict, was never grasped.

Yet who knows? Opportunities for conflict were never far from the surface during these contentious times. Even minor differentiations weren't exempt.

For instance, in the north Country of Maine, the Pilgrims had their outpost on the Kennebec at a period when the Plymouth colony was separate from Massachusetts Bay and determined to maintain its independence. So in May 1654, the Pilgrims sent Thomas Prence, Governor William Bradford's top aide, up to the Sagadahoc country to organize a government. This he did, in the Merrymeeting Bay home of Thomas Ashley, in a meeting not unlike those "loving and friendly" ones held to the south. In this case, the 16 signers pledged their fidelity to Plymouth Colony, not to Massachusetts Bay.

Earlier, Thomas Prence had tried to get the Puritans to help

48

Plymouth regain its trading post at Castine. An armed attempt by
Miles Standish and a man named Girling had failed. Massachusetts
refused, citing an inability to "procure you sufficient supply of men
and munition."

Plymouth acted at Merrymeeting Bay in part to forestall
competition for the fur trade. A well-connected interloper in this
northern area was Thomas Lake, a Boston merchant who had
flanked the Pilgrims by buying land above and below them on the
Kennebec at Waterville and Pittston. In the ensuing race to buy up
Indian property, Lake acquired political clout by teaming up with
Thomas Clarke, a fellow Hub merchant and one of the city's
representatives in the General Court.

This potential competition was changed to cooperation
through the good offices of William Paddy, ex-treasurer of the
Plymouth colony and a neighbor of Lake's in Boston. The Pilgrims
and the Clarke and Lake Company agreed to pool their merchandise in a single venture. That their enterprise failed had much to do
with "coasters," who defied Plymouth's weak authority and traded
illicitly with the Indians. One such was Joshua Tead who sold
liquor and possibly gunpowder to the Abnakis. The problem grew
worse in 1659 when "coasters" killed and kidnapped a number of
Indians and brought the fur trade to a temporary halt.

Already, Plymouth had lost interest. The extraordinary growth
of Massachusetts had begun providing markets to its farmers, so
that cash from the northern outposts became less vital. As
Plymouth's role waned, the Clarke and Lake Company expanded.
What's more, they diversified from furs into lumbering, farming,
fishing and local merchandising. At a "mansion house" in
Arrowsic, the two owners spelled each other as directors on the
scene. The company also brought many settlers into the area and
owned a shipyard where reputedly Sir William Phipps worked as
an apprentice.

The political nature of Maine was changing. The Massachusetts way, not exactly democracy but tending toward it, was
advancing and taking hold. Land distribution was an important
criterion. Rather than the feudal idea of great proprietors, giving
out grants, with tenants renting lands from those grantees, land
ownership by individuals was the touchstone of Massachusetts
policy. At first confined to church members, in Maine this require-
ment was set aside. Common lands were distributed in "towns,"
where formerly there were "chartered cities." "Selectmen" and
"town meetings" came into being. Even on the northern frontier, as

49

shown by the Clarke and Lake Company, a mercantile, money-making class—itself transforming Puritan society—had implanted its values. By the start of the 1660's, Maine was a much different place from what it had been 20 years before.

Maine's New Government—the Courts

Regulation of people's behavior was the essence of government to those rude settlers. A hardy and sometimes unreasonable individualism marked the Maine personality then (as it still does today). The court records show many examples of this "down east persnicketiness," none more glaring than that of the notorious Andrews family in Kittery, the first town in Maine to accept the Massachusetts promise of law and order and security.

Actually, prior to the Massachusetts takeover, Edward Godfrey's last court had this entry on October 14, 1652:

> We present John Andrews for threatening Mr. Godfrey and Mr. Withers that he would beat them.

Less than a year later on June 30, 1653, the first court held by Massachusetts saw another member of the family appear before it:

> Joanne Andrews, wife of John, presented for abusing a Grand Juryman with many threatening and reviling speeches.

Joanne pled guilty, was admonished and paid the court fees. Within four months she was back—for "selling a firkin of butter to Nicholas Davis which had two stones in it containing 14 2/3 pounds."

Convicted, she had to post a £5 bond until she satisfied her sentence, which was to stand at York and Kittery town meetings with her offense "written upon a paper in capital letters pinned upon her forehead."

In the session of June 1654, Joanne was *presented again*, this time for "stealing of certain things from Goody Hale." Not only did she have to pay 30 shillings restitution, but also additional fines for cursing and lying, since she had made "several Asservations, such as wishing the earth might open up and swallow her if she had any goods of Goody Hale," and then confessing to the thefts.

50

During the session of July 6, 1657, the Andrews' outdid themselves. Daughters Sara and Joanne were on the docket for breaking into the house of Robert Wadleigh. Father John was hauled in for threatening Wadleigh. And mother Joanne hit the jackpot with triple offenses:

1. for frequenting the company of Gowan Wilson at unseasonable times at home and abroad very suspiciously to the great discontent of the wife of the said Wilson.
2. for threatening Goody Whitte at York.
3. for contempt of authority, saying she cared not a turd for Rishworth nor any magistrate in the world.

This last offense, not surprisingly, brought the most condign punishment. Joanne was to be tied to a post and given 20 lashes on her bare skin. But being pregnant, she got off with a £5 fine.

While the Andrews family's assaults on authority may have been emblematic solely of untamed personality traits, political overtones are discernible in some of these court cases. Thus, William Wardell of Wells found himself in trouble "for casting an aspersion on the magistrates of Massachusetts Bay" and the irascible John Bonython of Saco was arrested when he labelled Massachusetts men "rogues and rebels against His Majesty."

The 1660's would witness a seesaw struggle for power in Maine, but overall, the firm grip of Massachusetts was molding the land.

General conditions

In 1663, John Josselyn came back to Maine. A quarter of a century had elapsed since his first trip and the America he described— from New York to Nova Scotia—was flourishing. Somewhat defensively, he fears the skepticism of his readers: "...you never heard nor saw the like, therefore you do not believe me..." And consequently, in this second piece, he is less prone to such wild stories as Michael Mitton and the Merman.

Yet Josselyn is always a lively, colorful writer. Although styling himself John Josselyn Gent.—*Gentleman* was close to a title in those days and Josselyn, himself, was the son of a nobleman—he could use in the most artless manner language that is picturesque, to say the least.

51

...the black currants which are larger than the red smell like cat's piss, yet are reasonable pleasant in eating...

...Fuss-balls (apparently a type of mushroom)...called by the fishermen Wolves-farts, are to be found plentifully...

...the old man falls asleep and lying upon his back gaped with his mouth wide open enough for a hawk to shit into it...

The latter snippet is from a "whopper" Josselyn tells of an old *planter* (farmer) at Black Point (Scarborough) who on a warm, sunny day did, indeed fall asleep on a grassy bank, with instructions to his 12 year old son to wake him in two hours. Out of his opened mouth a large bumble bee suddenly, inexplicably, flew and not until the bumble bee returned could the boy rouse his father. The insect "lighted upon the sleeper's lip and walked down as the lad conceived into his belly," whereupon the old man awoke.

Descriptions of nature abound in Josselyn's work. Some will make a Mainer of today feel right at home.

The country is strangely incommodated with flies, which the English call mosquitoes, they are like our gnats, they will sting so fiercely in summer as to make the faces of the English swelled and scabby, as if the small pox for the first year. Likewise, there is a small black fly no bigger than a flea, so numerous up in the country that a man cannot draw his breath but he will suck them in; they continue about thirty days say some but I say three months, and are not only a pesterment but a plague to the country.

It was a world at once familiar yet different. Foxes were hunted in the dead of winter by dumping a sledgeload of cod heads on one side of a "paled fence." When the moon would shine, the animals came to the bait and were shot by the score. Hot fox fat was used for ear ache. A *rout* of wolves (12 or more) was likely to be nearby. Mothers hung wolf fangs around their children's necks and rubbed their gums with them when they were teething.

The moose was known, but Josselyn was afraid his readers would consider its size—antlers 12 feet wide, etc.—to be "monstrous lies."

He described the wonder of the passenger pigeon:

...I have seen a flight of pigeons in the spring...that to my thinking had neither beginning nor ending, length nor

52

breadth, and so thick that I could see no sun, they join nest to
nest and tree to tree by their nest many miles together in pine
trees...

But he adds:

...of late, they are much diminished, the English taking them
with nets. I have bought at Boston a dozen of pigeons ready
pulled and garbaged for three pence.

He writes of lobsters so prolific that he has seen an Indian boy
spear 30 in less than two hours. One crustacean specimen weighed
20 pounds. Clam beds a yard deep and a quarter mile long are
cited. Huge oysters, "very fat and sweet," need to be cut in three
pieces before they can be eaten. The fish life had no end: trout "in
every brook, ordinarily two and twenty inches"; 3,000 salt water
bass taken at a single set; silver-bellied eels, which in London
would cost 8-12 pence apiece, sold by Indians at 3 pence the half
dozen. The herring were stupendously abundant and he saw a
phenomenon that still happens in modern times.

In *Anno Dom* 1670, they were driven in Black Point Harbor
by other great fish that prey upon them so near the shore,
that they threw themselves (it being high water) upon dry
land in such infinite numbers that we might have gone
up...amongst them for near a quarter of a mile...

On Maine people, Josselyn is more sparing in his remarks. "I
shall only speak a word of the people in the province of Maine and
the Duke's province..." (from the Sagadahoc area to Nova Scotia).

...Of the magistrates, some be Royalists, the rest perverse
spirits, the like are the planters and fishers, of which some be
planters and fishers both, others mere fishers.

Craftsmen were rare—a few coopers, smiths and carpenters—
and no shop keepers. Massachusetts merchant supplied all needs.
Their stores had English goods, but at excessive prices, he thought.
The farmers, if diligent, could become rich.

...but if they be of a dronish disposition as some are, they
become wretchedly poor and miserable, scarce able to free

53

themselves and family from importunate famine, especially in the winter for want of bread.

The fishermen sold their catches to Boston merchants who in turn shipped them, with boards and staves, overseas to Lisbon, Bilbao, Bordeaux, Marseilles, the Canaries, etc. Too often the pay was in strong spirits—rum, brandy, Madeira, etc.—the fishermen "becoming thereby the merchants' slaves," and the same thing happened with careless farmers.

Concerning individual Mainers, Josselyn writes little. He does mention a "Mr. Purchase," presumably Thomas Purchase, who cured himself of sciatica with bear's grease. Most unforgettable is "the waggish lad at Cape Porpoise who baited his hooks with the drowned Negro's buttocks."

The Royalist Counterattack

A dyed-in-the-wool King's man, John Josselyn could not forego occasional partisan comments. Directly discoursing on the politics of Maine, he declared "The Province of Maine...is a colony belonging to the grandson of Sir Ferdinando Gorges," and that Gorges had "his Province encroached upon by the Massachusetts colony who assumed the government thereof."

His narrative then turns to the Royal Commissioners sent over by Charles II (restored to the throne in 1660) with instructions to re-introduce the King's authority in New England. In Maine, a putative Royal government was put in place. Josselyn disgustedly continues:

> But as soon as the Commissioners were returned for England, the Massachusetts enter the province in a hostile manner with a troop of horse and foot and turned the judge and his assistants off the bench, imprisoned the major or commander of the militia, threatened the judge and some others that were faithful to Mr. Gorges's interests...

The "judge," in this case, was Josselyn's own brother Henry and he was one of 11 Justices of the Peace whom the King's emissaries had appointed. Later, when the Puritans deemed this action void, their excuse was that only three Commissioners had been present—their chairman, Colonel Richard Nicolls, being absent in New York, which he had just conquered from the Dutch.

The three Commissioners spent two months in Maine. After they had effectively severed Maine from Massachusetts, or so they thought, they journeyed beyond Pemaquid into the "Duke's Province" and set up another government, in what they called *Cornwall County*. They were emphatic that their task was solely to re-impose His Majesty's writ, not to help the Gorges heirs who had already previously sent over an agent, John Archdale.

The Commissioners had something Archdale didn't—400 soldiers. And except for Nicolls, who was tactful, they could not have antagonized the Puritans more. They even accused the United Colonies of having joined in a "war combination" to throw off the rule of England. Uniting, itself, they declared, was the King's *prerogative*, and they wanted democratic words like "commonwealth," "state," etc. stricken from the law books. In Maine, they pronounced the Bay Colony's government one of "rebels and traitors."

Most likely, it was with sternly suppressed whoops of inner glee that the Boston elders saw the trio leave for England.[1] The Puritans bided their time, then finally went north with their "Troop of horse and foot."

Puritan apologists have stated the soldiery was purely ceremonial. Henry Josselyn, who went to meet the delegation at York saw things as more intimidating. Beating drums and armed men on horseback with drawn swords hardly offered the calm atmosphere for a man of his refined temperament to argue the legal niceties of the King's prerogative. In a rather comic opera series of rival meetings, Josselyn's people took seats in the local church that their opponents had vacated to go to dinner. But the Massachusetts folk returned, demanded their places back and the Scarborough squire gave way. Thus were "the judge and his assistants turned off the bench"—literally.

Persecuted Massachusetts partisans jailed under the Royalists, like Peter Weare and Nathaniel Masterson, were rewarded with public office. Opportunists like Edward Rishworth who had served Massachusetts, then the Royal Commission, had to be nimble; initially, he was fired, but once he made a public apology to the Bay Colony, he was elected again. Watching Rishworth—and he was to make one final flip-flop under James II—was like a political science lesson in the vagaries of early Maine government.

FOCUS

The Dutch in Maine

Windmills down east? Wooden shoes and tulip beds beside the Penobscot? The images are anachronistic, but a corner of Maine once was officially titled *New Holland*. All of the territory north and east of the Penobscot (Nova Scotia included) was claimed "in the name of and for the High and Mighty and Privileged General (Dutch) West India Company."

This unlikely event occurred in the summer of 1674. After Colonel Nicolls took New York from them, the Dutch promptly recaptured it. Since the Sagadahoc area also belonged to the Duke of York, the Dutch decided to claim it, too. The skipper of a warship at Curaçao in the West Indies, Captain Jurrien Aernouts, received orders to sail his frigate *Flying Horse* to the north country and capture Pentagoët (Castine), then held by the French.

Aernouts stopped in New York City first. There, he met an English adventurer, John Rhoades, who swore fealty to the Prince of Orange and joined in the attack on Pentagoët Fort. Aernouts was successful. To add insult to injury, he carried de Chambly, the French commander, off to Boston and ransomed him for 1,000 beaver skins.

Here at Pentagoët and elsewhere in Acadia, the Dutch buried glass bottles containing their written claims. The local French swore allegiance to the Netherlands.

But it was not to last. The buccaneer Rhoades, left in charge, was apprehended by English ships off Machias and his Dutch flag torn down. Tried in Boston for piracy, he wasn't executed, although convicted. The Boston magistrates at the time were distracted by an event far more damaging to the public weal than a mere foray of sea rovers under a foreign flag. King Philip's War had erupted in Massachusetts and soon would spread to Maine.

CHAPTER Five

A TIME OF TROUBLES

King Philip's War

The ever-useful John Josselyn is again indispensable in bringing to life the Indian population of Maine just prior to the "War." How big was that population? Howard S. Russell in his book "Indian New England Before The Mayflower" calculates that after the epidemic of 1616-17, the whole of Maine had around 5,000 Indians. Pre-plague, he estimates 36,000 to 38,000.

Josselyn mentions the plague, too, and says it reduced the Indians of Massachusetts from 30,000 to 300. He somehow relates the local Indians to the Tatars of Central Asia, describes them as "pale and lean and Tatarian-visaged" and ascribes their speech to a dialect of Tatar, "as also is the Turkish tongue." These Indians, he states, are a "tall and handsome timbered people, black-eyed, which is accounted the strongest for sight, and generally black-haired..." They had no beards or "very rarely," he said, and their teeth were "very white." As comparisons were perceived in his day, with Austrians being known for their great lips, Jews by their goggle eyes, so Indians are distinctive because of "their flat noses," but those in Maine, Josselyn adds, are less depressed than those farther south.

Female Indians, whom he calls "Indesses," are "some of them very comely," with bodies "as smooth as mole skin," which they dye tawny while their old women he deems lean and ugly but goes on condescendingly, "are of a modest demeanor, considering their savage breeding," and he admits they shame "our English rustics whose rudeness in many things exceedeth theirs."

Josselyn also displays much of the prejudice of his time. He likens the Indians to the Irish, whom the Britons of that period considered savages, too, partly to excuse their usurpation of Ireland. The Indians are accused of cannibalism as "were formerly the heathen Irish, who used to feed upon the buttocks of boys and women's paps." The mourning cries over deceased Indians are likened to "the howlings of the Irish."

The Indians' relations with the English seem benign enough in Josselyn's writings, as indeed they were at this period. He does however touch upon the trading of rum to the Indians by both

King Philip

French and English and how it has killed many of them, "especially old women who have died when dead drunk." The cruelty of the natives to their enemies is graphically portrayed. As an eyewitness to the death by torture of two Mohawks, Josselyn introduces his readers to a scene of horror soon to be visited upon individual Englishmen who fell into Indian hands.

Josselyn mentions King Philip, as well, (he calls him Prince Philip) but actually only in the context of discussing how Indian notables adorn themselves with wampum. Philip came to Boston, he said, wearing a broad wampum belt and wampum beads on his buskins, an outfit worth £20 pounds.

Philip, of course, was not this Indian leader's real name. He was Metacom, son of the Pilgrims' friend Massassoit. Why he went to war in July 1675 has been the subject of fierce polemical discussion for hundreds of years. Was he justifiably goaded or was he of "a subtle and mutinous temper?" The precipitating incident was the murder near Plymouth of a Christianized Indian named John Sassamon, for which three Wampanoags were tried and hanged, perhaps unjustly. Philip responded with war, despite the attempt by a group of Rhode Island Quakers to mediate.

Maine might have stayed out of the conflict except for an act of supreme folly. As the story goes, a group of English sailors were drinking on the banks of the Saco River and discussing a theory then held that Indian babies knew instinctively how to swim. Spying a canoe with an Indian mother and tiny child in it, they deliberately upset the craft. The infant died as a result and since the victim was the son of an important chief—Squando of the Sacos—dire revenge was not long in forthcoming.

An interesting sidelight to this famed tale is revealed by John Josselyn. Talking about Indian customs, he does mention how the Indians will throw a baby into the water to see if it will swim. The reason is to test a suspicion that a child might have been fathered by a member of another tribe; should the child swim, it is accounted their own—a weird if not barbaric custom perhaps known to those English louts on the Saco.

The timing of the drowning has never been pinpointed, but it has to have been between the first raid by King Philip (against Swansea, Massachusetts) on June 24, 1675 and the first attack by Squando (against Saco) September 18. As early as July 11, word had reached York of the fighting in Massachusetts and 700 Maine militia readied themselves for possible action.

The first trouble downeast came when a group of

59

Anasagunticook Indians (Androscoggins) ransacked the trading post of Thomas Purchase at Pejepscot. Purchase was away and his womenfolk weren't harmed, but the natives made off with his liquor and ammunition and out of spite ripped up his feather beds and killed his sheep and cows. They were settling scores with the wily old trader for his adulterated liquor and outrageous prices.

Far more dire was an incident in the Falmouth area, when seven members of the Wakely family were massacred. Only 11 year old Elizabeth survived—taken captive—and reputedly carried off to Rhode Island.

At Saco, the people were forewarned. It was through rascally John Bonython, whose faithful Indian friend had alerted him, and this allowed the inhabitants to crowd into the fortified garrison house of Major William Phillips. With a brief exchange of musketry, the settlers repulsed the attack of Squando and his allies, who then set fire to Phillips's saw mill, corn mill and tenants' quarters. "Cowardly English dogs," the Indians shouted. "Come out and fight the fire." Seeing that maneuver fail, the attackers advanced again behind an ox-drawn cart filled with straw, birch bark and powder. Major Phillips, wounded in the arm, let them come within pistol range. A wheel stuck, the cart slanted and the Indians became exposed to a murderous fire. Six were killed, 15 wounded and they broke off the siege.

Scarborough's turn was next. At Blue Point, they killed a Mr. and Mrs. Nichols, then assaulted Foxwell's Garrison at Dunstan (West Scarborough). Killed there were the Alger brothers, Andrew and Arthur. A shallop was burned, as were grain stores at the Landing Place on the Dunstan River. Arriving from South Berwick, a Captain Wincoll and his small group of men found themselves confronted at Black Point by 150 Indians. In this skirmish, one Joseph Ring was captured and burned alive.

All that autumn, western Maine suffered. By December, it was calculated that 50 English had been killed between the Piscataqua and the Kennebec. Lieutenant Roger Plaisted and his two sons were ambushed and slain at South Berwick. In the Cape Neddick section of York, the Jackson family was wiped out. Settlements around Casco Bay were visited by marauding bands. Most Biddeford Pool homes went up in flames.

Then came winter, always a hard time for Indians to find food, so they sued for peace. But this lull proved to be only a temporary truce.

On August 12, 1676, King Philip was hunted down in the

swamps of Rhode Island. But the awful spectacle of the Wampanoag chief's severed head in the marketplace at Plymouth brought no surcease to Maine's difficulties. A day before Philip's death, a raid was made at Casco Bay by a party of Androscoggins led by a Wampanoag named Simon who had escaped from Dover jail. A day after his death, the trading post of Richard Hammond at the mouth of the Kennebec was torched. No less hated than Purchase, Hammond wasn't as lucky; he and two others were slain and 16 of his people taken prisoner. The sole escapee, a young girl, walked 12 miles through dense forest to warn settlers along the Sheepscot. On August 14, this war party fell upon the Clarke and Lake Company garrison at Arrowsic. The residents, sound asleep despite having heard shots the night before, were easily overcome. Four men, alone, escaped by canoe. Among them was Thomas Lake himself, but he was overtaken on the tip of Georgetown Island and killed by an Indian named Sagamore Sam. Sylvanus Davis was also one of these fugitives. Wounded, he crawled into a cleft of rock under a cliff, hid for two days and lived to participate in subsequent battles.

The major cause of Indian discontent in the Sagadahoc area was a ban on sales of firearms and ammunition to them. So dependent had they become on guns for hunting that they protested the prohibition would cause them to starve to death. Another sore point was the practice by some unscrupulous English sea captains and others of seizing Indians and selling them as slaves overseas. Evidence of its impact was documented to the Massachusetts General Court in 1677 by a Bernard Trott who, in asking to be reimbursed for having procured "the freedom of a couple of Indians" sold at Faial in the Azores, stated that the act perpetrated "by one Waldron...*made the first Indian war.*" Waldron was Major Richard Waldron of New Hampshire who had secured his captives by luring them to a meeting on false pretenses.

Active in Maine, Waldron led a rescue column up to Sagadahoc, which was deserted, its inhabitants all refugees on Monhegan. Waldron re-garrisoned Arrowsic (under Sylvanus Davis) and returned to Boston. After further Indian attacks, the whole Duke's Province was abandoned until June 1676 when New York, which claimed jurisdiction, sent out a force of four sloops and erected a new fort at Pemaquid on the burnt-out ruins of the old one.

Meanwhile, in Maine proper, the fiercest fighting was again at Black Point in Scarborough. A newcomer to the area, Captain

61

Joshua Scottow, had a garrison there. As a Bostonian and a Puritan, he had been none too welcome in this heartland of Royalist sentiment. But he had bought land of Henry Josselyn and had built the primitive fort at his own expense. In October 1676, it was attacked by a local chief from Saco, the famous Mogg.

The personalities involved form a drama out of which John Greenleaf Whittier was to fashion an epic poem, "Mogg Megone." The title approximates the real-life sachem's name of *Mogg Heigon*. In the fictional account, Mogg is inflamed to go to war because of the perfidy of the infamous John Bonython, who offers him his daughter Ruth for a wife, receives land in return and then reneges. The model for "Ruth" may have been Bonython's actual daughter Elinor, a lady of doubtful virtue.

The real-life Mogg moved on Scottow's fort while Scottow was away and the courtly Henry Josselyn in command.

> Grey Josselyn's eye is never sleeping
> And the garrison's lights are burning clear
> For the eyes and ears which are watching for Mogg
> Are keener than those of the wolf and the fox.

So writes Whittier, but the truth was that when Mogg called on Josselyn, whom he knew, to surrender, the old gentleman went out to parley and soon caved in. That he did was due to an unpleasant surprise back at the fort. Everyone had fled, except his own family and servants.

True to his word, Mogg treated Josselyn well. But he, himself, was ill-treated when he went to Boston to arrange a truce. Clapped in jail, Mogg was finally able to extricate himself and go back to Maine.

In May, 1677, Lieutenant Bartholomew Tippen fired a sharpshooter's shot that downed the leader of Indian charge against the Black Point blockhouse. His first conjecture was that he had killed Simon, the "arch incendiary." But this fallen chief turned out to be Mogg and his death thoroughly disheartened the local warriors. Still, there was to be one more major battle at Black Point. An expeditionary force of 40 English and 200 friendly Indians under Captain Benjamin Swett of Hampton landed nearby and fell into an ambush at Moor's Brook. Among those killed were Swett and Lieutenant Tippen.

It was this disaster that spurred the Governor of New York, Sir Edmund Andros, to send sloops of war to Pemaquid. Peace came about a year later with a treaty signed at Casco Bay. Squando promised to release all prisoners while the colonists pledged a peck of corn in annual rent for each English family in Maine. King Philip's War had taken 3,000 Indian lives and those of 500 whites, 360 of them east of the Piscataqua. The English survivors returned to the blackened ruins of their homes and began rebuilding. Unconsciously, too, a metamorphosis in political thinking had been triggered. Thrown together by the common danger, men of different allegiances saw they had to cooperate. Joshua Scottow, the Puritan in Anglican Scarborough, might still be criticized by certain of his fellow townsfolk, but he had fought side by side with them. Maine settlers now realized they had to rely on troops from Massachusetts. For the Bay Colony, Maine had become an important buffer against any threat from the north. And before long, the challenge of the French would be continually testing the resolve of these two merging populations.

A Political Interlude

In "Flintlock and Tomahawk," Douglas Edward Leach writes:

> The shortness of tempers in Massachusetts during July of 1676 can be explained largely in terms of three things—Indians, drought and Edward Randolph.

> Of the three annoyances, Randolph was conceivably the worst. The younger son of an impoverished landed family in Kent, he first came to Massachusetts as a special courier for the King's government. The drought passed, the Indian troubles faded, but Randolph stayed off and on for almost the next fifteen years to plague the colony's political leaders.

> Randolph's goal was to pick up where the failed Royal Commission had left off, i.e., to reduce proud Massachusetts to obedience to the King's prerogative—and, incidentally, to profit personally, himself. In the eyes of the Royalist bureaucracy, the Bay Colony had been brazen beyond belief; they had literally ignored an order to send agents to London to defend their conduct, and, more astonishingly, had been allowed to perpetuate their disobedience for a whole decade, 1665-1675.

> Worse, these Puritans had even dared to enunciate a doctrine of quasi-rebellion. Thomas Danforth, Deputy Governor of the

Province and later "President of Maine" declared to the General Court that Massachusetts owed allegiance to England only in external affairs.

When the pro-Puritan Earl of Shaftsbury fell from power in 1674, the ten year hands-off hiatus ended. The Privy Council created a Committee for Trade and Plantations and once again, Massachusetts was ordered to send agents to London—this time to dispute a claim by the heirs of Sir Ferdinando Gorges and Captain John Mason for all of Maine and New Hampshire.

Edward Randolph, a cousin of Mason, was sent in May 1676 to deliver the demand in person. He also received instructions to report back on conditions in Massachusetts.

A memorandum entitled "The Present State of Affairs in New England" resulted. It made eight damaging points about Massachusetts. The sixth was that the government established in Maine by the Royal Commissioners had been overthrown by force—a charge basically true. Other charges, while true, were exaggerated or distorted. Massachusetts, Randolph claimed, had become a "commonwealth" (never officially) and violations of the Navigation Acts had cost the Treasury £100,000 a year (highly inflated). His anti-Puritan spleen was such that he declared the Bay Colonists had no rights to either their land or their government.

Clearly, an assault of this magnitude had to be answered. The two agents sent by Massachusetts, ostensibly to argue the case for political control over New Hampshire and Maine, soon had to defend the very existence of their own government.

On the issue of Maine and New Hampshire, the Chief Justices of England voided any right to govern New Hampshire except by the King, thus making it a crown colony, while Maine was given back to the Gorges family. However, an adroit maneuver allowed Maine to stay under Massachusetts. Working through John Usher, later Lieutenant-Governor of New Hampshire, the Massachusetts Bay Company surreptitiously bought out the Gorges rights for £1,250. Taken by surprise, Charles II was furious,[1] but Massachusetts had legitimized its claim to Maine.

Edward Randolph, though, was far from through with the Puritan colony. Appointed Collector of Customs for New England in the fall of 1679, he arrived in New York that December, met with Sir Edmund Andros and the two men joined forces. In time, Andros was put in charge of a catch-all Royal government called the Dominion of New England. It stretched from New Jersey to

Maine and represented the ultimate triumph of the Royalists in
quashing colonial independence. By then, 1686, James II was King,
Massachusetts had lost its charter and the military martinet Andros
ruled arbitrarily, without an elected assembly, ignoring his Council,
loosing Randolph and other fortune-seeking carpetbaggers upon
the settlers and threatening land titles. In the spring of 1688, he set
out on a special expedition to Maine, with Randolph along,
specifically to survey land titles. But the ultimate consequence of
his trip was to provoke war. Andros attacked the French settlement
at Pentagoët and plundered the possessions of its commander, the
Baron de St. Castin.

Focus

Andros and Castin

Two aristocrats, one born on the
Channel Islands, the other in the
Pyrenees, one English, one French, are
fitting symbols of the polarized national
interests that tore Maine apart following
King Philip's War.

Both Sir Edmund Andros and the
Baron Jean Vincent D'Abbadie de St.
Castin had made marginal contributions
to that initial conflict. Andros, as
Governor of New York, established Fort
Charles at Pemaquid. Less visible, Castin
was rumored to have been active behind
the scenes, egging on the Penobscots
against the English.

A decade of peace then descended
upon Maine. Andros emerged as the
virtual dictator of the Dominion of New
England, while Castin led a felicitous
life, married to Mathilde,
Madockawando's beauteous daughter,
and engaged in lucrative trade, not
infrequently with Boston merchants.

Castin's business activity eventually embroiled him in the thorny issue of
who controlled the Penobscot country.
The trouble arose over a shipment of

Baron de Castin

65

wines. Who had the right to collect the duty on them? Was it Andros's man, the high-handed John Palmer, *"le juge de Pemaquide,"* as Castin called him, or was this French territory?

The disputed cargo was mostly Malaga wine, 70 pipes of it, sent from Spain and consigned to the Boston merchants, Nelson, Watkins and Company, whose senior partner John Nelson knew Pentagoët well, since his uncle Sir Thomas Temple had surrendered it to the French after the Treaty of Breda.

But now, the French claim was no longer recognized. "Judge" Palmer sent a ship to seize the goods. There is no doubt he would have sold them for his own profit had Castin and Nelson not protested so vociferously and in the end, the wine shipment was returned.

Far more serious, two years later, was the raid on Castin's establishment. One account has Castin away salmon fishing at Lake Alamoosook at the time; another says he hid in the woods at the approach of the frigate *Rose.* The house that was plundered by Andros had crude furniture hand-made by Denis, Castin's man-servant, who, Sancho Panza-like, had accompanied his master from the Baron's family estate in Béarn to the New World. The furniture, as well as all arms, powder, shot, iron kettles and trading cloth was carried off by Andros's orders. Then, in his usual, insufferable haughty manner, he sent word to the Frenchman that he could have his belongings back if he came to Pemaquid and swore fealty to the King of England.

Castin did come to Pemaquid, but not in the prescribed humble manner. On August 2, 1689, an Indian attack, planned by Castin and the Jesuit priest Father Louis-Pierre Thury, captured Fort Charles.

Three and half months earlier, on April 19,[2] the Andros government had been overthrown by a bloodless mini-revolt in the streets of Boston. What caused the upheaval was news of the "Glorious Revolution" in England that toppled the secret Catholic James II and replaced him with the Protestant monarchs William and Mary. But one effect downeast was to weaken defenses, leaving a mere 40 men at Pemaquid, officered by Lieutenant James Weems.

The struggle for Fort Charles was bloody. After an all-night battle, the wounded Weems surrendered on promise of a safe conduct, but the terms were broken. All but Weems and six of his men were butchered. Nearby, the unlucky Gyles family, out haying, was set upon. The father, Thomas, was mortally wounded and sons John and James made prisoner (poor James was later tortured to death for trying to escape). All along the Sheepscot and the Kennebec, further deadly attacks cleared out the English settlers.

Andros, kept in jail in Boston, was finally sent back to England. Despite charges by the Massachusetts authorities that he had conspired with the Indians, the Crown restored him to office, but in the more congenial Cavalier climate of Virginia.

As for Castin, he continued his enmity toward the English. He also continued his commercial activities, which reputedly netted him a fortune.

Maine poet Henry Wadsworth Longfellow celebrated Castin as a romantic figure of the American past. In "The Baron St. Castin," poetic license is taken to picture the French aristocrat-gone-native about to return to the family mansion in 1701. "His father, lonely, old and grey; sits by the fireside day by day," staring mournfully out at the Pyrenees, awaiting news of his errant son. The old Baron learns that his heir has married an Indian, *une sauvage*, not a noblewoman of his own class - and he promptly dies of chagrin. It makes no difference that his "dusky Tarratine" daughter-in-law, according to Longfellow, was "beautiful beyond belief."

The historic Castin wrote how his feelings grew for the light-complexioned young girl as he watched her paddling a canoe against the tide and catching lobsters, "her every movement a poesy of motion." He had known her since she was a papoose on her mother's back. She was baptised Mathilde Mataconando and bore Castin several children. The first-

born, Anselm, had a French cradle built for him, but when, Indian-style, it was hung from the bough of a tree, a red squirrel dropped an acorn on his nose.

The Castins' idyllic life in the wilderness did come to an end. The Baron had to return to answer charges in France about his profitable dealings with the English. In his native town of Escout, Mathilde opened a school for the peasants. She taught them her native crafts of weaving willow baskets and making blankets while they, in turn, taught her the manufacture of silks, tapestries and lace.

Anselm, whom they left behind, became Chief Sachem of the Tarratines and a 2nd Lieutenant in the French Navy.

King William's War

Perhaps the most implacable foe of Sir Edmund Andros in Massachusetts was the Reverend Increase Mather. This illustrious Puritan clergyman had to flee his Cambridge home in the middle of the night and sail to England, where he was able to carry on his fight for the Bay Colony's liberties. An important ally of Mather's was the Province's High Sheriff, the Maine-born William Phips— who also played a major role in King William's War.

If anyone epitomized the new type of Englishman in North America, it was Phips, the quintessential "self-made man." Born on his father's farm in Woolwich, he was one of 26 children. Raised in conditions of poverty as the son of a simple carpenter, it could never be predicted that he would rise to become the first American knighted by the British Crown and the first to be named a Royal Governor. Leaving home at 18, he went to Boston, was a shipwright's apprentice, married a wealthy widow and acquired his own ship, which, with a crew described as "cutthroats indulged in every known form of vice," he sailed to the West Indies. Obtaining the financial help of the Duke of Albemarle and the involuntary assistance of native sea divers, he retrieved a fabulous sunken treasure off the Island of Hispaniola. The recovered loot had a value of over £300,000, an immense fortune in those days. Phips's share made him instantly rich, while the gratitude of the King, whose government got its cut, won him his knighthood and the post of High Sheriff. After the Glorious Revolution, Increase Mather's influence at court obtained him his governorship. Mather, who counted Phips among his parishioners in Boston's North Church, had deemed that the transplanted Mainer would be highly sympathetic to Massachusetts's Puritan establishment.

Even before his appointment, Phips had led a New England pre-emptive strike against French Canada, capturing the Gallic stronghold of Port Royal in May 1690. He returned triumphantly to Boston with his prisoners, only to learn the enemy had counter-

Sir William Phips

68

attacked in Maine and destroyed Fort Loyal in what is now Portland. Poor Sylvanus Davis, in command, saw his men massacred
after they'd surrendered, but he, himself, was spared.

The up and down nature of the war was further revealed
when Phips tried to capture Quebec. Facing him this time was the
redoubtable French Viceroy, Count Frontenac, and the assault was
easily beaten off. Phips had to retreat ignominiously back along
the St. Lawrence. Yet his prestige hardly suffered. Bostonians were
led to believe the defeat was God's will, in part through the intervention of Increase Mather's son Cotton, also a Puritan minister of
great influence.

Cotton Mather had baptised Phips, then 40 years old, just
before the expedition started. At the time of Phips's birth on the
Maine frontier, no clergy had been available. The roughness of his
origin never left Phips. His temper was prodigious. As Governor,
he wasn't above using his fists or his cane on a political opponent.[3] One day on Boston's Scarlett Wharf, he beat a man named
Richard Short and fractured his head; he nearly did the same to
the Customs Collector, Jahleel Brenton, for seizing certain goods
against his orders. When the Speaker of the Massachusetts House
opposed him, Phips declared, "No more Speaker," and then sent
the Legislature home.

Yet for all his faults, he was popular as "a man of the people"
and indefatigable in his efforts against the French. A lull in the
fighting ended in January 1692 with the infamous "York Massacre," when the entire Maine shire town was essentially wiped
out. Phips responded by ordering the construction of a powerful
stone fort at Pemaquid. It was a large expense, adding to a debt that
had already caused the General Court to issue the first paper
money in America. In August, to create a show of force on the
Maine border, Phips set sail for Pemaquid.

When he came back to Massachusetts, he encountered a
Province not burdened by the tensions of war but gripped by
witchcraft hysteria. The Salem madness had started, abetted to an
extent by the writings and preaching of Cotton Mather. Maine
had no trials, although one downeaster did pay with his life. This
victim was a minister, too, the Reverend George Burroughs. His
crime seemed to be that he was inordinately strong. He could pick
up a fully loaded barrel just with his thumb hooked through a
bunghole—obviously the work of the Devil, his accusers charged.

Sir William Phips, irascible and unorthodox himself, finally
ran afoul of the London authorities. Ordered to England, he sailed

69

in 1694 and never returned, dying after only a few months ashore.

King William's War continued. The most important event of these latter years was the French capture of Phips's stone redoubt at Pemaquid.[4]

Pierre Le Moyne d'Iberville, a figure of note in the colonial history of America (he is credited with being the founder of Louisiana) led the forces that converged upon Fort William Henry in August 1696. Castin was also in the attacking group, having paddled with 200 of his father-in-law's warriors to New Harbor. Iberville came on a French warship.

There wasn't a battle. The fort commander, Pascho Chubb, surrendered without a fight after an ultimatum from Castin that there would be no quarter for himself and his men if he didn't. Chubb had reason to be afraid. Six months earlier, he had lured some Indians into the fort and treacherously shot to death Chief Egeremet and his son. Yet once Chubb accepted the terms, the French couldn't control their allies, especially when an Indian prisoner found chained inside claimed he'd been tortured. A number of English prisoners were struck down before the leaders could intervene. Among those saved was Chubb, but a year later, relentless Indian revenge seekers caught up with him at his home in Andover, Massachusetts.

Frontenac had ordered the attack on Fort William Henry. He had even more ambitious plans for 1697 when he intended to capture Boston. But the promised French naval fleet was detained by headwinds.

September 11, 1697, at Ryswick in Holland, a peace treaty was signed, concluding the European phase of the war. On this side of the Atlantic, a gathering at Casco Bay in 1699 officially terminated hostilities. However, neither pact defined a border between Acadia and New England.

Out of a conflict costing the English colonists around 650 casualties, the prime lesson learned in Boston and elsewhere in America was that, to quote Howard H. Peckham in his book "The Colonial Wars"

...the only way to achieve permanent peace was to push the French off the continent.

This notion became an article of faith in Maine for the next 65 years.

MAINE GROWS AGAIN

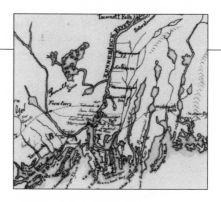

War, and More War

The impoverishment of the inhabitants of Maine at the close
of the war was dreadful, almost beyond comprehension.
Houses, barns and mills, with all the implements of agriculture, had been consumed by the flames. The people of York
wished for a grist mill. They were unable to build one. They
offered a man in Portsmouth, if he would put up a mill, a lot
of land to build it upon, liberty to cut such timber as he
needed, and their pledge to carry all their corn to his mill so
long as he kept it in order.

    The worn and wasted people gradually returned to the
desolated spots which had once been their homes. Log cabins
again began to arise in the solitudes of Falmouth, Scarborough
and at various other points, over which pitiless war had rolled
its billows...

So writes a 19th century Maine historian, John S.C. Abbott,
in a book he published in 1875. This graphically imagined description of the aftermath of King William's War was to be repeated
again and again. For not until 1763 was the French and Indian
threat totally removed.

    Meanwhile, Maine was a frontier buffer zone. The General
Court in Boston went so far as to command it to stay that way. In a
notorious piece of legislation passed on July 1, 1701, entitled "An
Act To Prevent The Deserting Of The Frontiers Of This Prov-

ince," Kittery, York and Wells were included among 21 border
towns from which the inhabitants were forbidden to relocate
without permission. Failure to obey led to forfeiture of all property
or a £10 fine for those who had no property.

A plea by Kittery for a tax abatement stated the fact that the
locals were "a poor scattering people necessitated to watch, ward,
scout, build garrisons and fortifications...and at every alarm driven
from our employment." York's post-massacre plight drew the pity
of the Chief Justice of Massachusetts, Samuel Sewall, who had
relatives there. He sent corn to "the poor families that are in
distress," having solicited relief supplies from Connecticut friends.

After less than half a dozen years of relative tranquillity,

Scenes of the Indian Wars

European politics caused war to break out anew—Queen Anne's
War (or the War of the Spanish Succession). And in America,
much of the early fighting took place in the south against the
Spaniards. Yet Maine wasn't spared. War parties under the Sieur de
Beaubassin descended upon Wells, Saco and Casco Bay in August
1703 and a few months later, other previously scourged areas, like
Black Point and York, experienced fresh raids. In response, old
Colonel Benjamin Church, the great Indian fighter, now 65, was
trotted out and sent up to the Penobscot country. So obese that his
men had to push him to mount steep inclines, Church accom-
plished little, aside from capturing Castin's daughter and burning
Grand Pré in Nova Scotia.

Indeed, the primary theater of operations remained Canada.
Port Royal was attacked twice and captured in 1710 by a British
regular, Colonel Francis Nicholson, with 500 Royal Marines. It was
renamed Annapolis Royal, in honor of the queen. A year later,
incompetent British commanders bungled a siege of Quebec City
and the largest military task force North America had ever seen—
5,000 soldiers and 60 ships—lost 1,000 men when eight transports
foundered in the St. Lawrence River before any battle could occur.

The Treaty of Utrecht, signed April 11, 1713, ended Queen
Anne's War. Its most significant aspect, from Maine's standpoint,
was that France lost Acadia—at least the Nova Scotia portion.
This was a decided improvement even if the boundaries between
overlapping French and English territory were left vague and a
prime mistake was made by allowing the French to keep Cape
Breton Island. Here, a new fortress destined to bedevil the New
Englanders was hastily constructed at Louisbourg.

In Europe, a long period of peace followed the settlement at
Utrecht. Irregular warfare, however, continued to rage throughout
the no-man's land of the Maine frontier. Along the Kennebec and
by the upper Saco, two major incidents erupted during this period
and each has found an enduring niche in Maine history.

The first of them, the massacre of the French Jesuit Father
Sebastian Rasle and a goodly number of his Norridgewock Indian
converts, had its genesis in the destruction of York by Madockawando in 1692. Most of the colonial rangers who descended upon
the village of Norridgewock in August 1724 came from the York
area. One of the commanders, Jeremiah Moulton, had been spared
as a feisty child of four during the infamous Candlemas Day raid,
beating at the Penobscot warriors with his little fists, much to their
amusement, running away unscathed and living afterward to

73

avenge manyfold the deaths of his parents and neighbors. Revenge, too, for the killing of the Protestant minister at York, the
Reverend Shubael Dummer, may have led to the killing of Rasle.
A controversial personage, a saint to the French and the Indians,
an instigator of terrorism to the Yankee settlers, Rasle apparently
was shot at point-blank range by an English lieutenant with the
French-sounding name of Richard Jacques. The priest was scalped,
as well. Jeremiah Moulton was furious with Jacques. He had
wanted to capture Rasle alive and feature him in a show trial to
prove the contention of a contemporary Boston newspaper that
the Jesuit was "the Head of the Indians in their Rebellion and...the
Chief Fondater of this war."

The smashing of the Indian village at Norridgewock was a
blow from which the Kennebec tribe never recovered. A large
number of them fled down east or to Canada.

A year later, the battle of Lovewell's Pond, although not
decisive for either side, proved to be another stroke of ill fortune
for the Indians. The scene had shifted to western Maine near the
present-day town of Fryeburg. Captain John Lovewell had gone
with a company of men in the direction of the White Mountains,

Father Rasle Monument

scalp-hunting at a time when scalps fetched £500 apiece. An Indian fired at them as they were being led in prayer by their chaplain Jonathan Frye and the entire group took off in pursuit. The quarry turned and fired, wounded Captain Lovewell and was gunned down. Meanwhile, the Pegwacket chiefs Paugus and Wahwa discovered the campsite where the men had left their knapsacks. They prepared an ambush.

During the fierce firefight that ensued, the wounded Lovewell was hit again and fell dead. Retreating to the shores of a pond, the English fought furiously. Chaplain Frye was mortally wounded. Paugus was bested in a gun duel by one John Chamberlain who was quicker to load and shoot, downing the herculean-sized Indian leader with a single musket ball. Some 40-50 Pegwacket warriors died in the eight-hour battle. Although the English were badly

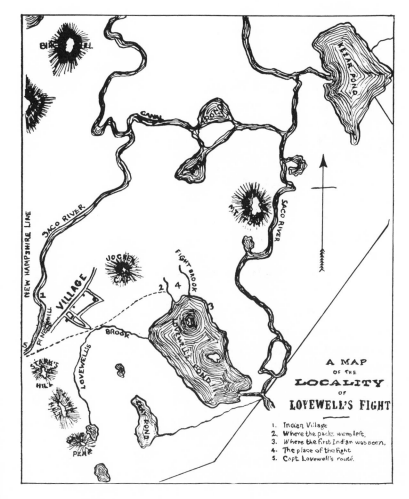

Map of the Battle of Lovewell's Pond

decimated, the survivors reached safety and as William Williamson wrote in his pioneering "History of Maine":

> The battle of Pegwacket broke the heart and spirit of the Sokoki natives. In a short time they withdrew and resided no more in those pleasant and ancient dwelling places...After this event the star of the tribe, pale and declining, gradually settled in darkness.

The peace treaty that followed has been given several names, "Dummer's Treaty," after Massachusetts Governor William Dummer, and the "Treaty of Casco Bay," where it was ratified in 1726. The English officials referred to it as "The Treaty of Pacification," and the term then also had its modern connotation—that of a cessation of guerrilla warfare achieved by the surrender of the guerrillas. The Indians had been whipped and wanted peace. The Penobscots did most of the negotiating, which took place in Boston throughout November 1725. Captain Loron was the Indian spokesman, representing all the other eastern tribes as well who wanted a "Cessation of Arms."

Of the seven points in the treaty, the most controversial required the Indians to join in putting down any tribes that broke the peace. The Indians had wanted to be assured that new settlements would not encroach upon their lands and asked to have the forts at St. Georges and Richmond removed. This request was sternly refused, but it was agreed those forts would be used as trading houses where the Indians could obtain supplies. The English agreed, at least temporarily, to halt settlement beyond the Kennebec and the Androscoggin and above Merrymeeting Bay. The caveat was that it would be done only until English titles could be proved so the Indians would have "the full knowledge and understanding of such right and title."

The latter was a real sticking point—forcing Indian minds to grasp that when their chiefs sold and deeded away land, it stayed that way forever. A special committee of the Massachusetts General Court was set up under the treaty to study the deeds in Maine—all 29 of them.

"To which," the committee reported, "the Indians replied that they had been shown Deeds and Papers enough to last them to the fall of the year, and that they did not desire to see anymore..."

This was in August 1726, at the scene of the ratification in Falmouth. And the difficulties of maintaining good relations were apparent even at that time. A man named Richard Jaquis was arrested for providing rum to the Indian delegates. He was bound over for trial in Suffolk County. Could it be that the *Richard Jaquis* of the court deposition was Lieutenant Richard Jacques, the same impetuous militia officer who had shot Father Rasle?

More ominous was a letter received from Captain Loron the following January. He said he was writing to disown the Articles. Specifically, that he was not acknowledging King George as his king, but only agreeing that he was indeed the King of England, and that he did not understand he had agreed to join forces with the English to fight rebellious natives. It was acknowledged that the letter had been written for him by Father Étienne Lauverjat, a Jesuit, who signed for him in the French manner.

It came to pass a number of years later that Massachusetts tried to invoke the provision by which Maine Indians would have to fight hostile Indians. The targets, in this case, were Nova Scotian tribes and the occasion was the next major outbreak of warfare in 1744-45.

Nothing less than a world war enveloped most of Europe, North America, the Caribbean and parts of Asia in the following years. For Maine, for New England, "King George's War," as the colonials called the War of the Austrian Succession, provided a seminal experience. The New Englanders, led by a merchant from Maine, were to capture a mighty French fortress, defeating French regulars, and do it pretty much on their own.

The merchant was a man from Kittery, William Pepperrell, rich and popular, achieving as commander-in-chief of a fairly rag-tag army the first real success Americans had in fighting foreign foes. And by then, these rough colonials did consider themselves "Americans," as opposed to purely English. At the siege of Louisbourg, the hugely expensive stone fortification Louis XIV had erected on the east shore of Cape Breton Island, the Yankees drew the contempt of the detachment of British Marines that had come with a Royal Navy squadron and they reciprocated with equal disdain for the spit-and-polish "Lobsterbacks." They considered it *their* victory when the French were forced to surrender. On previous expeditions under English leadership, they had often lost because of high command incompetence.

Louisbourg was thus an extraordinary feat and recognized as such by London. Pepperrell was made a baronet by the King, the first American ever to be ennobled. Ringing church bells and fireworks greeted the Yankee triumph on both sides of the Atlan-

77

tic. One third of the volunteer soldiery had come from Maine. An end to the French menace seemed at hand.

But there were still problems with the Indians. The troublesome clause of Dummer's Treaty, invoked after Nova Scotian tribes had joined in an attack on the English at Annapolis Royal, caused great soul-searching among the Abnakis left in Maine. Could they fight their brothers in Canada? No, they could not, the Massachusetts authorities were informed.

Accordingly, on August 23, 1745, the General Court declared war on the "Eastern Indians." Bounties were offered for captives or scalps, preferably the latter. The fighting, if anything, was more ferocious than ever—bands of marauders on either side, out prize-hunting. Many of the Indians were driven to Canada. A Reverend

Sir William Pepperrell

78

Mr. Smith of Falmouth wrote on October 2, 1745 that not a single Indian had been seen on the eastern frontier for a month. When they did appear, it was in hit and run raids, slaughtering cattle, often taking only the tongue, and carrying captives back north. One such was Captain Jonathan Williamson of Wiscasset. His captors told him the Governor of Quebec had asked them to bring back a high-ranking prisoner who could provide information on the "plans of the English."

When the mother country made peace in the Treaty of Aix-La-Chapelle of 1748, it was expected the French defeat at Louisbourg would be acknowledged. Instead, the English ministry handed the fortress back in exchange for Madras in India. The New Englanders were aghast and outraged, and the ill feelings engendered were to help lead directly to the American Revolution.

Eight months after the Treaty of Aix-la-Chapelle, delegates of the Indians of Maine journeyed to Boston and requested a peace treaty for themselves. A gathering was arranged at Falmouth, where 19 chiefs signed a "Submission and Agreement" of the tribes.

Proprietors, Big and Small

Sir William Pepperrell, the Kittery squire, represented a certain aspect of development in Maine. It was said he could ride a horse from his "mansion" in Kittery Point to Scarborough, a distance of 30 miles, and never leave his own land. But although known as one of the "River Gods," those titans of power, wealth and political influence who dominated Massachusetts (and Maine) in the mid 18th century, he was not a feudal lord in the aristocratic sense that Sir Ferdinando Gorges would have understood.

Pepperrell was simply a very successful businessman. The land he owned was not populated by tenant farmers paying him quitrents. He subdivided what he bought, like any latter-day developer, sold it and, in effect, created not housing projects but whole towns.

Like Saco and Biddeford. When, at the age of 21 his father helped him buy 10,500 acres on either side of the Saco River, a deal was first made with two local operators to set up a saw mill. Then, the rest of the four and a half by two mile parcel was broken up into residential lots, with public roads and landings laid out. Young William kept the choicest plot for himself, an 80 rod strip bordering the site of Saco's main street. Along the Saco River, a Pepperrell complex of commercial enterprises—gristmill, wharf,

warehouse, etc.—grew up to accommodate the budding community. For much of its early existence, Saco was called "Pepperrell-
borough."

The Baronet's name no longer graces any community in
Maine.[1] But Waldo—the surname of one of his colleagues, Gen-
eral Samuel Waldo—still exists for both a county (Waldo) and
two towns (Waldoboro and Waldo). If anything, the fact reflects
the efforts of this son of a petty German nobleman, originally Von
Waldow, to populate Maine. He worked strenuously to bring
Protestant settlers from continental Europe—Germans and Swiss-
Germans—to the Broad Bay area of mid-coast Maine. His agent
was a Swiss with the barely pronounceable name of Sebastian
Zuberbuhler. Concentrating on the section of the Rhineland-
Palatinate around the city of Speyer, Zuberbuhler recruited more
than 200 of the locals, all Lutherans feeling hostile pressure in this
Catholic corner of Germany. Not all reached Maine—30 elected

General Samuel Waldo

80

to go to Pennsylvania and some of the young men joined up as
mercenaries in the English army. But a nucleus of more than 150
arrived to add a new ingredient to Maine's ethnic mix.

The land to which Waldo brought them was part of the
Muscongus Patent, an ancient land grant of 600,000 acres given by
the Council of New England to several English gentlemen from
Lincolnshire. By 1714, it had devolved upon Thomas Leverett,
President of Harvard, who formed the "Lincolnshire Company and
Ten Associates."

In time, Samuel Waldo became their agent in England. He
had the daunting task of fending off a takeover by a group of
powerful Londoners, who had implanted their own man in the
contested region, a mercurial, Scots-Irish, ex-colonel, David
Dunbar. Bringing Scots-Irish immigrants to Pemaquid, Dunbar
proposed to establish an entirely new province, to be called "Georgia" and he laid out six towns named for important Whig ministers
(two of which, Walpole and Newcastle, have survived).

Waldo, a consummate politician, was too clever for Dunbar.
He lobbied the Privy Council to eject Dunbar from Pemaquid and
was finally successful after an incident caused the Sheriff and his
deputies to storm Dunbar's Fort Frederick and carry off a number of
his men to York Gaol.

Waldo's reward for his success was a grant of half the land,
and later, with the aid of his son-in-law, Thomas Flucker, Secretary
of the Massachusetts General Court, he extended his holdings to
two-thirds of the Muscongus Patent. Ironically, Waldo had originally expected his daughter Hannah (Flucker) to marry Sir William Pepperrell's son Andrew, but the young couple broke up after
a long and intermittent courtship.

The Lincolnshire Company or Waldo Patentees or Muscongus
Proprietors, whichever they were called, represented only one of
several large commercial land-holding operations in Maine.

There were the Kennebec Proprietors who traced their title to
the original Council of New England grant to the Pilgrims. It
comprised 15 miles on each side of the Kennebec River. Among
those active when it was reorganized in 1753 were Dr. Sylvester
Gardiner and such noted Boston businessmen as Thomas Hancock
and James Bowdoin.

The Pejepscot Proprietors descended from the Council of
New England grant to Thomas Purchase and George Way and
included later Indian deeds bought by Thomas Gyles and Purchase.
Among the Boston businessmen involved were Thomas Hutchin-

son, Adam Winthrop and Steven Minot.

Finally, to round out these major developers, were the Pema-quid Proprietors, arising out of the grant to Robert Aldworth and Giles Elbridge.

Settlers were brought from different parts of Europe. Waldo wasn't the only one to lure Germans. The Kennebec Proprietors, using a man named Joseph Crellius, settled 30 Germans at Frank-fort where they built Fort Shirley. The Pejepscot Proprietors successfully sought Scots-Irish families in Ulster and settled them around Merrymeeting Bay. Some land was sold to individuals. Between 1732 and 1740, William Vaughan bought all of Bristol, Bremen, Damariscotta, Nobleboro, most of Newcastle and parts of Jefferson and Waldoboro. Indefatigably energetic, Vaughan is often credited with having been the earliest proponent of an attack on Louisbourg.

The large proprietorships, with their thousands of acres, were not the whole picture. Other types of proprietorships, involving war veterans and ordinary people, were also instrumental— perhaps even more instrumental—in Maine's growth.

Focus

New Marblehead

The large proprietorships stressed devel-opment from the top down; the smaller, *grass roots* ones illustrated a different maxim, that:

> ...almost any man of whatever station who yearned for a share of frontier territory did somehow find one, either free or at a very small cost.

The Massachusetts Charter of 1691 made it clear that the attempted land grabs of Royal officials like Edward Randolph were over. The General Court was given the power to confirm land transactions.

Thus, land could be granted by the Boston lawmakers to groups of small proprietors. Since defense was a major concern, the creation of a line of settle-ments across Maine was encouraged, then actually ordered in 1727.

One of the communities to emerge was New Marblehead—today's Windham.

The creation of New Marblehead offers an excellent case study of growth "from the bottom up."

It began on November 20, 1734. Two Representatives to the General Court from Marblehead, Massachusetts, Abra-ham Howard and Joseph Blaney, intro-duced a bill to provide "A Tract of Land for a Township for such Persons belonging to said Town of Marblehead as will settle thereon."

82

A grant six miles square in Maine adjoining Falmouth was voted and a committee formed to lay out 63 lots, three of them specially set off for the minister, his ministry and the school. The land survey was accepted by the General Court on June 18, 1735.

The grantees (or proprietors), 60 in number, met at Marblehead on June 27 to dispose of the lots. Almost all of them were Marblehead residents except for one from Beverly, one from Haverhill and one from Newbury. The first lot went to the school, the second to a man named Calley Wright, the third to a sea captain Robert Parramore. The occupations of those present were highly varied, but mostly modest, although also in this socially mixed body were three "gentlemen" and four "esquires." Not all or even many of these proprietors went to Maine. Two who did and played a leading role in the early life of New Marblehead were Thomas Chute, a tailor, who received lot #12 and William Mayberry, a blacksmith, granted lot #57.

The proprietors met regularly in Marblehead and wrangled over such items as whether or not to build a saw mill, a meeting house, a bridge over the Presumpscot, etc. It was only two years later that they did decide to build a meeting house and the next year learned from Chute that Indian hostility had prevented the workmen from erecting it.

The local Indians were a small group under Chief Polin who lived along Lake Sebago. They complained the Presumpscot had been dammed and the movement of fish obstructed, despite promises to the contrary by Colonel Thomas Westbrook, a developer of the river. The proprietors back in Marblehead chose a committee to deal with the Indians and included their Representative Joseph Blaney and the sea captain Robert Parramore. The upshot was a meeting between Chief Polin and Governor Jonathan Belcher on August 10, 1739.

The problem of the dammed Presumpscot was discussed. The Governor promised to tell Westbrook to open his dam. Polin said the Indians did not want a dam any higher than at Sacarrapa, about 7 miles above the New Marblehead saw mill. The Chief also asked for a small quantity of rum, "but not so much to get drunk, for that is contrary to our religion," and he complained that his young men wanted to dance but had no drum.

The disputes with the Indians might have hindered development at New Marblehead, but could hardly permanently retard it. Active people like Thomas Chute were not only building on their owns lots, but were buying others and clearing the land.

William Mayberry, the blacksmith, a tall, bony man of great strength, originally from Antrim County, Northern Ireland, set up his forge under a gigantic oak tree, with his anvil on a nearby stump. His dry wit may have been a forerunner of "Maine humor." Accosted one day by a stranger on horseback from "Away," asking "how far is it to the blacksmith's shop?" Mayberry pointed to the woods around them and said in proper dead-pan down east style, "Yer in it right now, but it's three miles to the anvil."

His daughter, who bore the unlikely first name of Sea Fair, married the holder of Lot #4, Stephen Manchester, after he was widowed. Manchester, himself, had come to New Marblehead in pursuit of his first wife Grace, whose father John Farrow of Tiverton, Rhode Island, had deliberately fled to the wilderness in a vain attempt to keep her away from Manchester.

83

From Ulster, from Rhode Island, from Massachusetts, settlers came and the work of clearing and building proceeded apace. On Lot #33, initially set aside for the ministry, a "Province Fort" was erected and completed by the summer of 1744, just before war broke out again. It was one of a series in Maine authorized by the General Court and other defenses were built at Scarborough, Gorham, Sheepscot, Broad Bay, Medomak, Damariscotta, Buxton, etc.

The New Marblehead "Province Fort" was 50 feet square, two stories high, with walls of hewn hemlock one foot thick. The proprietors in Massachusetts voted to pay for its gunpowder—£20/9 shillings worth.

Dominicus Jordan was put in charge of a "Snowshoe Company" of 50 men. Desultory fighting with the Indians took place from the late 1740's to the mid 1750's. The culmination came in a showdown battle with Chief Polin in 1756. An ambush was laid by the Indians at Lot #21, where Ezra Brown was shot through the heart and killed and Gershop Winship was wounded and left lying on the ground, scalped. A group of settlers rushed to the scene. Winship was rescued (he lived another 10 years) and Stephen Manchester fired a shot that fatally wounded Chief Polin. The Indians fled with his body, which they allegedly buried on the shores of Lake Sebago. After that, the Indian troubles ended.

The proprietorship continued. The town grew and diversified. By 1759, 594 acres had been cleared, with 29 habitable dwellings for the 29 families in residence. In 1762, New Marblehead became Windham.

And Still They Come

Maine was filling up, slowly but steadily, during this more than half a century of intermittent warfare with the French and their Indian allies. The war, itself, helped contribute to the populating of the region. Soldiers who came to protect the frontier were attracted by the availability of land and stayed. And in some cases, the government designated property in Maine to be used for veterans' bonuses.

The Narragansett grants were intended by the General Court to reward those who had fought in King Phillip's War. Two Maine communities directly resulted: Narragansett #1 became Buxton and Narragansett #7, Gorham. Canada townships were for veterans of the expedition against Quebec in 1690. The most prominent in Maine was Sudbury Canada, now Bethel.

It took many years before most these land grants were settled. Several of them fell within territory that after 1741 was deemed to be part of New Hampshire, which assumed a separate government that year. This happened to a Captain William Raymond, a survivor of Phips's expedition to Quebec, whose 1735 grant, being lost to New Hampshire, was later replaced by the General Court with a township bordering Lake Sebago. Thus the town of Raymond came into existence.

Once a town was established, it didn't necessarily stay that way. The breaking off of a distinct section to form another town is a time-honored method of establishing new municipalities in Maine. The most recent case transpired in 1981, when the Legislature permitted Ogunquit, after years of dispute, to secede from Wells.

The first instance occurred in Kittery in 1713. A special commission was created to oversee the setting off of *Upper Kittery*, transforming it into the town of Berwick. Then, over the years, this "precinct of Berwick", itself subdivided, spawning the present-day legal entities of South Berwick and North Berwick, while Eliot was yet another town carved from Kittery.

The Massachusetts General Court had to become active in policing these changes. In the 1715-16 session, they heard the report of a committee for establishing the line between Berwick and Kittery and had to clarify if the inhabitants between Sturgeon Creek and Thompson's Brook belonged to the Upper Parish of Kittery or not. They also had to deal with specific individual problems. Like that of Francis Allen who had arranged with Kittery for £12 a year to take care of Thomas Younglove, "a blind impotent Man of that Town." Once the separation had left Younglove in Berwick, Kittery would no longer pay and Allen could get no help from the law since the Justices of the Inferior Court were all citizens of Kittery.

That same legislature received petitions for settlements at Casco Bay and Arrowsic, for a ferry across the Saco River, for aid to a budding community at Cape Porpoise and heard the report of a committee looking into a road from Wells or from Newitchawanock (South Berwick) to Pejepscot Falls (Brunswick). The General Court also took a pro-active role in populating its District of Maine by establishing a committee to "Prosecute the Regular Settlements of the Eastern Frontier." On June 2, 1715, this group, composed mainly of representatives from Maine towns, proposed the establishment of two new towns, each of six square miles. One from Pejepscot Falls to Maquoit on Casco Bay was to be called Brunswick; the other, from east of the Androscoggin to Merrymeeting Bay, would be Topsham. Having done this, the lawmakers then voted £500 to repair the fort built by Andros at Pejepscot Falls. "It would be the best bridle to the eastern Indians," they declared.

In the cases of Berwick, Brunswick and Topsham, new towns were being created in already settled regions. As the 18th century advanced, the coast began to fill up and an inland movement, mostly along waterways, such as at Windham and Raymond, took place.

In York County, Sanford was laid out in 1734. Originally, it was called Phillipstown for Major William Phillips who had received an original Gorges grant. The name Sanford came about because Phillips's wife had once been married to a man with that name and her son, Peleg Sanford, was among those to whom her second husband's large estate was willed. Hollis, when it became a town, first took the name Phillipsburg, also to honor the Major.

Another town to the westward that received settlers in the first half of the 18th century was Lebanon. Until then, it had been known by its Indian name of Towweh. Its own proprietors listed it with the mouthful of "The-new-town-lately-granted-by-the-General-Court-at-the-head-of-Berwick," and, as an afterthought, "on-the-easterly-side-of-the-Salmon-Falls-River."

To quote a chronicler of the populating of Maine during this era, Charles Clark, in "The Eastern Frontier":

> No single rule...can explain the push into the northeastern interior during the first half of the eighteenth century. No all-inclusive generalization can accurately describe the origin of all the towns that were established to accommodate the new breed of Yankee settler...

Thus, settlers could be found at North Berwick as early as 1736, although as a separate town, it wasn't incorporated until 1831. Among these initial residents was the Hussey family, whose name is noted still in today's Hussey Manufacturing Company of North Berwick.

Other interior York County places like Hollis, Lyman and Waterboro received settlers in the 1750's and 1760's.

Movement was continued all the way west to Fryeburg in 1763, after land was granted General Joseph Frye, a hero of the French and Indian War. Oxford County, which would not be created until 1805 out of York and Cumberland Counties, was in the process of being born as a migratory route. People came on horseback, and in oxcart and on foot, driving their cattle before them—first John Stevens and Nathaniel Merrill and Limbo, their black slave, then others from York or Berwick or Sanford or Francisborough (Cornish) across the Ossippee River to "Pequawket," which the Indians had deserted. A large number came from Andover, Massachusetts and some of these went on to establish the present-day town of Stowe, Maine.

Cumberland County, like York, had a variety of new communities. Actually, due to the Indian wars, some of the older communities needed help from the General Court to re-establish themselves. In May 1717, a petition was presented from former proprietors of North Yarmouth (incorporated 1680) asking for permission to "Settle a Towne" and particularly for assistance against timber thieves. About five years later, after a few of the old proprietors had acted on their own, the Legislature established the "Committee for the Resettlement of North Yarmouth."

North Yarmouth, called such to distinguish it from the existing town of Yarmouth on Cape Cod, then contained today's Yarmouth, North Yarmouth, Cumberland, Pownal, Freeport and Harpswell. Dominating the legislative committee was Elisha Cooke, a political powerhouse in Boston, leader of the "Popular Party" and a large Maine landowner. Further Indian warfare drove out the 25 families Cooke's committee initially settled in 1722 but by 1728, some 34 "proprietors and settlers" were back. Friction between the locals and the committee, especially over how to pay the salary of the minister Ammi Ruhamah Cutter, led to the town's creation by 1740 of a full-fledged municipal government with a seat in the General Court.

Moses Pearson was an outstanding individual, connected with three Cumberland County communities. First, Falmouth, to which he moved in 1728, then Gorham, the Narragansett #7 township, where he became one of the chief proprietors and finally Standish, granted to him and the company of men he'd raised for the Louisbourg expedition, and which for a while went under the name of Pearsontown.

A solid, Massachusetts-type Congregationalist, Captain Pearson was considered part of the Falmouth gentry, holding local offices, representing the town in the General Court and serving eventually as Cumberland county Sheriff. Among his fellow luminaries in the future Portland was Colonel Thomas Westbrook, who had received an appointment as royal mast agent in charge of commandeering all pine trees of more than 24 inches in diameter for the Royal Navy. His employer, Ralph Gulston of London, the Navy's general contractor, had moved his operation to Maine "By reason of the great waste of late years of white pine trees in the Province of New Hampshire." Westbrook's building of a sawmill at Sacarappa Falls on the Presumpscot helped launch the city that now bears his name.

Farther up the Presumpscot lay Windham and while citizens of Marblehead, Massachusetts were organizing growth in the Maine woods, so, too, were others in Gloucester and Boston. New Gloucester was settled in 1737 and has kept its name to this day. New Boston, granted about the same time, was populated somewhat later and became the town of Gray.

Another early Cumberland County community was Harpswell, incorporated as a town in 1758, after it broke off from North Yarmouth. Settlers from the same parent town were in its Harraseeket section by 1750, and later seceded to form Freeport. Likewise Pownal, inhabited since 1756, acquired an independent identity.

There were people in Bridgton by 1769. Five years earlier, the General Court had granted it to one Moody Bridges of Andover and others, to make up for land lost to New Hampshire. Bridgton followed naturally from Bridges, although at first the place was called Pondicherry. Whether this was in honor of an obscure French territory in India or because of a profusion of ponds and wild cherry trees isn't known for certain.

The inland thrust became blunted as one moved farther north. No towns beyond York, Oxford and Cumberland Counties were as far to the west as Lebanon, Fryeburg and Bridgton, but places like Dresden, Bowdoin and Richmond in the Sagadahoc area had received settlers leaving the coast by the 1750's. A decade later, people headed into Androscoggin County, stopping to build Poland, Lewiston and Livermore. Different ethnic groups entered the scene. To the Germans who had been at Waldoboro since 1740—the Walleazers, Waltzgriebers, Cramers, Ludwigs, etc.—were added the French Huguenots at Dresden—the Pochards, Hudelottes, Gouds, etc.—and the Scots-Irish that David Dunbar had brought into the Newcastle-Pemaquid region— McCobbs, McClintocks, McFarlands, Kennedys and Cargills.

Pownalborough was the major town in what became Lincoln County, which then covered three-fifths of Maine. Thomas Pownall, Governor of Massachusetts from 1757-60, was responsible not only for the name of the municipality—embracing today's Wiscasset, Dresden, and Alna—but for the county, too, since he was a native of Lincoln, England. By 1764,

Pownalborough's population was an impressive 880 inhabitants.

And, indeed, all down east along the coast, settlements were growing. Scots-Irish spread into Warren. Both Rockland and South Thomaston received settlers before the end of the 1760's.

In 1762 major grants were made by the General Court in what are now Hancock County and Washington County; six townships west of the Union River were given to David Marsh of Haverhill and others, while six townships east of the Union River went to David Bean and others. Modern towns included were Sullivan, Trenton, Surrey, Sedgwick, Bucksport, Penobscot and Steuben (which then included Milbridge). Nearby Gouldsboro was originally granted to a group of Boston businessmen, two of whom were Francis Shaw and Robert Gould. An offspring of their combined families was the great early 19th century Boston merchant

Mid-18th Century map of Maine

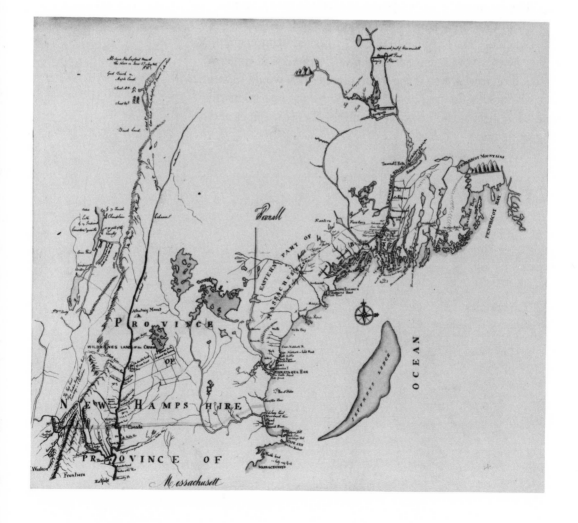

Robert Gould Shaw.

Not only did Hancock County fill up, but an earlier outpost of Yankee activity in Washington County—Machias—was reoccupied in 1763. Sixteen men from Black Point, Scarborough, in a large whaleboat, were searching for extensive supplies of salt marsh hay, plus an ample crop of timber, and found both at Machias. Their first season, they sawed 1,600,000 board feet, an astounding amount.

Parallel to the coastal population this far north was the trickle of Yankees mounting the Penobscot River. Before the break with Great Britain, there would be putative Americans at Orrington, Brewer, Bangor and Hampden.

Maine, having survived the vicissitudes of the French and Indian Wars, was still a vast wilderness, but here and there, the thick forests were giving way to the bustle of rudimentary civilization. The ending of France's power in Canada meant untold opportunities.

But doubtlessly unimagined by the rugged frontiersmen, as well as by the more sedate, church-going farmers and traders of the budding towns, was the next challenge they would soon unexpectedly face. A fight—not against Indians and foreigners this time—but against their own kind and for their own lives and independence.

CHAPTER Seven

On TO THE REVOLUTION

Some Milestones

How did Englishmen become Americans? How was a political mutation nourished to the point that rebellion occurred? In Maine, what factors built up a climate in which the local people could identify with a desire to break from the mother country?

It was a long time coming. Maine, actually, had started with inhabitants well attuned to the establishment in England. The Gorges ideal was of a class-conscious society based on feudal landholding, obedient tenantry and squirearchy; it was certainly not to be a democracy. Massachusetts had other ideals. Their democracy was only for elitist church group, but their land-holding patterns broke the medieval mold.

How many of York and Kittery and Scarborough's early denizen rejoiced in the spontaneous uprising against Governor Andros in 1689? Probably most of them because they saw their land titles threatened by home government officials. And the Indian attacks that cost many of them their homes and lives—what feelings did these engender toward a home government that couldn't or wouldn't protect them? Self reliance—they learned to fend for themselves militarily. Johnson Harmon and Jeremiah Moulton, homegrown soldiers, led their sons up to Norridgewock and shattered the Indians, with no help from the British regulars. A generation later, another homegrown leader, William Pepperrell, commanded a contingent from all New England that produced a major victory over the French. This victory, it must be admitted, was accomplished with the help of a Royal Navy squadron and a small detachment of Royal Marines. But the alienation of the "provincials" was only increased by that fact. They had to endure the scorn of the Marine commander because they didn't "march regularly enough" (although they fought much better) and they hand to stand by and watch the Royal Navy officers and seamen pocket all of the money from the captured French prize ships that were sold. Worst of all, they later saw their conquest—the proudest event of their lives—rendered meaningless when the mighty French fortress was handed back to the enemy for political reasons. As a letter to a Boston newspaper complained, "...this goodly land, itself...may be the purchase of a future peace."

Even when the corrupt and incompetent Whig government was put in the more competent hands of Sir William Pitt and the French were driven from the continent, the psychological effect was the opposite of what might have been expected. The logic then became that without a French menace, what further need had the colonists of any ties with England?

One of the major irritants already noted had been the pine tree controversy. Even such normally pro-English stalwarts as Sir William Pepperrell were quick to bedevil the Crown on this issue. At least in his younger days as a legislator, he joined Elisha Cooke's "popular party" in the General Court, which conspired to frustrate the Surveyor of the King's Woods whenever possible. As a York County judge, Pepperrell presided over the notorious *Frost versus Leighton* law suit where he ruled against the King's forester Leighton and, in the end, had to be overruled from London.

William Pepperrell, had he lived until the Revolution, would no doubt have stayed on the British side. (His descendants did). Yet as a *self-made* aristocrat, he was still an American type. The Sons of Liberty at Wells recognized this fact in November 1774 when they publicly declared that:

> the late Sir William Pepperrell, honored and respected in Great Britain and America for his eminent services...gave the highest evidence not only of his being a sincere friend of the rights of man in general, but of having a paternal love of this country in particular."

That they thought of America as *this country*, before they had a country, was mostly an unconscious evolution. One looks at old documents of Maine life in the 18th century and sees these people

nine of them, whom they dispatched to Worcester jail. These were true prisoners of war, British seamen, captured during the first naval battle of the Revolution, fought at Machias in the same month of June, 1775.

The Taking of the *Margaretta*

As naval battles go, the dust-up at Machias was no Trafalgar. It had elements of comic opera, but also overtones of tragedy. It might well have been a forgotten footnote in the military archives, except that it happened so early in the war.

And in Maine, it is almost like a folk tale. It began when a local sea captain, Ichabod Jones, arrived at Machias from Boston, carrying provisions and also under orders from General Gage to return with a load of Maine lumber. Escorting Jones was a small British warship, the cutter *Margaretta*, commanded by a Captain Moor, a veritable "slip of a boy." At a stormy town meeting, the Machiasites refused to supply Jones; furthermore, they provocatively erected a liberty pole and defied Captain Moor's arrogant demands that they cut it down.

A leader in this resistance was Benjamin Foster, a middle-aged veteran of the Louisbourg expedition. His suggestion, unanimously accepted, was to put an end to Moor's threats by capturing the young coxcomb when he came ashore to church on Sunday.

All would have gone well that morning had it not been for the inadvertent cry of the minister's black slave during the service as he spied a group of armed men approaching. Alarmed, Moor jumped out a window and, amid a flurry of ineffective shots, safely got back to his own vessel.

The few volleys from his four cannon presaged worse revenge from Moor. Foster then had another idea; grab Jones's sloop and go after the *Margaretta*. But this time, the locals were less quick to agree. Tired of their arguments, Foster leapt across a small stream and challenged the others to join him. All eventually did. Someone with a knowledge of the classics and Caesar's wars dubbed the event "Foster's Rubicon."

Having thus crossed the line to irreversible action, the patriots appropriated Jones's ship *Unity*, sailed below Machiasport and came to close quarters with the *Margaretta*. They rammed her, drifted off, then sped back and rammed her again. Meanwhile, a furious discharge of musketry was in progress. The Yankees,

Monument to "Foster's Rubicon"

Burnham's Tavern, Machias

100

brandishing pitchforks like bayonets, piled aboard the cutter. Captain Moor had gone down with two musket balls in him. His next in command, a frightened midshipman, promptly surrendered.

Carried ashore to Burnham's Tavern, Moor expired within a day. He was to have married a niece of Jones's upon his return from Machias.

The aftermath of the seafight was that the *Margaretta*, renamed the *Machias Liberty*, roamed the nearby waters and at Bucks Harbor captured another small British vessel. News of these exploits was sent to the Provincial Congress, along with a plea for "advice and support." Later, more specifically, Foster and a second of the Machias heroes, Jeremiah O'Brien, asked for grain and provisions to feed the people of Northern Maine.

Mowatt and Falmouth

Other Maine militia companies besides that of Captain Johnson Moulton of York had been set marching toward Boston by the news of Concord and Lexington. From Falmouth, Captain John Brackett went forth with his men, while other Cumberland County units under Captains Hart Williams, Wentworth Stuart and Abraham Tyler were not far behind.

None of these outfits reached the battlefield. Finding their services unneeded, they turned back and many went on guard duty, particularly along the coast, which was obviously vulnerable to British naval attack.

In York county, Colonel James Scammon's regiment was formed out of such former "train bands" and marched off to join George Washington's Continental Army at Cambridge. In Cumberland County, the task of organizing the first regiment was left to Colonel Edward Phinney of Gorham.

An incident at Falmouth Neck delayed the Cumberland County contingent's appearance among Washington's troops. This event, occurring on May 9, was to have a sequel of dire consequences.

Two of the most prominent Tories in Falmouth were Admiral Edward Tyng and Captain Samuel Coulson. Tyng had led the New England naval forces at Louisbourg and was a much respected local figure. Coulson, on the other hand, was deeply hated.

Not only was he an Englishman, but a loud-mouthed one,

unsparingly critical of the American cause and eager to defy any boycott of trade with Great Britain. Ostentatiously, he launched a vessel to carry masts to the mother country. Taking no chance, he also made sure Admiral Graves in British-held Boston dispatched a warship to protect his enterprise.

She was the sloop of war *Canceau*, and her captain, another supercilious young naval officer, was surnamed Mowatt, a name that was to echo through the ages in Maine, inspiring fear and wrath...Mowatt, the destroyer of Falmouth...but that is getting ahead of the story.

The news of Mowatt's arrival aroused the countryside. Into Falmouth swarmed a group of backcountrymen, 50 of them from Brunswick led by Colonel Samuel Thompson, plus Phinney's bunch from Gorham and Windham. Mowatt, strolling ashore with a local Tory, was captured by Thompson's men in an ambush on Munjoy Hill.

When threatened with bombardment by Mowatt's second- in- command, the most prominent citizens of Falmouth urged Thompson to release his prisoner. He finally said he would if Mowatt gave his word of honor to return the next day. Mowatt swore a solemn oath, but reneged as soon as he was free. The militiamen consoled themselves with the rum they found in Coulson's cellar. One well-oiled patriot went down to the waterfront and blazed away with his musket at the *Canceau*.[1]

The British vessel sailed away with Coulson aboard and the Falmouthites no doubt thought they'd seen the last of her. Another small British warship, the *Senegal*, did arrive on June 8 to pick up Coulson's masts, but they'd been hidden by the colonists. The wives of Admiral Tyng and Captain Coulson went aboard and were carried safely into exile.

Then, on June 24, the Provincial Congress ordered Colonel Phinney to send 400 of his men at once to Cambridge. Four companies were dispatched. Once there, one of the officers, Lieutenant Bartholomew York, was deputized with 37 men to stand guard over General Washington's headquarters—a signal honor for the men from Maine. Included in Colonel Phinney's regiment was Windham's pioneer settler Stephen Manchester, the celebrated killer of Chief Polin. Despite his age at the time, 58, he soldiered in the Revolution for five more years and lived until 1807, when he was 90.

The English may have known that Falmouth was relatively defenseless by now. That they harbored a grudge against the

102

community was evident. Admiral Graves considered it a principle supply depot for Washington's army. And on October 16, when Mowatt reappeared with a squadron, assembling his warships off India Street, cannon trained on the town, a proclamation read to the people was unequivocal in its condemnation:

> ...After so many premeditated attacks on the royal prerogative of the best of sovereigns...you are guilty of most unpardonable rebellion...

Mowatt's orders, he said, were "to execute a just punishment...I previously warn you to remove without delay, the human specie out of said town, for which purpose I give you the time of two hours..."

The signal to fire would be the hoisting of a red pennant to the main top gallant masthead. A group of English sympathizers, members of the local Anglican parish, tried to intercede with Mowatt. He agreed to hold off, provided the townspeople surrendered all their weapons. This, they eventually refused to do. At 9:00 a.m. the next morning, the red pennant went up. A barrage of more than 64 naval guns rained burning shot and shell on the settlement. The firing continued for almost twelve hours and landing parties added to the havoc by torching waterfront buildings. More than 130 structures were destroyed, including the public library, the town house and the Anglican St. Paul's Church. Miraculously, no one was killed.

One vivid image remaining from the firestorm that descended upon Falmouth is of the Widow Greele, coolly picking up a bomb that fell in her yard with a pair of tongs and removing it a safe distance. She also single-handedly put out fires on her roof whenever they started. All through the bombardment, she never left her place.

By the time the vindictive Mowatt ceased his "rod of correction," Falmouth lay flattened, a smoking, shattered ruin.

Arnold's March to Quebec

It is an oft-told tale, the epic of human endurance and failure that resulted when Benedict Arnold moved an army through Maine to attack the heart of Canada. There were two ostensible purposes for the maneuver. Capture of Montreal and Quebec would deprive the

British of bases from which to strike south into the colonies; secondly, the French inhabitants might well join the American revolt, since they had no great love for their British masters.

But they had even less love for the Protestant Americans with whom they'd fought for nearly 100 years. At least the British had given them the Quebec Act, which allowed them to practice their Roman Catholic Religion and keep their French language and customs. Sensing that the Yankees might not be as tolerant, they declined to rise up and join the invaders and Arnold's bold gamble thus became doomed almost from the start.

The drive on Canada was to be a two-pronged affair. General Richard Montgomery, starting from Fort Ticonderoga, would ascend Lake Champlain, capture Montreal, continue up the St. Lawrence and fall upon Quebec from the west. Coming from the east, Arnold would traverse Maine, following the Kennebec to the Dead River, enter Canada via the Chaudière River, reach the St. Lawrence at Levis, cross over and besiege the city.

Arnold earlier had been credited with the capture of Fort Ticonderoga in May 1775, although Ethan Allen and his Green Mountain Boys strongly disputed the claim. Vain, pompous, arrogant and hyperactive, Arnold nevertheless was a born leader of men. It is interesting, if not ironic, that another difficult figure in American history, Aaron Burr, was also a member of the mixed force of New Englanders, Pennsylvanians and Virginians who marched from Cambridge to Newburyport in September 1775 and then embarked for the Kennebec River.

Their first major stop was in Pittston at the Colburn and Agry boatyard. Here, they loaded themselves and their supplies into 200 bateaux—dory-shaped vessels—that had been banged together by local carpenters. Up the river to Fort Western in Augusta, they paddled and poled, and next began to experience the falls and ripples of the Kennebec. Past the particularly difficult rapids of the Waterville-Winslow area, they camped at Skowhegan, then halted to repair their boats at Norridgewock. Finally, they came to the Dead River and entered a maze of ponds, swamps, bogs and meandering streams. Starved for food they were reduced to eating wax candles and leather shot pouches. Not until they reached the Chaudière and French farmland could they procure sufficient supplies. Arnold restricted each famished soldier to one pound of beef but even so, one man died of overeating.

Getting to Quebec was easier. By November 9, Arnold had 700 men on the St. Lawrence, opposite the old French citadel, and

104

the dark night of November 13, the entire force slipped across. But they didn't assault the walls immediately. While waiting for scaling ladders, their presence was discovered and the advantage of surprise was lost. They also had to wait for Montgomery who had captured Montreal, according to plan, and was hurrying his 300 plus men toward the agreed-upon rendezvous.

Unhappily, the combined Americans weren't ready to attack until New Year's Eve. A snowstorm covered their charge, but the British were ready with withering fire. Arnold was hit in the leg. A chance shot by a British cannoneer killed Montgomery. Left fairly leaderless, although Dan Morgan, head of the Pennsylvania and Virginia riflemen, tried to take command, the cold, ragged Yankee troops eventually abandoned their siege.

Colonel Eddy and Colonel Allen

A much lesser known assault on Canada, and one potentially more promising, also had Maine connections. Nova Scotia, which then included New Brunswick, had large populations of settlers from Massachusetts and Connecticut. Pro-revolutionary sentiment was especially strong in the western counties. Only five persons could be found in the Cumberland County towns of Truro, Onslow and Londonderry to take an oath of allegiance to the British Crown. In Kings County, locals were ready to hoist a liberty pole when British troops intervened and prevented them. The town meeting at Maugerville in Sunbury County, held on May 14, 1776, sounds amazingly like those in Maine of the same period. They passed resolves that declared:

> ...we can see no shadow of Justice in that Extensive Claim of the British parliament (viz) the Right of Enacting Laws binding on the Colonies in all cases whatsoever...
>
> ...that as tyranny ought to be Resisted in its first appearance, we are Convinced that the united Provinces are just in their proceedings in this Regard.
>
> ...that it is our Minds and Desire to submit ourselves to the government of the Massachusetts Bay and that we are Ready with our Lives and fortunes to Share with them the Event of the present Struggle for Liberty...

Given such potential for detaching a part of Canada, it is not surprising that a military expedition was soon organized. Its leader was Colonel Jonathan Eddy, a native of Massachusetts who'd become a Nova Scotian landowner. What *is* surprising was its relative lack of resources. The prime target was Fort Cumberland, a well-guarded post near the Quebec border, and Eddy's original force consisted of only 28 men. When Colonel John Allan, a Nova Scotian fighting for the Americans, met Eddy in Machias Bay and saw his paltry "army," he tried hard to desist him from continuing. But Eddy, convinced he would gain recruits, moved on into Canada. When he did arrive before the fort, his effectives numbered 80, including a group of Indians. The commander of Fort Cumberland, Lieutenant Colonel Joseph Gorham, declined Eddy's invitation to surrender and, in turn, called upon Eddy to capitulate. The stand-off erupted in battle on the night of November 12, 1776. The pro-Yankee Nova Scotians brought scaling ladders into play, but the British Regulars held. One Indian was wounded. The landing of 400 British reinforcements from Halifax sealed the fate of the expedition. A surprise attack routed Eddy and the Americans retreated to the St. John River.

Reprisals against American Sympathizers were particularly fierce near Fort Cumberland. The house John Allan owned was burned to the ground. His wife and five children fled to the woods and only avoided starvation by creeping back to the ruins, finding potatoes baked by the fire and eating them. When British soldiers later discovered Mrs. Allan at her father's home, she was arrested and thrown into prison.

John Allan was not like most of the other pro-Americans in Nova Scotia. His family had not come from New England. They were Scottish and seemingly a part of the British establishment, his father an army officer and his mother the daughter of a knight of the realm.

Several months before the Eddy attack, the 29 year-old Allan had fled his home in Cumberland, having heard that his life was in danger. After time spent in Machias and Gouldsboro, he journeyed south, arriving in the Boston area in November 1776, where he preached to the Provincial congress about the opportunity for taking over western Nova Scotia and the extreme importance of maintaining the loyalty of the local Indians. To spread his message even farther afield, he travelled to Philadelphia and on December 22, dined with George Washington at his headquarters. Two days later Washington wrote letters to the St. Johns (Malecites) and

106

the Passamaquoddies. The former, he addressed to "My good Friend and Brother Governor Perre Tommar"[2] and the latter to "Brothers of Passamaquoddia" and in both missives, he expressed his appreciation that the "Chain of Friendship" had been kept "bright and unbroken," warned "never let the king's wicked counsellor turn your hearts against me" and told a cautionary tale of what had happened when certain southern tribes had turned against the Americans. Allan's influence seems obvious in these communications. After a trip to Baltimore to visit the Continental Congress, he returned to Maine with the official positions of Superintendent of the Eastern Indians and Colonel of Infantry.

Allan's efforts from then on were concentrated on keeping the Indians supplied and content, and trying to generate support for another invasion of Canada. On both accounts, he had mixed results.

Although the Indians, in regard to George Washington, "adored him as a Saint," they did so, said Chief Ambroise St. Aubin of the Malecites, because Washington told them to be at peace. As the old Indian expressed himself in a meeting with Allan: "How comes it that old England and new should quarrel and come to blows? The father and son to fight is terrible. Old France and Canada did not do so." Such sentiments of neutrality were sporadically penetrated by Allan who was able to prevail on the tribes to side, at least temporarily, with the Americans.

In an expedition to the St. John River, which he planned and began scouting in the spring of 1777, Allan made use of Indian auxiliaries. He had told the Massachusetts Provincial Congress that: "Nova Scotia is at present very weak. Easy would it be to overset the whole British power." but the forces sent him were insufficient. A skirmish in which the British drove the Americans from the settlement that later became St. John, New Brunswick suspended the campaign and Allan returned to Machias.

It was none too soon. On August 13, British warships appeared off Machias and on the 14th, under cover of fog, Royal Marines landed and captured an American battery. With the aid of a group of Penobscots, plus Passamaquoddies and Malicites who'd come with Allan, this assault was beaten back; a British brig, the *Hope*, which had sailed boldly up the Machias River, ran aground and was peppered with Yankee bullets and cannon balls. The Indians, running about and yelling war cries, gave the English the impression of larger forces than existed, and they soon sailed off.

The failed British raid, the brainchild of Sir George Collier,

107

Commander-in-Chief of Nova Scotia, was alleged by him to have been a successful pre-emptive strike to abort Allan's invasion. As such, this hit and run foray would not have done the trick by itself. But within days, orders arrived from Massachusetts that any further expeditions into Canada were being abandoned for lack of resources.

During the rest of the war, Colonel John Allan held down the eastern front. It wasn't easy. He had to plead for supplies again and again, faced with competition from the British Indian Superintendent, Michael Franklin, who had unlimited resources for wooing Indians. Allan had a price of £400 on his head and he suffered a number of narrow escapes, once from a gigantic Indian who came into his house after him with a hunting knife and was subdued by other Indians and once having to skate to safety and clear a large opening in the ice with an olympian-sized running jump.

But Allan succeeded in the end. Machias remained an American outpost. His ability to keep the Indians from entering the fray on the British side was the key, perhaps, to the present-day existence of Washington County as part of Maine. His own wish, that several other counties now in New Brunswick could have joined, too, never came to pass, but not for want of effort on the part of this extraordinary Nova Scotian-turned-American.

The Penobscot Campaign

Sir George Collier was a determined and aggressive British naval commander. He had led the pre-emptive strike on Machias even after the army commander in Halifax, General Massey, had refused to supply his troops. Moreover, Sir George had taken part personally in the battle and it was his Marines who, upon his express orders, had set fire to military supplies but spared people's homes. He was smart enough to try leniency with the Americans.

Thus, it is no surprise to find Sir George Collier involved in the next English invasion of Maine—one that was far more successful.

The focus in the late spring of 1779 was Majabigwaduce (now Castine.) The original British landing on June 17 did not involve Sir George Collier but was led by Brigadier General Francis McLean who sailed from Halifax with a small flotilla of naval vessels and 700 men. Among the fleet commanders was the hated Captain Mowatt. McLean's forces took the peninsula without

108

opposition and proceeded to build a fort, which they named for George III. In the King's name, too, they issued a proclamation inviting all local inhabitants to swear loyalty to his Majesty. Before long, the occupation was a magnet to Maine and Massachusetts Tories who had fled down east.

With unaccustomed haste, the Massachusetts Provincial Congress reacted by organizing an expedition to recapture Castine. In less than four weeks, an armada of 19 armed vessels, carrying 344 guns, and 24 transports with 1,000 soldiers, was assembled. The stage was set for a defeat of American military forces that was to be unequaled until Pearl Harbor Day.

Most of the blame for the fiasco has been put on the naval commander, Admiral Dudley Saltonstall of Connecticut. No doubt, he deserved the opprobrium, which left him condemned never to hold another command. A few years earlier, he had let a British frigate escape, but somehow had been exonerated by a board of inquiry. This time, through inexplicable inaction, Saltonstall let an entire British expeditionary force escape.

He had a significant advantage in men, vessels and firepower. His army commanders, Generals Solomon Lovell and Peleg Wadsworth, were brave and vigorous officers. Paul Revere was in charge of his artillery. Yet despite overwhelming superiority, the first American naval attack on Castine was half-hearted. Several landings were repulsed before 200 men took over Nautilus Island.

Relics of the Penobscot expedition

Intelligence was brought to Saltonstall via Colonel John Brewer that the British defenses upriver were extremely weak. According to Brewer, the Admiral "hove up his long chin and said, 'you seem to be damned knowing about the matter! I am not going to risk my shipping in that damned hole.'"

On July 28, the Americans stormed a high bluff and received heavy casualties. But with their forces on the heights, Saltonstall called a council of war and refused even to demand that the British surrender. Every proposal the land officers made to him was turned down. And as days passed, Saltonstall still refused to attack. On August 11, General Lovell addressed a blunt letter to him: "Do not delay any longer. Go in and destroy the British ships. The operations of the ground troops are confined so long as the British ships are safe in the harbor. There is an absolute necessity to destroy these ships or quit the place."

In vain did Lovell argue. Then, on August 13, time ran out for the Americans. "Some strange sails in the offing," as a Tory writer put it, revealed that a British rescue fleet had arrived.

It was Sir George Collier with seven warships and 1,530 men.

Had the Americans fought, they might well have overcome the attackers. At first, it looked like they would. Sir George Collier wrote: "...the rebel fleet presented themselves to our view, drawn up in a crescent across the river and seemed inclined to dispute our passage..." But, as Sir George continues: "...their resolution, however, soon failed them and an unexpected and ignominious flight took place."

Four British ships pursued the entire American flotilla up and down the Penobscot River. The transports, now loaded again with Lovell's men, tried to flee. some went aground; others, seemingly in danger of British capture, were purposely driven ashore and burned.

The Americans totally scattered. Sir George Collier's flagship ran down the "Hunter," trying to escape near Islesboro. Another Yankee gunship, the "Hampden," was also taken, as were nine transports. All the other American craft were burned, 10 at Bangor, alone, leaving a trail of wrecked and scuttled shipping from the mouth of the river up to Kenduskeag.

A Court of Enquiry, headed by Major-General Artemus Ward, investigated the route. The tribunal had praise for General Lovell and even more for General Wadsworth who had conducted himself, it said, with "great activity, courage, coolness and prudence." Saltonstall, in effect, was cashiered, nor was Colonel Paul

110

Revere entirely exonerated until his appeal was heard several years later and a court martial acquitted him of all charges.

The effect of the British occupation of Castine was felt farther south. Constant raiding by the invaders made life on Vinalhaven and other of the Fox Islands a hazardous affair. Captain Eleazar Crabtree, who raised a militia company to defend the islands, had to abandon his home on North Haven, while John Perry who singlehandedly battled 15 British marauders on Vinalhaven saw his house burned to the ground. Life in Belfast for patriotic Americans became untenable and many fled to Camden. Yet even this strongpoint could be penetrated, as demonstrated by the famous kidnapping of General Peleg Wadsworth.

Wadsworth was living at Thomaston in February 1780 when the fiery British commander at Castine, a Colonel Campbell, sent a commando force of 25 soldiers to surprise him in his quarters. During a sharp but vain resistance, the General was badly wounded. Taken to Castine, he was incarcerated with another American, Major Benjamin Burton, and both were slated to be sent to England where they faced severe imprisonment, if not hanging.

So they escaped. It was an epic adventure, boring holes in the ceiling of their cell, plugging the gaps with chewed bread, breaking out in the dead of night, Wadsworth hampered by his wound not finding Burton again until the next morning, fleeing in a canoe and finally crossing the American lines to safety. It has always been a mystery, as well as a shame, that the General's grandson, Henry Wadsworth Longfellow, who wrote about Baron Castin and Paul Revere, never chose this daring episode as a theme for one of his poems.

New Ireland

A Tory haven had been established in Castine. The King's rule had been re-established over his unruly American subjects, sometimes mild as it was under the perspicacious General McLean, or harsh, as it was under his successor, the choleric Colonel Campbell.[3] One of the most noted of the Loyalists to come to Castine was Dr. John Calef of Ipswich, Massachusetts. Calef, whose name was pronounced "Calf," had been a member of the General Court. As such, he was one of the notorious "Rescinders" of 1768—that is, one of those who, on a vote of 92-17, supported Governor Thomas Hutchinson's demand that the lawmakers *rescind* a circular letter to

111

other colonies in defense of American liberties. The 17 yea voters were vilified up and down the Province and Paul Revere made a copperplate caricature of the hated group, with Dr. Calef's figure topped by the head of a calf.

It is no surprise, therefore, to find Calef, a former legislator, involved in the scheme to create a new British province out of most of Maine.

The plan first surfaced in August 1780, a year after the defeat of the Americans on the Penobscot. The idea was to separate all of Maine from the Saco to the St. Croix and form it into New Ireland, with the 30 mile sliver of land between the Piscataqua and the Saco being given to New Hampshire.

In the governmental structure proposed for New Ireland can be seen what the English had in store for the American colonies should they have defeated the Revolution. There would be a Governor and Council, a Chief Justice and Civil Officers, all to be paid by Parliament, and no Legislature until the King decided conditions were propitious. Even when a Legislature was established, it would not be democratic. The upper house members were to be appointed for life by the Crown and the Governor's Privy Council would also sit in this august body. An American House of Lords.

Quit rents would be back. The only exemptions would be as rewards to distinguished Tories. Every grantee of land would have to take a loyalty oath to the Crown, and the Church of England was to become the established religion. To "lay the ground of an Aristocratic Power," large tracts of land would be leased to the "most meritorious and to be by them leased to the lower people in manner as has been practiced in New York, which is the only Province in which there is a Tenantry, and was the least inclined to Rebellion." A salary schedule was even drawn up, with a budget of almost £5,000. Calef, as clerk of the Council, was to get £50.

However, the project languished in the higher echelons of the British establishment. Possibly there was strong behind-the-scenes opposition from Thomas Hutchinson, who did not want to see Massachusetts dismembered.

Two years later, Calef was writing as "agent for the inhabitants of the territory of Penobscot", beseeching the Crown to sever the District from Massachusetts and "erect it into a government under your Majesty's own authority." The 16,000 Mainers would become "usefull Subjects, Raise Oscen (sic), Grain, Sheep, etc... haul Masts for the Royal Navy..." open a post road from Halifax to Boston and another from Quebec to Boston. The Indians would convert to Anglicanism, the cod fishery would be secured and other parts of British America supplied with copious Maine provisions.

Despite such blandishments, the British government finally said no. Calef went over to England to lobby and did so until one morning when he entered Lord North's office and was told without explanation, "Doctor, we cannot make the Penobscot the boundary. The pressure is too strong."

In 1783, when British troops evacuated Castine, Calef's dream of an aristocratic "down east" lost any lingering flicker of hope.

Mainers Elsewhere in the Revolution

The "times are very dubros at present for there is no news of Peace as yet," Jonathan Burrows, a Mainer serving in the 5th Massachusetts Regiment wrote home from West Point on April 6, 1782. It was a letter he failed to send right away and on May 21, he added a postscript that he had "the pleasure to write now that we have the greatest prospect of Peace."

Burrows was one of thousands of Maine soldiers and sailors who fought in the Revolution.

They were everywhere—at Ticonderoga, the siege of Boston, Trenton, Valley Forge, Saratoga, Yorktown, Quebec, on the seven seas. Lieutenant Moses Banks of York was on George Washington's staff; another York man, Thomas Simpson, took over command of John Paul Jones's *Ranger*. Jonathan Knox of Berwick was present when General Burgoyne surrendered. Taking a cargo of tobacco to France in 1778 was a Kittery sailor, James Brown, and it was a cargo that the three American Commissioners, Benjamin Franklin, Arthur Lee and John Adams took a special interest in seeing was safely delivered and sold. A year earlier, Adams had been on his way to France aboard a ship captained by Commodore Samuel Tucker of Bristol, Maine when an armed British cruiser was encountered and a fierce battle ensued. In the middle of it, Tucker noted the future second President on deck, blazing away with a musket. He rushed over, yelling, "You have no business here, sir! I am commanded to carry you safely to Europe and, God helping, I will do it!" Whereupon, he pick up Adams in his arms like a child and carried him down to his cabin.

Jonathan Britton of Otisfield was at Valley Forge, Yorktown and the battle of Monmouth. Luther Carry of Turner fought on Long Island. John Gardner of Hebron, a sailor, was captured twice

113

at sea, taken twice to Halifax and escaped twice. Then, he enlisted in the army, was captured again and remained a prisoner in England until the end of the war. Some of these veterans who later qualified for Maine pensions were not originally from Maine. James Boaz of Portland was living in Plymouth, Mass. when he enlisted in 1780. He was a Black man. Simeon Moulton was from Exeter, New Hampshire. Caleb Gordon who stormed the Quebec City walls with Arnold, and was shot off a ladder, came from Brentwood, New Hampshire, but emigrated to Augusta. A New Brunswicker, Benen Foster, sought a pension for his services in three down east incidents—the capture of the *Margaretta*, Allan's expedition to St. Johns and the defense of Machias.

The best known veteran to settle in Maine was Henry Knox, Washington's first Secretary of War. Knox was a Bostonian who came to public notice when he transported the artillery captured

General Henry Knox

114

by Ethan Allen and Benedict Arnold at Fort Ticonderoga all the way from Vermont to Massachusetts. A close confidante of Washington's and his prime artillery commander, Knox also later became head of the first veterans organization in the United States, the Order of the Cincinnati. He married Samuel Waldo's granddaughter and inherited the vast Waldo lands in Maine, part of which became a county named for him.

ON TO STATEHOOD

Post-Revolutionary Conditions and the Bingham Purchase

After the establishment of American independence, several European aristocrats visited Maine and left with less than favorable impressions of the District.[1]

The Duc de la Rochefoucauld-Liancourt, a member of one of France's oldest families, came on two occasions—in 1795 and 1796—to stay with Henry Knox at Thomaston. Knox had just finished building "Montpelier," his elaborate mansion. Despite Knox's hospitality, the Duke was scathing in his assessment of the region. He wrote:

> In short, of all America, the province of Maine is the place that afforded me the worst accommodation...the condition of human life in that place is exceedingly wretched...this country is still in its infancy and in a languid and cheerless infancy.

Ten years earlier, an Italian nobleman, Count Luigi Castiglioni, was nowhere near as critical after a visit to York, but he, too, paints a picture of primitive conditions. "The land of old York is dotted with poor cabins where dwell the cultivators...whose food consists of rye bread, and maize with pork and salt beef and whose drink is Grog and spruce beer..."

The illustrious French diplomat usually known only by his

116

surname of Talleyrand (he was Charles Maurice de Talleyrand-Perigord) also added his comments. There is a traditional rumor that Talleyrand was actually born in northern Maine when it was under French influence and taken to France as a young boy. In any event, he was not flattering about Maine people during his travels when he was in exile in the U.S. in the mid-1790's.

> ...ignorant and grasping, poor but without needs, they resemble too much the natives of the country whom they have replaced.

The Frenchman claimed a lack of hard money had led Maine people to the habit of making cunning, if not fraudulent, bargains at the drop of a hat. Mainers, he said, were more interested in buying and selling than in producing, resulting in a surplus of would-be entrepreneurs, merchants and salesmen, and a definite dearth of craftsmen. Debts, bad business, lawsuits and insolvency were the results.

An exception to this spate of negative comment came from the English banker Alexander Baring (later Lord Ashburton). He found, to his surprise, that the people were not as "wild and savage" as he had expected and he was pleased with their "disposition and character."

But Baring, it must be noted, had just sunk a lot of money into purchasing Maine land. Furthermore, he married the daughter of William Bingham of Philadelphia, a man who had bought more than 2 million acres of Maine land. And Baring, himself, had nothing good to say about the lumbermen he'd encountered, while he was openly annoyed about "a pack of fanatical itinerant Methodist preachers" who'd crossed his path.

One important background to the extraordinary Bingham purchase was the burden the Revolutionary War had placed on Massachusetts. A $3 million debt led to intense pressure for relief from taxes, including a regressive poll tax that helped set off Shays rebellion. Land sales were urged as a substitute—and most unsold land in the Commonwealth lay in Maine.

Available for sale were some 17 million acres. Furthermore, selling it would relieve another problem bedeviling the Boston lawmakers—that of protecting the wilderness against trespassers and timber rustlers. A committee of the General Court produced its recommendations in 1784; townships six miles square were to be laid out between the Penobscot and the St. Croix and sold either

117

privately or in public auction. By 1786, however, a mere 100,000 acres had been bought.

That same year, therefore, a land lottery was devised. Tickets costing $60 each were issued—2,720 of them—calculated to bring in $163,200. But only 437 of the ducats were sold. The biggest winner was a William Dall, who took the first prize of 5,440 acres. No more than a disappointing 165,000 acres was disposed of in this fashion.

It was Henry Knox who precipitated the first immense block sale. Always the speculator, he teamed up with William Duer, an Assistant Secretary of the Treasury, in a scheme to buy "not less than 1 million nor more than 4 million" acres of Maine land, at a price not to exceed 12 cents an acre.

The actual work of negotiating with the Massachusetts General Court was left to two close associates of the pair—General Henry Jackson of Boston and Royal Flint of New York City. Tough bargaining finally led to a sale of 2 million acres—half in the Kennebec area and half between the Penobscot and Schoodic Rivers. Other purchases were added to the tract, like Mount Desert and Trenton from the DeGregoire family, heirs of the French pioneer Lamothe-Cadillac, and the Gouldsboro area from the Shaws. Most of the sale was on credit, with Knox and Duer expending a paltry $10,000 in a transaction worth $400,000-500,000. Lack of cash thus became a critical problem for the speculators. In 1792, Duer failed in his affairs and went to debtors' prison, leaving Knox to look with increasing desperation for an "angel" to bail them out.

William Bingham, a Philadelphia socialite, banker, ship-owner and U.S. Senator, was a friend of Knox's. While serving as Washington's Secretary of War in the then nation's capital, Knox was a frequent visitor to Bingham's home. The two men began to talk about a possible deal for the Maine lands. After they reached an agreement, another go-between, Major William Jackson, was sent with $50,000 to the New York debtors' prison to secure Duer's acquiescence. It took only a minimum of haggling before Knox's partner was persuaded to sell out.

The eventual purchase price was to be $300,000. Knox was promised a share in any surplus profits and so remained keenly interested in all of Bingham's efforts to develop this vast territory.

Bingham did his best to promote these forest tracts whose principle drawback seemed to be their remoteness. He contacted General Benjamin Lincoln, the man who had put down Shays'

118

Rebellion, to go around Maine with a testimonial that consisted of 44 questions and 44 positive answers. Lincoln's previous exposure in Maine had included serving on a committee to determine the true location of the St. Croix River and as chief negotiator for Massachusetts to buy Maine Indian lands. In addition to Lincoln's rave reviews, Bingham procured favorable comments from such distinguished Mainers as Charles Vaughan of Hallowell, Daniel Cony of Augusta and John Gardiner of Gardiner.

But these lands didn't sell. So Bingham looked to Europe where wealthy Dutch, French and British interests had begun

Bingham's Kennebec Purchase

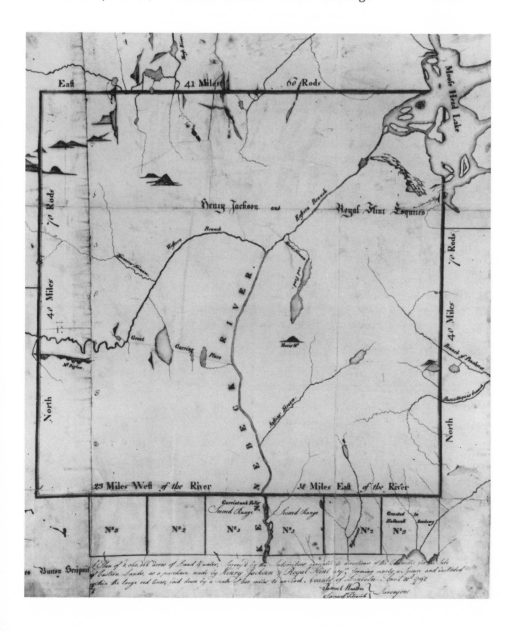

119

dabbling in American real estate. He sent Major William Jackson
to prospect, but in several years overseas, Jackson succeeded in
attracting only the most tentative of bites—a show of interest from
the British banker, Sir Francis Baring.

In time, Baring and Henry Hope, another English banker,
would start actively seeking investments in the United States.
Meanwhile, Bingham tried to promote "retail sales"—selling off
the land parcel by parcel—and to this end he hired as his agent
General David Cobb, a close friend of Knox's, an ex-Speaker of the
Massachusetts House and one-term Congressman. Cobb set up
shop in Gouldsboro and proceeded to a "manufacture of land,"—
building roads, advertising, seeking individual buyers.

Key to the thinking of Cobb and Bingham was that lumbering
had to be discouraged and agriculture boosted. They felt that only
in this fashion would the lands become most attractive to settlers.
Bingham's feelings toward lumbermen may well have been colored
by his attitude toward the omni-present timber thieves in Maine.
"It gives me pleasure to find that you have been able to combat
with success the dangerous prepossessions of the inhabitants
relative to the right of plundering timber," the great landowner
wrote to Cobb in 1795.

In the autumn of that same year, Bingham had reason to be
even more elated. He received a letter from Sir Francis Baring
stating that his son, young Alexander Baring, was sailing for the
United States with the definite intent of investing in American
lands. Baring, then but 21 years old, carried a letter of credit for
£100,000 and authorization to spend £25,000 more. Despite his
youth, he was a cool, hard-headed businessman who had served his
apprenticeship in Henry Hope's banking firm in Amsterdam,
Holland.

During the summer of 1796, a "party of pleasure," in the form
of an expedition to Maine, was undertaken by Bingham, his beauteous wife, his sister-in-law, his two teen-age daughters, a French
aristocrat guest and Baring and his English friend John Richards.
How *pleasurable* a trip seemed doubtful at the outset when the
ladies became violently seasick on the crossing from New York to
Newport, Rhode Island. The journey by stage to Boston, then
Portland, was more agreeable, and they risked another sea journey
on a packet to Thomaston. There, the ladies were left in the
comfort of Knox's "Montpelier" and the men went on to
Gouldsboro and farther down east.

Baring liked Maine, was impressed by the people and the fact

120

that in settling an area "their first wants are a church and a school." He noted that Wiscasset, alone, had more shipping than all of New Hampshire and foresaw the day when Maine would have its own government.

It is expected that the District of Maine will be formed into a separate state. Two years past a petition was presented to the state of Massachusetts to desire they would take the general sense of the people on this question in Maine, which was complied with and three-quarters were averse to this separation. It is now to be tried a second time and expected to succeed, the growing importance of the country having rendered it necessary to have their state government nearer them...The constitution will be modelled after that of Massachusetts and I have no doubt that our friend Knox will be made Governor...

In June 1797, Baring bought half of Bingham's holdings, paying $263,901 for 593,778 acres in what was deemed an extremely good bargain.

Knox's mansion, "Montpelier"

A year later, the young Englishman capped his triumph by marrying one of the Bingham sisters, Ann, and still later, the two families became even more intertwined when his brother Henry married the other sister, Maria.

Despite Baring's business acumen and the energies of John Richards, whom he instituted as his agent, the properties still didn't sell. There was no significant migration down east. Annsburgh and Mariaville were created in newly-formed (1789) Hancock County. Some roads were built and saw mills erected. And yet the profits Bingham and his son-in-law had envisaged did not materialize.

Then, tragedy struck. In 1800, Bingham's wife took sick after a difficult birth and she died in Bermuda whither he had rushed her. Grief-stricken, he decided to go and live in England with Alexander and Ann.

Soon, political changes in Maine threatened to have an impact on the Bingham-Baring holdings. The Jeffersonian Party, known as Democrat-Republicans, were gaining in strength, partly through their loud opposition to big landowners and their championing of the rights of squatters. William King, a converted Federalist representing the Bath area in the General Court, sponsored the Law Betterment Act of 1807, which protected squatters who had held land more than six years by requiring proprietors to pay for any improvements if they evicted the people.

By 1807, William Bingham was dead. The terms of his will had placed his vast acreage into a trust, with Baring and his brother, among others, as trustees. "Hard-ball" politics were about to be played by the Massachusetts solons. Bingham had never fulfilled Knox's contract with the General Court, which called for settling an agreed-upon number of colonists on the lands; as a result, his heirs faced "settling duty" penalties of $70,000. Worse, a ten year moratorium on taxes had ended and worse still, there was a move to void the entire original sale on the grounds that the contract hadn't been observed. William King had been pushing a bill to investigate all land contracts to see if their terms had been followed. David Cobb, as President of the Senate, was just able to have it killed.

Enter Charles Willing Hare, a relative of Bingham's wife and one of the Bingham trustees. At the height of this crisis, the canny Philadelphian travelled to Boston and used a time-honored device to defuse the situation: he bought off William King. In return for the bargain price of $5,000, King was to have a share in Township

122

No.'s 1, 2 and 3 on the west side of the Kennebec. The Bingham
Trust was delivered from the danger of having its lands confiscated
and given more time to bring in the required settlers. Harrison
Gray Otis, a prominent Federalist lawyer, was in on this deal that
crossed party lines, as was Peleg Tallman, a crony of King's from
Bath. The one long-lasting result of this nifty arrangement was the
town of Kingfield.

FOCUS

Sam Ely—Troublemaker

Surveying land for Henry Knox in 1793
had its perils, as stated by a professional
named Jennison whom the General had
hired. Wrote Jennison:

> On our tour, we had the pleasure of
> seeing the famous Drinkwater, one of
> the great Samuel Ely's disciples who
> among others are going to prevent our
> surveying the seashore by Duck Trap,
> etc., knock us on the head, break our
> instruments, moor us in Owl's Head
> Bay...and they even carry their threats
> so far as to say that even General
> Knox himself will share the same fate
> if he attempts to take an active part in
> the enterprise.

Squatters who had come upon
Knox's land since 1775 were protesting
in every way they could and their leader
was a charismatic if not overly scrupu-
lous ex-clergyman from Connecticut
with the reputation of being a tireless
agitator. Samuel Cullick Ely was a graduate of Yale who had been removed from
his pulpit in the town of Somers and
deprived of his license to preach. "He
was voluble, vehement in address, bold,
persevering, active, brazen-faced in
wickedness, and under the accusation

and proof of his crimes would still wear a
face of piety," read the indictment
against him. Of a more political nature
was the complaint, "Wherever he went,
he industriously awakened the jealousy of
the humble and ignorant against all men
of superior reputation."

Anti-establishment, Sam Ely most
certainly was. After a brief stint as a free-
booting Revolutionary War volunteer at
the Battle of Bennington, he settled in
western Massachusetts and became involved in disturbances that were precursors to Shays' Rebellion. Arming himself
with a club at Northampton, he offered
to lead a mob against the County courthouse and declared he would rather fight
the local judges than the King of Great
Britain. When arrested for this secular
blasphemy, he was freed by his friends,
then rearrested, and after he was allowed
out on bond, went to Maine.

Here, Henry Knox became one of
those "men of superior reputation" upon
whom Ely's ire became fixated. His fiery
and satirical pamphlet, "The Unmasked
Nabob of Hancock County" mercilessly
pilloried Knox. An appeal Ely wrote to
the General Court for squatters on
Knox's land in the Muscongus area
begins respectfully enough, asking

123

consideration for "inhabitants so poor in purse and property that it is beyond their present ability and...will remain so during their lives, to purchase or pay for their present possessed premises..." but ends with yet another fierce diatribe against Knox.

> 1st Query, what ought to entitle General Knox to a grant of a tract of land superior in extent to any Lord in Europe or America, has he done more for his country than hundreds of us, no verily...
> 2nd Query, whether it would not be as just as to make a grant to every faithful soldier, of thirty miles square as to Knox and others—yes–

And so on...

Ely's purported henchman, Micajah Drinkwater, penned an addendum of his own to the petition:

> We the subscribers do solemnly declare that General Knox told us a number of positive falsehoods relative to peoples signing his general would never have paid no attention to him nor his spurious errand among us.

But the General Court offered no relief and the tension down east continued. Knox went so far as to urge the creation of a county defense association to repel attacks by Ely, who openly advocated violence. Ely's pen was as busy as his mouth. Attacking Knox again was a pamphlet entitled "The Deformity of a Hideous Monster discovered in the Province of Maine by a man in the Woods, looking after Liberty."

Massachusetts authorities, asserting that Ely had violated his bond to behave himself, had papers served on him by a Deputy Sheriff, and the agitator went into hiding. A "Last Petition of an Innocent Man, a Plaintive Worm..." made it to the House of Representatives in Boston as Ely's final broadside; it also contained a pat on the back for himself:

> I believe it can abundantly be proved that Knox and his agents have said repeatedly that if it were not for my pen and damn tongue, he could make all the settlers pay for their lands at his own price, meaning in other words he could cheat them as he please.

From this point on, Sam Ely disappears from history, his last known address Ducktrap (Lincolnville). But the problem of squatters in the wildlands continued. A particularly shocking example occurred in 1809 at Malta (Windsor), just outside Augusta. A four-man surveying crew was attacked by nine masked, armed men disguised as Indians. One of the surveyors, Paul Chadwick, was shot and killed, but before he died, was able to name his assailants, who were arrested. Public support for the accused reached the point where a rescue mob had to be routed. The "Malta War" only ended when a jury, unable to ascertain who had fired the fatal shot, found all of the defendants not guilty of murder.

While there is no evidence that Sam Ely was anywhere in the vicinity, his irascible, populist spirit could only have rejoiced.

Focus

The Madawaska Settlement

In contrast to his unfulfilled prophecy that Henry Knox would become Governor of an independent Maine, Alexander Baring was astutely clairvoyant about the future of the Madawaska area he visited in 1797. The young Englishman came away convinced it would become part of Maine when the "true St. Croix River" was determined, as it would have to be under the terms of Jay's Treaty between England and the United States. Little did Baring expect that many years hence he would play a major role in settling the Maine-Canada boundary. Thus, he was able to make his prediction come true— that the pocket of French exiles living in a governmental limbo between Quebec, New Brunswick and Maine, would, most of them, become American citizens.

Baring was impressed with the land and its people. He saw summer wheat producing 25 bushels an acre even amid stumps of ill-cleared fields. Moreover, no doubt thinking of his own investment, he saw the area becoming joined to father-in-law William Bingham's upper tract.

The French settlers in this remote valley were, in an indirect fashion, further victims of the American Revolution. They were originally among the refugees scattered when the British had expelled the Acadians from their Nova Scotian heartland in the early 1750's. Some twenty years later, a goodly number had drifted back into what is now New Brunswick. Hundreds were squatting on land along the lower St. John.

Then came the peace treaty of 1783, ending the Revolution and bringing thousands of Loyalists into New Brunswick. The lands of the French refugees, who'd basically been neutral despite France's aid to the Americans, were confiscated and given to exiled Tories.

Sometimes, there was compensation. A Lieutenant John Coombs of the 2nd New Jersey Volunteers paid more than £65 for the improvements François Cyr had made on his land. Frederick de Peyster of the New York Volunteers paid £87 to Joseph and Marie Theriault. But by then, the exodus upriver of Cyrs, Theriaults, Daigles, Martins and Heberts had already begun.

Legend has it that the first Frenchman there was Pierre Duperre, in search of his half-brother Pierre Lizotte who'd wandered off and been taken in by Indians. Supposedly, this occurred in 1783.

From New Brunswick, groups of Acadians travelled to the region while other harassed French groups from Quebec (then called Lower Canada) joined them in their quest for a sanctuary. These were actually two distinct populations—the Acadians from Poitou, Brittany and the west of France the Canadians from Normandy, Picardy and the French Province known as Maine. The mingling of these types produced in time a *Madawaskeyan* nature, described as:

> Breton and Norman all at once, stubborn and shrewd, honest and gay, active and intelligent, generous and full of initiative, hospitable, particularist without exclusiveness...

The fledgling colony had its problems. The year before Baring was

125

impressed by its abundant crops, *la grande disette* had visited the Madawaskans—"the great famine" when early snow had destroyed two-thirds of the harvest. It was a time when the wife of Joseph Cyr, forever known as *Tante Blanche*, achieved near sainthood for her acts of mercy to the sufferers.

But little by little, a civilization developed; a church was built and a rudimentary government developed through the appointment of Joseph Daigle as church warden and Louis Mercure as

colonization agent. Mostly, however, it was a self-regulating community where a man's word had the force of law. The greatest shame was to *perdait sa parole*—to go back on one's word.

Thus, they lived and developed in peace, generally left alone by the British authorities in Fredericton and Quebec. As for the Americans far to the south, they most likely had no idea that Madawaska existed, never mind that it would someday become a unique corner of the State of Maine.

Focus

The Indian Treaties

The omniscient Alexander Baring, in 1797, wrote apropos of northern Maine:

I shall confine myself certainly to what I have done...and particularly (about) the Penobscot Indian land, which we shall have an eye to when the state sells. The purchase of the Indians has already been made and persons appointed by the state of Massachusetts to examine and report the situation and nature of the lands. They have excited so much curiosity and attention that I fear they will sell for more than we shall choose to give...

With such pronounced anticipation among the business community, it is no wonder Massachusetts brought strong pressure on the Penboscots—and the Passamaquoddies—to part with the bulk of their land. As early as 1786, the Penobscots were being coaxed to sell by General Benjamin Lincoln, who met

with the tribe at Kenduskeag. As others had before him, the tough old soldier argued that the Indians had more land than was necessary for their subsistence, but also, he claimed, they had lost their land rights because of a treaty they had signed in Governor Pownall's day. Only the action of the Massachusetts Provincial Congress, Lincoln said, meeting at Watertown in 1775, had given them any claims at all, which were to a 6 mile strip on either side of the Penobscot from head of tide.

That the Penobscots acceded to Lincoln's blandishments proceeded from several causes. They were anxious, because of encroachments by white settlers, to have their boundaries firmly fixed; furthermore, if they ceded their riverfront territory, they were under the impression that their hunting grounds in the hinterland wouldn't be included; finally, they were in want and Lincoln was offering supplies—blankets, powder, shot, flints...

126

So they agreed, with the proviso they keep Old Town Island and all islands in the river from Sunkhaze to Passadumkeag, plus their hunting grounds. Legislation was passed in Boston, confirming the deal, and Lincoln met with Chief Orono and placed the promised trade goods and unsigned deed with a John Lee of Castine, expecting the Penobscots would ratify the accord.

They didn't. Impatience in Massachusetts grew. Voices began calling for militia troops to enforce the act. But Governor John Hancock was reluctant to use force. Instead, he dispatched an emissary, a Reverend Daniel Little.

Little brought a parchment document with him. At the meeting at Old Town, he had to wait for an aged blind member to be led into the council. He produced his document and argued, "You asked then for blankets, powder, shot and flints. Government now gives you all which you then asked and has fulfilled their part...This parchment, signed by the Governor, conveys four times as much land as you had before."

Orsong Neptune answered for the tribe, pleading their right to the soil from 500 years of possession. He cited promises made to them by George Washington and the Massachusetts General Court that they would forever occupy their lands. "We know nothing about writing... We do not mean to have anything to do with the treaty at Kenduskeag or that writing..."

This adamant refusal to cede stood unchallenged for another decade. That it did, or that the year 1790 passed with the land still in the possession of the Penobscots, was to have momentous consequences almost 200 years later. For had the Penobscots given in before 1790, they would have lost all subsequent claims, due to a law passed by Congress requiring all Indian treaties to be ratified in Washington. All treaties Massachusetts did ultimately make with Maine Indians occurred *after* 1790 and were *never submitted to Congress*.

The Passamaquoddies became the first tribe to finalize a treaty after 1790. On September 29, 1794, they and "others connected with them" (presumably Malicites and Micmacs) relinquished their land in return for certain considerations. John Allan had represented them. The tribe, nearly destitute, had expressed through him their willingness to cede their land if they could be guaranteed their "ancient occupation and a suitable tract for their use." Allan, whose job as U.S. Superintendent for Eastern Indians had just been terminated by Congress then became one of the Massachusetts commissioners treating with his former Federal wards. The price paid to the Passamaquoddies was to leave them 100 acres of islands in the St. Croix, a 23,000 acre township, 100 acres nearby at Nemcas Point, 10 acres at Pleasant Point along the coast, several other islands and use of a camping site on the Bay of Fundy. The cost to the Commonwealth was £200, paid to John Frost, an associate of General Lincoln's, for his land at Pleasant Point.

Paying off the Penobscots was more expensive. In 1796, when they ceded riverfront land on both banks for 30 miles upstream of head of tide, they were paid 149$^{1/2}$ yards of blue cloth for blankets, 400 pounds of shot, 100 pounds of powder, 36 hats, 13 bushels of salt, 1 barrel of New England rum and 100 bushels of corn. These amounts were boosted later on and a second treaty, taking additional land, upped the ante even more, threw in 6 boxes of chocolate, 7 barrels of clear pork and changed the blanket cloth to red one year and blue the next.[2]

By 1833, all the Penobscot land, with the exception of Indian Island at Old Town and the other islands in the river, had been sold. The last purchase was for four townships and it brought $50,000 that was put into a trust fund, theoretically to be managed for the tribe's benefit.

Through this series of coerced treaties, millions of acres of prime land became available for settlement or lumbering in Maine.

Statehood, 1785-1820

Professor Stephen Marini of Wellesley College in an interesting book about the growth of religious sects in New England during the late 18th century, discusses the drive for Maine statehood, seemingly an unrelated phenomenon. Marini links the 35 year effort of Maine to break free from Massachusetts to a series of disturbances in what he calls the "hill country," the northern and western parts of New England, which experienced massive immigration in the 1770's and 1780's, and increased their populations by 50% again in the 1790's and 1800's. Maine had less than 10,000 people before 1770 and Vermont about the same. By 1820, the numbers respectively were 298,335 and 235,754. As Marini says, "Between the Revolution and the War of 1812, the northern frontier received the largest and most intense population growth of any region in the new United States."

Hill country society was strongly egalitarian, its people "poor but not in need," mostly farmers, patriot in sympathy during the Revolution and fiercely democratic. Clashes with existing authority after the war led to three notable disturbances: the struggle of Ethan Allen and his Green Mountain Boys to bring Vermont into the Union as a state separate from New York; Shays' Rebellion in Massachusetts, which ultimately helped prod the scrapping of the Articles of Confederation for a new Constitution, and Maine's long-sustained effort to break from Massachusetts.

Paradoxically, it was not back-country Jeffersonians who led the first thrust for Maine statehood. The leading proponents were men who became Federalists, those supporting James Madison, Alexander Hamilton, etc. in the move for a stronger, centralized national government. In 1785, a year before Shays' Rebellion and three years before the Constitution would come up for ratification in Massachusetts, an article appeared in the *Falmouth Gazette*, Maine's first newspaper; rather, it was an oblique hint in the form

128

of an acrostic about Falmouth, to the effect that the town might soon be the capital of "a rising state". It was signed by "a benevolent Gentleman in a neighboring Town."

Subsequent supporting comments bore pseudonyms like "A Farmer," "Ruricola," "Impartalis" and "Philadelphos." Massachusetts writers who attacked the separatists were reprinted and answered. The *Gazette's* editorial policy was evidenced by its retort to a Bostonian's sneer at Maine Statehood.

> The above paragraph, while it proves the writer to be an ignoramus, with respect to the subject he scribbles, or a liar, or both—proves also, that, from interested motives, he fears the event...

The *Gazette's* issue of September 17, 1785 had a notice, summoning all citizens of York, Cumberland and Lincoln counties to the First Parish Church in Falmouth on October 5 to discuss separation.

It was an establishment group that gathered. The two ministers of the church were among them. General Peleg Wadsworth took part; so did Stephen Longfellow, a gentleman farmer from Gorham. In all, some 30 men attended. A seven man committee headed by Peleg Wadsworth drew up a circular letter, inviting delegates to a convention scheduled for January 4, 1786.

This initiative was received with hostility. In Boston, Governor James Bowdoin attacked it as "a design against the Commonwealth of very evil tendency, being calculated to the dismemberment of it." The separatists had to defend themselves against charges their action was insurrectionary by proving such gatherings were lawful under Article 19 of the Massachusetts constitution. They also had to deflect charges that statehood for Maine would open the door for Tory refugees to return from Canada. At the appointed date, 33 delegates appeared and cited a list of grievances. Included were a general lack of understanding, the location of the Supreme Court and especially its clerk's office in Boston, trade regulations that "reduce the price of lumber to the enrichment of Boston," the lack of representation for Maine towns under 150 population, a system of taxation unfair to Maine people: they claimed a sheep raised in Maine, which cost more to feed yet sold for less, should not be taxed the same rate as in Massachusetts, that Maine people drank more rum and thus the tax on rum was a greater burden and since property changed hands more often in

Maine, the fixed fee on deed transfers was inequitable.

Another convention, set for September 1786, was decided upon, but in the meantime, Shays' Rebellion broke out, leading some separatists to change their minds. The 31 delegates who did arrive stuck with separatist sentiments yet two groups emerged, one fairly radical, supporting not only separation but also the emission of "soft currency," i.e., paper money.

The leader of this latter group was none other than hot-headed General Samuel Thompson, the Brunswick militia commander arguably responsible in part for the bombardment of Falmouth. Thompson was "steeped in localism and distrustful of all authority," to quote the late Maine historian, Ronald Banks. A committee dominated by Thompson bluntly demanded independence. "You feel yourself distressed and your distresses will continue until you legislate for yourself," their report declared.

The moderates moved to delay presenting such a demand for separation to the General Court until after the furor of Shays' Rebellion had died down. By a vote of 15-13, the radicals reversed the decision. Thompson was authorized to go to Boston. For strategic reasons, he held off, hoping further conventions would give him stronger backing. They didn't. The separation movement sputtered to a halt after four more inconclusive and poorly attended meetings between September 1788 and March 1789.

Thompson then seemingly became more worked up over the proposed U.S. Constitution whose ratification by Massachusetts he fought tooth and nail. Topsham elected him to the ratifying convention and he travelled to Boston as part of a Maine contingent of 46 men, joining 309 other delegates. With William Widgery of New Gloucester and Major Samuel Nasson of Sanford, Thompson provided some of the most vocal opposition heard in the old meeting house on Brattle Street. Continually, he harped on the lack of a bill of rights in the proposed document. "The safety of the people depends on a bill of rights," he insisted. "If we build on a sandy foundation, is it likely we shall stand?...There are some parts of this constitution which I cannot digest; and, sir, shall we swallow a large bone for the sake of a little meat?...I say, let us pick off the meat and throw the bone away."

Arguing as vociferously, if not as colorfully, on the other side was Maine-born Rufus King, a Federalist legislator now living in Newburyport, and one day to be a U.S. Senator from New York; also, ironically, the half-brother of William King who would later lead Maine to statehood. Rufus King chided Thompson who had

130

uncharacteristically demanded a property qualification for Congressmen. "We never knew that property was an index to abilities...the men who have most injured the country have most commonly been rich men. Such a qualification was proposed at Philadelphia (at the Constitutional Convention in which King took part) but was resisted by the delegates from Massachusetts."

Thompson was never convinced. He acted, the *Falmouth Gazette* reported, "as if the Devil had possessed him," and after the vote was taken, refused unlike Widgery, Nasson and others, to announce he would support the new government. The Massachusetts ratification was a key one, built on the compromise of a promised bill of rights, and passing by a mere 19 votes out of 355. The Maine vote was 25-21. Another early exponent of statehood, Stephen Longfellow Jr., also voted in the negative.

An infuriated Thompson left Maine for New Hampshire and the direction of the statehood movement once more fell into moderate hands. Phoenix-like, the urge for separation rose repeatedly from the ashes of neglect during the last decade of the century. A leader of the effort was the conservative Portland lawyer Daniel Davis who became especially active around 1790 with the disappearance of the radicals. Aiding Davis were two other like-minded gentlemen, the Harvard-educated Portland barrister William Symmes and John Gardiner of Wiscasset whose Tory father, Dr. Sylvester Gardiner, had been one of the great land-holding Kennebec proprietors. Their efforts were successful in persuading the General Court to hold an election on separation in the District of Maine. Held May 7, 1792, this first broad sampling of Maine voters had disappointing results. Statehood was beaten, 2,074-2,524.

There was some solace in the defeat. The question actually received a majority in 83 of the 89 communities and lost overall because of large negative pluralities in just six York County towns: Wells, Arundel, Kittery, Sanford, Lebanon and Berwick. York County went more than 4-1 against statehood; Cumberland County gave it a thin majority; and Lincoln County favored separation by 2-1. Strangely enough, the two new frontier counties, Hancock and Washington, were strongly opposed.

Consequently, when a new initiative was discussed, the suggestion was made that Hancock and Washington be left with Massachusetts. York County's overwhelming opposition was based in part on the perception that the capital of the new state would be farther away than Boston (a prediction eventually true). Even

131

more of a stumbling block was the "Coasting Law" the U.S. Congress had enacted in 1789. It required ships sailing along the coast to stop in states non-contiguous to the state from which they'd embarked. Thus, a Maine vessel, (in essence, a Massachusetts vessel), could sail non-stop to New Jersey, since the intervening states of New Hampshire, Rhode Island, Connecticut and New York were all contiguous to Massachusetts. An independent Maine would be contiguous only to New Hampshire. This argument became a powerful objection in Maine's seaport towns.

The next vote was five years later, in May 1797. Separation won—but by a whisker—2,785-2,412. The Massachusetts General Court did not consider this a sufficient mandate, in an election in which little more than 5,000 persons out of a population of 100,000 had bothered to vote.

Not until 1807 was there another successful attempt to wring a vote on separation out of the Boston legislators. New leadership had taken over the statehood drive in Maine. But despite the vigorous efforts of William King and his allies in the Jeffersonian Democrat-Republican Party, the results were a disaster for partisans of Maine's independence. They were beaten by an almost 3-1 margin, 9,404-3,370.

The explanation was that the timing had been wrong. Economic conditions were simply too good. Politics had had nothing to do with the outcome. Indeed, the Federalist Party, which no longer supported statehood, had actually dwindled. The Democrat-Republicans, full of ambitious leaders like King and Henry Dearborn, Jefferson's Secretary of War, and General John Chandler and John Holmes and William Pitt Preble, were now fully in the ascendant. They had courted and won the vote of the greater part of the settler-squatter population of inland Maine and had strong pockets of support along the coast and in the newly-created upriver counties of Kennebec and Oxford. In the gubernatorial election of 1805, they had carried Maine for the first time and even while statehood was being trounced in 1807, their candidate for Governor of Massachusetts, the Maine-born attorney James Sullivan, was winning the District by 12,408-8,983.

William King was originally a Federalist but became disenchanted after he ran against an anti-separatist choice of the party leaders for Congress and lost. The following year, King was calling himself a Democrat-Republican and the year after that, he challenged David Cobb, Bingham's man, for his State Senate seat and lost again. Only in 1805 did he finally win—by one vote—taking

132

the State Representative's seat in Bath. Once in office, however, his political popularity grew and grew.

After the crushing defeat of separation in 1807, the Federalists gloated, their newspaper in Boston, the *Repertory*, stating sarcastically:

> Mr. King and Mr. Widgery[3] are really to be pitied. These individuals with a few of their associates, who wished to be greater men than even their own party...were willing to make them, had supposed themselves of sufficient influence to persuade the inhabitants of Maine to request a separation; and thus make a new little Empire for these aspiring demagogues... but it seems that Maine is far from inclined to dissolve her connexion with Massachusetts proper.

William King

And the editor came down particularly hard on King, alluding to his "deal" with the Bingham Trust:

> ...A gentleman should not set himself up for a great intriguer who has so little talent at concealing his selfishness...

But the gleeful Federalists could not foresee the War of 1812. Maine's experiences during that difficult and unpopular conflict were to give statehood irresistible political momentum. Most Maine people, especially in the north, were to end up feeling betrayed by Massachusetts.

It was Jefferson's attempt to avoid war that caused the first problems. In December 1807, his infamous "Embargo" passed congress and the affluent economy of Maine entered a precipitous decline. William King, himself, one of the district's foremost ship-owners, soon found he was losing more than $5,000 a month. Within two years, there was 60% unemployment along the down east coast and soup kitchens had been set up in Portland.

Jefferson had been trying to keep American ships out of the war zone that the entire Atlantic had become. Both England and France, the principal belligerents, were harassing American merchantmen as they attempted to carry on normal trade. Shipping from Maine had been primarily directed to the West Indies, to islands that were Spanish, Dutch, English, French and Danish. Bath, where William King lived, was then as now a shipbuilding center; between 1801 and 1807, 77 vessels were constructed there. In 1802, King had begun sending ships to French-held Louisiana, following the close of America's undeclared war with France, in which 1,700 American craft, many from Maine, were captured by the French.

But bad as the French had been, the English were worse. The failure of Jefferson's plan caused a brief revival of Federalist sentiment in Maine. Yet the Party's anti-war position, once Congress declared war on England in June 1812, lost it most of its popular support. The Federalist governor of Massachusetts, Caleb Strong, actually refused a request from Washington to let his militia leave the state, while condemning "Mr. Madison's War" and calling for a day of public fasting to underline opposition. In December 1814, the Federalists, in the eyes of some Americans, came close to treason with their convening of the Hartford Convention, an event that gave rise to speculation about New England's secession from the United States.

134

Earlier, an English invasion force, striking south from Canada, had captured the islands of Passamaquoddy Bay, including Eastport, then had taken Castine and most of eastern Maine down to Belfast.

William King was major-general of the 11th Division of the Massachusetts militia. He quickly mobilized to meet any further British advance. But he was given little support from either Washington or Boston. The Federal government had no money to spare. Massachusetts, under Governor Strong, borrowed money, but used it only to beef up protection for Boston and surroundings. As Ronald Banks wrote in *Maine at Statehood*, "No event...so blatantly revealed the extent to which the interests of Maine could be sacrificed to those of Massachusetts proper."

Repeated pleas by King's friend, Senator Mark Hill of Phippsburg, for the General Court to raise an army to liberate eastern Maine were just as repeatedly ignored. When President Madison nationalized the Massachusetts militia and King was selected to lead an offensive, no money was available to pay the men and the Boston banks declined to lend it. A personal visit by King to Governor Strong produced yet another refusal of help.

The anger in Maine led to renewed calls for separation. A convention of Democrat-Republicans in Oxford county met on December 28, 1814 and resolved "that it is inexpedient that the District of Maine constitute a part of the State of Massachusetts..."

The War of 1812 was over by then, although the people of Maine and Massachusetts wouldn't know it for another two months. A new Maine State Senator, Albion Parris of Paris, had introduced a fresh statehood measure into the General Court. His resolution was being debated when news arrived of the peace signed at Ghent. The Senators rejected Parris's bill, 17-10, but the political war between Maine and Massachusetts continued unabated.

William King was a complex and unforgiving man. Tradition paints him as a barefoot youth, leaving the family homestead in Scarborough with his only inheritance—a pair of oxen—and, by chance, electing to go north rather than south to seek his fortune. The actual truth is obscure, but apparently less romantic. His father, Richard King, had been a commissary with Sir William Pepperrell's forces at Louisbourg, had used that lucrative position to his advantage and with the proceeds, had bought property at Dunstan's Landing. William was the son of a second marriage. At Topsham in 1792, he went into business with his brother-in-law,

135

Dr. Benjamin Jones Porter. And because of Porter, too, King became embroiled with Bowdoin College in a controversy that sheds another light on the movement for separation in Maine—religious differences.

Bowdoin was a Congregationalist institution. William King was a Congregationalist, too, and he served on Bowdoin's board of trustees, along with Porter, who was the College treasurer. In the spring of 1814, the Androscoggin River flooded, causing Porter considerable losses. The unlucky merchant had to default on his bond as treasurer of Bowdoin.

Another trustee, Benjamin Orr, acting for the college went after King who had guaranteed his brother-in-law's obligation. Orr also did it in a particularly nasty fashion, attaching all of King's holdings in Bath. Able to pay off the debt, King nevertheless was furious and blamed not only Orr but President Jesse Appleton of Bowdoin, whom he intimated had been a British collaborator during the war.

This vendetta led to King's dogged support for a new educational institution in Maine, meant to challenge Bowdoin's monopoly. The Maine Literary and Theological Institute, a Baptist college, was promoted, as well, because it would bring religious pluralism. Said King, championing the cause of sectarian tolerance in demagogic terms:

View of Bowdoin College

Bowdoin College must go down...One of the classes of graduates of Bowdoin College has turned out to be principally
drunkards and another appears to have been religiously mad...

Baptist students there, he insisted, were not even allowed to
attend their own services.

The Baptist institution, which became Waterville College and
in time, today's Colby College, was a going concern by 1818 when
it received its first students. King tried to pry funding for it out of
the Massachusetts General Court, but they kept turning him down.
On February 19, 1819, the lawmakers declared:

It is believed that in the present state of the country, it is not
expedient to attempt the establishment of two considerable
universities in the District of Maine. Every consideration...
requires that the public funds...should be concentrated in one
flourishing institution and not be divided between two that
are inefficient...

Statehood would overturn that logic. Although Bowdoin had
political clout enough to see that it was protected under Article 7
of the Act of Separation, King's later power as Governor was para-

*View of Waterville
(Colby) College*

mount. Article 8 of the Maine Constitution, which he no doubt
inserted, gave the Legislature the right to interfere in higher
education matters; consequently, the governing board at Bowdoin
was packed and a Democrat-Republican, William Allen, put in as
President after Appleton died. More cutting still, legislative support was given to Waterville college.

The growth of the mainstream Baptist churches of Maine
(called Separate Baptists) was extremely rapid, especially in the
decade 1800-1810. No fewer than 110 were created, as opposed to
the establishment Congregationalists' mere 15. Other non-con-
formist congregations multiplied in the same period; the Free-Will
Baptists, an entirely different offshoot, added 22 new pulpits and
the Methodists 14. It was in Lincoln and Kennebec counties, hot-
beds of separatist sentiment, that the Baptists showed their greatest strength. In 1820, more Separate Baptist churches existed in
Maine than Congregationalist ones.

The exact relationship of religious sentiment and separatist
sentiment is hard to pinpoint. There were two successive votes on
separation in 1816—May 20 and September 2—and while certain
Kennebec County towns showed overwhelming support—Malta
(Windsor) went 50-0 and 56-0 and Augusta 248-24 and 258-39—
equally Baptist Lincoln County turned it down.

In both elections, the Separatists were victorious, but political
considerations nullified the results. The May election was called
into question because of the low turnout—16,892 out of 37,828
registered. Opponents of statehood argued that the stay-at-homes
were negative votes. The General Court formed a joint committee
to study the returns and report.

The committee was dominated by its Senate chair, Harrison
Gray Otis of Boston. He was not without his own interests in
Maine, as a partner with William King in the three townships
wrested from the Bingham estate. Statehood might help attract
settlers to their property. Besides, Otis was a Federalist and the
Federalists were eager to shed all those Democrat-Republican
voters in Maine.

As legislators will, Otis and his colleagues devised a complex
solution. They first called for a constitutional convention in
Maine whose delegates could vote yes or no on statehood; then, an
amendment wiped out the delegates' powers and required another
direct referendum of the people to instruct the delegates; yet
another amendment stipulated a 5-4 plurality. The statewide election results reported to the convention were 11,969 yeas and

10,347 nays—not a 5-4 majority, but the committee appointed by King to examine the returns used a twisted method of aggregating the majority of yeas in the favorable towns versus the aggregate of nays in the unfavorable ones and came out with a 5-4 ratio. Their specious reasoning was duly forwarded to the Otis committee in Boston and although Otis wanted to see Maine go free, even he couldn't swallow such a political slight of hand. The General Court dissolved the convention (held at Brunswick) and declared it inexpedient to adopt any further bills pertaining to separation.

Statehood for Maine once more seemed dead.

What helped revive the cause was a bit of astute political maneuvering by William King. The period directly following these defeats in 1816 had not been a happy time for King. He had vainly sought an appointment as Secretary of the Navy from President James Monroe and, in an attempt to gain control of Massachusetts for his party (and thus assure statehood for Maine), he had run for Lieutenant-Governor on the same ticket with old General Henry Dearborn. They were badly defeated in 1817. His sole victory was to be elected to the State Senate the next year. But this positioned him for the decisive act that made separation palatable for a broad range of Maine people—his success in having the "Coasting Law" repealed in Washington.

A mission to the nation's capital during late October 1818 found King enlisting the support of his half-brother Rufus and, more importantly, that of the Secretary of the Treasury, William Crawford of Georgia. Crawford had presidential ambitions and was counting on King's help in Maine and Massachusetts. On March 2, 1819, the bill was passed in Congress that resulted in one huge contiguous naval district from Eastport, Maine to the Florida-Alabama border on the Gulf of Mexico. No longer would Maine merchants have to fear that statehood would mean their ships couldn't go beyond New Hampshire without paying duties.

Two principle Maine opponents of statehood promptly changed their minds and said so in public. Moses Carlton Jr. of Wiscasset, a prominent shipowner, and General David Payson signed a letter in the *Eastern Argus* and other down east newspapers, acknowledging that the law passed by Congress "does away with all coasting objections."

The change of mood in Maine became evident, too, through the attitude of those who stayed opposed. The *Hallowell Gazette*, a consistent foe, published a scathing attack that was, nevertheless, utterly defeatist in tone. In an attempt at satire, they invented an

139

absurd constitution for the new political entity; among other things, the seat of government was to be Owl's Head, the proceedings to be held at night and the members to decide by *Hoot* and *Toot*, instead of *Yea* and *Nay*; the coat of arms was to be an owl with the motto on its beak, "Success by hook or crook"; the governor's title was to be "his Mightiness" and his two chief aides "the Governor's Dandies," and alluding to King, whose speech was not always grammatical, "No man shall be a candidate for Governor who cannot speak his mother tongue as correctly as Sancho Panza spoke the Spanish."

The sour grapes of Federalists in Maine was not reflected to the same degree in Boston. On June 9, a committee headed by Senator Josiah Quincy, a staunch opponent of separation, reported out a bill that pretty much incorporated the "Act of Separation" previously devised by Harrison Gray Otis. It included a referendum vote scheduled for late July. A plurality of 1,500 would be needed and, if obtained, would trigger a constitutional convention to be held at Portland on October 2. Quincy, although his committee had reported out the measure, still was opposed. His two hour harangue against the bill was followed by the two hour defense of it from his fellow committee member, Leverett Saltonstall of Essex. On June 19, 1819, after it had passed by wide margins, Governor John Brooks signed this authorization for yet another Maine statehood vote.

King and his allies organized to get out their vote. The opposition, without leaders, proved ineffective. A few Federalists, all friends of Bowdoin College and fearful for its future, held the only anti-separation rally of the campaign. As it so happened, the margin of victory for statehood far exceeded 1,500 votes. Every county (there now were 9) supported independence. The final tally was 17,091-7,132.

Two more steps were needed to make statehood a reality: the constitutional convention called for by the Quincy Committee bill, and ratification by the U.S. Congress, also called for, but with a deadline of March 4, 1820.

The first part was easier than the second. On October 12, 1819, 274 delegates gathered in Portland at the First Parish Church. They represented nearly all of Maine's 236 incorporated towns—a cross-section of the Maine population, with perhaps one element missing—the "establishment" Federalists who had opposed separation. For example, there was only one Congregational minister, but eight Baptist clergy and four Methodist. Staunch Federalists who'd

140

been at the Brunswick Convention, like Stephen Longfellow, Benjamin Orr and Samuel Fessenden, were notably absent.

William King, to no one's surprise, was elected to preside and he appointed his cohorts to the various key committees, such as rules, style and title, and constitution drafting.

An initial controversy had to do with a name for the new State. King's people suggested the "Commonwealth of Maine." Yet *Commonwealth* was deemed too fancy. As one delegate argued, "What was use of giving the name Jonathan when it would always be called...plain John?" And *State* was substituted only by a razor-thin margin of 6 votes. Then, it was moved that "Columbus" be substituted for "Maine". Daniel Cony of Augusta, who favored this move, offered an ingenious argument. He cited the fact that the U.S. Navy had begun practice of naming its battleships after states and complained that *Maine* would have to wait a long while for such an honor. However, there already *was* a major dreadnought called the *Columbus*.

His tortured logic failed to convince. *Columbus* might make people think of the Columbia River or a place in South America, foes argued.[4]

A more substantive battle was over the size of the Legislature. The large towns wanted a smaller House, so their votes would have more weight, and the rural communities wanted the Massachusetts model of one representative for every 150 taxpayers, which might have created a body of from 700-1,000 members. A committee, headed by the veteran politician John Holmes of Alfred, offered various formulas and settled on population ratios that eventually produced the compromise number of 151, where it still remains. The Senate, Holmes recommended, should also be based on population, a departure from Massachusetts, where the wealth of a county was the standard. A maximum of 31 members finally was allowed (since raised to 35).

Other departures from Massachusetts were that Maine refused to impose property qualifications on voters and candidates for office. In Massachusetts, to vote, you needed an income of $10 or an estate of $200. Without a word of dissent, the Maine delegates also agreed not to have a Lieutenant-Governor, another Bay State institution.

The role of religion was hotly debated. Freedom of religion, as proposed by the Holmes Committee, would be absolute—so that an attempt to introduce the Massachusetts clause that people had "a duty to worship" was soundly defeated. The convention had

141

gotten a petition from a small group of Roman Catholics around Damariscotta, led by Edward Kavanagh, asking for equality with Protestants. The anti-Papist grousing of William King was ineffectual in overcoming the strong sentiments of those present for toleration. Referring to Catholics, Jews and Moslems in a floor speech, one delegate declared, "The liberal principles of our government ought to make no difference between them...there is no ground for the exclusion of either of these great divisions."

The debate over the education article, which came to center on Bowdoin College, had a religious underpinning, too, as well as being a partisan political question. The Democrat-Republicans of Maine were determined to assert influence over what they saw as a closed Federalist corporation. Therefore in Article VIII, entitled "Literature," a section was inserted that no grant of funds could be made to "any Literary Institution now established" (i.e., Bowdoin) unless the Governor and Council had the power to overturn decisions of the trustees. Ether Shepley of Saco amended this to give the Legislature that power and the re-worked article then passed. Thomas Jefferson was credited by King with having inspired the wording of much of Article VIII during a visit the "Sultan of Bath" made to Monticello.

A considerable amount of controversy surrounded another feature proposed for Maine government—an Executive Council, like that of Massachusetts. Dr. Daniel Rose of Boothbay argued that a Council was unnecessary and a waste of money. He pointed out that the President of the United States had no such Council, nor did governors in many states.

Despite the arguments of Rose, John Holmes and others, a Council was accepted, composed of seven members (Massachusetts had nine), elected by both legislative branches (in Massachusetts, just the Senate) and having the power to "advise and consent" on numerous governmental matters.

Rufus King had warned in a letter to his half-brother William that an Executive Council (New York had one) "is worse than useless, it is the scene of intrigue and destroys executive responsibility."

Similar arguments were unavailingly made in Maine until 1975 when the combination of a Republican Senate, a Democratic House and an Independent Governor once and for all did away with this institution.

The constitution formulated in Portland was presented to Maine voters on December 6, 1819. It received almost universal

142

approval, with only 797 dissenters out of a vote total of about 10,000. On January 5, 1820, the members of the convention re-assembled to deal with several housekeeping items. Yet an air of uncertainty spoiled what might have been a time of celebration and self-congratulation. The word from Washington was that the politics of the North-South debate over slavery's extension threatened to delay Maine's admission into the Union beyond the deadline of March 4.

It was all started by a Democrat-Republican Congressman from New York, James Tallmadge. He stuck an amendment on the Missouri Statehood Bill to prohibit slavery in that territory. Rufus King tried the same thing in the Senate, but lacked the votes. Northerners threatened that without the amendment they would block Missouri's admission.

Then, Henry Clay declared he would oppose Maine without Missouri. In the Senate, where the Southerners had the votes, a bill was in the offing to couple the two admissions. Senator James Barbour of Virginia said he was all for Maine but "thought it best the Mother should have twins this time."

Power politics was being played to the hilt. The Senate Judiciary Committee tacked a rider on the Maine Statehood Bill, allowing slavery in both Maine and Missouri. A pro-Southern Senator from Illinois, Jesse Thomas, next offered a compromise that, except for Missouri, slavery would be banned in the Louisiana Purchase north of the 36° 30" line.

The House, after a lengthy debate, (600 pages in the record) said no.

A committee of conference then sought to break the deadlock.

The problem for those in Congress from Maine was a moral dilemma. To win statehood, they would have to accept slavery in Missouri. Only Mark Hill and John Holmes eventually could bring themselves to do so. Yet their votes were crucial on a key House vote that struck the anti-slavery proviso from the Missouri Bill by a mere three votes, 90-87. William King, given Rufus's reputation as an anti-slavery pioneer, was deeply torn. At first defiant, he promised to organize a state government in Maine regardless of Congress. But the practical politician in him prevailed. He was successful in persuading the Massachusetts General Court to extend Maine's deadline by two years and when word reached him from John Holmes about the Thomas Amendment, he supported it. He now shared his friend Mark Hill's position that to be for a compromise was not to be for slavery. He even lobbied the other five

143

Massachusetts Congressmen from the District of Maine, trying to convince them "that a compromise on those principles (the Thomas Amendment) would be highly proper, and more interesting to the north than anything which the most sanguine had ever contemplated."

Holmes and Hill were savagely attacked in Maine. Holmes was called a "Demagogue and Parasite" and both were accused of having "leagued themselves with southern slave drivers." In their defense, the two Congressmen wrote long letters to the press and to national figures. Hill heard from James Madison who commiserated that "As long as the conciliatory spirit which produced the Constitution remains in the mass of the people...these stormy subjects will soon blow over."

John Holmes

Thomas Jefferson, in his reply to Holmes, was less pollyannish.

In a passage destined to become famous, the illustrious Virginian prophesied about slavery:

> But this momentous question, like a firebell in the night, awakened and filled me with terror. I considered it at once the knell of the Union. It is hushed, indeed, for the moment, but this is a reprieve only, not a final sentence...

On March 15, 1820, Maine became the 23rd state of the Union.

CHAPTER Nine

A STATE TAKES SHAPE

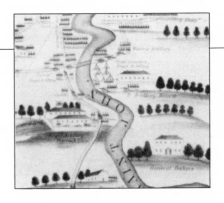

The First Steps

There had to be celebrations. On March 16, cannon salutes were fired all day in Portland until sunset, the public buildings were lit in the evening and a magnificent ball crowned the festivities. William King, the hero of statehood, came to Portland for the dance and on his return home, was escorted in triumph from Brunswick to Bath by a detachment of cavalry.

Even before the gubernatorial election in April, in which he was unopposed, he had begun to work. His mail was already filled with petitions from office seekers. To add to a governor's usual problems in filling jobs, he had let it be known he would find places for the opposition Federalists. The ratio was to be one Federalist to every three Democrat-Republicans.

The election came and went. King garnered 21,083 votes out of 22,014 cast. The Legislature, elected then, too, assembled at Portland the last day of May, in quarters built on the site of an old stable. For as long as they stayed there, they complained of the swarms of flies on warm days.

King addressed the solons June 2. The agenda of this first message ever of a Maine chief executive included the need for a Supreme Judicial Court, a new and revised code of statute law, a revision of the Militia Law and the election of two United States Senators. King also touched upon four of the principle resources of the state: agriculture, which he wanted encouraged; fisheries, where he felt the regulatory laws needed re-examination; lands,

146

which he asked to have protected from speculation; and manufacturing, for which he requested a complete tax break. In discussing finances, he reported that $21,131 had been spent on the constitutional convention, that Massachusetts was defraying this cost by $7,742 and the balance was in a loan of $14,000 that had to be repaid. Receipts were: from the State tax, $28,786; from the Bank tax, $17,700; from Licenses probably $6,000; plus $8,000 from Massachusetts—total revenue of $60,486. "What is to be the amount of the expenditures of the State is by the people confided to you," he went on, and expressed the hope there would be a surplus.

King was highly complimentary to Massachusetts. The image of "a great and powerful Commonwealth yielding up her jurisdiction over a large portion of her citizens and territory" was deemed a memorable phenomenon. And he was particularly grateful the Massachusetts legislators had been so fair in dividing the public lands fifty-fifty when they had had "it in their power to dictate the terms."

Having heard from their Governor, the Maine lawmakers went to work.

During that initial session, which ran until June 28, they passed 32 Acts and 36 Resolves. The very first Maine law put on the books was "An Act to Incorporate the Augusta Union Society," signed on June 10.

As in most legislative sessions, there were concerns ranging from the most trivial to the most critical. One insignificant measure legalized a series of personal name changes, allowing, among others, John R. Lisherness of Vassalboro legally to call himself Ranlet Ness. Of more pressing importance was a resolve that legitimatized several marriages performed 15 years earlier by a Baptist preacher in Topsham who had not been properly ordained.

Bills relating to towns are always a perennial: this maiden session saw a major one—creating the town of Kennebunk out of Wells, and several minor items: changing the name of East Andover to Andover, setting the north line of Alna and confirming the "doings" of Rome, Pownal and Montville.

The Bowdoin College controversy was well-represented. "An Act to modify and limit the terms and conditions of the Act of Separation relative to Bowdoin College and encourage Literature and the Arts and Sciences" accomplished what William King had long wanted—a public control over the actions of the President, trustees and overseers. By way of a sop, a bill was also passed

147

establishing a medical school at Bowdoin. King's other higher education goal was incorporated in "An Act to enlarge the powers of the Maine Literary and Theological Institution," which authorized the future Colby College to grant B.A. and M.A. degrees.

A Supreme Judicial Court was set up and a State Seal created. Designed by a committee, it featured various symbols: a pine tree, a "Moose Deer," the north star, since Maine was then the northernmost state of the Union, and the motto, *Dirigo*, Latin for "I lead." One committee member expressed his disappointment with the final result, claiming he had wanted the aurora borealis plus the north star, with the motto a quote from St. Paul, "I saw in the way a light." William D. Williamson, Maine's second Governor, who was President of the Senate at the time, was likewise displeased. In his monumental "History of Maine," he wrote:

> Owing to the hasty call for a metallic stamp, through a necessity of immediately using it, no part of it was very ingeniously wrought...and hence people of taste and judgment have not been altogether pleased...

Another task of the first Legislature was to approve a salary schedule for top government officials.

The Governor was to receive $1,500, the Chief Justice $1,800, the State Treasurer $900, the Attorney General $800 and the Secretary of State $700. Legislative per diem was $2, plus mileage of $2 for every 10 miles travelled. The Speaker of the House and the President of the Senate were to get an extra $2 a day.

Finally, they paid the State's bills. The largest was $500 to Francis Douglas for doing the State's printing. Samuel Hovey was paid $7.12 for sweeping and cleaning the State House. Ashur Ware, the Portland journalist who'd been elected Secretary of State, was reimbursed $5.66 for transporting certain books from Massachusetts and $15 for counting the Senatorial vote. Then, there was Robert Eastman. It had been his job to manufacture the State Seal—the work that Williamson had not considered "ingeniously wrought"—but he was nonetheless paid the $50 he had charged.

Poorly rendered State Seal or not, Maine was in business.

Early Politics

William King and his Democrat-Republicans were now thoroughly ensconced in Maine government. Two old war horses of the party, John Holmes and General John Chandler, were chosen by the Legislature to be U.S. Senators. The State Senate, House, Executive Council and Constitutional Offices were all dominated by the group that had pushed so hard for statehood. True to his word, King made some Federalist appointments. Chief Justice of the Supreme Court went to Prentiss Mellen, a former U.S. Senator (for Massachusetts), and Ezekiel Whitman was chosen to head the Court of Common Pleas. In other appointed positions, like Sheriffs, Clerks of Courts, Registers of Probate, etc., the Governor kept up his promised ratio of two-thirds, one-third.

His fairness, predictably, caused him grief among his own followers. The Wingate family, neighbors of King's in Bath, related to General Henry Dearborn, had long held the political plum of collector of customs in Bath and were miffed when various Sheriff's appointments were not given them. Their enmity to King, masked by social civility, was to cause trouble for the Democrat-Republicans in the years to come.

Nor was King's tenure as Governor untroubled. Re-elected without opposition in 1821, he still was unsuccessful in some of his most cherished endeavors. No tax breaks were given to manufacturing (King, by the way, owned a cotton factory) and another pet project, buying Massachusetts' share of Maine land, was rejected by the Legislature. Mid-way through his second term, King shocked the State by suddenly resigning.

Ostensibly, he was simply taking a more lucrative job. The Adams-Onis Treaty with Spain had given Florida to the United States, and in return the Americans had agreed to assume $5 million in claims against the Spanish governments. King was to be one of the commissioners who would settle those claims. He publicly announced that the pleas of Maine merchants with Spanish claims for someone they could trust had led him to accept the post. Cynics pointed to his political disappointments and a desire to be in Washington to help his friend William Crawford run for the Presidency.

Succeeding King was the President of the Senate, William D. Williamson, later Maine's esteemed first historian. Within six months, he, too, was out of office, having been elected to Congress, and the Speaker of the House, Benjamin Ames, became

149

acting Governor until the next election.

A three-way race for that vacant prize seemed to be looming between Senator John Chandler, General Joshua Wingate, Jr. and Albion Parris, a judge and ex-U.S. Congressman from Oxford county. Chandler soon dropped out and at county conventions, Parris was the clear favorite, prompting cries from Wingate that the meetings had been unfairly packed. The bitterness of the two intra-party rivals grew intense. An anonymous letter, signed *an old man,* was sent to Parris from Bath, telling him he would fail to win if nominated and should get out of the race, that only three persons in town would support him, "vis, Gov. King and his two creatures, Col. Robinson and Green," and maybe they could corral seven others, leaving the vote Wingate 450, Parris 10.

Naturally, it was suspected the Wingates had authored the letter. Later, it was found they were spreading vicious stories about King, saying he'd taken money from the Spanish claims to pay his debts, had borrowed $27,000 and had bartered away Maine's vote to Crawford.

Wingate's tactics were fruitless. Running anyway, without the nomination, he came in a distant third behind Whitman the Federalist and Parris, the winner.

The next year, Wingate did even worse in a three-way race among the same three men. Parris, who had to be begged to run for re-election, won in a landslide, taking more than 70% of the vote. In 1823, 1824, and 1825, Parris was re-elected without opposition.

Enoch Lincoln, another Oxford County resident, took his place. He was from a distinguished Massachusetts family, his father Levi Lincoln having served as Governor (and also as Jefferson's Attorney General) and his brother Levi Jr. likewise as Governor. Enoch Lincoln has been called Maine's first poet, because of an epic of 2,000 lines that he penned in 1816, more than a decade before he became Chief Executive.

At the time, he was living in Fryeburg and the title of the poem, "The Village," is ascribed to that upper Saco River community in the shadow of the White Mountains. But Lincoln's opus was not simply a bucolic idyll; it was filled with his political views, which, in a modern sense, could be described as extremely liberal. He addressed himself to "ye spoilers of all that the red men possessed...," railed against "slavery's plague" and asked "ye happy freeman" to behold "the poor Negro...seized (and)...yok'd like the ox...", declared that in regard to women, "Beauty's all subduing charms secures no conquest without mental arms," castigated the

150

cruelty of shooting song birds and declared that caprice ruled elections so that "too oft preferment falls to rogues and fools."

On the centennial of Lovewell's Fight at Fryeburg, he read a long paper he wrote commemorating the event and was in the process of completing a book on Maine Indians when he died unexpectedly at age 41. Only a few months earlier, the cornerstone of the new capitol in Augusta had been laid. Lincoln was buried across from the State House in Capital Park, by the banks of the Kennebec River. His mausoleum is still there.

FOCUS

Seba Smith, Political Humorist

The political "doings" on the state level soon produced a pioneer of Maine humor, the newspaper editor Seba Smith, who founded the *Portland Courier* in 1829. Smith's dry, satirical wit was a model for other 19th century writers like Maine's William Pattangall ("The Meddybemps Letters"), the Waterford, Maine native "Artemas Ward" (real name Charles Farrar Browne) and the Chicago columnist Finley Peter Dunne ("Mr. Dooley") who summered in York Harbor—all of whom poked incessant fun at politicians.

For this purpose, Seba Smith invented Major Jack Downing of rural Downingville, out of which he ventured into the real if bewildering world of politics. "Yes, sir," said Jack, "in the Fall of the year 1829, I took it into my head I'd go to Portland with no more capital than a load of axe handles, a cheese and a bundle of stockings." His rusticated father gave Jack a dollar to tide him on his way.

From Portland, Jack went to Washington where he hob-knobbed with Andy Jackson and other national luminaries and even pontificated on foreign affairs.

Here's Russia snapping her teeth like a great bear and is jest agoing to eat up the Poles. There's the Dutch trying to eat up Holland the Belgians trying to eat up the Dutch...and in fact all the

Major Jack Downing

Kings of Europe are trying to eat up
the people and the people are trying to
eat up the Kings...

But it was Cousin Ephraim who
kept folks informed of what was happen-
ing in Augusta, whither he'd gone to sell
apples from his orchard.

These Legislater folks cronch apples
down by the wholesale between
speeches and sometimes in the middle
of speeches too! That afternoon, Mr.
Clark spoke all day. I guess I sold nigh
upon half a bushel for cash and trusted
out most three pecks...

When in 1833, there was talk of
moving the capital back to Portland,
Ephraim was all excited because he estimated he could get more for his apples
there than in Augusta. Smith had him
support the idea on a satirical par with
arguments actually being voiced by Portland legislators.

They say it will be better all around.
They won't have so fur to go through
the snow-drifts to their boarding-
houses and won't have to pay much

more than half as much for their
board. And here in Augusta they have
to pay four pence apiece every time
they are shaved; but in Portland they
can get shaved for three cents apiece.

Andrew Jackson also came in for
his share of ribbing.

As Smith plotted it, Major Jack had
invited "Old Hickory" to Downingville
and he had promised to come. Everyone
scurried around, getting ready for the big
event. Aunt Keziah fixed up the house
and baked three ovens full of "dried
punkin pies besides a few dried huckle-
berry pies and cakes and a great pot of
pork and beans."

Alas, the perfidy of politicians!
Jackson didn't come. No wonder that:

Cousin Nabby said nobody in Downingville would vote for him now
except Uncle Joshua and he wouldn't
either if he wasn't afraid of losing the
post office.

Doonesbury would do it differently
today, but the genre of such topical satire
can be traced in a direct line to Portland's Seba Smith.

Lincoln had let it be known he wouldn't seek re-election.
Reflected in Maine just then was a political realignment, due to
the candidacy of John Quincy Adams for President. The old
Jeffersonian Party split, becoming *Democrats*—the inheritors of the
group's original populist mantle—and *National Republicans*, who
soon were Whigs and, in time, today's G.O.P. The Federalists,
meanwhile, simply disappeared, most of the members merging with
the new National Republican configuration.

In Maine, the Democrats nominated Judge Samuel Smith for
Governor. The National Republicans, already a force in the Maine
Legislature, put up Jonathan Hunton of Readfield. The election
was extremely close, and not only for Governor but also for con-

trol of the House and Senate. Hunton narrowly took the Governorship and his fellow National Republican, Daniel Goodenow, won Speaker of the House by a 73-71 vote. It took 50 ballots before the National Republicans were able to elect the Reverend Joshua Hall, as President of the Senate.

The following year, Judge Smith beat Hunton 30,215-28,639 and the Democrats also took control of the Legislature.

With the exception of several brief stints in the chief executive's chair by Edward Kent, a Whig, the party of Jefferson and Jackson held sway in Maine until shortly before the Civil War.

The State Capital Controversy

Cousin Ephraim wasn't simply joshing about cheaper barbering for legislators. The location of the State capital was a running controversy almost from the inception of statehood until a last attempt, in 1907, to move back to Portland. After that, an amendment to the Maine constitution guaranteed Augusta as the site.

It had been understood right from the start that Portland was only to serve as a temporary capital—as it did from 1820 to 1832. *Understood*, perhaps, but certainly never *accepted* by Portland partisans. The first action to start to leave Portland took place as early as 1821 when the Legislature formed a joint search committee that recommended Hallowell.

This thriving seaport was the largest and wealthiest community on the Kennebec River. so its primary disadvantage was not locational but political. It happened to be a Federalist stronghold. No one was surprised that the Democrat-Republican majority in the Legislature rejected Hallowell.

The next search committee, stacked with Democrat-Republican stalwarts, dutifully visited Brunswick, Hallowell, Augusta, Waterville, Belfast, Wiscasset and Portland before unanimously settling upon Weston's Hill in Augusta, a beautiful conical elevation overlooking the Kennebec. Along with their choice of site, they included a timetable—establishing the first Wednesday of January 1827 as the deadline for the initial meeting of the Legislature in its new home.

That this date was delayed by more than five years was due to stalling tactics by Portland supporters. When Judge Nathaniel Weston presented a deed of his land in December 1823, the

153

Senate accepted it, but the House refused by a 12 vote margin. Another vote was put off for two years.

Reuel Williams, an Augusta legislator destined to become a U.S. Senator, and Samuel Fessenden of Portland, whose son would also become one, led opposing sides in 1825. Fessenden had the votes, or rather, by one vote, 65-64, he was able to postpone the Augusta question once again.

In 1827, when the matter was thrashed out anew, the Kennebec Journal wearily wrote that the argument was "familiar if not tedious to most of our readers, having been published with little variation for five successive winters" and "all argument on the subject was exhausted years ago."

But during that debate, Portland outsmarted itself. A motion was passed to have the State capital at Hallowell. As a counter-move, Portland supported a capital at Augusta, to be established on January 1, 1832. Their Machiavellian thinking was that the 1832 date would give them plenty of time to overturn this expedient measure in the next Legislature.

Except the next year, they were unable to defeat a bill to plan the Augusta capital. Ex-Governor William King was appointed building commissioner, 10 public lots were sold for $60,000 to finance the work, the illustrious architect Charles Bulfinch was hired and the project was underway.

The cornerstone was laid on July 4, 1829. The handsome, granite-faced edifice, 150 feet long and 50 feet wide, took shape, but a cost overrun of more than $30,000 led to more opportunities for political mischief. The pro-Portland group tabled the appropriation and made a new bid for the capital. Augusta's response was to furnish a bond for any further expenses beyond a $25,000 appropriation for the cost overrun. In the end, at a final cost of $138,991.34, the Maine State House was built by 1832.

Five years afterward, Portland businessmen offered a Merchants Exchange they were building as an "eligible accommodation" for the State Legislature. Unsuccessful then, too, Portland tried again in 1860, 1889 and 1907 and just as doggedly, Augusta beat them back.

Back in 1829, on the day of the cornerstone-laying, the guest of honor, Major Augustus Davezac, personal emissary of President Andrew Jackson, talked about auguries and potential threats.

He wasn't thinking about Portland's attempts to wrest away the capital; his mind was on the State's undefined northern boundaries and he said: "The frontiers of Maine will never recede

154

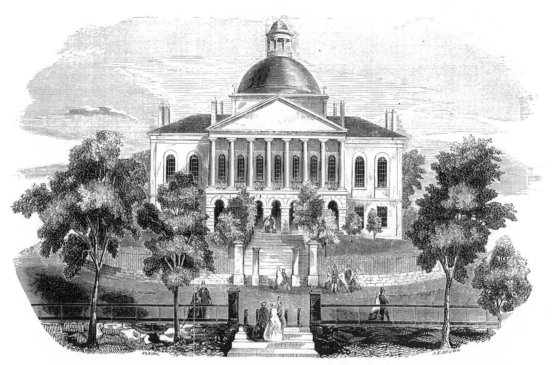

Maine's State House

before the footsteps of an invader and...her youth, in defense of
their native land, can never be conquered."

For the next 13 years, the State House would echo to concerns of warfare in the Aroostook wilderness and possible invasion
from Canada.

Settling the Northeast Frontier

Where were the Highlands? In Article II of the 1783 Treaty of
Paris, which ended the American Revolution, the north east
boundary between the United States and British Canada was to be
determined by a line drawn due north from the "source of the St.
Croix River" until it reached what were described as "Highlands"
dividing "those rivers that empty themselves into the River St.
Lawrence from those which fall into the Atlantic Ocean."

Once Jay's Treaty fixed the *true* source of the St. Croix in
1798, the due north line could be drawn. But that didn't help
matters much, for the "Highlands" still remained elusive.

The British rather brazenly picked out a single prominence in

155

the Aroostook region—Mars Hill—and maintained that here were the Highlands.

The Americans, on the other hand, staked their claim on the Notre Dame Mountains, only 20 miles from the St. Lawrence; if sustained as the Highlands, this marker would have given Maine parts of five Quebec counties.

It has been claimed that England knew the Notre Dame Mountains were the Highlands but refused to hand over the territory to the United States because of boundary squabbles elsewhere on the continent.

Map of the "Highlands"

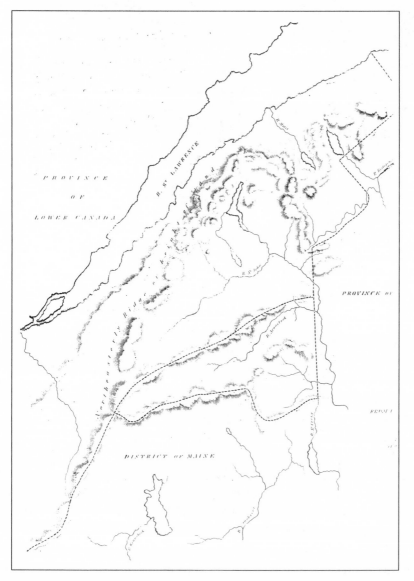

Thus, the land lay in limbo. During the War of 1812, it was reported by Bishop Joseph Octave Plessis who visited the Madawaska
area that many of the local males refused to become British soldiers.
"In two months, it may be decided that we are Americans," they
argued. Why should we exert ourselves in fighting against them
now?"

The close-knit French-speaking Madawaska community lived
in an isolated world of its own. Then, in 1817, the first Americans
arrived, settling north of today's Fort Kent at Meriumticook, now
Baker's Brook. The first American there, in fact, was Captain
Nathan Baker, but the most famous was John Baker, who came
somewhat later. At Baker's Brook, he built a saw mill, married
Nathan's widow, celebrated the 4th of July, established an American "Republic of Madawaska" and generally was a thorn in the side
of the English. Declaring the entire territory belonged to Maine,
John Baker petitioned the Maine Legislature for letters of ownership. The New Brunswick authorities protested his activities and
then took action.

Their first foray by Constable Stephen McNeil ended ignominiously for the Canadians. When McNeil seized a cow belonging
to an American, he was set upon, beaten and driven off. Next, a
special New Brunswick envoy, George Moorehouse, appeared and
ordered the Americans to take down a flag they'd raised on the 4th
of July. After the settlers demurred, Moorehouse lowered the
banner, himself, and took it with him to Fredericton. Mrs. Baker, as
dauntless as her husband, immediately borrowed some material
from a neighbor and produced another copy of Old Glory.

On the night of September 25, 1827, Sheriff W.E. Miller and
14 armed policemen surrounded Baker's "capital" of Meriumticook
and took the Madawaska Republic's "General" prisoner.

The arrest and subsequent incarceration of John Baker at
Fredericton became an international incident. The American
Secretary of State Henry Clay wrote Governor Enoch Lincoln,
expressing his outrage. Lincoln called on New Brunswick to free
Baker, saying he'd been arrested on Maine soil. Troops—Maine
militiamen—were sent to Houlton where they began building a
military road toward Canada, preparatory to invasion.

Cooler heads prevailed and the matter was turned over to an
independent arbiter, King William of Holland. The Dutch
monarch's decision, rendered on January 10, 1831, pleased neither
side and both quickly rejected it.

Shortly afterward, the Maine Legislature passed "An Act to

157

incorporate the Town of Madawaska and other purposes." Among its provisions was one to divide the entire Madawaska territory into three electoral districts and a rather comic-opera series of elections were held. The first was to be at Pierre Lizotte's house in St. David on August 20 to elect—in good old Maine town meeting fashion—a Moderator, Town Clerk and Selectmen. At the last minute, Lizotte refused to have the meeting in his home so the conclave had to be held outdoors. At a subsequent election, Pierre Lizotte was persuaded to run for State Representative. Opposing him was none other than John Baker, recently released from a New Brunswick jail. Lizotte won by five votes and, amazingly, the Americans all voted for him rather than Baker. But then Lizotte wrote Governor Smith of Maine that he never intended to swear allegiance to the United States, that he was a British subject and would die as such. When the Governor of New Brunswick, Sir Archibald Campbell, arrived with his militia, Lizotte was among those who presented arms to him.

The object of Campbell's expedition was once more to rout out the nest of Americans at Meriumticook. John Baker fled to Portland and sought help for four Americans who were arrested. President Andrew Jackson joined his protest to the clamor in Maine and the men were soon released.

After seven years of relative quiet, the next eruption of real trouble began in 1839 when tough-minded John Fairfield of Saco, a former Congressman, assumed the Governor's chair in Maine.

The "Aroostook War"

Portland's "Eastern Argus," the principle Democratic newspaper in the State, would have been well disposed to John Fairfield under any circumstances; they were especially pleased to point out, in an editorial on January 5, 1839, that Fairfield was strong on the boundary question.

> Meanwhile, we have no fears that our claim will suffer under the management of Mr. Kent's successor...He has already shown upon the floor of Congress that he understands our rights.

Indeed, Fairfield's maiden speech in Congress had been on the issue. Ironically, while waiting to deliver his peroration (it

158

John Fairfield

took more than a month before he was scheduled), an event
occurred thrusting him into the prominence that led to his nomination for Governor. This was the death of his fellow Maine
Congressman Jonathan Cilley in a duel with Kentucky Representative William Graves—a dispute sparked by aspersions of corruption against Maine's venerable U.S. Senator John Ruggles. Outraged by what he called Cilley's "murder," Fairfield broke
Congress's unwritten rule not to speak out against dueling. He
called for an end to the practice and, in so doing, achieved national notoriety. His two-hour speech on the north east boundary
was somewhat of an anti-climax, but was well-received. A key
passage of his letter home that day clearly articulates the temper of
Maine people on the question:

In Maine, there is but one feeling on this subject, that State, sir, feels that she has suffered deep and enduring wrong at the hands of the British government. She knows that she has been illegally and unjustly deprived of the property and jurisdiction in a portion of her territory; that the valuable timber upon that territory has been the subject of plunder and waste; that her citizens have been seized and imprisoned in foreign jails without law...and that the nation guilty of these multiplied and gross outrages not only denies redress, but refuses even to agree upon a mode by which the legality of her acts can be tried...

So one of Fairfield's first actions as Governor was to send a land agent to Aroostook to drive off the various New Brunswick trespassers cutting logs. An official report had indicated that illegal loggers on rivers like the Grand, the Green, the Fish and Little Madawaska were purloining timber valued at more than $100,000.

Rufus McIntire of Parsonsfield, a former Congressman, assisted by the Sheriff of Penobscot County and a posse of 200 men went up into the contested territory. They seized 20 of the interlopers but on a dark February night were caught sleeping by a large body of armed Canadians and hustled off to jail in Fredericton. Colonel Ebenezer Webster of Orono, who was then in New Brunswick, was himself arrested when he tried to gain their release.

These acts of aggression, as they were regarded in Maine, were further exacerbated by a declaration of Sir John Harvey, New Brunswick's Lieutenant Governor, characterizing McIntire's mission as an "invasion."

Fairfield fired off several special messages to the Maine Legislature. But he also went beyond mere words. He ordered the men assembled at Bangor as reinforcements for McIntire to be dispatched northward. Following them would be 1,000 more, whom Major-General Hodsdon of the Maine militia was authorized to draft. And another 10,343 officers and men were to be called up as reserves. The Legislature responded with a resolve appropriating $800,000 for "a sufficient military force...to prevent further depredations on the public lands and to protect the timber...already cut by the trespassers and to prevent its removal without the limits of the State."

The British were not idle, either. A regiment of 800 Irish Fusiliers landed in New Brunswick and marched west toward the

160

Madawaska territory while 500 more red-coated regulars moved east from Quebec. At Cabano on Lake Temiscouata, a detachment under Lieutenant Lennox Ingall built Fort Ingall. The Mainers, in turn, built Fort Kent and Fort Fairfield, named for their two most recent Governors.[1] Despite attempts to cool down the crisis by releasing prisoners, the situation remained inflamed. In Washington, Senator Ruggles startled his colleagues by announcing a battle had taken place in Aroostook and blood had been shed. There was a great sensation in the Chamber until Daniel Webster arose and said he doubted the report. Ruggles later told the Senate he'd been given false information.

The English were basing their actions on a supposed agree-

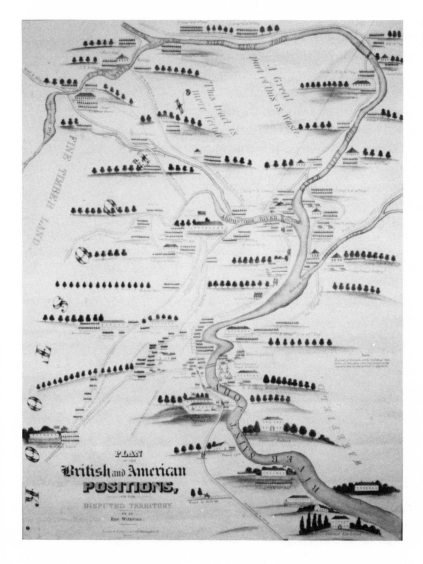

British and American positions during the "Aroostook War"

161

ment giving them jurisdiction over the disputed land until a settlement was reached. President Martin Van Buren declared there was no such agreement and the Senate Foreign Relations committee, after a study, agreed. Van Buren was empowered to resist the British, $10 million was voted and 50,000 volunteers authorized. During the debate in the House, Congressman George Evans of Maine melodramatically defended his State's position and warned that Maine would act unilaterally if the country didn't support her.

> The question for you is whether she shall be left alone battling for her rights...You may see her trod in the dust by military power which she cannot resist...You may see her cut off from the Union and incorporated with the colonial possessions of a foreign power, but you will not see her quailing before the enemy, nor abandoning the high ground she occupies, while she can lift an arm to uphold her flag.

On February 27, Governor Fairfield reviewed the Maine troops. Seated on a borrowed horse, a bareheaded Fairfield received the salute of 600-700 men drawn up outside the State House. Thousands of spectators watched. "The windows of all the houses were full, tops of houses covered, trees full of boys and the streets crowded with men," the Governor wrote.

The same day, the U.S. Secretary of State and the British

Fort Kent

162

minister signed a memorandum that the New Brunswick officials would not try to expel the Maine forces in Aroostook as long as the Yankees agreed to withdraw.

This "memorandum of Forsyth[2] and Fox" received a less than enthusiastic response, and not only in Maine. A man from Albany, New York wrote to Fairfield, "Sir, that Memorandum is a foul blot upon our nation..." The Maine Governor also heard from an Illinois Militia general, seeking help to have the President call up his brigade.

But Van Buren was treading carefully. He dispatched General Winfield Scott to Maine, carrying copies of the memorandum, one for Fairfield and one for his counterpart, Sir John Harvey, whom Scott had met during the War of 1812. "Peace with honor" was the goal the President outlined to Scott.

The General arrived in Maine on March 5 and learned of the fury created by the memorandum's implication that the Americans had to retreat. Scott was also astute enough to realize that political considerations were at work. Neither Democrats nor Whigs wanted to appear overly dovish.

So the key thinking, Scott grasped, was to drop the memorandum for a different formula and with Fairfield's support, this was done. The Governor stated that if New Brunswick would deny any intention of occupying the disputed territory, Maine *would* withdraw its forces, leaving only a "posse to protect the timber resource. On March 23, the Legislature passed a resolve authorizing the Governor to take such steps. Meanwhile, Scott met with his old acquaintance, Harvey. He proposed a statement for the Canadian to issue, alluding to impending negotiations and renouncing all use of military force. Harvey agreed. Then Fairfield agreed to pull back the Maine Militia. On March 30, all but four companies, which were left at Fort Fairfield, departed Aroostook and those remaining were soon replaced by civilians. The "Aroostook War" had ended. Diplomacy took over.

The Webster-Ashburton Treaty

Oh, have you heard how old Maine went?
She went hell-bent for Governor Kent
And Tippecanoe and Tyler, too
Tippecanoe and Tyler, too.

Gleeful Whigs in 1840 were singing this ditty as political power changed—first in Maine, which voted in September—and then in the nation. General William Henry Harrison and the ex-southern Democrat John Tyler carried the Pine Tree State by 411 votes. John Fairfield, despite his heroics during the Aroostook War, was replaced by the man he'd replaced. Actually, Edward Kent did not win the popular vote. In undoubtedly the closest gubernatorial election in Maine history, Fairfield nudged out Kent by nine votes, 45,588 to 45,579, but the existence of 70 other scattered votes meant a majority of all votes cast hadn't been reached, which by law left the choice up to the Legislature, and it was dominated by Whigs.

From Maine's point of view, the most important result of the 1840 election was the appointment of Daniel Webster as Secretary of State. With ties to Maine (he had taught school in Fryeburg), he was committed to a peaceful settlement of the northeast

Daniel Webster

boundary. In January 1842, his overtures to Whitehall paid off when he learned that the British would send Lord Ashburton to negotiate a treaty.

Lord Ashburton—Alexander Baring—what a happy choice, Webster had to think. Here was an Englishman who knew America well, and Maine, in particular. Nor was it amiss that Webster had once done legal work for the Barings. The two men met frequently in Washington after the 67 year-old Ashburton took quarters at 16th and H Streets, close to Webster's home. Critical to Webster was Maine's role and he invited the Governor of Maine, who by then was once more John Fairfield[3], to send representatives. He also invited Massachusetts.

The Maine Legislature voted to dispatch four commissioners, divided equally by party. The Democrats sent William Pitt Preble and Edward Kavanagh; the Whigs, ex-Governor Kent and John Otis. Massachusetts sent three representatives, among them Abbott Lawrence, the future industrialist.

Knowing he would have to make concessions, the canny Webster acquired a trump to play if Maine proved too recalcitrant.

Shortly before the Maine Legislature met, the Secretary of State paid a discreet visit to Boston, where he called upon Professor Jared Sparks of Harvard. Webster had somehow learned Sparks possessed a copy of a French map used during the Treaty of Paris sessions in 1783, bearing red lines drawn by Benjamin Franklin in the northeast that were far south of the present American claim; they approximated the British claim and could prove fatal to Maine's case if they saw the light of day. Sent to Augusta, Jared Sparks secretly shared his knowledge with top Maine officials.

Consequently, Lord Ashburton's offer to give the Americans territory from the St. John River south received a more favorable hearing than might have been expected. The Briton's proposal gave England only 5,000 of the 12,000 square miles in contention, a tad more than the rejected award by the Dutch King. To sweeten the pot, free navigation of the St. John was promised, Maine and Massachusetts were each to get $125,000 in Federal funds and Rouse's Point, a fortified ex-U.S. post on Lake Champlain, would be returned.

Ashburton, who was criticized in London for being too soft, made no bones about his eagerness to settle. Washington's stifling summer weather affected him. "I contrive to crawl about in this heat by day and pass my nights in a sleepless fever," he wrote home. "I had hoped that these Gentlemen from the North East

165

would be equally averse to roasting."

Webster smoothed the path by using $17,000 of a secret slush fund at his command—with the acquiescence of President John Tyler. Some of it went to pay Jared Sparks for his services. Most of it went to an interesting character named F.O.J. Smith, nicknamed *Fog*, a Maine Congressman and wheeler-dealer. Fog Smith spread money around judiciously in Maine. He was able to persuade the "Eastern Argus" to change its editorial policy and push for an accommodation. One of his most effective ploys was to place continual articles in favor of peace in the Portland "Christian Mirror," a religious paper.

Such public relations pressure had its effect on the Maine commissioners, who finally agreed to Webster and Ashburton's terms. Then, Senator William Rives, Chairman of the Foreign

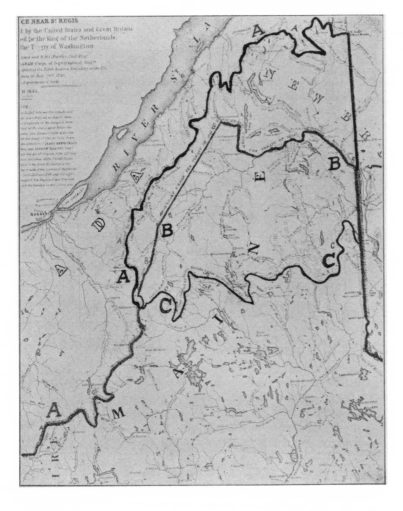

The different boundry claims settled by the Webster-Asburton Treaty

Relations Committee, guided the treaty to ratification. His use of Sparks' map behind the scenes helped overcome the opposition led by Senator Thomas Hart Benton of Missouri, a noted expansionist. The Senate vote was overwhelming, 39-9.

Genuine relief that the crisis was past brought plaudits to both Ashburton and Webster. The Englishman was feted with banquets in New York and Boston. At the one in New York, an uncomfortable incident showed the antipathy toward President Tyler even among members of his own party. When a toast was proposed to Queen Victoria, everyone rose, but when Ashburton lifted his glass to Tyler, no one stood.

Notwithstanding such rough edges, the Treaty was a success, even more so in America than in England, where officials were miffed when they finally learned about the hidden Sparks map.

By then, southern Madawaska was firmly a part of the United States and of Maine. Jose David Cyr had been elected to the Maine House and the territory divided into its three administrative "plantations"—Van Buren, Fort Kent and Madawaska. An unforeseen consequence of the boundary split was to leave John Baker, the fiery American patriot, on the Canadian side. But in time, he became a respectable citizen of his new country.

The State of Georgia Versus Maine

At Baltimore in late May 1844, the Democratic Party nominated James K. Polk of Tennessee for President on the ninth ballot. There was also balloting for Vice President and on the first vote, John Fairfield of Maine, by now a U.S. Senator, received the most votes, but not a majority. On the second ballot, George Dallas of Pennsylvania beat out Fairfield and went on to become Vice President when Polk was elected. In discussing his defeat, Fairfield explained:

> I am informed that I should have been nominated on the second ballot if it had not been thought that my course when Governor in the controversy between Maine and Georgia and my views on the treaty would operate against me in the South.

The *treaty* was for the annexation of Texas as a slave state, against which Fairfield voted. The *controversy* also involved slavery. It was a vivid example of the problems that differing attitudes toward slavery could cause between states and it had begun prior to Fairfield's election as Governor.

Early in May 1837, the Maine schooner *Susan*, captained by Daniel Philbrook of Camden, with Edward Kelleran of Cushing as mate, stopped at Savannah, Georgia, to undergo minor repairs. On May 4, she sailed north again. But unbeknownst to all, a slave named Atticus, one of the laborers, had stowed away and his presence wasn't immediately discovered.

The absent slave's owners, James and Henry Sagurs, conjectured that he might have gone off aboard the *Susan*. They hired a pilot boat to give chase, but the schooner was too far ahead. On May 9 or 10, Philbrook docked at Thomaston and a few days later, the pursuers in the pilot boat arrived at Rockland. James Sagurs went straight to a Maine court and obtained a warrant for Atticus's arrest as a fugitive slave. He also offered a $20 reward. Two local men betrayed the slave and Atticus was taken to the pilot boat, which sailed with him to Georgia. An angry demonstration at East Thomaston expressed the feelings of most Mainers, but Sagurs was allowed to leave with his "property."

And there the matter might have rested had it not been for Sagurs' slaveholder mentality that assisting a slave to escape was tantamount to outright theft. A month later, he went before a magistrate in his own county and was granted a warrant for the arrest of Philbrook and Kelleran, that they did "feloniously inveigle, steal, take and carry away without the limits of the State of Georgia, a negro man named Atticus."

When the Georgia authorities were informed that Philbrook and Kelleran could not be found, Governor William Schley of Georgia wrote to Governor Robert Dunlap of Maine, saying he had appointed an agent to bring the "fugitives from justice" to stand trial in the south. He asked Dunlap to apprehend the two and turn them over to this man.

The indignation of Maine people at what they judged to be an aggressive, vindictive act by the Georgians was reflected in Dunlap's response. "So far as I have received any information relative to Philbrook and Kelleran," he wrote back, "their visit to your state was in the course of their ordinary business as mariners. Their vessel being at the South, they navigated it homeward by the usual route and in the usual time. They had stated homes, to which they openly returned. At those homes they took up their residence, and conducted their affairs there without concealment

168

and in all respects conforming to the usages of innocent and unsuspecting citizens." Those last words, *innocent* and *unsuspecting*, were emphasized all the more by Dunlap's denial of Georgia's request. There was no "probable cause" for arrest, he asserted, as required by the U.S. Constitution.

Governor Schley cited the U.S. Constitution, as well. States were bound to obey the laws of sister states, he argued, and under Georgia law, Philbrook and Kelleran were fugitives from justice. The Georgia Legislature was called in to deal with Dunlap's continued refusal. They reluctantly rejected a proposal to close all Georgia ports to Maine vessels, for that *clearly* would be unconstitutional. So was the idea of seizing Maine citizens in Georgia as hostages. They contented themselves with strong words against Maine's *dangerous* course, requested again that the Governor of Maine comply and planned a special General Assembly if he didn't. The motivation behind Georgia's dogged persistence was well revealed in the statement of the legislative committee involved that it views:

> The doctrine of abolition as a moral and political pestilence, which if not checked will spread devastation and ruin over the land.

The antagonism continued with new Governors in both States. George R. Gilmer of Georgia asked Edward Kent of Maine to deliver the two men for trial, adding a charge that they had stolen Atticus for their own use. No more satisfaction was given to this demand than to the previous ones. The frustrated Georgian Chief Executive could only vent his spleen by declaring almost apoplectically in his annual legislative message that:

> ...all citizens of Maine who may come within the jurisdiction of this state...shall be considered as doing so with the intent to commit the crime of seducing negro slaves from their owners, and be dealt with accordingly by the officers of justice.

To which Governor John Fairfield, in *his* message in 1840, responded:

> ...The proposition so clearly violates the constitution of the United States...that the intelligent Legislature of that distinguished and gallant state will never sanction it.

169

Fairfield was right. The Georgia Legislature wisely refrained from acting on this hot-headed and childishly vengeful suggestion.

The controversy eventually died down. Long after the Civil War, Philbrook's grandson, Captain Eugene Cookson, visited Savannah and was accosted by an aged Black, the boss of a gang of stevedores. It was Atticus, himself, full of grateful memories of his brief moment of freedom.

The episode of Atticus and the *Susan*—an obscure one amid the many more famous explosive conflicts over slavery—was like Jefferson's "fire bell in the night" on a muted scale. It brought into sharp relief the depth of feeling on an issue that was to grip all States until its resolution through five years of bloody and destructive warfare.

CHAPTER Ten

THE FORTIES AND THE FIFTIES

An Overview

It could be said half-seriously that Secession and Civil War came almost as a relief in 1860-61; the two decades preceding the hostilities had been times of such tension, such agitation, such uncertainly and such divisiveness, that red-hot war, when it came, acted like a catharsis.

The three main issues dominating American public life during those twenty years had emotional power so great that each, in its way, bore seeds of violence. Abolition, Prohibition and Nativism, they are known to history. They existed nation-wide and in Maine. They contributed to the demise and reformulation of the two major political parties. They created riots, the burning of public buildings and sudden deaths, even within bucolic Maine. There were Mainers—prominent ones—who combined all three, as anti-slavers, temperance men and know-nothing upholders of White Anglo-Saxon Protestant "Americanism."

Maine was burgeoning with economic growth during the 1840's and 1850's. Shipbuilding and shipping reached a peak. Railroads were being built. For one brief moment, Portland bid fair to outrival Boston as the major city of New England. Bangor was the lumber capital of the world. Immigrants arrived—mostly Irish people of the Roman Catholic faith, and as their numbers grew, so did discrimination. The nation's political leaders struggled to avoid war, but each compromising of the extension of slavery created thousands of new abolitionists. *Freedom* became the rallying cry, too, of those who sought freedom from the slavery of demon rum.

171

The trio of themes—much later joined alliteratively as *Rum, Romanism* and *Rebellion*—haunted the two decades, riveting Maine's attention now that its boundary had been settled.

Focus

Edward Kavanagh

After finishing his unforgettable "Evangeline," Henry Wadsworth Longfellow wrote an eminently forgettable novella entitled "Kavanagh." He started his project in 1847, three years after the death of Edward Kavanagh, the first Roman Catholic Governor of Maine.

Longfellow may have had a fascination with Catholics, and in "Kavanagh," he uses a fictitious character descended, as he says, "from an ancient Catholic family" whose ancestors "had purchased from the Baron Victor of St. Castine a portion of his vast estates, lying upon that wild and wonderful sea-coast of Maine..." The twist here was that Longfellow made his *Kavanagh* a convert to Protestantism, and a minister of the church, no less.

The real-life Edward Kavanagh was always a devout Roman Catholic. His father James Kavanagh emigrated from New Ross, Wexford County[1] to Boston, and then to Maine with another young Irishman, Matthew Cottrill. They settled in the Newcastle-Damariscotta region, prospered, married Catholic girls and built St. Patricks, the first English-speaking Catholic church in Maine.

All of this happened before statehood. While neither man suffered any outright persecution, they did have trouble with the discriminatory laws of Massachusetts. Having built a church for his faith, the elder Kavanagh went to court to relieve Catholics from the burden of supporting the local Congregational minister. He lost. And dire legal action was taken against the French-born priest Jean Cheverus because he performed a Catholic wedding ceremony at Newcastle. If convicted, Cheverus not only would have been fined, but publicly pilloried. His trial ended inconclusively when the judge fell off a horse and was incapacitated.

Edward Kavanagh started his public career by authoring an eloquent plea to the framers of the Maine constitution for an article—subsequently included—on complete religious toleration. The young lawyer more actively entered public life in 1823 with his election to the school committee in Newcastle, then went on to Selectman, State Representative, and State Senator from Lincoln County. A Democrat and a Jacksonian, he assumed State-wide office in 1829 when the Legislature elected him Secretary of State.

In his next try for office—for U.S. Congress—Kavanagh experienced the only overt attack made against his religion. An itinerant preacher, described by a Catholic newspaper as "a prowling wolf of the Education Society," warned from the pulpit that a Kavanagh victory would unloose a "torrent of Catholicity" to deluge poor Lincoln County. Such appeals to prejudice may have been ahead of their time. In any event, they had no effect on Kavanagh's election. Indeed,

172

the Jacksonians jumped on the incident as a way to gain Catholic votes. "The attempt of the Clay Party to proscribe a gentleman because he is a Catholic and the son of an Irishman cannot be too much reprobated by all liberal men of every political and religious opinion," declared the Boston *Statesman*, a Democratic newspaper. The backlash proved useful nationally, as did the news that the first Catholic had been sent to Congress from New England.

While waiting to take his seat, Kavanagh participated in an official survey of the disputed northeast boundary lands. No doubt this influenced his choice as one of the four Maine Commissioners who worked with Webster and Ashburton in settling the knotty question. Not an unmixed blessing, however. The treaty was unpopular in Maine and the Commissioners, for having agreed to it, shared the opprobrium. Yet so highly regarded was Edward Kavanagh that he easily won re-election to the State Senate, while his fellow Commissioner John Otis, a Whig State Senator, was defeated.

Moreover, his fellow Senators almost unanimously chose Kavanagh to be President of the Senate, which meant he was next in line to succeed the Governor should the highest office become vacant.

And this was exactly what happened. Early in March 1843, the Legislature chose Governor John Fairfield to replace U.S. Senator Reuel Williams, who had resigned. On March 7, Edward Kavanagh became Governor.

Internal Democratic politics ordained that Kavanagh would not be renominated by his party. The major split nationally was between those who wanted ex-President Martin Van Buren to run again and partisans of John C. Calhoun. Edward Kavanagh was a Calhoun man. John Fairfield and his choice for Governor, Hugh J. Anderson, were with Van Buren. The State convention at Bangor narrowly settled on Anderson. The angry Calhounites refused to make the nomination unanimous and there was talk of running Kavanagh independently. He would have none of it. Publicly, he declared,"...I have explicitly stated my determination to support Mr. Anderson for Governor." Still, he received 3,221 votes in an election Anderson won by only 1,000.

It may have been just as well Kavanagh wasn't re-elected. His health had deteriorated badly (he probably had stomach cancer). Back in Augusta, he finished his duties as Governor, resigning on December 28. Within less than four weeks, Edward Kavanagh was dead at the age of 49.

Temperance

Temperance Flag! The Temperance Flag!
It is the banner of the free.
The Temperance Flag! The Temperance Flag!
An emblem of our liberty.
That flag proclaims us free from Rum
A foe we never will obey...

On the front page of the *Bangor Whig* and *Courier* in June 1842, this preamble to a longer poem appeared, showing that even in this sinful lumber boom town in the north woods, the State's major reform movement was making inroads.

The editors went on to cajole their readers:

A strong temperance delegation from Portland is expected...There will be fine times at the City Hall this evening, Let all work now and help root out the power of alcohol over the bodies and minds of men. Let an end come to the slavery of appetite. Let men be sober and free. One and all to the City Hall tonight!

Neal Dow

174

Neal Dow, the Portland volunteer firefighter, was the movement's leader in Maine and, as it turned out, a pioneer of prohibition for the entire United States. This feisty bantam (he was only five feet tall), unpeaceable descendant of Quakers, who took regular boxing lessons, had achieve local notoriety by persuading the members of the Deluge Engine Company to forego the customary liquor served at their annual celebrations. Dow's very connection with the fire department derived from his distaste for alcohol; as a fireman, he was exempt from duty in the militia, whose "musters" were notorious for being little more than drunken bashes.

Dow, whose prosperous family owned a tannery and speculated in real estate, took an active role in the embryo temperance movement fanned New England-wide by the Reverends Lyman Beecher and Justin Edwards. After Edwards's October 1827 visit to Portland, the Maine Temperance Society was formed and Dow, along with his cousin John Neal and the future U.S. Senator William Pitt Fessenden, became a charter member. One of their early prohibition efforts was against the practice of giving workers "rum breaks" at eleven o'clock and four o'clock, akin to our present-day coffee breaks, with the employers supplying their men free drinks.

Eventually, the Maine Temperance Society split over the question of banning wine. Members like ex-Governor William King and John Neal argued that wine, as a "gentleman's drink" should not be forbidden; purists like Neal Dow argued, as in our modern debate on marijuana and hard drugs, that wine led to stronger stuff. The result was a permanent division, and the creation of the Maine Temperance *Union*, promoting total abstinence.

The stage was now set to try for legislative action. Living in Portland since 1833 was a retired War of 1812 general named James Appleton, who had opened a jewelry shop. Many an hour, Neal Dow met with him in his store to discuss temperance—and particularly how Appleton, elected to the Maine Legislature as a Whig Representative, could help.

In February 1837, Appleton got himself made head of a joint committee on liquor laws. Dow, through the Temperance Union, flooded the legislators with petitions calling for prohibition. After three weeks of deliberation, Appleton's committee presented a report that called for an end to sales of liquor—except for doctors and druggists and wholesalers, who would have to sell 28 gallons at a time or more.

The report was tabled, but the first shot had been fired. The nation's earliest prohibition law had seen the light of day.

The "Maine Law"—the stringent teetotalling measure by which Dow gained national notoriety—was not enacted until 14 years later. On April 8, 1851, Dow was elected Mayor of Portland and lost no time in using his position, plus alliances with Free-Soilers and anti-slavery Democrats, to pressure the Legislature once more on temperance. He had almost succeeded in 1849, but Governor John Dana had refused to sign the bill. A new measure with the same title, "An Act for the Suppression of Drinking Houses and Tippling Shops," was brought before the Augusta lawmakers in May 1851. It was a tough bill, its key provision being a "search and seizure" mechanism whereby any three voters could apply for a search warrant if they suspected someone of selling liquor. Convicted sellers faced jail sentences of 3-6 months and to appeal, they would have to post four bonds and pay a double fine if they lost. On May 24, Dow appeared at the committee hearing and made an impassioned plea. Three days later, the House passed the bill by a 3-1 margin. The opposition in the Senate was led by an Aroostook County lumberman, Shepherd Cary, whose condemnation of the "inquisitorial edicts of the temperance fanatics of Portland" fell on no less deaf ears. A 2-1 vote propelled the bill to Governor John Hubbard and many legislators (even among those who'd voted for the bill) expected and hoped the Democrat chief executive would veto it. Dow went to see Hubbard. What they talked about was never revealed. No doubt it included Hubbard's re-election problems and how the Mayor of Portland could help him. On June 2, the bill was signed.

By the end of that summer, Neal Dow was being hailed nationwide as the "Napoleon of Temperance." In August, he was the featured speaker at the National Temperance Convention in Saratoga Springs, New York. Thousands of tracts describing the Maine Law were distributed throughout the country. Horace Greeley, the distinguished editor of the *New York Herald Tribune*, referred to Dow effusively as "a moral Columbus".

But there was a down-side too. The heavy-handed manner in which the Mayor enforced the law earned him increasing enmity. Among those alienated was his own cousin John Neal, upset over the arrest of one Margaret Landrigan, alias "Kitty Kentuck," and also over Dow's insinuation that Neal had a personal interest in the lady. Nor had Dow ever been temperate in expressing anti-Irish

176

sentiments, thereby angering a growing section of the voting population. The business community, too, was upset, as reflected in the *Eastern Argus's* claim that the Maine law was hurting the city's economic climate. All these factors, combined with the fact his opponents put up the much-revered, five-time Governor Albion K. Parris, caused Dow to fail of re-election by a significant plurality.

For the next three years, the Napoleon of Temperance crusaded. He travelled to Canada, Illinois, Maryland and Virginia. He preached continually and saw variations of the Maine Law enacted in Vermont, Rhode Island, Massachusetts, Michigan and Indiana. He lost another race for Mayor in 1854, but in 1855, with the open support of the new Republican Party and the secret support of the anti-Catholic Know-Nothings, he squeaked by with a 47 vote margin out of 3,745 ballots cast. And back in office, this pugnacious little man, attacked by one newspaper as "Pimp, Spy, Fanatic, arrogant at heart," promptly made a colossal error of judgment.

Under the Maine Law, a municipality could appoint an agent to sell liquor for "medicinal and mechanical purposes." As Mayor, Dow ordered $1,600 worth of liquor, but the bill for it bore his name, not that of the agent. A technicality, to be sure, and Alderman Joseph Ring even joked with him about it before he went to the newspapers to claim Dow would be making an illegal sale if he transferred the booze to the bonafide agent. Three men went to a judge and swore Dow was keeping liquor for an illegal sale and the judge had no choice but to issue a warrant for search and seizure. At this point, the whole affair seemed comic-opera, worthy of Gilbert and Sullivan. Soon, alas, it turned tragic. A crowd gathered outside the agency store where the liquor was held. Dow sent armed police to protect the place. The mob threw rocks. Dow, himself, appeared with hastily-summoned militiamen in civvies carrying rifles. More stones were thrown. Dow ordered the amateur soldiers to fire. They wouldn't unless their captain gave the word and he hesitated. Dow fumed and when reinforcements arrived, screamed at the officer in charge to shoot. A volley rang out. When the smoke cleared, one man lay dead and seven others were wounded.

Dow's response, told there had been a fatality, was to ask if the victim were Irish. But 22 year-old John Robbins wasn't; he had been the mate of a Maine sailing vessel. His funeral drew a procession of 300 sailors and a vast outpouring of anti-Dow sentiment. John Neal declared his cousin should be hanged for murder. A Connecticut newspaper termed him "a remorseless, unscrupulous tyrant, akin to Nero."

Put on trial for the original charge of illegal liquor selling, Dow had to be guarded by State militiamen. Prosecuting him was a Democrat, Nathan Clifford, soon to be the U.S. Attorney General. The defense attorney was William Pitt Fessenden. In the end, Dow was acquitted, but his reputation had suffered badly. Worse, due to his poor image, his candidate for Governor, Anson P. Morrill, was not elected and under Democrat Samuel Wells, his precious Maine Law was repealed in 1856.

Two years later, Dow's stock rose again when he helped Hannibal Hamlin become Governor. At the same time, he was elected to fill a vacancy in the Legislature. Astutely, he held back from pushing the Maine Law and stuck to business as Chairman of the Committee on Mercantile Affairs and Insurance. There was even talk of running him for Governor on the Republican ticket. And then, he suffered another crushing blow.

It seems that an associate of his in the temperance movement—a former Congregationalist minister named Benjamin D. Peck—then serving as Maine State Treasurer, and also as Chairman of the Republican State Committee, had been lending the State's money to private individuals—including Dow. This became known after Peck was jailed for defaulting and also that Dow had had Peck's safe rifled to rid it of incriminating documents. Although not jailed, himself, Dow was forced to repay the loan. In September 1860, he did not seek re-election. Mercifully, the Civil War intervened; he was able to use his political pull to be named a Regimental Colonel, then later a Brigadier-General, was captured by the Confederates and ultimately exchanged for a nephew of Robert E. Lee.

During the rest of his long life, Neal Dow pushed the cause of prohibition, to the extent of running for President on the issue. The glory days of the Maine Law were never quite revived and he was eventually seen as an irrelevant, even comical, political figure. His imprint on Maine, on the other hand, was hardly irrelevant. Long after Neal Dow, the temperance battle was a major ingredient of the success the Republican Party enjoyed in the Pine Tree State once it swept into office just prior to the Civil War.

Anti-Slavery

The saying was:

All abolitionists are prohibitionists.
Most prohibitionists are abolitionists.

This link between supporters of these two burning issues was nowhere better illustrated in Maine than during the gubernatorial elections of 1843 and 1844. The first candidate fielded by the brand-new Liberty Party was General James Appleton, the same man who had launched the temperance drive in the Maine Legislature. Appleton fared poorly at the polls on both occasions, but the mere fact that abolitionists had formed a party and were running was an indication of their growing respectability if not strength. Early on, abolitionists met with almost as much hostility in the north as in the south. The mob that nearly lynched William Lloyd Garrison in Boston was scarcely different from the gang in Mississippi that stripped an abolitionist of his clothing and dragged a frenzied cat by its tail back and forth across his naked body.

Some Maine sentiment toward slavery had surfaced in the controversy with Georgia in the 1830's. The State's first anti-slavery society was actually formed at Hallowell in 1833. But *abolition* was viewed, much like communism, as a radical step and concerned people mostly rallied around half-measures, like halting the spread of the institution or returning emancipated slaves to Africa through well-meaning "emigration societies." Yet political events constantly agitated the electorate; there was the thorny question of the annexation of Texas as a slave state; the "Wilmot Proviso" to ban slavery from territories acquired from Mexico; and most contentious, the Compromise of 1850. One part of that Henry Clay-engineered deal was a stricter Fugitive Slave Law. As in the Georgia controversy, the brutality of the slave system was brought right into the north and Maine people were obliged legally to become a part of it.

The Democrat establishment in Maine worked hard for acceptance of the Compromise. Nathan Clifford declared its opponents' position "...embracing as it does...the abolition of slavery everywhere in the United States" would mean the dissolution of the Union and a "consequent overthrow of our Federal Constitution." Governor Hubbard made a nasty speech at a convention in Bath, classing Negroes with monkeys. Another

179

delegate stated, "Resistance to the Fugitive Slave Law is as criminal as to any other law, and he who encourages it encourages anarchy."

Resistance, there was. Material on the Underground Railroad in Maine is necessarily skimpy, given the need for secrecy, but several well-known stops have been identified. Among them are:

> The Nason House in Augusta. Slaves would be kept here in a secret room behind a bookcase until they could be guided to the Reuel Williams House.
>
> The Reuel Williams House in Augusta. The home of the one-time U.S. Senator, it was a lovely 14 room mansion fronting the Kennebec River with its back door on Cony Street.
>
> The Farwell mansion on Riverside Drive in Vassalboro. This was a final destination for slaves hidden in Augusta, before they were sent to Canada. Ironically, the builder of this spacious home with five white columns in front, plantation style, was Captain Ebenezer Farwell, a slaver who had been killed in Africa.

Political resistance in Maine to pro-slavery attitudes had also grown. A leader here was Hannibal Hamlin, who, as a Democrat Congressman, voted against acquiring Mexican War territory without the Wilmot Proviso.

Hamlin, of course, as a Republican, was eventually to be the Vice President of the United States. Maine legend has it that an Indian princess in his native Oxford County, Molly Ockett, cradling him as an infant, predicted clairvoyantly that he would rise to great heights. His family had settled at Paris Hill and the children of his grandfather, a Revolutionary War captain, were named Africa, Europe, Asia and America until twins were born and called Cyrus and Hannibal. Later, Cyrus named one of his sons Hannibal.

This young Hannibal began his career in Hampden, practicing law, having studied under General Samuel Fessenden in Portland. After two terms in Congress, he returned to the Maine Legislature where he'd already served as Speaker of the House. In 1848, still a Democrat, he was elected by his peers to the U.S. Senate, defeating Nathan Clifford, the candidate of the pro-slavery Democrat "Hunkers".

The split in the Democratic Party grew. A rump convention of anti-slavery and pro-temperance Democrats nominated its own

180

candidate for Governor in 1853. He was the State Land Agent, Anson P. Morrill of Readfield, brother of Lot M. Morrill, the Democrat State Chairman, and he and the Free-Soil candidate drew a respectable 25% of the vote. Hamlin and the Morrill brothers were soon to lead their factions into the newly-formed Republican Party, whose national birth is said to have occurred in June 1854 at Jackson, Michigan. In Maine, the G.O.P.'s origin is traced to the town of Strong in Franklin County in the summer of 1855.[2] U.S. Senator Hamlin and Lot Morrill left their own party in 1856 over the Kansas-Nebraska Bill. Hamlin ran for Governor as a Republican, won in a landslide, then promptly resigned and was re-elected to the U.S. Senate.

The fissures in the political parties over slavery were echoed in other institutions, like the churches. There was a Free-Will

Hannibal Hamlin

181

Baptist anti-slavery group in Maine as early as 1841. The Methodists, too, had an anti-slavery movement in their ranks. In the Congregational church, members divided over the Fugitive Slave Law. On December 19, 1850, the conservative Reverend John Orr Fiske of Bath preached:

> That law ought to be obeyed unless some express written divine statute to the contrary can be produced. There is no such written statute to my knowledge in all the word of God.

The governance of Maine's Congregational church was vested in separate "conferences," based on county lines. From the Piscataquis Conference five weeks later came this stinging reply:

> We shall not obey its abominable mandate, but if the panting fugitive needs our aid, we shall give it, ever ready to pray and labor for universal liberty...

The Franklin Conference resolved:

> That we bear our earnest and decided testimony against the Fugitive Slave Law as a most Heaven daring attempt on the part of our government to nullify the Law of God...

Even before Fiske had spoken, the Waldo Conference had likened the act to the Code of Draco, whose laws were written in blood.

In 1852, the featured speaker at the Congregationalists' State conference was Professor Calvin Stowe whose speech was entitled "The Duty of American Churches respecting slavery and the colored population generally." His words have been lost, but can be imagined. It was the same year that his wife's book, "Uncle Tom's Cabin" appeared and became an overnight sensation. The Stowes had come to Maine two years earlier, settling in Brunswick where Calvin was returning to his alma mater, Bowdoin, as a Professor of Natural and Revealed Religion. Not long after their arrival, a relative of Harriet's—a Mrs. Edward Beecher—wrote her suggesting that she author a book on slavery, which the Stowes had witnessed first-hand when living in Cincinnati. But it was not until February 1851 that Harriet Beecher Stowe was almost mystically inspired. One morning in the Bowdoin chapel, she had a vision of an old slave being brutally beaten and then imagined

182

the dying black man forgiving his murderers. She set to work doing research, reading books like "The Life of Frederick Douglass" and meeting with former slaves. Printed first in magazine installments, the book was into a third edition within three weeks of its publication date. That first year, there were 120 editions and soon it was translated into the first of 40 languages. In all, 3-4 million copies were sold in the United States, $1^{1/2}$ million copies in Great Britain and 4 million in foreign countries.

The impact on the slavery controversy was devastating and far beyond what Mrs. Stowe had intended. She was anti-slavery, but not an abolitionist. One wonders about her private reaction when Abraham Lincoln greeted her as "the little lady who started the big war."

After she left Maine, Harriet Beecher Stowe wrote a novel based on her Maine experiences. "The Pearl of Orr's Island" is little read today, while the story of the south she conceived and fashioned entirely in Maine has become an immortal American classic.

The Know-Nothings

Harriet Beecher Stowe's father was the noted Congregationalist minister Lyman Beecher.[3] A powerful orator, he was at one point pastor of the prestigious Hanover Street Church in Boston. His thunderous sermons against Boston's Irish immigrants and their religion, employing incendiary phrases like "the foul beast of Roman Catholicism" and "the whoredom of Babylon" are credited with having incited a mob to burn down the Ursuline Convent in Charlestown—one of the earliest manifestations of the loosely organized hate movement known as "Know-Nothingism."

Its prejudice was fueled by ignorance and exaggeration. Lurid stories of sex orgies, rape and bondage behind convent walls were a type of political pornography that became popular. The sensational revelations of "escaped nuns," like Rebecca Theresa Reed and Maria Monk, usually deranged young women, were bestsellers. Respectable figures like Lyman Beecher gave credibility to these aspersions. Samuel F.B. Morse, the inventor of the telegraph, was another prominent and vocal anti-Catholic. So were the Harper brothers, founders of the venerable publishing company. Leadership of the organization that emerged from a national convention held on July 4, 1845 devolved upon a loud-mouthed ex-salesman named James W. Barker, the "King of the Know-Nothings." The official title was the American Party. A splinter group was called the Star-Spangled Banner Party. In the rough and tumble politics of America's big cities, violent gangs not unlike the storm troopers of modern times went to work with guns and clubs to disrupt their rivals. They bore colorful names. In New York City, the Know-Nothings fielded The Wide Awakes, The Plug-Uglies (after their plug hats), The Blood Tubs and The Red Necks. The Democrats, under their Tammany Hall umbrella, responded with the Dead Rabbits, the Shad Rows and The Butt Enders.

Bucolic Maine was not immune from this madness. Bangor incorporated itself as a city in 1838 after an incident in which the meeting house used as a Catholic church was torched by a mob of ruffians, the citizens feeling their town government had not been adequate to the emergency. By the 1850's, the *Kennebec Journal* had acknowledged the presence of the Know-Nothings in Maine and was charging that the Catholics, themselves, brought on violence because "outside agitators"—i.e., Democratic politicians—made them think they were oppressed.

Ellsworth, a rough logging and shipbuilding center, was the site of perhaps the worst anti-Catholic incident in Maine. As its local historian Albert Davis wrote in the 1920's, "Few towns ever experienced a greater crisis than did Ellsworth from 1850-1860. religious and political feeling ran high...Each party, the Democratic and the Republican, had its own press and their newspaper battles were frequent and hot..."

As in New York City, there were bully boy groups with colorful names and uniforms. The most notorious in Ellsworth were the Cast-Iron Band, The White Caps and The Rough and Readys. Water Street, termed "Rum Row," was the hangout of these lawless elements and, as Davis says, "Bloodshed and riots were often the principle amusements n that section."

Into this hothouse atmosphere in October 1854 came a gentle, courageous, Swiss-born Jesuit priest, Father John Bapst. There had been a Catholic church, St. Joseph's, in Ellsworth since 1840, but not without controversy in this overwhelmingly Protestant community. One major bone of contention was Catholic protests against use of the St. James version of the Bible in the public schools. Ellsworth had had a fiery debate on the issue. Bapst was no stranger to Ellsworth. He had been posted to Old Town in 1848 and the Hancock County shire town was but one of the outlying parts of his parish. In fact, he was on his way to Cherryfield

184

to pay a sick call the night of October 15 and decided to stay in Ellsworth, despite a town meeting resolution stating he would be attacked if he appeared. It was a Saturday evening when Bapst arrived at the Kent residence on High Street and he had taken no food or drink since he intended to say Mass the next morning. A mob gathered, broke into the house, pulled Bapst out, rifled his pockets, rode him to the outskirts of town on a rail, stripped him, and tarred and feathered him. Imperturbable, despite his pain and humiliation, the Jesuit returned to town, continued his fast and said Mass as planned.

Another serious anti-Catholic incident had occurred in Maine a few months before the attack on Father Bapst and may have been the inspiration for it. In this case, a well-known Know-Nothing fanatic by the name of Hector Orr came to Bath after he had terrorized Boston. Dressed in a long, none-too-clean, white robe and carrying a trumpet, he called himself "The Angel Gabriel." He had glowing black eyes, long black hair, a dark complexion and an accent he described as Scottish. Later, it was revealed that he was a native of British Guiana, half-Scotch and half-Negro. At the head of a mob he had harangued, this bizarre figure led them to the local Catholic church where they smashed the windows, tore the cross off the steeple and then burned down the entire structure.

Throughout Maine, the hostility toward Catholics was palpable. A priest in Portland declared, "Since the 4th of July, I have not considered myself safe to walk the streets after sunset...I am hissed and insulted with vile language...last week, a large rock entered my chamber rather unceremoniously about 11:00 at night."

The increase in Maine's Catholic population had been steady since the days of the Kavanaghs and Bishop Cheverus. An entire township in Aroostook County had been bought by Cheverus's successor, Bishop Benedict Fenwick and a first settlement of Irish pioneers implanted in *Benedicta* in 1834. There were soon outlying missions in Island Falls, Molunkus, Patten and Sherman. Augusta had its first Catholic pastor in 1833, plus the Kavanagh School, started with a $25,000 donation from Governor Kavanagh's sister Winfred. By the early 1850's, Bangor was one-quarter Irish.

This latter situation no doubt contributed to the fact that on March 13, 1855, a slate of Know-Nothing candidates, also referred to as the "Hindoo Sect," captured the Bangor city government on a platform of strict enforcement of the Maine Law and

185

an end to foreign influence.

The new Mayor, J.T.K. Hayward, handed most of his power to the Reverend Philip Weaver, who was made city marshall, constable, superintendent of schools and tax collector. Weaver, a friend of Neal Dow's, at once sought and received authorization to recruit 40 special police who wore leather hatbands emblazoned with "POLICE" in silver. The reverend-marshall loved to parade his para-military force, decked out in a black frock coat decorated by a silver star, a black cockade in his hat and a pair of Colt revolvers in his belt. They began a series of liquor confiscations, and the sobriquet of "the 40 thieves" bestowed on the deputies by a Bangor editor was soon shown to be more than political hyperbole. A City Council investigation revealed Weaver and his men had sold the rum they'd seized, were releasing people from jail for $20 and Weaver, himself, was a heavy drinker. The scandal marked the end of Know-Nothing influence in Bangor.

Elsewhere in Maine, Know-Nothing support helped elect Anson P. Morrill as Governor in 1855. But once the Republican Party gelled, the Nativist sentiment found a home within its confines, albeit in a much less extremist fashion. Ex-President Millard Fillmore ran on the American Party (Know-Nothing) ticket for President in 1856 and carried only one state, Maryland. This most virulent strain of anti-Catholic prejudice had run its course.

FOCUS

Bangor

Henry David Thoreau made three trips to Maine; in 1846, 1853 and 1857. He climbed Katahdin on the first occasion, went to Chesuncook on the second and descended the Allagash on the final visit. He was at Bangor, as well, and has left several memorable quotes about the city:

...the principle lumber depot of this continent with a population of 12,000, like a star on the edge of night, still hewing at the forest of which it is built.

Despite the great wilderness through which he had travelled, Thoreau was concerned about the rate at which it might be depleted.

The mission of the men there seems to be, like so many busy demons, to drive the forest all out of the country, from every solitary beaver swamp and mountainside, as soon as possible.

He went to see several of General Samuel Veazie's saw mills, describing one with 16 sets of saws—"some gang saws, sixteen in a gang, not to mention circular saws...The trees were literally drawn and quartered there..." Veazie, a Portland transplant, owned 52 local lumber mills. In all, there were 242 saw mills in greater Bangor, which included the towns of Veazie, Orono, Bradley and Old Town.

Thoreau, himself, relates how 200 million board feet annually were cut. "No wonder," he wrote, "that we hear so often of vessels which are becalmed off our coast, being surrounded a week at a time by the floating lumber from the Maine woods." Wryly, he summed up his attitude toward all this activity:

Think how stood the white pine tree on the shore of Chesuncook, its branches soughing with the four winds, and every individual needle trembling in the sunlight—think how it stands with it now—sold, perchance, to the New England Friction Match Company!

Oblivious to Thoreau's sensitivity, Bangor cut and cut, and when the white pine was gone, the loggers turned to spruce and fir. The boom began in the 1830's and lasted through the 1850's, creating an atmosphere similar to San Francisco's "Barbary Coast" during the heyday of the Gold Rush.

Fanny Hardy Eckstrom, in her classic book, "Penobscot Man," chronicled the lumbermen who included in her words: "White men, Irishmen, Provincemen, Bluenoses, Prince Edward Islanders, Canadian French, St. Francis, Micmac, Penobscot and Passamaquoddy Indians."

These "Bangor Tigers" came roaring

Early Bangor

187

into town as soon as they had their pay checks. In the infamous "Devil's Half Acre" were the bars and brothels that catered to this boisterous clientele, as well as the equally macho sailors off the lumber ships. Fan Jones's "house," with its sky blue chimneys,[4] was a noted Bangor landmark. The grog sellers of lower Exchange Street or "Peppermint Row," mostly Irish, carried on just as brisk a trade in a variety of saloons. One of them, Pat Moran, acquired the old Methodist Meeting House and turned it into a drinking emporium he archly dubbed *Moranbega Hall,* a punning parody of sedate, elegant *Norumbega Hall,* the city's civic auditorium, where illustrious speakers like Ralph Waldo Emerson gave public lectures and illustrious thespians such as Edwin Booth acted.

Timberland speculation brought rich and often overnight fortunes. The tale was told in a Baltimore newspaper that two paupers escaped from the Bangor almshouse and before they were recaptured the next morning had each earned $1,800 investing in forest property. Possibly less apocryphal was what was said of the local coroner; that if a body were found floating in the river and it had money on it, the ruling was suicide; if the pockets were empty, the verdict was murder.

In this sort of setting, it was hard to take seriously the poetic toast to an ideal Bangor made at a Mechanics Association Festival:

May every street
Be clean and neat
and free from filth and swine...
With no rude boys
To make a noise
With boisterous mirth obscene
Nor dirty shops

To sell vile slops
To swine, in shape of men.

Like Harriet Beecher Stowe's Topsy, Bangor just grew—from 2,868 in 1830 to 8,634 in 1840 to 16,408 in 1860. Riots, like the anti-Catholic disturbance of 1833, natural disasters like the giant logjam and flood of 1846 and illnesses, like the cholera epidemic of 1849, did not seem to affect the growth that made millionaires of lumber magnates like General Veazie and his arch-rival Rufus Dwinel.

The cholera epidemic, which killed 161 persons, contained a bizarre incident worthy of the pen of Bangor's modern-day master writer of the macabre, Stephen King. Most of the victims of the dread disease were poor Irish. In one case, the little daughter of an Irishman named Hangley was laid out in her coffin, awaiting burial, when she suddenly sat up and declared she had been to heaven and seen her mother, who had died of cholera, and the Casey children, including a third one whose death was not known at the time. The Hangley girl's miraculous recovery and glimpse into the hereafter was actually repeated when she took sick again, was on the point of dying and once more rallied, voicing more details from the beyond.

The year of the epidemic saw population drawn away to the new adventure of the California gold fields. Ships left directly from Bangor to San Francisco, among them a bark called *Gold Hunter.* The local newspapers were rife with tales of those who were prospering. There was an article about Warren Davis of Hallowell who was offered a job at $6,000 a year, a princely sum, after only 30 days in San Francisco. With him was young Calvin Spaulding who had no trade but could start at work paying $16 a day, with room

188

and board costing a mere $3.50 a *week*. A young man named Glines returned to Maine from California with an awesome nest egg of $15,000; he had left an almshouse to seek his fortune. The newspapers fed the exodus with such get-rich-quick tales and pollyannaish statements like, "It is very healthy in California and all immigrants are contented and happy."

Transportation out of the Queen City was short-range, too. Steamers went to Greenville on Moosehead Lake, to Castine, Deer Isle, Sedgwick, Blue Hill and Ellsworth, to Boston via Portland, where one boarded railroad cars for the last leg of the voyage, and from Enfield, a steamer would go to Old Town, where railroad cars carried passengers to Bangor.

This 12 mile line was the first steam railroad built in Maine and reputedly the second in the entire United States. By 1855, there was also railroad service from Portland to Bangor. The old Portland and Kennebec steadily had pushed north, reaching Waterville, then Pittsfield, then Bangor. The next step was the brainchild of a one-time Bangor lawyer, John A. Poor. But it is a story that belongs to Portland, to which Poor had emigrated as a young man.

John A. Poor and His Railroads

In a book published by Harvard University Press in 1948, "Men, Cities and Transportation," the author, Edward Kirkland, took the reader back to the 1840's and made this rather startling statement:

...for one brief, crowded, glorious interlude it seemed that, of all the cities of New England, Portland might be a rival, and not a satellite, of either Boston or New York.

Location is everything in transportation—and Kirkland explained the thinking in that era when England was the economic giant of the world:

...if Boston could dream of supplanting New York because she was nearer Liverpool, the same reason justified Portland's supplanting Boston.

Portland was *two days* nearer to Europe than New York and a *half-day* nearer than Boston. Plus, in the competition for a rail line from Montreal to the Atlantic coast, Portland was 100 miles closer to the Canadian metropolis. And the battle between Portland and Boston for this all-important route really heated up in the 1840's.

Mainers like John A. Poor reacted to the Boston rivalry by seeking an independent railroad policy for the State of Maine.

189

When he emerged as Maine's foremost railroad promoter, Poor would even insist that his ventures lay down track of a different gauge. His vision was certainly over-optimistic. "Maine will present at some future day, along our bays and harbors, a line of cities, surpassing those which are now found upon the shores of the English Channel or the Baltic Sea," he declared. But his devotion to securing a railway between Montreal and Portland was unlimited.

Thus, during the winter of 1845, Poor undertook an epic journey from Portland to Montreal by horse and sleigh in order to head off a group of Boston competitors. The weather was bad when Poor left Portland. The stableman from whom he'd rented the team refused to accompany him, so he prevailed upon a friend named Cheney to come along. Bundled in fur coats and fur caps and under fur lap robes, they rode through a raging blizzard. As Poor graphically described it, "Our only protection was the covering of ice which hung in masses from our eyebrows." To South Paris, to Rumford, then into New Hampshire to Dixville Notch, through which the proposed railroad would run, Poor and his friend sped over snow so deep that it covered stone walls and woodpiles. They were lost five times. The temperature was 18° below zero when they crossed the frozen St. Lawrence and entered Montreal at 5:30 A.M. After three hours sleep, Poor headed to the Board of Trade building, where Sir Alexander Galt and other interested Canadians had been considering a Boston proposal. Poor persuaded them to postpone any decision, arguing that the Maine Legislature had already granted a charter to the proposed line and Portland would provide a large loan to help finance it. A week later, Judge William Pitt Preble arrived in Montreal with a copy of the charter and Galt and his associates decided to choose Poor and the Mainers.

Massachusetts then tried to convince the intervening states of Vermont and New Hampshire to deny access to the newly-created Atlantic and St. Lawrence Railroad. But without success. On July 4, 1846, at Portland, William Pitt Preble, now president of the company, turned the first shovelful of earth with a silver-plated spade. The crowd cheered and was even louder when Governor Hugh Anderson wheeled off the first load of dirt.

Financing, however, did become a problem. Portland eventually had to loan the organization more than $2 million. Poor needed to convince the construction contractors, Black, Wood and Co. of Portland, to take half of their payment in bonds and stocks. The railroad was opened on July 18, 1853. Three weeks later, it was leased to the Grand Trunk Railway Co. of Canada.

190

The gauge, it should be noted, was 5 foot 6 inches whereas standard gauge was 4 foot 8 $^{1/2}$ inches. Thereupon, a battle over competing gauges erupted when the Legislature had to choose between routes for a link from Portland to Bangor. The result was a typical compromise: *two* roads were built: the Kennebec and Portland, which went through Augusta as standard gauge; and Poor's Androscoggin and Kennebec, following the Grand Trunk to Lewiston, by-passing Augusta to use Waterville as a terminal, then continuing its broad-gauged path to Bangor.

Poor's next vision was to carry this line eastward in an even more grandiose scheme. The European and North American Railway was certainly grandiosely named and it entailed nothing less than a roadway from Bangor to New Brunswick, into Nova Scotia and across the straits of Canso to Cape Breton Island, where its terminus would be the old French fortress town of Louisbourg. From Louisbourg, fast steamers would cross the Atlantic to Galway, a train would take the passengers to Dublin, the Irish Sea would be crossed, and another train would cover the last leg to London.

To promote his dream, Poor assembled a huge convention in Portland in the summer of 1850. Twin flags of the United States and England decorated the hall along with a gigantic map of the proposed route. One of the numerous speakers, a Canadian, brought down the house with a declamation in which he foresaw "the rose of England blending the colors of York and Lancaster and plucked from the gardens of Windsor...twined freshly in America with the Beautiful prairie flower...and bound together with the lilies of Canada...(to) compose a fragrant wreath wherewith to crown the Statue of Concord in the Temple of Peace." The rally ended with three cheers for Queen Victoria, three cheers for President Polk, three cheers for the "Mother Country," three more for "her American Children," and three final deafening ones for the "European and North American Railroad." Not long afterward, the Maine Legislature granted the enterprise a charter.

But it took 21 years for this ambitious project to be fulfilled. Poor, himself, died six weeks before the line reached the Maine-New Brunswick border at Vanceboro. Financial problems, aggravated by England's participation in the Crimean War, started the delay. Conversely, America's Civil War helped revive the scheme. The Maine Legislature in 1864 granted it various public lands. Eventually, broad gauge reduced to standard, Poor's railroad masterpiece, which had never achieved its potential, became part of the Maine Central system.

191

The Clipper Ships of Maine

While the railroads were uniting the country and the State of Maine with their prosaic bonds of iron and injecting a sylvan landscape with polluting bursts of noise and smoke, the romantic era of sail on the seas—the "tall ships" that so incite the nostalgia of modern man—was reaching its climax. Like a light bulb intensifying before it goes out, a half-dozen years in the 1850's saw the clipper ships come and go.

Maine, in 1855, was the ship building capital of the United States, accountable for 215,904 tons, yet by then, the clipper ships were totalling less than 5,000 tons. They were built for speed, these handsome vessels that Lloyds of London insured under a special category marked C. The Gold Rush in California was the inspiration for shipbuilders on the east coast to build the "sharpest" (i.e. speediest) craft they could. Essentially, four main yards dominated the effort in Maine: Fernald and Pettigrew of Kittery, Trufant and Drummond of Bath, Metcalf and Norris of Damariscotta and the Deacon George Thomas's yard at Rockland.

Famous clipper ships, with romantic and perhaps immortal names, like the *Typhoon*, the *Nightingale*, the *Snow Squall*, the *Flying Dragon* and the *Red Jacket* were the stars of the fleet. The *Snow Squall*[5] raced Donald McKay's biggest clipper *The Romance of the Sea* from China and beat her by two days. The *Nightingale*, built by Samuel Hanscom in Eliot, honored the Swedish singer Jenny Lind whose likeness formed not only the figurehead but was also sculpted on the stern in a reclining figure with a nightingale perched on her finger. Her owners offered to race her to China for a stake of £10,000, but found no takers. Actually, the record-breaker among Maine ships was the *Flying Dragon* from the Bath yard, which covered the run from Maine to San Francisco in 97 days. The *Typhoon* from Kittery earned the nickname "the Portsmouth Flyer" when she set the record from Portsmouth to Liverpool of 13 days, 10 hours. The *Red Jacket*, launched at Rockland before a huge crowd in 1853, has been called the largest, fastest and most handsome of all the Maine clippers. Fore and aft, as on the *Nightingale*, she carried life-like images of her namesake—the famed Seneca Indian Chief. Her cabins were finished in exotic woods, combining mahogany, black walnut, rosewood, etc. Fourteen staterooms could be found below and she had a crew of 62. On her first trip, she beat the *Typhoon's* record to Liverpool by almost nine hours. Bought up by the English White Star Line, she was soon off to Melbourne, Australia—and other records, including a spurt from the Cape of Good Hope to Melbourne of 19 days that was never afterward equaled.

An economic crisis in 1857 and a lessening need for speed wrote an end to this brief moment of sailing glory. A new naval era was coming. The Civil War would see the introduction of iron-clads to warfare on the seas. The modern industrial epoch that had begun to clank its way across the countryside with railroads was just around the corner. A last flash of beauty on the high seas made what was vanishing all the more poignant.

Schooner Governor Ames

MAINE IN THE CIVIL WAR

The Maine Battle Flags

Under the rotunda on the second floor of the State House in Augusta, there are large glass cases containing numerous tall, out-sized flags, most of them fading and worn. The area is known, un-surprisingly, as the "Hall of Flags" and also contains a pantheon of portraits of Maine's most outstanding political figures: Governor William King, James G. Blaine, Speaker of the U.S. House Thomas Brackett Reed, Governor Percival Baxter (represented by a bust), modern day U.S. Senators Margaret Chase Smith and Edmund S. Muskie, etc. The centerpiece, however, remains the flags—battle flags of wars from the Civil War to the Korean Conflict, but with an emphasis on the Civil War.

Many of these regimental colors from the War Between the States display battle names. Behind the cases, some of these are hard to read. What can be discerned are a few names that seem familiar but most of which would be known only to diehard Civil War buffs. One sees:

Kellys Ford
Coal Harbor
North Anna
Aldie Station
Brandy Station
Winchester
Sabine Crossroads, La.
Cane River, La.

194

none of which strike a familiar note. Others:

Cedar Mountain

Fair Oaks

Po River

Rappahanock

have a vaguely reminiscent ring to them. Then there are still others:

Petersburg

Fredericksburg

Appomattox

Bull Run

names that every American school child should know, while a number of these banners sport the most famous name of all:

GETTYSBURG

Close observation reveals the identities of some of the units that carried these flags:

The 4th Maine Regiment of Infantry

The 5th Maine Regiment of Infantry

The 1st Maine Regiment of Cavalry

The 17th Maine Regiment of Infantry

And what is left is the impression of a vast mobilization of forces within the State of Maine when war came in 1861. The statistics are that Maine furnished 32 infantry regiments, 3 cavalry regiments, 1 regiment of heavy artillery, 7 batteries of mounted artillery, 7 companies of sharpshooters, 30 companies of unassigned infantry, 7 companies of coast guard and 6 companies of coastal fortification. The army received 72,945 Mainers and the navy and marine corps 6,750. Killed in action in the army, alone, were 7,322. The cost of bounties for the troops of Maine raised was $9,695,620.

The baptism of fire for Maine boys came, as it did for so many other Yankee soldiers, at the first battle of Bull Run. Of the four Maine infantry regiments involved—the 2nd, 3rd, 4th and 5th— the latter three were in a brigade under the command of Colonel Oliver Otis Howard, a West Pointer, from the small Androscoggin County farm town of Leeds. Howard, then only 31 years old, had left his position as an instructor at West Point when elected to head the 3rd Maine, a regiment composed mostly of lumbermen from Kennebec County. It was an election, incidentally, engineered by Howard's friend James G. Blaine, the young editor of the *Kennebec Journal*. The 4th was commanded by Colonel Hiram G. Berry of Rockland, later cited for his heroism at Bull Run and the 5th was under a Portland man, Mark H. Dunnell.

They were all raw troops, all volunteers, hastily transported to Washington D.C. and then across the Potomac into Virginia as part of the initial Northern effort to advance on Richmond.

The 2nd Maine, a Bangor outfit in a separate brigade, was early thrust into the fighting at Bull Run when it seemed as if the Union forces would win a major victory. Their casualties were heavy, nearly half that of their whole brigade. Howard's troops were not brought up until the tide had begun to turn against the North. A forced march in the hot sun scattered his men. They managed to form two lines and advance up a hill in the face of furious rifle and cannon fire. But, as the Confederate commander Joseph E. Johnston wrote in his memoirs, "...they could not fight the battle alone and soon joined the rest of the army in its flight." Howard did what he could to halt the retreat. It was not enough to satisfy his wounded division commander General S.P. Heintzelman, who swore at him. The young colonel was finally able to re-assemble his men at their old camp at Centerville, where they took up new positions guarding Alexandria against any Rebel attack.

Bull Run took place July 21, 1861. On July 25, General George McClellan took command of the armies in Virginia and September 3, Howard was made a Brigadier-General and put in charge of troops not from Maine.

In McClellan's "peninsula" campaign, 7 Maine infantry regiments took part. Added to the veterans of Bull Run were the 6th., made up of Penobscot County lumbermen, the 7th from around Augusta and the 11th, whose colonel was John C. Caldwell of East Machias. This campaign, in essence, was an attack on Richmond from another direction—up the York and James Rivers—and Maine troops helped capture Yorktown and Williamsburg. McClellan visited the 7th. Maine after the latter battle and lauded them:

> Soldiers of the Seventh Maine, I have come to thank you for your bravery and good conduct in the action of yesterday. On this battle-plain, you and your comrades arrested the progress of the advancing enemy, saved the army from a disgraceful defeat and turned the tide of victory in our favor...In recognition of your merit, you shall hereafter bear the inscription "Williamsburg" on your colors...

But McClellan's entire campaign failed when Lee kept him from closing in on the Confederate capital. There were many fierce

196

battles, like Fair Oaks, where General Howard, his elbow shattered, had his arm amputated, and Cedar Mountain in the Shenandoah Valley where the 10th Maine was decimated.

Other famous Virginia battles, like Fredericksburg and Chancellorsville, saw Maine men in action. Rockland's Hiram Berry, promoted to Major-General, was the victim of a Confederate sniper at this second engagement. Two new Maine infantry regiments, the 16th and 17th, fought there.

When the Confederates counterattacked north, Maine men—four regiments of them—were at Antietam to stop the Secessionists. The deepest penetration into northern territory was, of course, at Gettysburg where the "high-water mark" of the South was reached by Pickett's charge. The 19th Maine, which helped contain it, was only one of many Downeast units on that "hallowed ground." The 20th Maine and its colonel, Joshua Chamberlain of Brewer, achieved immortality with their defense of Little Round Top. After Gettysburg, a major battle on this front was at Rapahannock Station, where the 6th Maine distinguished itself with a ferocious charge.

A campaign along the coastline of the deep South was undertaken simultaneously with McClellan's peninsula operation. New Orleans was captured and put in charge of General Benjamin Butler, nicknamed "the Beast" for, among other things, decreeing that Louisiana belles caught insulting Union personnel would be treated as ladies of the evening plying their trade. Maine units were involved in taking Fort Pulaski, on Tybee Island, at the entrance to Savannah. Offshore, the "low country" islands—places like Hilton Head and Daufuskie—and onshore, Beaufort, South Carolina—were captured. Charleston was besieged; Morris Island in its harbor was overrun, but Fort Sumter, although bombarded regularly, held out, as did the Rebel city, practically until the end of the war. The 8th, 9th and 11th Maine regiments played a part in this theater.

The 11th Maine has left an extensive record of its history. Mustered in Augusta, it was transported to Portland where its first disappointment was not to receive the munificent welcoming banquet expected of the home folks. When the men went off, they were grumbling, and reciting the following bit of improvised, sarcastic doggerel:

The rot took their potatoes
And the weevil took their grain

197

So they'd nothing left to give us
In Portland City, Maine.

Another couplet was added after weeks of boredom on the
Virginia peninsula, camped outside of Yorktown:

Here we labor, here we toil,
Shovelling Virginia soil.

And a story told of the capture of one of their number also
had a sardonic ring. Spotting a Confederate patrol, the man dove
into a pigpen, observed by a silent young slave boy. The "ungrate-
ful pickaninny," as the regimental historian called him, then
shouted to the Southern cavalry, "Hi, hi, Massa, there's a Yank in
h'yah with Unk Effum's shote."

The 11th Maine then boarded transports at Yorktown and
went to Hilton Head. A curious feature of the battle here was that
two of the opposing commanders were brothers—General Thomas
Fenwick Drayton, in charge the Confederate defense, and Percival
Drayton of the United States Navy. By now, command of the
11th. had devolved upon Lieutenant-Colonel Harris Plaisted, who
would one day become Governor of Maine. After Hilton Head,
the regiment moved to Beaufort and then to Fernandina on
Amelia Island, Florida. It was hard duty, in alligator and snake-
infested swamps "where a breed of the most sanguinary mosquitoes
filled the air at night to an extent that not only made it impossible
for a man to sleep, but force him to keep his already mosquito net-
covered head in a thick smudge of smoke."

Their transfer to the fight in Charleston harbor must have
been a relief. It was here they had their first glimpse of Black
troops, the 54th Massachusetts, under Boston's Colonel Robert
Gould Shaw, whose family had originated in Gouldsboro. The
Mainers were astonished by the sight of a red-headed Negro, a
Sergeant, with "skin light enough to appear freckled." In one of
the assaults on Fort Wagner, in which the 9th Maine took part,
Colonel Shaw was killed. The 11th, during this same campaign,
actively manned a famous battery of cannon called the "Swamp
Angel" because of its location in the marshes. Before they returned
to Virginia for more fighting, the regiment witnessed the execu-
tion of a deserter from the 3rd New Hampshire. The man had been
caught by the 9th Maine on Black Island. The prisoner was forced
to kneel on a coffin, shot and then buried. He originally was a

Southern deserter who'd gone north, collected a large bounty to enlist and was trying to escape with his money.

Texas, and more especially Louisiana, were other Southern states where Maine men fought. When Federal troops occupied Brownsville, Texas on November 6, 1863 and Corpus Christi ten days later, soldiers from Maine were among the contingents. But far more fighting took place in Louisiana and Maine units there included the 13th, 14th, 15th, 21st, 22nd, 24th, 29th, 30th and 2nd cavalry.

The campaign in Louisiana began as an effort to help Grant clear the Mississippi of Rebel forces. New Orleans and Baton Rouge had been captured to the south, Memphis to the north, and Grant was besieging Vicksburg. Yet the Confederates still held 200 miles of riverfront between Vicksburg and Port Hudson, La., which was about 20 miles above Baton Rouge.

The Northern commander was an ex-politician from Massachusetts, Nathaniel P. Banks, who had once served as Speaker of the U.S. House of Representatives. By all accounts, he was a far better lawmaker than General, having already been defeated twice in battle by Stonewall Jackson before coming to take over from "Beast" Butler in New Orleans.

The Yankee troops moved on Port Hudson. It was during this attack that General Neal Dow was shot in the arm and thigh. At a plantation in the rear, he was captured by a raiding party of Confederate cavalry. The news that Vicksburg had fallen to Grant on July 4 (1863) motivated the defenders of Port Hudson to capitulate four days later.

With the Mississippi under Union control, the next Yankee drive was an offensive up one of its tributaries—the Red River. But it met fierce Confederate resistance and at Sabine Crossroads, the hapless Banks was defeated by C.S.A. General Richard Taylor. The northerners retreated to a place called Pleasant Hill, the 29th. Maine acting as rear guard, and although the Rebels were beaten back, the Yankees continued their retreat. At Alexandria, La., the various lumbermen in the Maine regiments cut timber for a dam that raised the water level of the river so the Federal gunboats could escape. Once this ill-fated expedition ended, some Maine outfits were re-transferred to Virginia. The 2nd Maine cavalry, however, went to Pensacola, Florida, where it engaged in raids on Southern territory, including one into Alabama that netted a train of 50 wagons.

The campaigns in Virginia that culminated in Lee's surrender at Appomattox also had significant Maine participation. The 1st Maine Battery and 29th infantry fought well at Cedar Creek in the Shenandoah Valley. At Petersburg, a unit formed of veterans, known as the 1st Maine Veteran Infantry, was in the brigade that pierced the Confederate lines. Also storming Petersburg were the 8th, 11th and 31st Maine infantry. Richmond fell the same day as Petersburg—April 3, following Sheridan's seminal victory at Five Forks on April 1, where the 1st Maine cavalry played an important role. When Lee decided to surrender at Appomattox on April 9, two of his flags of truce came into General Joshua Chamberlain's lines. The honor of receiving the surrender was given to this heroic Maine officer.

A Maine historian, John C. Abbott, writing ten years after the event, described the scene:

> He (Chamberlain) drew up his troops in a straight line, a mile in length. An equal division of the rebel army was marched to a parallel line in front at a distance of but a few feet. All were silent. Not a bugle sounded; not a drum was beat; not a voice was heard.
>
> As the vanquished foe came up, Gen. Chamberlain ordered his men to present arms. This honor, paid to the heroic victims of a cruel rebellion in their hour of humiliation, brought tears to the eyes of many rebel officers. One said, "This is magnanimity which we had not expected." The defeated troops returned the courteous salute before they laid down their arms. As this division filed away, another came and another, until twenty-two thousand left behind them their arms and their banners.

The war was over, but its effects in Maine took shape in the statues and war memorials found in almost every town. The battle flags came to Augusta—43 national colors, 41 regimental colors and 28 guidons. Pride was expressed that no Maine regiment had ever surrendered its flag.

Poetry was also written about these banners. One day, a clerk in the Secretary of State's office, Moses Owen, overheard a discussion between two visitors who dismissed the display as "Nothing but flags."

Owen, already the author of several poems, immediately penned another entitled "The Returned Maine Battle Flags." In a

bronze plaque, it hangs near the glass cases, full of the ironic senti-
mentality of that bygone era.

> Nothing but flags—but simple flags
> Tattered and torn and hanging in rags...

> Nothing but flags—yet methinks at night
> They tell each other their tales of fright...

> Nothing but flags—yet they're bathed with tears.
> They tell of triumphs, of hopes, of fears...

> ...They are sacred, pure and we see no stain
> On those dear loved flags at home again.
> Baptized in blood, our purest best.
> Tattered and torn, they're now at rest.

Focus

An Officer's Experience—O.O. Howard

Oliver Otis Howard's name has endured in history more for his experiences after the war than during the fighting. As head of the Freedmen's Bureau, he grappled with the problems of the emancipated slaves and founded the nation's first institution of higher education for Blacks—Howard University.

On the battlefield, the one-time farm boy from Leeds was less than a success, prompting the estimation that "Howard was a man of only modest military abilities."[1] Despite this, he saw a good deal of action—at Bull run, at Fair Oaks (where he lost his arm), at Second Bull Run, South Mountain, Antietam, Fredericksburg, Chancellorsville and Gettysburg. At the latter two battles, he received strong criticism. His 11th Army Corps was surprised in the Chancellorsville fight by a daring 15 mile

flanking movement that Stonewall Jackson commanded. And on the first day at Gettysburg, he had to take over the Yankee left wing when General J.F. Reynolds was killed, with another precipitous retreat the result as his men were driven back to Cemetery Hill. Howard was miffed a day later that General Winfield Scott Hancock, who was junior to him, was placed above him in command.

Yet Howard still had a lot of fighting ahead of him. Ordered west to join General William Rosecrans in Kentucky, he met first with President Lincoln who urged upon him the necessity of isolating Tennessee. "General, can't you go through here and seize Knoxville?" the President asked, pointing to Cumberland Gap on a wall map. Speaking of the pro-Union mountaineers of the region,

Lincoln insisted, "They are loyal there, they are loyal." Howard played a key role in the battle for Chattanooga and then participated as commander of the Army of the Tennessee in Sherman's march through Georgia. At the war's end, he was still only 35 years old.

Howard had never intended to be a soldier and, in fact, as a Bowdoin graduate, was heading for a teaching career when his uncle secured him an appointment to West Point. In his class was J.E.B. Stuart, later the famed Confederate cavalryman, and the two became fast friends. The Superintendent of the Academy was Robert E. Lee and Cadets Stuart and Howard often visited with him and his family. Upon graduation, Howard's initial posting was to the Watervliet Arsenal at West Troy, N.Y. His commanding officer was married to the sister of the man who would beat the Yankees at Bull Run—Joseph E. Johnston. His closest companion was Lieutenant W.R. Boggs of Georgia who was to become a Rebel general. One of the guests at the commander's house was Jennie Pickett, sister of the Captain George Pickett of Pickett's charge.

None of these pre-war Regulars could foretell the future, but the strains in American society were never far from the surface. One day an escaped slave came to the arsenal and asked for food and enough money to go to Canada. Boggs laughed, but said he would give him food as he would anyone who was hungry. Then, he told Howard, "It is against my principles to help a slave escape from his master. But you can do what you choose."

Howard's one brush with hostilities

before the war came when he was sent to Florida in 1856 to take part in the Seminole War. He saw no actual combat, but did lead a daring expedition through the Everglades to find the Seminole Chief Billy Bowlegs to persuade him to make peace. Years later, Howard negotiated with various warring Indian leaders in the west, among them the great Chief Joseph of the Nez Perce. By then, he was known as the "Christian General" because of his piety and probity. It was during the Florida campaign that he became "a born-again Christian." It happened in Tampa, during a church service.

The outbreak of the Civil War found Howard back at West Point as an instructor. Lt. Colonel John F. Reynolds, whom Howard would replace at Gettysburg, was Superintendent. The young captain had written home to the Governor of Maine, offering to lead one of the volunteer regiments the State was organizing. News of this reached James G. Blaine, then Speaker of the House in the State Legislature. He won Howard the necessary votes. Jumped three ranks to full colonel, the slender, bearded West Pointer was soon in Augusta, addressing his troops. Not all of them were impressed. "Under Tucker (the other candidate), we could have had a good time, but this solemn Howard will keep us at arm's length," one of them groused. Yet Howard soon won them over with his honesty and dedication.

The 3rd Maine was then off to Washington, D.C. Within less than a month, Howard was made a Brigadier-General.

His rise from second-lieutenant to general had taken only seven years.

FOCUS

An Enlisted Man's Experience—John W. Haley

The 17th Maine was made up of men from York, Cumberland, Androscoggin and Oxford Counties and formed after the war had been in progress for a year and a quarter when a call went out for 600,000 troops. On August 6, 1862, John West Haley enlisted, along with five others in his Sunday School.

Haley was from one of the oldest families in the Saco area. His ancestor Samuel Haley had settled in Winter Harbor (Biddeford Pool) in 1638. At the time of his enlistment, he was unemployed, the textile factory where he'd worked for 50¢ a day having closed in 1857. The Federal-State-Local bounties he could collect, a princely sum of $125, no doubt figured as highly in his motivation as youthful impetuosity and patriotic fervor.

Twenty-two years old, Haley was remarkably articulate, with a wry, spare Maine quality about many comments in the war diary he kept.

The 17th saw as much combat as any unit. They were at the battles of the Wilderness, Po River, Spotsylvania, Cold Harbor, Fredericksburg, Chancellorsville and Gettysburg, and Haley went through them all unscathed.

His impressions are recorded with a biting honesty. Pomposity and posturing drew his immediate scorn, while those he admired like General Hiram Berry and General Daniel Sickles, elicited unabashed hero worship.

Here is Haley at his critical best, lambasting the newly-elected Governor of Maine, Abner Coburn, who'd come to Virginia to review the home troops and score a few political points. Not with Haley:

> Governor Coburn is, without exception, the most wretched speechmaker that ever punished the cushion of the Governor's chair. What sin have we committed that we should be so punished and on the eve of battle, too. He acted more like a great blubbering schoolboy than like the Governor of Maine. The sum total of his remarks was the sum of all flattery, piled so thick it fell off in great chunks.

Also reviewing the troops during this lull after the battle of Fredericksburg, was Abe Lincoln, accompanied by his wife and son Tad. Haley's tone changed out of respect, but still has a sly wisp of Maine humor.

> Mr. Lincoln is one of the plainest of men, while his wife is quite the reverse. He had a kindly expression that made us forget his plainness. Mr. Lincoln on horseback is not a model of beauty such as an artist would select...It shows him off at a horrible disadvantage. There was a fearful disproportion between the length of his legs and the height of the horse. It seemed as if nothing short of tying a knot in them would prevent them from dragging the ground...

The next day, at another review, Haley was touched that Lincoln was weeping as he rode by the men.

Haley speculated that what saddened the President was the thought of all the men lost in the charnel house of Fredericksburg. But worse was to come. The battle on whose *eve* they were was Chancellorsville, one of the bloodiest of the war. It was here Stonewall Jackson died, shot by mistake by his own men. The death of General Hiram Berry, hit by a sniper bullet through the shoulder and heart, devastated the Maine soldiers. Wrote Haley, "He was carried off the field on his horse, supported by two of his aides, a sad sight to us who fairly idolized him." And not only did Maine men mourn. General "Fighting Joe" Hooker, Berry's superior, openly wept, crying, "Oh, my God, Berry, why wasn't I taken and you left!?" and kissing his dead friend again and again. Vice President Hannibal Hamlin travelled from Washington to Rockland to attend Berry's funeral.

Another officer the Maine men adored was General Daniel Sickles. The men named their camp in honor of him and Haley, who proudly referred to him as a "game cock" and "gamey-looking bird," also declared, which was high praise, indeed, that there was "no braver or better-looking officer." Yet Sickles was a highly controversial person. He had been a member of Congress from New York and one day in Lafayette Square, opposite the White House, had shot to death Philip Barton Key, son of Francis Scott Key; the reason: Key had been trifling with Sickles's wife. Defended by Edwin Stanton, later Lincoln's Secretary of War, Sickles was acquitted—the first instance in which the plea of temporary insanity was used in the United States. But many people in Washington still referred to him as a *murderer*.

At Gettysburg, Sickles held up the Rebel advance in furious fighting around an area known as the Peach Orchard. A

bullet smashed his leg and it was amputated on the field and Haley describes him as coolly smoking as he was carried off to the rear. In later years, when Sickles was Chairman of the New York State Monuments Commission, he was accused of mismanagement of funds and wrote Haley, asking him to: "...organize a movement of those who served under me to come to my relief now..." Haley had troubles of his own at the time with a law suit and it's not known if he were able to help his old general.

Haley's diary is full of sharp observations: the soldier punished for drunkenness with a barrel put over him on which was written, "RUM DID IT"; the protest of General de Trobriand, an exile from the France of Louis Napoleon, who declaimed, "Ze 17th of Maine says I eat frogs. I *do not* eat frogs!"; a wisecrack about Colonel Tommy Egan of an Irish regiment (Haley was outspokenly prejudiced against the Irish and Blacks) that he had said there was no sense in buying meat since half of it is bone, when you can buy whiskey with no bones it; the Southern woman who'd been told Yankees had horns almost fainting away when a Union soldier took off his cap to show a big wen sticking up through his hair; "Dutch Mary," wife of a soldier in a Zouave regiment dressed in the same colorful uniform beating a soldier over the head with a wet shirt when he tried to kiss her; a description of General Winfield Scott Hancock pulling a louse out of his hair.

After Lincoln's assassination, the new President, Andrew Johnson, paid a visit to the troops. Haley's estimation of him, centered on his large nose, was withering:

It has the look of one that is trying to

204

get away from an unpleasant odor. If current rumor is true, his own breath is sufficiently pungent to cause this recoil.

Each of his comrades was also estimated at the end of his diary:

James S. Clark: Noted only for gluttony. Could eat four men's rations.

Josh W. Small: Most always sick. Suspected of eating soap and other choice edibles.

William Lamberton:If he was good for anything but lying and swearing, there is gross omission in the records.

J.W. Jose:Wounded at Petersburg. An excellent soldier. None better or braver.

James M. Brown: Away much. Loved rum more than country.

Etc., etc...And also, Haley, on Haley, himself.

John Haley: Below criticism. Poor fighter. Attained successful mediocrity as a soldier. Present all the time.

Other Military Highlights

The 20th Maine at Little Round Top

Joshua Lawrence Chamberlain of Brewer (called "Lawrence" by his brothers) was not the original Commander of the 20th Maine. Offered a regimental command by Governor Israel Washburn, this 33 year old professor at Bowdoin was modest enough to admit he had some learning to do about military matters. So he became a Lieutenant-Colonel under a West Pointer, Colonel Adalbert Ames, who hailed from Rockland, and only after Ames was promoted to Brigadier-General following Bull Run, did he take over the 20th Maine.

The regiment's moment of glory was at Gettysburg and by then, they were a hard-fighting, well-disciplined group with plenty of battle experience.

Gettysburg found Lee on the attack, invading Pennsylvania, carrying the war to the North. The armies met at this little village pretty much by chance. The crucial position where the 20th Maine found itself was at the extreme left of the Yankee line. The Union troops were stretched along an extensive height known as Cemetery Ridge, which terminated in two hills, Little Round Top and Big Round Top. Initially, neither side occupied them.

About a mile to the west of Cemetery Ridge was Seminary Ridge, held by the Confederates. Their right wing went all the way to the vicinity of Big Round Top. A concerted push here could outflank the whole Federal army.

General Governor K. Warren, a minor Union commander, discovered the Round Tops weren't manned, except for a few signalmen on Little Round Top. When he conveyed the news to the General Staff, the 5th Corps under General George Sykes was ordered to take possession of this section.

The 5th. Corps' leading brigade had four regiments: the 44th New York, the 16th Michigan, the 83rd Pennsylvania and the 20th Maine.

Up the wooded slopes of Little Round Top, the Yankee soldiers scrambled, peppered by Confederate artillery fire. The 20th was sent to the very end of the line, farthest to the left, on the brink of a smooth, shallow valley, with Big Round Top looming across from them. As a latter-day historian of the regiment, John Pullen, has written, "Holding the left of the entire 4 or 5 mile Union line, the 20th Maine had stepped all unawares into the spotlight of history." As Pullen also characterized it, "one of the world's decisive small unit military actions" was about to begin.

But it wasn't just the luck of the draw that gave such notoriety to the 20th Maine. Two decisive acts ordered by Chamberlain turned away what could have been a disastrous outflanking move by the Southerners.

Facing the Yankees was General Evander Law's brigade of Alabamans, plus the 4th and 5th Texas. The 15th Alabama led

Joshua Chamberlain as a young officer

206

off, capturing Big Round Top. Colonel William Oates was in command. His first instinct was to lug artillery up the large hill, from whose elevation the Yankee lines could be mercilessly bombarded. Turned down on his artillery request, Oates was ordered to send his men down into the valley between the two hills and skirt the Northerners left flank, while at the same time, an attack was made on Little Round Top by the 4th Alabama. Through the smoke of the volleys that cut down the charging Rebels, Chamberlain could see Oates' men in the valley.

The Maine commander then issued the first of his extraordinary orders. He was able to swivel his line of men so that one part was a right angle to the other, ready to meet any flanking attack.

This complicated maneuver came just in time. The Alabamans charged up what they thought was an unguarded flank. Instead, they were met with a fierce, unexpected volley from the 20th Maine that stopped them cold.

But these were tough men and they rushed on again, with fixed bayonets. The Mainers used their rifles as clubs and chopped at the Rebels as if they were wielding axes. There were charges and counter-charges in this bloody hand-to-hand fighting. A third of the Maine regiment became casualties, and worse, they were running out of ammunition.

Then came Chamberlain's second act of genius, a sublime instant of military instinct, for which he belatedly received the Congressional Medal of Honor. He ordered his outnumbered men to fix bayonets and charge down the hill. The Alabamans were taken completely by surprise and when the men of Chamberlain's Company B, who had managed to get behind them, opened fire from the rear, they panicked and broke.

The 20th Maine took 400 prisoners. Their own losses were 130 killed and wounded. Oates lost half his regiment. Years later, he wrote:

> There never were harder fighters than the 20th Maine men and their gallant Colonel. His skill and persistency and the great bravery of his men saved Little Round Top and the Army of the Potomac from defeat. Great events sometimes turn on comparatively small affairs.

Gettysburg wasn't over until Pickett's futile charge the next day, which took place with the 20th Maine being held in reserve.

The 27th Maine Medal of Honor Mix-Up

It was not until 1893 that Joshua L. Chamberlain received specific official recognition for his actions at Little Round Top when he was awarded the Congressional Medal of Honor. Shortly before his death, writing in 1914, he expressed his feelings about the medal he had received:

> ...we trust that no self-seeking plea nor political pressure shall avail to belittle the estimation of this...seal of honor whose very meaning and worth is that it notes conduct in which man rises above self. May this award ever be for him who has won it, at the peril of life, in storm of battle...

In so speaking, Chamberlain may or may not have been alluding to the most notorious instance in which the medal was issued to non-combatants—the transmittal of 864 individual medals to *all* members of the 27th Maine!

How did this fiasco happen?

To begin with, it is useful to go back to the origins of the Congressional Medal of Honor in 1861. The idea was the brainchild of Gideon Welles, the Secretary of the Navy. Welles, wanting a medal to reward the heroic actions of his sailors, convinced Congress to pass a bill for a Navy Medal of Honor, found a designer and manufacturer and ordered 175 of them struck. Then, the Army, under Secretary of War Edwin Stanton, produced a similar-looking medal. However, Stanton saw the decoration as having a slightly different purpose: an inducement rather than simply a reward.

Congress, in legislation it passed in 1862, incorporated Stanton's philosophy in the bill regulating the medals use. It could be issued for gallantry in action but also for *other soldier-like qualities*.

The 27th Maine had been formed n the summer of 1862. The men were volunteers, enlisted for a nine month period. All were from York County and one of the chief recruiters was a patriotic medical doctor from Kittery, Mark Wentworth. In time, he became their Colonel.

It was an outfit that never saw combat. Sent to Washington D.C. and then into northern Virginia, the regiment was kept on picket duty. Finally, in June 1863, with the nine months up, the men prepared to go home.

But this was the same period when Lee was invading Pennsyl-

vania and the capital's defenses were being depleted to send troops
to Gettysburg. Lincoln and Stanton decided to appeal to the 27th
Maine, and the 25th, also due to go home, asking them to stay and
guard Washington.

To this end, they sent a Maine Congressman, Daniel Somes,
to talk to the regiments. Colonel Francis Fessenden of the 25th was
sympathetic, but his men flatly refused to agree. Then, Somes went
to see Wentworth, who drew his men up in formation, relayed the
request, stated he would be staying and asked those who would join
him to step forward two paces.

It was a difficult decision for many soldiers. Haying time had
started at home; a large number had made plans to return. Out of
more than 800 men, 550 decided to go; slightly more than 300
joined Wentworth.

As it turned out, these volunteers were in Washington only
three days longer than their comrades who left on July 1. By July 4,
news had come of Lee's defeat and the 27th. was no longer needed.

But Stanton had decided that their act of volunteering
deserved reward and his solution (made in a promise to Wentworth) was to give each one the Congressional Medal of Honor.
To compound this watering down of the medal, a bureaucratic
snafu issued it not just to volunteers but to the entire muster list of
the regiment—864 members!

Mark Wentworth went back to the war after a short stay in
Kittery as commander of the last regiment raised in Maine—the
32nd. Seriously wounded, he was sent home and while recuperat-
ing, had to deal with the problem of the medals, 200 pounds of
them, sent in a barrel to Governor Daniel Cony.

Wentworth had Cony ship them to Kittery. He made sure
that only those 315 who had volunteered received them. The rest
he sent back to Augusta but they were sent back to him and he
stored them in his stable. Over the years, they were lost and have
never been found.

Somewhere in Maine, more than 500 unpacked Medals of
Honor in their leather cases bear testimony to the vagaries and
ironies of government.

The Home Front

In addition to all of the fighting men that Maine sent to the various
battle sectors, companies of Home Guards also were raised. Mark

Wentworth, in Kittery, for example, transformed the militia unit he'd drilled before the war into the Kittery Artillery and they moved into Fort McClary in order to protect the Navy Yard. It was feared that Rebel privateers might sail up the Piscataqua and attack this Federal facility.

The vulnerability of the Maine coast was a real concern. Companies of volunteers were put into other forts, as well, like Fort Scammel in Portland Harbor and Fort Sullivan at Eastport.

In October 1861, Governor Israel Washburn appointed three distinguished Mainers—Vice President Hannibal Hamlin, ex-U.S. Senator Reuel Williams and railroad magnate John A. Poor—to pressure the U.S. Government to beef up Maine's shore fortifications. As a result, some batteries were erected. Rumors of Confederate cruisers offshore led to the dispatch of cannon to the larger Maine cities, and not all of them on the coast.

Politics in Maine did not relax because of the war. Within the Democratic Party was a large faction that refused to support the Northern cause. These "Breckenridge" Democrats actually succeeded in controlling their party convention in 1862 where they nominated one of their own, after the "Douglas" Democrats walked out en masse.

This particular convention was being held in Augusta. The Breckenridge group had originally scheduled their own meeting for Bangor. However, even the very call for this anti-war gathering was provocative, seeking delegates "...who are opposed to this unholy civil war and in favor of the immediate restoration of peace by negotiation and compromise." At a huge rally in Bangor, the local people protested against the proposed anti-war meeting and declared the "Bangor Democrat," whose editor Marcellus Emery was one of its organizers, a treasonous publication.

From words, they went to action. Rufus Dwinel, the lumber tycoon, stirred up a crowd that broke into the newspaper's offices where a blacksmith took apart the press, after which all copies were publicly burned. Emery arrived in the middle of the riot, but his friends hustled him away before he could be harmed. Not long afterward, he put out an edition headlining the outrage, having had it secretly printed locally on the promise he would say it was printed in Portland. The anti-war Democrats were wise enough to know they should cancel their convention. Besides, the corporators of Norumbega Hall had refused to rent it to people they said were "traitors."

So these former supporters of the presidential campaign of

210

John Cabell Breckenridge, who was now a Confederate general, went to Augusta and took over the conclave called by those party regulars who had supported Senator Stephen Douglas for president in 1860. In the majority, they chose an aged ex-Governor and U.S. Senator, Judah Dana, as their gubernatorial candidate. The "War Democrats," caucusing in another hall, nominated Colonel Charles Jameson of Bangor, the commander of the 2nd Maine.

The Republicans, suffering no such split in their ranks, easily re-elected Governor Israel Washburn, with Jameson coming in second.

Republican domination continued throughout the war; Washburn was followed by Abner Coburn who was followed by Samuel Cony. But Cony was elected in the name of the Union party. The change had been the idea of James G. Blaine, then Chairman of the Republican State Committee, alarmed at Coburn's fairly poor showing under the Republican rubric. Cony had been a Democrat until the outbreak of the war and was very popular because as Assistant-Paymaster General of Maine, he had advanced money from his own private fortune to the soldiers before State funds became available. He was able to win the nomination from Coburn and went on to beat the Democrat Bion Bradbury, 68,339–50,676.

That the anti-war Democrats gathered as many votes as they did was a testimony to the unpopularity of some of the Lincoln Administration's measures. The draft, for example—and what was often perceived as a bungled prosecution of the war. Lincoln, himself, had to face one of his own generals, George McClellan, when he ran for re-election. Ironically, the Cabinet blamed McClellan for the poor performance of the Union army.

Anti-draft riots in major cities like New York took dozens of lives. In Maine, the one outburst of anti-draft feeling had a typical downeast flavor. This was the so-called "Kingfield Riot." When 34 Kingfield men were called up, Samuel Law of Phillips, the enrolling officer, arrived in town to deliver the notices and was met by a crowd of 50 men who prevented him from doing his duty. In the neighboring communities of Freeman and Salem, the homes of the enrolling officers were broken into and the notices carried off. The Governor called up the Lewiston Light Infantry, who were mostly returned veterans of the 10th Maine. Given ten rounds of cartridges each, 100 men reached Farmington by train, then marched to Kingfield. On the outskirts of town, they were met by young girls who invited them to a community feast. Tables laden with food had been set out in the center of town, the soldiers ate and in this convivial atmosphere, the notices were delivered and the law upheld.

Maine's contribution was not only soldiers provided—the most proportionately of any state—but also defense work. A famous Yankee ship-of-war, the *Kearsarge*, which defeated the Confederate raider *Alabama* off the Coast of France, was built at the Kittery Shipyard, where more than 2,000 workmen completed 26 wartime ships. Two of these were ironclads, the *Passaconaway* and the *Agamenticus*. Another vital contribution of the Maine economy to the war effort was in the manufacture of gunpowder. It has been estimated that the powder mills on the Presumpscot, at Gorham and Windham, produced 5% of all the powder used by the Union forces.

FOCUS

Confederate Attacks on Maine

While Lee's army never penetrated farther north than Gettysburg, the Union states, no matter how far from the South, were not immune to individual Rebel raids. This included Maine, especially because of its closeness to Canada where Confederate agents and escaped prisoners could gather and plot.

But the first incident in Maine did not involve Canada. It was the end result of a privateering expedition during the spring of 1863 led by a daring Confederate naval lieutenant named Charles W. Read. On board the brigantine *Clarence*, a Yankee ship captured off the Brazilian coast, Read began an extensive raid north on Union shipping, capturing at least five prizes before he transferred his crew to one of them, the *Tacony*. Despite pursuit by the U.S. Navy as they headed still farther north, Read and his men captured 15 vessels in less than two weeks. By late June, they were 45 miles off the entrance

to Portland harbor, where they proceeded to take a number of fishing schooners. One of these was the *Archer* and Read, worried the *Tacony* was too well known, again transferred his crew. Off Damariscove Island, the Rebels took aboard two local fishermen, Albert P. Bibber and Elbridge Titcomb. Through them, Read learned of the existence in Portland Harbor of the U.S. revenue cutter, *Caleb Cushing*.

Read's next idea was boldness, itself. He decided to sail right into Portland Harbor and steal the *Caleb Cushing*!

Three granite forts guarded Portland Harbor—Fort Scammell, Fort Preble and Fort Gorges. Read sailed past them without incident. Between Fort Gorges and Munjoy Hill, the *Archer* dropped anchor. Another target also presented itself—the *Chesapeake*, a 460 ton steamship that ran between New York and Portland, but the Rebel engineer with

212

Read said he couldn't handle such large engines. So it was back to the *Caleb Cushing*, whose skipper, ironically, had died of a heart attack the day before, leaving in command an officer of Southern origin, Dudley Davenport of Savannah, Georgia.

Read launched two small boatloads of armed raiders. It was after midnight and Lieutenant Dudley was asleep in his cabin when four men burst in, overpowered him and handcuffed him. When he learned who his assailants were, he protested he shouldn't be handcuffed because he was a Southerner.

The rest of the crew was also easily overcome. Since the wind had died, the *Caleb Cushing* had to be towed by the two small boats. Once a breeze sprang up, she was maneuvered into Hussey Sound and open ocean.

As soon as the revenue cutter's disappearance was noticed, a pursuit was organized, which included the *Chesap-*

eake. About to be overtaken on their prize, the Confederates opened fire with the ship's only gun. The *Chesapeake* fired back and bore down on the cutter. Out of ammunition, Read saw he was cornered; he released his prisoners, then gave orders to scuttle. A mass of bedding was set alight and the Rebels abandoned ship. Not long afterward, the *Caleb Cushing* exploded. The captured Confederates, taken ashore on the *Chesapeake*, were the object of strong local anger, so they were sent to Fort Warren in Boston Harbor. Read later escaped from this naval prison, but was soon recaptured.

The *Chesapeake* figured in another episode of Confederate privateering that occurred about six months afterward. The vessel was en route from New York to Portland in early December 1863, her cargo including wine for H.H. Hay, a prominent Portland drugstore, bales of cotton and boxes of starch for the Bates Mill in Lewiston and rags for a paper mill

The blowing up of the Caleb Cushing

in Gardiner. On December 8, off Cape Cod, 14 of the ship's 22 passengers turned out to be hijackers. Armed with pistols, they swiftly took over the *Chesapeake*, but not without a struggle in which the second engineer, Orin Schaffer, was shot and killed and two other crew members wounded.

A one-time confidence man by the name of John Cribben Brain was the organizer of the attack. An Englishman, Brain had used British diplomatic pressure to get himself released from a Northern prison and then had gone to Canada. In St. John, New Brunswick, he'd gathered a group of conspirators together. One of them, another Englishman named Vernon Locke, claimed to be a commissioned Confederate privateer and gave Brain orders to go to New York City and "there engage passage on board the steamer and use your own discretion as to the time and place of capture."

Having commandeered the Maine-bound *Chesapeake*, the Rebel hijackers headed for Canada. They first sighted land again off Mount Desert and continued to Grand Manan, where they stopped for fuel. Deeper into the Bay of Fundy, they stopped again, at sea to take on Vernon Locke. After freeing their prisoners near St. John, they steamed for Nova Scotia.

The American consul in St. John, J.Q. Howard, alerted authorities in Washington and Portland. Yankee warships were soon on the way. The *Ella and Anna*, commanded by Lieutenant J.F. Nickels of Searsport, finally located the *Chesapeake* at Sambro Harbor, close to Halifax. Nickels put a boarding party onto her and most of the hijackers fled. One who didn't get away was George Wade, the man who had shot Engineer Schaffer. But through the connivance of

local Southern sympathizers, Wade was able to escape as did Brain. The Nova Scotian authorities made an appropriate fuss about the intrusion, then turned the *Chesapeake* over to the Yankees.

Among those charged with piracy in the affair yet never extradited was David Collins, a 30 year old Irish immigrant. His youngest brother, William, was a captain in the Confederate forces, ostensibly visiting the family in New Brunswick in the spring of 1864 when he became the pivot of yet another Rebel foray against Maine—this time by land.

William Collins had but one serious failing as a plotter—he liked to boast. His open talk about a raid on Maine so alarmed his sister Mary that she wrote to still another brother, John Collins, serving as a Methodist minister in York, Maine.

John grew alarmed, too. He hurried to St. John to confront William and told him, "I don't know what your plans are, but I shall do all in my power to block them. Knowing you are a spy, I should be a traitor to my country if I did not deliver you over to the hands of the authorities."

Then, John Collins went to see Consul J.Q. Howard. The clever diplomat hired detectives to go underground among the pro-Confederate circles in town. They discovered William Collins's plan was to rob the bank in Calais, Maine and steal a large supply of gold. A U.S. Army deserter named William Daymond was infiltrated into the ranks of the raiders.

Moreover, Howard sent warning telegrams to Maine's Governor Samuel Cony and the cashier of the Calais Bank, Joseph A. Lee.

At noon on July 18, 1864, four men in civilian clothes walked into the Calais Bank, produced some gold coins and

214

asked to have them changed into paper dollars. Then, one of them went for his pocket, which held a small revolver. Immediately, another of the gang yelled out a warning to the bank officials and seconds later, the place was bristling with guns!

It was Daymond, needless to say, who had given the signal. His reward was to be cleared of all desertion charges. William Collins and his two companions were jailed, then tried and sentenced to three years in Thomaston State Prison as common bank robbers.

One of them, a young Missourian named Francis X. Jones, claimed they were, in actuality, the vanguard of a Rebel invasion force of 5,000 meant to mesh with an underground uprising of southern sympathizers—"Copperheads"—to overwhelm the Pine Tree State. Jones also described a Confederate agent, Major Dudley Harris, operating out of Portland, as the coordinator. The existence of Harris in Portland was verified, although no amphibious landing of grey-clad hordes on the down east coast ever took place.

A final postscript: William Collins and four other convicts escaped Thomaston on November 26, 1864. Collins swam the frigid St. George River, got to New Brunswick and eventually returned to the South.

Two Mainers in Washington

Hamlin and Fessenden

Most Maine people, probably, know that Hannibal Hamlin was Abraham Lincoln's first Vice-President. But few, no doubt, have any idea of what he *did* as Vice-President or how he happened to be chosen or why he was dropped after only one term. It can also be speculated that had he been given a second term, he would have become President.

Hamlin never sought the Vice-Presidency. He was a U.S. Senator at the time and happy with his position. In fact, he had asked his friends not to put his name in nomination for either President or Vice-President at the Republicans 1860 convention in Chicago.

The apparent favorite for the G.O.P. nod that fateful year was not Lincoln but Senator William H. Seward of New York. Hamlin's objection to Seward was ostensibly his concern that the New Yorker couldn't carry enough states, yet it might also have reflected a split in the Maine party where Hamlin was the leader of the former Democrats and his rival William Pitt Fessenden of the former Whigs. Besides, Hamlin was genuinely impressed by what he'd heard of Lincoln. He therefore worked hard to see that the Maine delegation, which might have committed to Seward, was sent unpledged.

215

Lincoln was chosen. Then, Hamlin's friends did allow his name to be circulated. David K. Cartter of Ohio, who had swung the last deciding votes to Lincoln, nominated the Mainer. His only serious rival was the fiery anti-slavery radical, Cassius Clay of Kentucky. Hamlin outpolled Clay on the first ballot, but was shy of a majority. On the second ballot, he had the G.O.P. nod.

But would he accept? The Maine Senator hadn't the slightest inkling of what was going on. At the Washington House in D.C. where he roomed, a large group of friends suddenly thronged into his quarters.

"Good evening, Mr. Vice-President," they chorused.

"What do you mean!?" Hamlin shot back.

"You've been nominated for Vice-President," he was told.

"But I don't want the place," he replied.

It was an honest answer, not a politician's coyness. Later on, he often talked about his historical overview that most Presidents and Vice Presidents didn't get along and he frequently likened the job to "the fifth wheel on a coach." But what persuaded him to give in was the logic of Senator Benjamin Wade of Ohio that if he rejected them, the Democrats would claim he did so because he thought the G.O.P. ticket was too weak to win.

Hamlin and Lincoln had never met. Following the election, Lincoln wrote him, "It appears to me that you and I ought to get acquainted...You first entered the Senate during the single term I was a member of the House of Representatives but I have no recollection that we were introduced." Hamlin journeyed to Chicago and the two of them hit it off well.

In setting up the administration, Lincoln allowed Hamlin to choose the one New England member, who was to fill the post of Secretary of the Navy. Hamlin opted for Gideon Welles of Connecticut, a decision he was to regret. He also helped Lincoln fill other Cabinet slots and was particularly useful in persuading Seward to become Secretary of State.

But the influence afforded a Vice-President *was* minimal, as he had feared. As a Senator, he had had far more patronage. On the military side, he was able to aid the advancement of some worthy constituents, like Hiram G. Berry, who advance to Major-General, or Hiram Burnham of Cherryfield, who made Brigadier,[2] but on the civilian side, he was not able to place more than half a dozen Mainers. His biggest disappointment came in his dealings with Gideon Welles. The final straw occurred when Welles promised a contract for building gunboats to Captain William

McGilvery of Searsport and General Samuel Hersey of Bangor (Hamlin's best friend) and then reneged after Hamlin told them to go ahead and start the work. Worse, the sole naval contract given to Maine went to a political foe of Hamlin's, a man he considered a Southern-sympathizing "Copperhead".

Hamlin's prime duty was to preside over the Senate. Quite often, he was absent—once, for two and half months—and as soon as Congress recessed, he headed back to Maine. There, he did a good deal of politicking, helping Republican candidates, and also recruiting soldiers for the Union army. Early on, before muskets were issued, he drilled a company of the 2nd Maine in his hometown of Hampden using pickets he had them tear from a fence. He also served, himself, as a corporal in Company A of the Maine Coast Guard and spent the summer of 1864 at Fort McClary in Kittery.

Hamlin was not without influence on Lincoln. Along with other Republican "Radicals," he continually urged the President to free the slaves. Before issuing the Emancipation Proclamation, Lincoln did confer with his Vice-President whom he credited with having pushed him to his epic act.

There are strong indications Lincoln would have liked Hamlin to continue. But he made no effort to intervene at the 1864 Republican Convention when a move was made to substitute a War Democrat, Andrew Johnson. More than a little Machiavellian maneuvering lay behind the move to dump Hamlin. The principal actor here was Massachusetts Senator Charles Sumner. This vain, difficult man, made all the harder to deal with after the savage beating he'd received from the Southerner Preston Brooks, fiercely hated Maine Senator William Pitt Fessenden. Sumner diabolically reasoned that if he could deny Hamlin the Vice-Presidency, Hamlin would run against Fessenden for his Senate seat and defeat him.

The scenario did not work out. Hamlin never ran against Fessenden. Lincoln offered him the job of Secretary of the Treasury and he also turned that down (ironically, it went to Fessenden). But finally, facing financial pressures, he did take the lucrative post of Collector of the Port of Boston,[3] which he held a short while until a U.S. Senate position opened up and he was once more sent to Washington by his peers.

It was also during his Vice-Presidency, in 1862, that the Morrill Act established land grant colleges. As a trustee of Colby, Hamlin was interested in education, but he resisted the efforts of

217

both Colby and Bowdoin to attach such an institution to their own campuses. His choice was Orono and, apparently, he persuaded the trustee who cast the deciding vote.

William Pitt Fessenden held no great enmity toward Hannibal Hamlin. They were simply opposites who, on the same side politically, found themselves thrown against each other. Even physically, they presented a deep contrast: Hamlin, fleshy and dark-complected, so dark that Southerners like Robert Barnwell Rhett created the myth he was a mulatto; Fessenden, lean and dour, stiff, gaunt, the epitome of the dry, brainy Yankee. Fessenden's father had taught them both law in his offices in Portland. William Pitt, elected to the Legislature, to the Congress and then to the U.S. Senate, had been in politics more than 20 years when the outbreak of the Civil War found him Chairman of

William Pitt Fessenden

the all-important Senate Committee on Finance.

The Committee had seven members and they handled all measures relating to public finance and the Treasury, all loans, all coinage bills and all appropriations for the army, navy and other departments. Fessenden's major role was to defend the administration's finance bills and beat back the myriad amendments his colleagues tried to tie to them. Some of those bills were as complex as any passed in Washington today. One tax bill had 119 sections, an omnibus tariff bill had 182 sections. The government repeatedly needed to borrow money. At the start of the war, revenues were $25 million; expenditures the first year were $474 million. Fessenden had to handle a Legal Tender Bill allowing for $150 million in paper money, plus $500 million in bonds. Expenditures soared; soon, they ballooned to $715 million and the last year of the war were more than $1 billion.

An example of Fessenden's problems could be seen in the debate on the Fortification Bill of 1862. One item in it was $550,000 to build defensive earthworks at Portland Harbor. A raft of amendments followed. One senator wanted the same thing in Narragansett Bay, another on the Great Lakes, another on the Pacific, another said that earthworks were no good and should be stricken from the bill. Fessenden spent his nights researching each suggestion so he could defeat it during the next day's debate.

Non-military appropriations bills had to be dealt with, too, war or no war. Most troublesome for Fessenden were the Indian Appropriations Bills. None gave more opportunity for pork barrel and fraud and Senators from states where reservations were located tried to load them with self-seeking amendments. When Fessenden complained, opposing one such amendment, how certain states didn't enforce their own laws to protect Indians, the author of the proposal shot back that Maine didn't enforce her own laws since he could always buy liquor there. Fessenden good-humoredly replied that the gentleman must have used superior skills learned in the West to do so.

With the war going badly in its early stages, Republican Senators focused on Secretary of State Seward as a prime scapegoat. Fessenden took a major part in the effort to persuade Lincoln to drop Seward and reorganize his Cabinet. In a meeting that lasted until one o'clock in the morning, Fessenden bluntly urged Lincoln to accept Seward's resignation.

"Mr. Seward lost my confidence before he became Secretary of State," Fessenden told the President, "and had I been consulted

I should not have advised his appointment."

The entire Cabinet was upset over the confrontation. Salmon P. Chase, the able if ambitious Secretary of the Treasury, offered his resignation too. He urged Fessenden to take the job.

Fessenden responded, "You know very well that the part I have taken in this movement would effectually exclude me from a Cabinet appointment..."

Lincoln ended the crisis by refusing to accept any resignations.

Yet, ironically, when Salmon P. Chase did resign from the Treasury in the summer of 1864, Fessenden was appointed in his place. Originally, Fessenden had gone to the President to urge the choice of a fellow Mainer named Hugh McCulloch. Unbeknownst to Fessenden Lincoln had just prepared an order naming him and before seeing the Maine Senator, had the nomination sent over to the Senate. Once Fessenden began his plea for McCulloch, Lincoln smiled and revealed what he had done. Fessenden was aghast. "You must withdraw it! I cannot accept," he cried, springing to his feet.

Again, this wasn't coyness. His heavy responsibilities as Chairman of the Finance Committee had taken a toll on his health. But before he could return to the Senate, his nomination had been unanimously confirmed. His colleagues pressed him to accept. The next morning, he met again with Lincoln, who used all his powers of persuasion. What finally decided Fessenden was his fear of a financial crash if he refused and its effect on the economy and the war effort.

Lincoln had promised him he could leave as soon as it would not cause any "public injury." That time came in March 1865 after a stint of approximately nine months at the Treasury in which he earned high marks for controlling expenditures and inflation. Shortly afterward, he was back in the U.S. Senate and his most famous act—his vote *not to impeach* Andrew Johnson—was still several years ahead of him.

CHAPTER Twelve

THE REPUBLICAN ERA

Reconstruction

Had Hannibal Hamlin become President, the history of the "reconstruction" of the defeated South would have been very different from what it was. But initially, the "Radical" wing of the Republican Party, epitomized by Charles Sumner, his fellow Senator Benjamin Wade of Ohio and Congressman Thaddeus Stevens of Pennsylvania, was delighted with their choice of Andrew Johnson. As leader of the Unionist forces in Tennessee and military governor there, Johnson had pronounced himself as vengeful against the South as any "Radical" could hope to be. He would, the G.O.P. extremists were sure, undertake to fulfill literally as well as figuratively the promise in the old Union war song to "Hang Jeff Davis from a sour apple tree."

But Johnson's hatred, it turned out, was not against the Confederacy for its rebellion, but rather a social peeve against the ante-bellum aristocracy.[1] Born poor, self-made, a lowly tailor by trade, Johnson had simply struggled all his life against the planter class. Now that their power had been broken, he wished to transfer authority to those Southerners, whether they had been rebels or not, with whom he could identify. For the 4 million ex-slaves who had been emancipated, he had little or no sympathy. He met with their leader, Frederick Douglass, but offered only platitudes.

Soon, the Radicals' reservations due to Johnson's personal deportment (he showed up drunk to be sworn in as Vice-President by Hamlin) became open warfare because of his political actions.

221

Johnson's legalistic position—that the rebellious States had never left the Union—clashed diametrically with the Radicals' view that the Southern States were, in effect, conquered foreign entities. The Presidential plan was to allow the Confederate States back into the Union as soon as they could organize, swear allegiance and pledge to ratify the 13th. Amendment, outlawing slavery. With Congress adjourned from April to December 1865, the President was able to work his will. In May, he issued an amnesty proclamation, restoring civil rights to all Rebels except those with property worth more than $20,000. By the end of 1865, every Secessionist State except Texas had organized a government.

They also passed discriminatory laws against ex-slaves, known as Black Codes. Negroes were uniformly denied the vote. Those whites elected to office were often notorious supporters of the Rebellion. Alexander Stephens of Georgia, Vice-President of the Confederacy, was actually elected to the U.S. Senate, although not allowed to take his seat.

The counter-thrust by the Radicals found several Maine men intimately involved. The Joint Committee on Reconstruction had William Pitt Fessenden as its Senate Chairman. The report it issued on June 20, 1866 set the framework for much of what happened later, declaring that the ex-Confederate States were not entitled to representation and that "reconstruction" was a Congressional not an Executive responsibility. A major clash ensued over a bill to extend the life of the Freedmen's Bureau, the government agency created while Lincoln was alive to look after the ex-slaves. Johnson's veto was overridden. Thus the Bureau, led by Maine's General O.O. Howard, was allowed to continue its social and educational work, but not without sustained harassment from the President.

What happened to Eliphalet Whittlesey was a perfect example. This close friend of Howard's, a professor at Bowdoin before the war, had been made Assistant Commissioner[2] of the Bureau in North Carolina. His loyalty to Howard made him an ideal target for the President who, unable to stop the Bureau with his vetoes, sent investigative agents to sniff out incidents that could discredit its work and personnel. The most notorious were Colonel James Scott Fullerton, formerly a confidante of Howard's, and General John B. Steedman, a Democrat hostile to blacks.

In 1866, Fullerton and Steedman pounced upon an incident at a plantation in North Carolina run by another Yankee, the Reverend Horace James of Massachusetts. This particular plantation was intended to be a model—part school, part church, part workplace—where ex-slaves were treated well, paid well, educated, and helped to lead productive, religious lives. But one of the freedmen stole some clothes, was caught, ordered to dig a ditch as punishment and when he fled, shot and killed by a white overseer. Since Whittlesey was part-owner of the place, along with a Brunswick, Maine neighbor, Winthrop Tappan, the President's men saw an ideal opportunity to embarrass the Bureau. Whittlesey, James and nine other Bureau officials were arrested and charged with a range of crimes, including torturing blacks.

The trial resulted in Whittlesey's acquittal, but he was forced to leave North Carolina. Howard was able to put him on his staff in Washington, where he stayed until 1872.

Another Mainer deeply involved in Reconstruction was Adalbert Ames of Rockland, the original commander of the 20th. Maine. When Congress, getting tough with Andrew Johnson, produced its "Military Reconstruction Plan," Ames ended up as Military Governor of Mississippi.

The Republicans of Mississippi, gathered in convention on July 2, 1869, were jubilant.

> We confide in and will support Major General Adalbert Ames, military commander and Governor of this State. We look to him as the representative of the President and of Congress and regard him as able and firm in peace as in war... For his order relieving the poor of a heavy burden and unequal taxes, and for the order abolishing distinction of color for the jury...the loyal people owe him a debt of gratitude which they can never repay...

Ames was outspoken about his support for the rights of the ex-slaves. "I found when I was Military Governor of Mississippi that a black code existed there, that Negroes had no rights...I felt I had a mission to perform in their interests..."

Thus, both in words and actions, he did not endear himself to the so-called "Bourbons," who rallied around the terrorist Ku Klux Klan. In 1870, Ames reported that 63 murders had been committed by night riders in his State in the course of only three months. In Congress, his father-in-law, the redoubtable *bête-noire* of the South, Benjamin Butler, tried to push through a "Force Bill" or "Ku Klux Klan Bill," aimed at curtailing these vigilante activities. During this debate, Butler coined a lasting phrase in American

223

politics—"the Bloody Shirt"—waving the blood-soaked shirt of a carpet-bagger County Superintendent in Monroe County, Mississippi named A.P. Huggins, who had been horsewhipped by Klansmen.

Before long, Adalbert Ames was in Washington, too, as one of the U.S. Senators from Mississippi. The other Senator elected by the Legislature was a black minister, Hiram R. Revels. It took three days of debate and a rousing speech by Senator Sumner before the Senate would agree to seat Revels.

Ames was soon voting for acts to enforce the 14th and 15th Amendments, which legalized the franchise for all Americans. In his brief stay in Washington, he also strongly supported the Northern Pacific Railroad and the enormous land grants given to it by Congress. Then, he was back in Mississippi once more as Governor. His Lieutenant-Governor was a black man, as were his Secretary of State and Superintendent of Education. Rather than being profligate, a charge made against many carpetbagger Governors, Ames sought to reduce state expenditure by 25%. He cut the state printing bill and sliced the state debt by almost a third. Despite the Mainer's admirable record, an attempt to impeach him was made when the Bourbons sought to recontrol the state after the disputed Presidential election of 1876 and President Rutherford B. Hayes' removal of Federal troops from the South. So anxious were the Mississippians to get rid of Ames that they didn't try to accuse him of theft, a usual practice. They attacked him because of a fight he'd had with his Lieutenant-Governor. Long afterward, when Ames was back in the North, he would comment whenever there was violence nearby that the Mississippians were still after him.

Yet another major Maine player in the Reconstruction drama was James G. Blaine. This quintessential Republican politician—ex-teacher, ex-newspaperman, ex-Pennsylvanian who had married into a prominent Augusta family—had become Speaker of the U.S. House by 1869. In the debate over the 14th Amendment, he introduced the principle that if any state denied the vote to persons because of race, their population as a basis for electoral vote and members of Congress would be reduced accordingly. It was considered an important provision at the time, although never implemented later on.

Another "Blaine Amendment" was to the Miltary Reconstruction Act, the backbone of the Radical Republicans' program. The act was so tough that James Garfield declared it "written with

224

an iron pen, made of a bayonet." The wielder of that pen was
Thaddeus Stevens, the most fanatical of the Radicals. Blaine tried
to soften it with a proviso that any Southern state could come out
from under military rule by ratifying the 14th Amendment and
allowing blacks to vote. A compromise version became part of the
final bill, vetoed by Johnson but overridden by both bodies.

In such actions, Blaine showed the instincts of a true politician—a feel for compromise. This talent brought him far, along
with his intelligence, his affability, his writing skills and penchant
for hard work. From the rough and tumble of Congress's clash with
Andrew Johnson over Reconstruction, James Gillespie Blaine
went on to the most illustrious, if controversial, national career of
any Maine public figure up to that time.

Focus

Blaine

Blaine!—the very sound of his surname
provided rhythm for a bit of political
doggerel, chanted publicly like an adult
nursery rhyme:

> Blaine, Blaine—James G. Blaine,
> The Continental Liar from the State
> of Maine.

What was the flaw in this brilliant
man's character? Throughout his career,
he was dogged by distrust, and accusations of dishonesty.

A less than admiring biographer[3]
provided the following perception:

> All his natural instinctive inclinings
> were for the society of the rich. His
> sympathies were with them, he
> snuggled close to them...It was
> impossible for him to conceive that a
> rich man could do wrong.

A sense of mystery always surrounded his affluence—wealth that gave
him his "mansion" in Augusta opposite
the State House and a summer home in
Bar Harbor called "Stanwood" from his
wife's family name. The Credit Mobilier
scandal of 1872 lifted a tantalizing corner
on Blaine's involvement with big business and, as was to happen several times,
ended in a sort of ambiguous vindication
of the man. That year, there was a deep
split in the national Republican Party; a
"Liberal" faction was running Horace
Greeley for President against incumbent
Ulysses S. Grant and the New York Sun,
supporting Greeley, broke a story of
"colossal bribery" in Congress. Various
Congressmen and Senators, according to
the testimony of the ringleader, Congressman Oakes Ames of Massachusetts,
had been given Credit Mobilier shares in
exchange for favorable votes that en-
riched its parent company, the Union
Pacific Railroad. At the head of the list
was Speaker James G. Blaine, who

225

allegedly had received 3,000 shares.

Blaine hotly denied the accusation. He temporarily stepped down as Speaker and had an investigating committee appointed. Then another newspaper expose, claiming he had received nearly $2 million in stock in a division of the Union Pacific allowed him to strike back with ridicule. He pointed out that this supposed transaction had taken place before he had been elected to Congress. "I had no more to do with that congressional legislation than the fish wardens and tide-waters on the Kennebec River," he declared. It was next discovered that the holder of the stock in question, was a J.E. Blaine, Blaine's brother John, who had $10,000 worth. Blaine made fun of the accusation he was hiding his assets behind his brother's name by citing a passage from an old play:

"Does your brother like cheese?"

"I have no brother."

"If you had a brother, would he like cheese?"

In such glib fashion did Blaine exonerate himself and he also got Oakes Ames to refute the Credit Mobilier accusation.

Yet the taint never totally receded and four years later, when Blaine seemed inexorably headed for the Republican Presidential nomination, a far more serious scandal broke around him. Once more it involved a railroad, this time the Little Rock and Fort Smith Line in Arkansas.

The sensationalism beloved of tabloids focused on an item headlined as "The Mulligan Letters". James Mulligan was the clerk for an obscure stockbroker in Boston and had once worked for Jacob Stanwood, Blaine's brother-in-law. Blaine had just convinced a Democrat-dominated Congressional Committee he

James G. Blaine

had never used $64,000 of Little Rock and Forth Smith bonds as collateral for a Union Pacific loan he had never had to pay back when the startling news was revealed that James Mulligan had letters from Blaine, himself, to prove he was lying.

Summoned to Washington, Mulligan appeared before the Committee and on his first day of testimony, gave only verbal and inconclusive evidence. The letters were not yet produced.

226

When they saw the light of day, it was in the most sensational manner. While Mulligan was at his hotel in Washington, he was accosted in person by Blaine, who asked for his letters back. There are two versions. Mulligan claimed Blaine threatened suicide so he took pity on him and returned the letters. Blaine's side of it was that he asked to examine the letters, then coolly pocketed them since they were his private property.

The latter theme was Blaine's defense for not immediately handing over the letters to the Committee. His legal counsel, he said, advised him that the Committee had no more right to examine his personal correspondence than it did to influence the education of his children. The matter might have rested there had it not been for political considerations.

The Republican Convention was only about two weeks away. Blaine's implacable enemy in the G.O.P., Senator Roscoe Conkling of New York, was taking advantage of the scandal to consolidate votes against the Mainer. Learning that he was losing ground, Blaine decided on a bold stroke.

He appeared before the Committee with the Mulligan Letters in hand and read them aloud while a large, sympathetic audience cheered as it became apparent they contained nothing incriminating. Then, Blaine created something like pandemonium when he charged that the Chairman of the committee, Proctor Knott of Kentucky, had suppressed a telegram from a former official of the Little Rock and Fort Smith, totally exonerating him. When Knott admitted receiving the telegram, the crowded chamber went wild.

The date was June 5, 1876. Several days later, the Committee, recovering from Blaine's theatrics, began to dig a little deeper. Then, there was another coup, perhaps staged, perhaps not. Walking to church on a hot, muggy Sunday, Blaine collapsed. For a full day, he lay in a coma. As the Republicans gathered in Cincinnati for their convention, word was sent that Blaine was recovering. The New York *Sun* sardonically proclaimed, "BLAINE FEIGNS A FAINT."

The nominating speech for Blaine by Colonel Robert Ingersoll of Illinois was an oratorical triumph in its oblique reference to Blaine's masterful handling of the Mulligan Letters. "Like an armed warrior, like a plumed knight," Ingersoll declared, "James G. Blaine marched down the halls of the American Congress and threw his shining lance full and fair against the brazen foreheads of the defamers of his country and the maligners of his honor." Even afterward, James G. Blaine was the *Plumed Knight*.

But Conkling had done his work too well. Enough delegations had entered favorite sons so that Blaine, although clearly ahead, had no majority on the first ballot. His two main opponents were Senator Oliver Morton of Indiana and Secretary of the Treasury Benjamin Bristow of Kentucky. On the sixth ballot, Blaine was only 71 votes shy. Then, the bombshell burst. Morton and Bristow withdrew and the votes of their states, plus a New York-Pennsylvania alliance arranged by Conkling, went to the dark-horse candidate who'd been quietly making progress—Governor Rutherford B. Hayes of Ohio. When the seventh ballot ended, Hayes had the nomination by five votes.

The ever-so-close election of 1876, as is well known, was a crucial turning point in American history. Because Hayes needed the electoral votes of

227

three Southern states where the results were in dispute—South Carolina, Florida and Louisiana—an unwritten agreement was concluded with Southern leaders whereby Reconstruction effectively came to a halt. The Southern blacks were, to all extents and purposes, abandoned and America delivered over to a possibly far more dire Civil Rights struggle than would have ensued. Had Blaine been President, things might have been different since he clearly opposed the "Great Swap" that left Southern Republicans in the lurch.

Blaine's career, of course, did not end with his failure to win the 1876 nomination. Eight years later, he *was* the G.O.P. standard bearer and lost in another close Presidential election. Meanwhile, on the state level, he became involved in yet another disputed election that was one of the most tumultuous events in the whole history of Maine—a partisan quarrel so rancorous that it almost led to civil war!

The Great Count-Out or "The State Steal"

The Presidential election of 1876 held a warning for Maine Republicans that was not seriously heeded: Hayes' plurality in one of the most Republican states was shaved to 17,500, whereas U.S. Grant had triumphed by 28,000 and 32,000 votes previously. Disappointment that local hero Blaine hadn't gotten the G.O.P. nod was no doubt seen as a major cause. But in hindsight, some saw the reason as the "Greenbackers."

Forever associated with the Greenback movement in Maine was a long-faced, long-nosed Androscoggin County farmer by the name of Solon P. Chase. But a much less notorious Mainer from Kennebunk, Hugh McCulloch, also played a key role in the fierce *hard money-soft money* controversy that erupted after the Civil War. McCulloch, the successor to William Pitt Fessenden as U.S. Secretary of the Treasury, was a quintessential hard money man. His goal was immediate reduction of the $450 million in unbacked paper money issued to finance the Civil War and a return to specie payments, i.e., money backed by gold. Opposing McCulloch were soft-money advocates like Chase, wanting inflation so they could pay off their debts more cheaply. After the financial panic of 1873, various groups, particularly farmers, were hard-pressed. Grant's veto of an Inflation Bill set the stage for the creation of a nation-wide Greenback Party.

In the 1876 election, their candidate for President garnered a mere 81,737 votes. In Maine, the Greenbackers gubernatorial candidate won a laughable 520 votes. But "Uncle" Solon Chase

was hard at work; he'd been to Indianapolis in 1876 to help
organize the Greenback Party and now began to traverse Maine in
an oxcart pulled by a pair of steers. His reference to "them steers"[4]
became a political by-word as he explained how hard money was
robbing him of the value of the animals (he could now only get
half the price he'd paid for them.)

The 1878 election found Chase on the ballot against a strong
Republican Congressman, William Frye, and almost beating him.
More startling still, the Greenbackers did elect two of the five
Maine Congressmen. And most astounding—unheard of—was
that the Republican Governor, Selden Connor, was denied a
majority due to the 41,371 votes given to the Greenback candidate. By Maine law, the election went into the Legislature and lo
and behold, the Legislature of 1878 was not under Republican
control! Democrats and Greenbackers dominated the House,

"Uncle" Solon Chase and
"Them Steers"

229

which sent only the names of a Democrat and Greenbacker to the Republican Senate. For them, the Democrat was the lesser of two evils. Thus, Alonzo Garcelon of Lewiston became the Democratic Governor of Maine, the first since before the Civil war, in a state "where for 24 years, a Democrat had been looked upon as a natural curiosity or a perverted criminal."

Greenbackers and Democrats also collaborated on choosing the Constitutional Officers and the Executive Council. This "Fusionist" effort continued during the next election.

That election—in 1879—was nasty, possibly corrupt and again hotly contested. The Republican candidate for Governor, Daniel Davis, whom the Fusionists dubbed "Diarrhea Davis," intimating he'd faked an illness to escape combat while a corporal in the Union Army, did not receive a majority. The Greenback candidate—who came in second—was Joseph Smith and the G.O.P. labelled him "the Shylock of Old Town," emphasizing his wealth, which they claimed he'd built up by lending money at usurious rates. Democrat Governor Garcelon escaped much of the mudslinging, but hadn't been expected to do well this time around.

Once more, the key was control of the Legislature. At first, it looked like the Republicans had a solid majority there.

But the Fusionists soon began to cry foul, insisting the G.O.P. had bought many of their votes. James G. Blaine, still Republican State chairman even after he'd gone to Washington, stated the Party had only spent $8,000. Opposition newspapers ran a story that Blaine's son Emmons admitted spending $30,000; one estimate was as high as $150,000.

A letter of Blaine's, which he later denied writing, was suggestive:

See every man in your district, and find out how he is going to vote. If he is a Republican and weak-kneed, see what will strengthen him. If he is a Democrat or a Greenbacker, see what will induce him to vote with us. Make up a statement of what you will need for expenses, and forward at once.

Intimidation was also charged. Businessmen ordered their employees to vote Republican or be fired. Fusionists had indictments against them dropped if they switched. A U.S. Pension agent threatened to withhold Civil War pension payments. This was an era when voters publicly had to take the ballot of a party,

230

so it was easy to know how they voted.

The Fusionists played hard ball, too. Their prime instrument was the Governor and Council, who, under law, had to certify the winners of all legislative races. Here were opportunities for untold mischief.

For example, when voters in a Penobscot County district marked their ballots for Francis W. Hill of Exeter in one town and F.W. Hill in another, it was counted as votes for two different men, and Republican Hill was "counted out" and an election certificate given his Fusionist opponent (who happened to be his own brother).

At least 37 apparent Republican victors lost their seats because of such spurious tactics, masterminded by a clever veteran politico, and ex-Copperhead from Franklin County, named Eben F. Pillsbury.

These 37 seats denied the Republicans what had seemed to be a G.O.P. majority of 29 seats in the House and 7 in the Senate. The crisis brought Blaine back from Washington in mid-November 1879. On November 17, he led a large crowd of Republicans into the State House to confront the Governor and Council. The "Plumed Knight" dramatically demanded the returns be opened to public inspection.

Unawed, Garcelon and his Council refused. "The Council decided...that no mob should wrest from them the sacred trusts

Scene from the "Great Count-Out"

231

committed by the people," one councillor pompously put it and heaped scorn on the "ex-Governors, editors, pothouse politicians... filling the ante-room, stairways and corridors..."

For the next month, the Republicans resorted to petitions, plus dozens of lawyers who represented the "counted-out" candidates.

On December 16, the Governor and council issued House certificates of election to 78 Fusionists and 61 Republicans, leaving 12 seats vacant. Senate certificates went to 20 Fusionists and 11 Republicans.

The new Legislature was set to assemble on January 6. Tempers were rising statewide. Blaine organized "indignation meet-ings." A Greenback Councillor in York was threatened with tar and feather-ing by the local G.O.P. chairman while another one in Rockland was ordered out of a store. Hannibal Hamlin, now over 70, threat-ened the opposition with physical punishment and a national Democratic newspaper editorialized that "if Mr. Blaine resists Governor Garcelon openly and with arms and takes life with those arms, it will be right and proper to shoot Mr. Blaine."

Rumors were rife that Blaine was plotting to use armed force, so Garcelon ordered the State Militia Arsenal at Bangor to dispatch arms and ammunition to Augusta. Christmas morning, two wagon-loads of weapons left. But they were stopped by a mob and had to be sent back.

Five days later, the Governor did succeed in having the weapons shipped. The State House was turned into what the Republicans sarcastically called "Fort Garcelon," where at night 75 members of a Fusionist para-military force guarded every window and door. This ad-hoc army had been assembled by Garcelon because he didn't trust the State Militia. Technically, the Militia's commanding officer was ex-Governor Joshua Chamberlain, now the President of Bowdoin, although he'd never been sworn in. Garcelon and Chamberlain were on good terms, despite the latter's Republican affiliation, and when the Governor asked the war hero to intervene, he finally took a leave of absence from his college. The deadline of January 7 was fast approaching. Chamberlain made arrangements with Western Union and various railroads to mobi-lize his troops if necessary. Chamberlain was concerned by contin-ual rumors of intentions "to fight the matter out by force and settle the question by mob law." The man who had held the line at Little Round Top was now besieged by politicians on both sides. He told Thomas Hyde, future founder of the Bath Iron Works and pur-ported leader of a Republican assault on the capitol, "Tom, you are

232

as dear to me as my own son (Hyde had been one of his officers.) But I will permit you to do nothing of the kind. I am going to preserve the peace...I want you and Mr. Blaine and the others to keep away from the building."

The G.O.P. offered Chamberlain a U.S. Senate seat, but he wouldn't budge.

Next, the ever-active Republicans simply carried off a bloodless *coup d'etat*. At 5:30 P.M. on January 12, a large group of their supporters quietly took physical possession of the two legislative chambers in the State House The Fusionists appealed to Chamberlain to eject them. He responded that his sole responsibility was to keep those chambers open to members.

A crowd of angry Fusionists gathered outside the State House did not like his explanation. The General's life was threatened. Chamberlain calmly unbuttoned his coat and told the armed men

Joshua Chamberlain at the time of the "Great Count-Out"

233

among them to go ahead and shoot. A man in the crowd shouted, "By God, the first man who lifts a hand against you, General, is a dead one." And the tension was broken.

Yet in the following days, as more partisans flocked to Augusta, the atmosphere grew ugly. Chamberlain ordered a regiment to assemble at the Gardiner Armory on January 16. That same day, the State Supreme Court declared the Republicans had legally organized the Legislature. The Fusionists replied by electing the Greenbacker Joseph Smith as Governor and "Governor" Smith then tried to dismiss Chamberlain and some Fusionists even tried to arrest him for "treason." Both actions were ignored.

The next day was a Saturday when the State House normally is empty. This day, it had *two* Legislatures meeting in it. The Republicans went ahead and elected Daniel Davis and his Council. They presented the results to Chamberlain and he announced he felt his special mission had concluded.

When Daniel Davis arrived that Saturday night, he found the Governor's office locked and it had to be pried open with a jackknife. The Secretary of State's office was also locked; moreover, the Fusionist Secretary of State, Prince A. Sawyer, had made off with the official State Seal.

Monday morning, when "Governor" Smith and the Fusionist legislators appeared at the State House, they were barred by armed Augusta police.

The shut-out government held a rump session outside the building. They voted to adjourn and meet the next day at a rented dance hall. Worried the Fusionists were organizing to take back the State House by force, Davis called up the Militia. Soldiers encamped in the capitol. At the main entrance, they posted a Gatling Gun.

This final image of a primitive machine gun on the State House steps was intimidating enough to quell any further thoughts of rebellion. A week later, the Gatling Gun was back in storage at the Lewiston Armory. For better or worse, Maine had a functioning government.

Focus

Blaine (continued) and other G.O.P. Notables

In the hyperbolic imagery beloved of the late 19th. century, Lewiston's William P. Frye extolled the role of James G. Blaine in the "count-out."

> The grand old ship, 'The State of Maine,' had just encountered such a tempest...A true man was at the helm...Calm, he restrained the impetuous, and brought the imperilled ship, with her precious cargo, into the port of safety...That man, too, was a hero and his name is James G. Blaine.

Frye, who was to enter the U.S. Senate two years after the "month of madness" in Augusta, was one of the Maine Republicans who played a prominent role on the national stage during the latter part of the 19th century. Another was Nelson Dingley, Jr., also of Lewiston, whose name graces a tariff famous in the annals of American economics. Still another was Senator Eugene Hale of Ellsworth, frequently teamed with Frye, and both having strong ties to Blaine. Hale and Frye acted as co-counsels for the Plumed Knight during the Mulligan Letters affair. They were also linked by critics like the muckraker David Graham Phillips in his scathing book, "The Treason of the Senate." His jaundiced view contains remarks like:

> Thus Hale and Frye have their Senatorial seats from Legislatures ruled by 'the interests' and would lose those seats if they developed however shadowy symptoms of 'demagoguery'...

Neither Hale nor Frye is in the Senate for the people. In the vital matter, the people *versus* the confiscators of their property, Hale sits for his millions well invested with the 'interests' and Frye for his dear friends in politics and social life...

According to Phillips, Theodore Roosevelt called Hale:

> ...the Senator from the shipbuilding trust...the most innately and essentially malevolent scoundrel that God Almighty ever put on earth...

Nor does Phillips spare another Maine giant of that age in Washington, Thomas Brackett Reed, who, like Blaine, became Speaker of the U.S. House—conceivably its most famous Speaker ever.

> ...he (Reed) is corporation every time...there isn't a man in the U.S. whose election would be so dangerous to the labor cause...

Despite such criticisms, Maine's star did shine brightly on the national scene. As the Maine Writers Research Club later boasted:

> It might well be said that from 1880 to 1889, Maine controlled the legislation of Congress and largely directed the destinies of the Republic...

In 1880, Blaine saw the Republican nomination go to his friend James Garfield after 35 convention ballots. The

235

new President made Blaine his Secretary of State. Then, on July 2, 1881, he was shot by a disappointed office seeker and died of his wound several months later. Blaine was with him in a State Department carriage when the assassin's bullet struck.

With Chester A. Arthur, a Conkling man, as President, Blaine resigned his post and spent the next three years writing a monumental if dry autobiographical treatise entitled "Twenty Years in Congress"—1,400 pages. In 1884, Blaine won the Republican Presidential nomination.

The campaign between Blaine and Grover Cleveland is one of the more famous in American history. Blaine's defeat was attributed to his loss of New York State by 1,040 votes, which, in turn, was traced to the public outcry over a reference to the Democrats by the Reverend Samuel Buschard as the party of "Rum, Romanism and Rebellion." The Catholics in New York, offended by Burchard's alliteration, which in hastily-printed handbills was blamed on Blaine, turned out en masse to vote against the G.O.P. standard bearer; ironically, Blaine, himself, was born of an Irish Catholic mother, but raised Protestant. Grumped one Republican afterward, "...the Lord sent us an ass in the shape of a preacher and a rainstorm to lessen our vote in New York."

Blaine served as Secretary of State once more, under President Benjamin Harrison. He made an abortive attempt to gain the G.O.P. Presidential nomination in 1892 and died the following year. His prime accomplishment as Secretary of State was to establish the first Pan-American Congress, held in 1889-90, out of which came the creation of the Pan-American Union. Today, we know it as

Thomas Brackett Reed

the Organization of American States.

Thomas Brackett Reed entered Congress when Blaine went to the Senate. Physically an imposing man, six foot two inches and almost three hundred pounds, he had an intellect to match. His articulate, spontaneous and often cutting wit was much feared. Historians still record his aphorisms.

Such as:

A statesman is a politician who is dead.

All the wisdom in the world consists of shouting with the majority.

When a particularly pompous Democrat Congressman declared, "Mr. Speaker, I would rather be right than President," Reed shot back, "The Gentleman need not worry. He will never be either."

After putting down on obstreperous

236

member with similar sarcasm, Reed declared, "having embedded that fly in the liquid amber of my remarks, I will proceed."

Reed's rise to the Speakership took a number of years. In December 1885, with the Democrats in control of the House, Reed was chosen by the Republicans to be their titular leader. William McKinley, the future President, nominated him. But in 1888, when the House went Republican, McKinley challenged Reed for the Speakership. The Mainer won on the second ballot.

Soon came the dramatic moment that made Reed's reputation. A pernicious parliamentary practice of those days was the "silent quorum" in which a minority could hold up the business of the House by simply refusing to answer to a roll call. On January 29, 1890, when the House assembled, the Democrats demanded a roll call to see if a quorum were present. Reed needed 166 votes for a quorum. But he had only 163 and the Democrats refused to answer to their names. Reed then announced, "The Chair directs the Clerk to record the names of the following members present and refusing to vote" and he proceeded to read off the names. The House erupted, the Democrats shrieking in protest, the Republicans wildly applauding. When Reed got to McCreary of Kentucky, this member jumped up and said, "I deny your right, Mr. Speaker, to count me as present." Reed paused until there was silence, then replied, "The Chair is making a statement of fact that the Gentleman is present. Does he deny it?" When he finished, Reed airily ruled "there is a quorum present within the meaning of the Constitution."

The constitutional argument was Reed's trump. His position was that the Constitution had intended a quorum to be based on those present, not on those voting. This ruling was challenged and for three stormy days, the House fought out the issue. Reed was called a "czar," a "tyrant" and other names but through it all, he remained steadfast and, above all, cool. In the end, he won his point and the Rules Committee brought out a set of rules, known ever since as Reed's Rules, that are still in use today.

When the Democrats took over the House two years afterward, they threw out Reed's reform, but had to reinstate it because, as minority leader, he deliberately used the silent quorum technique against them.

The author of the Rule had achieved national notoriety. He was mentioned as a possible Presidential candidate. Nor was he loath to run. But his sarcasm and rectitude in refusing to chase after campaign money hurt his chances. He quarrelled with President Benjamin Harrison, saying, "I had but two enemies in Maine and one of them Harrison pardoned out of the penitentiary and the other he appointed Collector of Portland." Back as Speaker in 1895, he actively sought the Presidency. His main rival was William McKinley whose adroit manager, Mark Hanna, rounded up delegates in the South and swamped Reed at the convention, despite his strong support from Teddy Roosevelt and Senator Henry Cabot Lodge.

Reed's friendship with Roosevelt was personal, not ideological. For on the question of American expansion overseas—"imperialism"—T.R. was the hawkest of hawks and Reed the dovest of doves. The speaker was an active member of the anti-Imperial League. On the question of annexing the Phillipines, he went out of his way to have himself re-

237

corded "opposed" when absent because of illness. Then, he went one step better. He resigned from Congress to express his disgust with McKinley's policies.

A contemporary called him "the ablest running debater the American people ever saw." Another proclaimed him, "the greatest parliamentary leader of

his time...far and away the most brilliant figure in American politics." Historian Barbara Tuchman characterized the illustrious G.O.P. Speaker from Portland as "uncompromising to the end, a lonely specimen of an uncommon kind, the Independent Man."

Some Opposing Views—the Democrats during the Republican Era

"The Plunderer"

Morgan Hale succeeded the last Captain James G. Blaine who converted the Ship of State into the Plunderer of that day. It was he who covered her hull with corporation planks... and shipped as his sailors the members of both the Republican and Democratic State Committees.

The above paragraph is from an obscure work of Maine fiction, published in 1907 by Dr. George Langtry Crockett of Thomaston and entitled, "The Plunderer, A Political Story of Maine, Exposing the Piratical System and Explaining the Remedy." Dr. Crockett describes himself as an "Ex-Member of the Democratic State Committee of Maine." The introduction is by none other than William Jennings Bryan who declares, "If I had Doctor Crockett's voice I could stand on my back porch in Nebraska and talk to the people of Maine, any time they desired to hear me."

The tone of Dr. Crockett's loud voice seems one of the perpetual and universal political indignation. It is full of the condemnatory language the frustrated Democrats of his day used against the entrenched Republican hierarchy: favoritism to special interests, high taxes, failure to enforce prohibition...A satirical question and answer scene in the novel emphasizes these points:

"Who's governor of Maine?' Answer: 'The State House Ring.'"

"What's the capitol of Maine?' Answer: 'Maine Central Railroad.'"

"What's the government of Maine?' Answer: 'Ring Rule.'"

"To what country does Maine belong?' Answer: 'The Trusts.'"

"What's the leading import of Maine?' Answer: 'Whiskey.'"

"What's the leading crop of Maine?' Answer: 'Moral Hypocrites.'"

But Crockett differs from the usual partisan muckraker by striking out at both sides. The prime villain of his book, in fact, is a Democrat, a "boss," William J. Morgan. Crockett's thesis is that Maine's sad condition derives from this Democratic leader's willingness to abet the Republican majority's control and live off the political crumbs thrown to him. In one scene, Crockett hammers his point home in discussing what Maine did with land received under the Federal Morrill Land Grant Act, an allotment of 310,000 acres for establishing a University of Maine.

"Where's the land, Mr. Packard?'" a young Democrat reformer is asked.

The reply: "'Most of the other states kept theirs, but Maine sold hers.'"

"'To whom?'"

"Packard truthfully answered: 'To the Plunderers of Maine, the state house Ring and their allies who are now leading the Democratic Party...'"

Whether apocryphal or not, this tale of what allegedly happened when the Orono campus was created is symptomatic of Crockett's theme of unabashed political boondogglery in Maine. He sardonically observes that "if Moosehead Lake were whiskey... and the proprietor received word a sheriff was en route to search the place, the lake would disappear." The Morgan Hale (note the combination of Democrat and Republican surnames[5]) who takes charge of the Republican machine at the end is finally pictured going down to defeat when more than two-thirds of a newly-elected Legislature are "men who believe in direct legislation and self-government for all political parties."

Crockett characteristically comments:

> It could not be called a Democratic victory for until that election the Democrat Party had been the ally of the trusts. It could not be called a Republican victory...It must be called a people's victory, for it resulted in constructive legislation.

Wishful thinking by a naive and disillusioned reform politico? More than likely, it was. For, in reality, the following years were filled with the most biting broadsides of political satire Maine has

239

known—William R. Pattangall's tongue-in-cheek classics—"The Meddybemps Letters" and "Maine's Hall of Fame."

Pattangall was an out-and-out Democrat and his vehicle was a newspaper he published in Waterville called the "Maine Democrat." Earlier, he had edited the "Machias Union," where "The Meddybemps Letters" was born, following in the tradition of Seba Smith. Indeed, *Smith* is the name of the fictional author of this wry correspondence—Stephen A. Douglas Smith.

Real political personages are involved in the hokey interviews that Pattangall has Smith, as correspondent for the "Machias Union" (and agent of the Chicago Plow Co.) conduct all around Maine. On a visit to Rockland, Smith even meets up with Dr. Crockett. William Jennings Bryan may not have been exaggerating the power of Crockett's voice, since the following excerpt from a Meddybemps letter dated December 10, 1904 plays on the tremendous timbre it must have had:

> The first thing I did was to hunt up Dr. Crockett.
> I heard him speak once.
> It was at Calais that he spoke, in City Hall.
> I drove in as far as Milltown, three miles away and listened.
> He made a first rate speech and the distance softened his voice
> a little so that it sounded real pleasant.

In joking further about the Doctor's booming speaking style, Smith touches on Crockett's ambition to be the next Democratic candidate for Governor. The comment is that Crockett could campaign like McKinley did in 1896, speaking from his own doorstep, but it wouldn't be necessary to run excursion trains to have people hear him. Everyone could just stay home and listen, although you might have to raise your window if your hearing was bad.

Pattangall then has Smith tell Crockett Meddybemps would go for him. "That seemed to satisfy him and it let me out easy," the interview ends.

Then, it's on to visit the local Knox County Republicans whose favorite son candidate is William T. Cobb, who did become Governor in 1904 after a bruising nomination fight with Bert M. Fernald.

The lost world and forgotten names of turn-of-the-century politics in Maine makes "The Meddybemps Letters" seem essentially dated today. And the "Hall of Fame," because it is more non-fictional, somehow stands up better

Here is Pattangall at his acid best, with some inspired bits of low key, downeast, dry wit:

> Colonel Hale (Frederick Hale) is neither a communist nor a socialist but, like William Randolph Hearst and a few other wealthy young reformers, he believes in uplifting the poor even to the extent of dividing a certain percentage of his own money with them on election day and when caucuses are held. He has not yet gone as far as Tolstoy, who divided his entire estate among the peasantry of his neighborhood, but he may do so between now and next fall...
>
> During his first winter at Augusta, Mr. Fernald (Bert M. Fernald, later Governor and U.S. Senator) was principally noted for his unfailing good nature and for his ability and willingness to sing. If anyone had told the members of the 1897 House that Bert Fernald was ever going to be governor they would have accepted the statement as a joke. If the same person had ventured the prophecy that he would someday lead a minstrel troupe, it would have been regarded as a fairly safe prediction.
>
> Senator Frye (U.S. Senator William P. Frye) never took a very prominent part in debates in Congress, notwithstanding his great ability as a speaker. Perhaps this was because they keep shorthand reporters there who take down what a man says and print it the next day in the Congressional Record. Some of those fancy mathematics of his would have looked funny in print.

Pattangall, himself, served in the Legislature and was elected Attorney General when the Democrats controlled n 1911 and 1915. He also ran unsuccessfully for Congress and Governor. His last years in public life saw him switch to the Republicans, but even before his conversion, a G.O.P. Governor had appointed him to the State Supreme Court. A few years later, another Republican Governor made him Chief Justice.

Pattangall had been born at the very end of the Civil War in the small Washington County town of Pembroke (not far from Meddybemps). As a boy, he shipped out on a square-rigger built at his family's shipyard in Pembroke. After his stint at sea, he worked in shoe factories in Massachusetts and New York. His life thus spanned an important transition period in the economy of the nation and the State of Maine. The political effect of the change

241

was one with which this intelligent, Washington County-bred writer-lawyer grappled all of his life, as the post Civil War period saw the dominant political party in his state—the Republicans—solidify their gains through association with the major industries that were emerging as powerful influences in Maine—the railroads, the public utilities and the paper companies.

CHAPTER Thirteen

Economic Maine— Some Examples

The Great Northern Paper Company

The epitome of Maine's paper industry can be found in the sprawling Great Northern Paper Company mills at Millinocket and East Millinocket. There were numerous paper mills in the state earlier, some quite large. but Great Northern became the real giant and remains so to this day.

In 1846, Henry David Thoreau wrote of the Penobscot County location:

> As we stood upon the pile of chips by the door, fish hawks were sailing overhead and here, over Shad Pond, might daily be witnessed the tyranny of the bald eagle over that bird. Tom pointed away over the lake to a bald eagle's nest, which was plainly visible more than a mile off...

This gloriously natural scene lay close by the West Branch of the Penobscot in Indian Township 3, along Millinocket Stream. The "Tom" Thoreau mentions was Thomas Fowler, the first settler. And for almost forty more years, the site remained in its sylvan simplicity, until events transformed it into a brand-new industrial complex.

As so often happens, one form of development spurred another. The completion of the Bangor and Aroostook's branch line from Old Town to Houlton in 1892 inspired a Bangor man, Charles Mullen, to envisage the possibility of a major paper mill nearby and he bought a number of lots in Indian Township 3. He also approached the manager of the Rumford Falls Paper Co., an enterprising New Jerseyan of Dutch origin, Garrett Schenck. By 1897, $1 million in capital had been raised, mostly from Bangor men, and then Schenck, through his contacts with publisher Joseph Pulitzer and prominent New York financiers, was able to raise the rest. In 1899, the Maine Legislature created the Great Northern Paper Co., Tom Fowler's old homestead on Millinocket Stream was acquired and the Bangor and Aroostook ran a spur to the site. A year later, there were 2,000 people in the area.

Interestingly enough, given the G.O.P. domination of Maine, most of the early financial backers were leading national Democrats, albeit wealthy ones. Colonel Oliver H. Payne, his brother-in-law William C. Whitney, Daniel Lamont and Pierpont Morgan all had close ties to Grover Cleveland. Their interest originally had been in a Madison, Maine paper company and was extended through Schenck to Great Northern.

An unusual facet of the project was its introduction of foreign-born laborers to northern Maine on a large scale. Under their generic term of "Polacks" were lumped Poles, Finns, Hungarians, Latvians, Lithuanians, Estonians, Czechs, etc., but the most prominent ethnics here were the Italians. Some had already done railroad work in Washington County. They lived in a jerry-built community of shacks that sprang up overnight and inevitably became known as "Little Italy." The labor contractors, the *padrones*, kept them more or less in thrall, taking part of their pay and selling them provisions. Notable was Ferdinando Peluso— "Fred" Peluso—who set up a store on the east side of Millinocket Stream and, in the best American tradition, became a bank director and active in the Chamber of Commerce.

A contemporary who described the scene, the rough huts chinked with mud and grass, the sound of Italian music played on a harmonica, the smells of exotic cooking, expressed amazement at yet another feature alien to Maine. "There is not a saloon in the place," he said.

If he had stayed long enough, once Fred Peluso and others began making wine, he would have understood the popularity of nocturnal visits to "Little Italy," and the fights and knifings that occasionally took place.

But raw Millinocket was hardly the wild west. On March 16, 1901, it became the State of Maine's 467th town. George W. Stearns, an ex-school teacher from Rumford who'd come with

244

Schenck to be the company's land agent, headed up the initial group of Selectmen. Churches were established and, in a reverse of the usual Maine pattern, the Catholic church came first, followed by various Protestant denominations.

Within record time, the largest newsprint mill in the United States had been built. Owning thousands of acres, contracting with hundreds of loggers, employing a large work force, the economic influence of this huge paper company became enormous. Put together with other major companies in the paper field,[1] such dollar power was also translated into political power. Therefore, it could be said about Maine, as one observer from "away" did, that he'd seen company towns before but never until now a "company state."

The Central Maine Power Company

During a 1910 debate in the Maine Senate, a Senator Kellogg of Penobscot was eloquent in his opposition to "An Act to Amend the Charter of the Messalonskee Electric Company, Now called The Central Maine Power Company." He referred to the company as an "Octopus," swallowing other companies at Clinton, Dexter,

Paper machine at Great Northern Paper Company

MILLINOCKET, ME.   PAPER MACHINE ROOM IN GREAT NORTHERN PAPER CO'S MILL.
FINISHED PAPER 152 INCHES WIDE, REELED OFF 500 FT. PER MINUTE.

Skowhegan, Solon, Vassalboro, etc., and he tried to hold the bill over to the next session by which time, he averred, the state might have a Public Utilities Commission. Then, as if to underscore the political power of this particular lighting company, Kellogg reversed himself that very same afternoon.

This was an era when power companies were cropping up in Maine like mushrooms after a rain. Electricity, itself, was still fairly new. The first power plant in the United States, Thomas E. Edison's Pearl Street Station in New York City, had begun its operations only in 1882. The genesis of what was to become Maine's foremost power company occurred in 1899 when a young Oakland native, Walter Wyman, bought the Oakland Electric Company for $4,500. It served just Oakland and Belgrade. Expansion began two years later with a contract from Waterville for street lighting and

Walter Wyman

the building of a hydro station at the head of Messalonskee Stream.
In 1910, the name Central Maine Power Company came into
being. The Kennebec Light and Heat Company was acquired next,
a steam plant was built in Farmingdale and the cities of Augusta,
Gardiner and Hallowell were added to Wyman's empire. True to
Kellogg's prediction, companies in the towns he'd cited were also
gobbled up.

Described as a man of "foresight, ambition and daring,"
Walter Wyman was to see the full blossoming of CMP in the early
1920's as it spread into Lincoln, Oxford and Androscoggin Counties. A culminating acquisition came in 1942, with the takeover of
the Cumberland Power and Light Company—14 merged companies covered Cumberland and York Counties.

Along the way, the canny Wyman brought his company under
the financial umbrella of a Chicago-based holding company belonging to Samuel Insull, an Englishman who had started his American
career as Edison's private secretary. Then, just as adroitly, Wyman
maneuvered CMP out of danger when Insull's overextended structure collapsed in the 1930's. Wyman bought manufacturing plants
in Maine, so he could sell them electricity, enticed others here and

*Central Maine Power
Company dam at
Azicohos Lake*

gained a reputation for himself and his firm as a powerhouse in Republican politics. An admiring if sycophantic Portland newspaper called him "Maine's greatest builder." His *Octopus* remains the state's largest and richest power company today.

The Maine Central Railroad

Railroads preceded paper companies and power companies as an industrial economic entity in Maine. The Maine Central, eventually encompassing some 50 lines, was chartered in 1856 and organized in 1862. The first annual report, issued by President William Goodenow on June 16, 1863, spoke of a road that ran from Danville Junction (near Auburn) to Bangor, "a fraction less than one hundred and ten miles in length." He was pleased to inform the stockholders the trains had run "with regularity and without injury to anyone."

The new railroad combined two earlier roads, the Androscoggin and Kennebec and the Penobscot and Kennebec. Both used what is known as "wide gauge"—a width of 5 feet 6 inches for their tracks, as opposed to the "standard gauge" of 4 feet 8$^{1/2}$ inches.[2] A *war of gauges* followed with several rival lines, chief among them the Kennebec and Portland. This fierce rivalry no doubt underlay Goodenow's understated remarks in his report that it was unnecessary to relate the obstacles to the Maine Central's creation by "adverse interests in the Legislature." However, the railroad learned its political lessons well for soon among its presidents were two ex-Governors, Anson P. Morrill and Abner Coburn.

In 1870, after a protracted battle, the rival Kennebec and Portland was leased to the Maine Central, which bought it four years later. Another road out of Portland, running to the west, the Portland and Ogdensburg, was likewise leased to the Maine Central. This line was famed for its engineering feat of having cut through the White Mountains at Crawford Notch; originally slated to run from Portland to the Great Lakes, it had reached no farther than St. Johnsbury, Vermont.

John A. Poor's European and North American Railway, completed to Vanceboro on the New Brunswick border in 1871, was yet another acquisition. The ceremonies celebrating this link to Canada drew the President of the United States, Ulysses S. Grant. In 1882, the Maine portion was leased to the Maine Central. It was the site of a little known near-international incident during

248

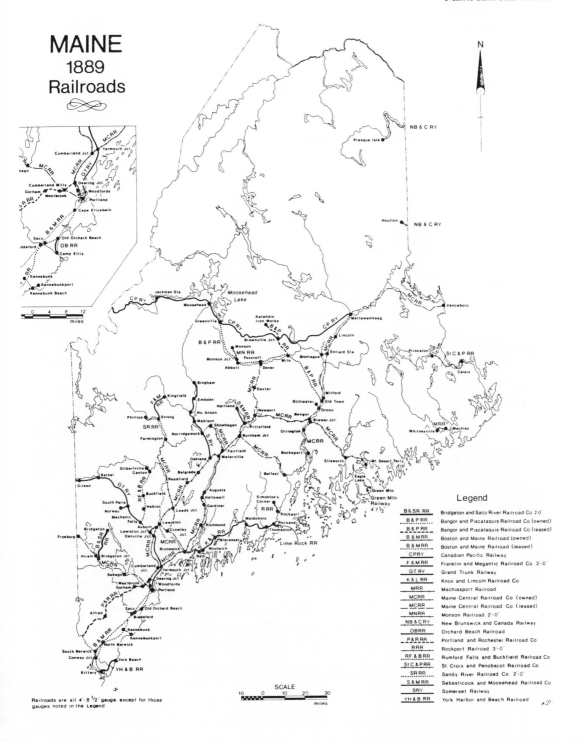

Maine Railroads in 1889

MAINE
1889
Railroads

Legend

B & SR RR	Bridgeton and Saco River Railroad Co 2'0"
B & P RR	Bangor and Piscataquis Railroad Co (owned)
B & P RR	Bangor and Piscataquis Railroad Co (leased)
B & M RR	Boston and Maine Railroad (owned)
B & M RR	Boston and Maine Railroad (leased)
CP RY	Canadian Pacific Railway
F & M RR	Franklin and Megantic Railroad Co 2'-0"
GT RY	Grand Trunk Railway
K & L RR	Knox and Lincoln Railroad Co
MRR	Machiasport Railroad
MCRR	Maine Central Railroad Co (owned)
MCRR	Maine Central Railroad Co (leased)
MN RR	Monson Railroad 2'-0"
NB & C RY	New Brunswick and Canada Railway
OBRR	Orchard Beach Railroad
P & R RR	Portland and Rochester Railroad Co
RRR	Rockport Railroad 3'-0"
RF & B RR	Rumford Falls and Buckfield Railroad Co
StC & P RR	St. Croix and Penobscot Railroad Co
SR RR	Sandy River Railroad Co 2'-0"
S & M RR	Sebasticook and Moosehead Railroad Co
SRY	Somerset Railway
YH & B RR	York Harbor and Beach Railroad

Railroads are all 4'-8½" gauge, except for those gauges noted in the Legend

SCALE

the early years of World War I when the U.S., in violation of its
neutrality, allowed Canada to transport its troops through Maine.
Since German protests were ignored, a lieutenant in the Kaiser's
army was sent over and, in full uniform so he wouldn't be treated
as a spy, he placed a dynamite charge under the Vanceboro Bridge.
Luckily, before he could touch it off, he was arrested by the Sheriff
of Washington County.

Another Maine Central acquisition was the creation of Hugh
J. Chisholm, the industrialist who organized International Paper.
His Portland and Rumford Falls Railway Company was supposed to
have gone to Quebec but never got farther than the Rangeley
Lakes.

Maine's tourist business, such as that to the Rangeley Lakes,
was developing rapidly around the turn of the century. Most
people went to the big summer resorts by train and the Maine
Central not only transported guests, it also managed the facilities.
Some of the most famous were the Mount Kineo House on Moosehead Lake and the Samoset Hotel at Rockland.

Steamships and ferry boats, owned by the Maine Central, also
carried passengers to the most renowned of all Maine summer
resorts—Bar Harbor on Mount Desert Island.

Mount Kineo Resort

Mt. KINEO HOUSE

Tourism Develops—The Two Types

Eden, Maine sounds like a town in one of today's new-fangled novels of *real* down east life. But until 1887, it was a genuine Hancock County community. Then, the townspeople elected to exchange their name for one seemingly more prosaic, yet now emblematic of high-toned holiday retreats—Bar Harbor!

Popularized by James G. Blaine, visited by Presidents, summer home to millionaire socialites, Bar Harbor and the island on which it sits has since turned into a mecca for all tourists visiting Maine. Millions annually swarm to Acadia National Park. And the bi-polar nature of Maine's tourism—the exclusive and the popular—amply illustrated here—is reflected up and down the coast, where the *Vacationland* heralded on the state's license plates, in effect, had its origin.

An interesting community for studying the evolution of tourism in Maine is the ancient town of York. The local economy had declined precipitously by the year 1857 when it could be said that the first tourist, a summer boarder, appeared. Gone was the shipping industry that had made York prosperous before Jefferson's Embargo. Lumbering wasn't possible, nor was papermaking, and the water power necessary for the textiles that developed elsewhere in York County wasn't available. A somewhat agricultural backland and a desultory fishing industry were all that was left in 1871 when the first major hotel was built. This was the Marshall House, the work of a transplanted Englishman named Nathaniel Grant Marshall. The site, picturesque "Stage Neck," where executions once were held, had been a local slum ever since refugees from the Isles of Shoals had been resettled there during the American Revolution. Marshall, in an early form of urban renewal, uprooted their descendants and created an exclusive resort, York Harbor, that mirrored Bar Harbor, albeit on a minor scale.

Then, cheek by jowl with tiny York Harbor, plebeian York Beach was created—a Coney Islandish amusement center whose initial attraction was a "Marine Car," a wagon-like device that ran on rails out into the ocean. It was followed by St. Aspinquid Park, which contained a casino, restaurant, menagerie, walks, carriage drives and rustic arbors. Even today, York Beach has a zoo and Luna Park-like rides and carnival booths.

To York Harbor came celebrities such as John Jacob Astor, President Charles W. Eliot of Harvard, General Charles Devens,

251

Alice Longfellow, the poet's daughter, and the ubiquitous James G. Blaine. Literary types like Finley Peter Dunne, the Chicago political humorist who created the character "Mr. Dooley" and Thomas Nelson Page, diplomat, friend of Woodrow Wilson and Southern novelist, helped form the York Harbor Reading Room, modelled on the Bar Harbor Reading Room, an elitist retreat for gentlemen professing literary interests but actually a masculine refuge wherein to tell good stories and quietly defy Maine's prohibition laws.

To York Beach, on the other hand, came the masses, to be amused and to bathe on a stretch of magnificent open beach. When their camping area threatened to spill over into York Harbor, the Reading Room stalwarts rushed onto the books Maine's first zoning law.

That consummate snob, Kenneth Roberts, writing about the event afterward, declared York Harbor "was in danger of being almost completely swamped by young ladies in shorts, young men in soiled undershirts and fat ladies in knickerbockers," but thanks to the "wise men who founded and maintained the York Harbor Reading Room, York Harbor will always be one of Maine's outstanding resorts and proudest possessions..."

To a large extent, the division between these two summer communities within a larger community still exists. Ironically, the current major public thrust being resisted is no longer the democratization but the gentrification of York Beach, which, beneath a somewhat honky-tonk exterior, contains many architectural jewels from the period when it was developed.

Tourism—Maine's second largest industry (after paper) and fastest growing—spread rapidly from these small beginnings in the guest houses, summer cottages and pioneering hotels along the coast in the decades that followed the Civil War. It was aided by steamships and especially by the railroads that were reaching into every corner of the state. Maine entered the American consciousness as a place to relax, to commune with nature, to hunt and fish, and to rediscover simple values.

Two Traditional 'Industries'—Lobsters and Potatoes

"Vacationland" is no longer the sole distinguishing trademark on the Maine license plate. Thanks to a group of schoolchildren from

Saco, the Legislature was persuaded to embellish it with the animal symbol most identified with the state—the lobster. While some grumped that the logo should have been a potato or a pine tree or a moose—the lobster was voted in—bright red and looking, to the jaundiced eye of one critic, like a "boiled cockroach."

The emblem on the license plate does admittedly seem undersized. But lobsters and Maine are synonymous in this day and age, and all the more so as the crustaceans become scarcer and more expensive. The lobster landings for Maine unmistakably are the most valuable part of the seafood haul, worth almost twice as much as the rest of the catch put together. Yet dollars and cents aren't really the main issue—all of Maine's marine products are minor compared to the economic weight of paper or tourism or textiles or agriculture; the lobster "industry" is an image thing—it conjures a distillation of the Maine essence: picturesque scenery, rugged individualism, humans against the elements and a sense of tastiness, a distinctive flavor.

Huge lobsters four feet long—maybe even five or six feet—greeted the colonial settlers and normal crustaceans were so plentiful that they littered the beaches after a storm and had to be pitchforked off for fertilizer. Even by the late 1820's, when a small fishery had started, they were still being used as bait for cod. In 1828, one of the first conservation measures was passed in Maine; it forbade out-of-state "smacks", or sailing vessels with holding tanks from picking up local lobsters unless they had a permit.

Early lobstering scenes

253

Those permits, by the way, could be sold by towns, like the one
Harpswell sold to a Connecticut captain for $100 in 1835.

Lobstering then was seasonal work, augmenting farming, done
in contraptions that resembled eel pots. The first lath traps were
set in Casco Bay around 1830. Systematic records of the catch
weren't kept until 1880 when 1,843 lobstermen set 104,500 traps
from 1,800 boats and landed 14 million pounds.

In 1885, the use of color-coded wooden buoys came into fashion and also a law prescribing penalties for interfering with a person's gear. Even earlier, there were laws passed to prevent the
taking of females with eggs and establishing closed seasons. The
peak of the Maine catch may have been reached in 1889, with 25
million pounds.

Early lobstering scenes

A hundred years later, lobsters were still being caught—a total estimated at more than 90% each year of the available stock. Concern for the future of the fishery has spawned endless debates over proposed legislation—limiting the number of traps, increasing the minimum size, doing away with the maximum size limit imposed during the Depression on oversized lobsters, raising license fees, trying to freeze out part-timers,—a perennial host of arguments that have become as traditional as the business of lobstering, itself.

Will the lobster fishery remain? Despite the lobsterman's habitual pessimism, it probably will, a small portion of Maine's economy that looms in the national consciousness as the one major product people can always associate with Maine, alone.

Maine potatoes, on the other hand, have rivals. Idaho has staked out the same territory, and so have Michigan and California. It is not well know, but the potato is not even the most valuable agricultural crop in Maine. That honor belongs to the brown egg.

However, Maine's history as a potato producing state *has* ingrained the notion of Maine potatoes in the American mind. It is estimated that the tuber has been in Maine since the 1750's, brought by the Scots-Irish. They can be, are, grown everywhere in the state, but their prime identification is with Aroostook County, where 90% of the commercial crop is raised. Supposedly, Joseph Houlton planted the first spuds in the "County" in 1807.

By the start of the Civil War, Maine was growing 6.4 million bushels. The Penobscot River valley was initially the leading producer with Aroostook catching up fast as trees were felled for shingle-making. Rising demand from the budding Maine textile industry for potato starch and even more so the extension of the railroads led to a potato boom in the far north. In 1890, Aroostook had 28,000 acres under cultivation, producing 5 million bushels, and 42 starch factories at work.

Farm machinery came slowly. As one Aroostook planter put it:

Our machine for digging potatoes is the Madawaska Frenchman and his wife and children. And when they will dig, sort and put potatoes at 10¢ a bushel, we calculate that is cheap enough...My potatoes were all dug by one man and three children...the oldest seven years old and the others coming along in order.

But after 1890, the *Hoover digger*, a horse-drawn, traction drive

rig was introduced and tractors appeared following World War I.

Maine still supplies some 15% of the U.S. potato crop—about 60 million bushels. It is a risky business, subject not only to he vagaries of weather and insect but especially to the roller-coaster variations in the price paid per barrel. Aroostook potato farmers are often described as "gamblers." When prices on the mercantile are good, they can drive Cadillacs; when prices drop, they go back into debt. The fixation with potatoes in this rolling country bordering Canada was aptly summed up a few years ago by a Fort Fairfield farmer:

Potato field in Aroostook County

> We eat potatoes, work potatoes, thrive, flourish and starve on 'em.

The Mills

Certain Maine communities are *milltowns*, or once were, their most prominent features a set of large, sprawling brick buildings that impart an aura of the industrial revolution. They are, for the most

256

part, located along waterways, often close to a set of falls, which produced power before the age of electricity. Nowadays, most of them no longer hum with textile machines or shoe production; they are likely to have been turned into collections of boutiques or condominium apartments.

In places such as Waterville, Augusta, Biddeford, Sanford, Brunswick, Topsham, Lisbon, Auburn, Old Town, etc.—these mills were located, flourished and faded. Textiles predominated, woolens, and particularly cottons. And, as far as Maine was concerned, the grandaddy of them all was Lewiston—the Lowell or Lawrence of the Pine Tree State.

The city traced its origins to the Pejepscot Proprietors, who gave a grant in 1768 of five square miles at the upper falls of the Androscoggin. Water power was used for grist and saw mills and descendants of one of the first developers, Moses Little, hung onto those rights. Michael Little started the first woolen mill in 1819 and Edward Little (for whom the High School in Auburn is named) along with holders of other distinguished Lewiston surnames, John Frye and Alonzo Garcelon, branched into the even more profitable business of cotton manufacturing several decades later with the Lewiston Falls Cotton Mill. It was at this point, in the 1840's, that the pattern of Lewiston's textile industry was set— *Lewiston Mill*

the complex of five and six-storied brick mills with Italianate towers and mansard roofs along tree-lined canals spanned by bridges. This complex was the creation of the Lewiston Water Power Company, which had absorbed not only the enterprise of Little, Frye and Garcelon, but also an entity with the ambitious name of the Great Androscoggin Falls Dam, Lock and Canal Company. Furthermore, the new organization had reached beyond Maine to capitalists in Boston and among the investors in its stock, finding a prize in Benjamin E. Bates. He raised half a million dollars in Massachusetts and poured in a good deal of his own money to create the mill site that soon bordered the Androscoggin.

The Civil War saw Bates's faith (and shrewdness) rewarded. He foresaw a long war, stocked up on raw cotton at 12¢ per pound., saw the price go to $1 per pound., and made large profits from government contracts he procured.

Lewiston grew with the mills. Its population was 5,000 in 1850 and 23,700 in 1900. The nature of the work force had also changed. At first, young Yankee girls, off the farm, living in boarding houses, heavily chaperoned, tended the machines. Then came rough Irish immigrants and finally, the eventual mainstays of the mills, the French-Canadians, actively sought, good workers, and even more important to management, uncomplaining. During the hey-day of the mills' prosperity, 70% of the local work force had jobs there.

The decline came much later, accelerated after World War I thorough competition from synthetics like rayon and the lure of the South, offering even cheaper labor. A crisis in the 1920's was only averted by the intervention of Walter Wyman of the Central Maine Power Company, acquiring the three principal Lewiston mills, the Bates, the Hill and the Androscoggin.

By 1970, textile manufacturing in Lewiston employed only 1,800 out of 17,600 workers.

Some of the vacant buildings attracted shoe manufacturing operations, always know as "shops," rather than "mills," Shoes were important throughout Maine and like textiles, which relied on cheap labor, experienced a rise and decline, faced with competition not only from the South but abroad.

Textiles have not totally disappeared from Maine, nor have shoes—and, indeed, in 1987, Maine was still the third largest shoe producer in the U.S., although the number of shoe workers had dropped by half since 1980. Yet, currently the economies of the milltowns have diversified in ways unimaginable to those who have

258

known their telltale landmarks—the brick monuments that served as a magnate for many of the immigrant groups coming into Maine after the Civil War. Thanks in large degree to the mills, a Maine of considerable ethnic diversity now exists.

CHAPTER Fourteen

ETHNIC MAINE

Rock-ribbed Maine conjures up images of rock-ribbed Yankees—
folks of English origin—Anglo-Saxons—transmuted by their American experience into doughty, *Ayuh*–speaking, dry-humored Down-
easters. That Maine harbors people of other backgrounds is less well-
known. Maybe 20% of all Mainers are Franco-Americans, and there
are significant Irish pockets in Portland and Bangor. An even closer
look shows many more bits and pieces of the American ethnic
mosaic—in surprising as well as unsurprising places. We have already
noted the "Little Italy" in Millinocket, but there are Italian enclaves,
too, in Stonington (where they were quarry workers) and Calais
(where they worked on the railroad). There are Finns in South Paris
and Slovaks in Lisbon, Albanian-Greeks in Saco, Armenians and
Poles in Portland, Lebanese in Waterville, Lithuanians in Lewiston,
descendants of Germans in Waldoboro, groups of European Jews in
Portland and Bangor—each just large enough to make an impression. Plus some really special circumstances, like the Swedish colonies brought to Aroostook County, now forming towns like Stockholm and New Sweden, or the most recent colonization after World
War II of Russians and Ukrainians in Richmond. There is the
vanished community of Blacks and near-Blacks on Malaga Island
and various Native American groupings. The "Melting Pot" hasn't
missed Maine—and refugees still come—Cambodians, Afghans,
Soviet Jews, Vietnamese, etc. It is a facet of Maine often hidden
beneath the homey Maine Yankee mystique.

260

The Franco-Americans

In the popular mind, Maine's French heritage is confined to emigrants from the Province of Quebec, Roman Catholics, who flooded into the state after the Civil War to work in the mills. Settling in ghetto sections often called "Little Canada," they proceeded to form Maine's largest ethnic minority and in cities like Lewiston, Biddeford, Sanford, they were soon a distinct majority. But Maine's ties to France are not limited to this one group of *Quebecois*. There is also the large Acadian population in the St. John River Valley, retaining a separate identity that extends to their having their own Acadian flag (a tri-color with the yellow star of Notre Dame de Lorette, as opposed to Quebec's fleur-de-lis). And before the displaced Acadians had been removed from their ancestral homes in Nova Scotia[1], even before the French government had given up its claim to half of Maine, a colony of different French refugees had come to the state. These were Huguenots—French Protestants—living in Germany, enticed by the promotional efforts of Samuel Waldo and his agents in the Rhineland.

Actually, at the time (the 1750's), Germany as such did not exist and most of these settlers who eventually created the town of Dresden in Maine were citizens of the County of Montbéliard, an independent, French-speaking component of the Holy Roman Empire. Under the aegis of Joseph Crellius, a local promoter who worked for Waldo and the Kennebec Proprietors, families with names like Goux, Pochard, Malbon and Houdelette, staunch Lutherans, were persuaded to leave for America. While in Boston in 1751, awaiting spring before heading north, Pierre and Daniel Goux wrote back home of their initially favorably impression of the New World:

> You will be surprised to see the meat that comes into the city—meat in abundance and the best you can imagine and of delicious taste—as well as the fowls ready to cook and cheap... and the most remarkable, the wild chickens...and here they give the beef heads to the dogs...

Later, they would not be sanguine about the quality of the land they had received or the harshness of conditions in Maine.

Letters went to the Proprietors, complaining that Crellius had shipped their relatives to Halifax instead of Boston, that English settlers were encroaching on their "line," which they had been promised would group the French all together, that their requests for "sundry articles we are in very great need of" had been ignored. Such articles included "smoak tobaca, barrel of rum, black pepper, hats, thread."

The English encroachment no doubt hastened the process of assimilation as did the Protestant religion of these French, and the Huguenots soon passed from sight as an alien element in the composition of Maine.

Not so the Acadians. Isolated in the farthest northern reaches of the state, with Canada just across the river, the community that migrated to the Madawaska region in the last 18th. century has kept its identity to a degree unmatched anywhere else in Maine. It has also spread since its early days. From Fort Kent, knots of settlers headed south down the Fish River to found Wallagreass Plantation and Eagle Lake, or swung westward to St. Francis, Van Buren (originally Violette Brook) sparked a movement east to Hamlin and south toward Caribou; from Madawaska and Frenchville, other southern migrations occurred, which then met Swedes pushing north into what is now the Stockholm area. Some say the Swedes were brought over deliberately to serve as a buffer.

This St. John Valley group, several writers have claimed, is not a wholly unalloyed Acadian population. Beatrice Craig, writing in the Quarterly of the Maine Historical Society, maintains the *Acadian* element was simply the elite of a "stratified society," composed in part of migrants from French Canada (i.e., Quebec). She writes:

> Consequently by 1850, the Madawaska settlement was quite different from what it had been a generation before...At the bottom were the recently arrived French Canadians. Numerous and poor, they were perceived as intruders and shunned socially. At the top of Madawaska society was a core of old families who counted the Acadians among their ancestors, who were more prosperous and who were connected to each other by multiple ties of blood and marriage...

Further, she blames Americans for perpetuating a legend of the Madawaskans as refugees from British persecution who fled to an unreachable wilderness beyond Grand Falls. The reports of two American Commissioners sent during the Aroostook controversy, John G. Dean and the future Maine Governor Edward Kavanagh, sound this self-serving theme. But the wealthier members of the

262

community were all, to the disgust of Dean and Kavanagh, supporters of the enemy. "Simon Hebert is a partisan of the British
and hostile to our state," they wrote. "The English protect him and
with their help, he has dislocated several families from their properties." David Cyr likewise met with their disapproval. He was the
tax collector and school teacher and paid by the Province of New
Brunswick. At his house, they ate rancid food, of which they
complained, as they did of the fare in several other houses, yet it
was pointed out rather slyly by a local historian: "Readers will note
that the meat and butter were only rancid at the houses of the
settlers who were hostile to the American delegates."

Among the households enumerated in their report by Dean
and Kavanagh, a number were cited as having come from "Canada," while a few were listed as Irish and had Irish names. Unmistakably, the denizens of the St. John Valley are a population of
mixed origins that has amalgamated over years, but resolutely this
has been done under the rubric of *Acadian*. In their discussion of
themselves, the term *Acadian* is used again and again. Thus, the
long-time Speaker of the Maine House of Representatives, John L.
Martin, a native of Eagle Lake, writes of a local history course at
Madawaska High School as *l'histoire acadienne*." The Valley's chief
historic museum is the "Acadian Village"; a landmark monument
at St. David is the "Acadian Cross." One eats *ployes*, Acadian
buckwheat pancakes, and there is a special Acadian historical
heroine, "Tante Blanche" Thibodeau Cyr, who ministered to the
sick and hungry during a terrible famine in 1796.

Whatever the original composition of its peoples, the Franco-
American community in northern Aroostook perceives itself today
as Acadian and as distinct. While non-Francos might unthinkingly
lump all those of Canadian French origin together, a closer look
reveals one subtle but very real difference. The St. John Valley
Acadians, once rooted during the 18th. century, were never again
uprooted and have remained a stable island of French culture
within an American society somewhat remote from them. Those
who came from Quebec to Maine during the 19th. century were
the uprooted, leaving home and cultural stability, many thinking
they had come for only a temporary stay.

Three main movements have been discerned by historians of
this immigration. First, a nucleus of seasonal workers in the Penobscot and Kennebec river valleys evolved into more permanent centers at Old Town and Waterville. Then, large numbers of permanent workers came to the woolen and cotton textile mills in Lew-

iston, Biddeford, Sanford, etc. Finally, the pulp and paper mills drew *Quebecois* to Rumford, Jay and Westbrook.

The Grand Trunk Railroad, that creation of John A. Poor connecting Montreal and Portland, helped produce the exodus. Lewiston had built a spur to this trans-national line and the Grand Trunk Station on Lincoln Street became an Ellis Island-like gateway for the arriving Canadians. They had large families, averaging a dozen children, and they came as families, having, in effect crowded themselves off the land in Quebec. With them, these *Habitants* also brought, as political scientist Norman Sepenuk has written, "the attitudes of a rural, clergy-oriented, anti-intellectual, anti-State society." Another scholar, A.R.M. Lower, was somewhat more complimentary to the individual Quebecker of the 19th century diaspora:

> He has the Norman qualities of thrift and industry, all the Latin's sociability and that virtue for which the Latin is not conspicuously famous, honesty...He is medievally conservative...Essentially religious and spiritual in his outlook on life, he stands at the opposite pole from Protestant materialism and individualism.

Kinder still were the authors of a 1929 Maine Writers Research Club publication who described the Lewiston citizens of French-Canadian descent as "thrifty, energetic, intelligent and ideal homebuilders." An image that sticks of this simple, country-bred, strongly patriarchal folk, to whom the local priest or curé was the most respected figure in their lives, lies in the memory of a descendant when he arrived at the Lincoln Street Grand Trunk Station. The mill bell was tolling the noon hour. "*Aux genoux*," commanded his father, "On your knees." And there and then on the station platform, the entire family recited the "Angelus".

They were coming in droves by the 1870's. It has been estimated that in June 1873, one-third of Quebec's farmland was already vacant. At the end of the 70's, there were 125,000 French Canadians in New England. And still they came. By 1884, that figure had shot up to more than 450,000.

The mills were running night and day. The immense toll of the Civil War had left a severe labor shortage, exacerbated by rapid industrial growth.

Lewiston, sometimes called the "Franco-American capital of New England" overtook Biddeford on this score as early as 1868.

264

Unlike the Irish immigrants who preceded them, the French had a language problem. Their experience with an English-speaking world led to misunderstandings, some comical. In Lewiston, a Yankee told a Franco friend that he had to go to a church "meeting." The sound was transformed to "mitaine," a French word for *mitten*. Local French residents for years would refer to non-Catholic churches as "mitaines." Conversely, a Yankee interpreted the sign "Loyer" on buildings in Little Canada as meaning lots of *lawyers* among the French. The French verb "loyer" means *for rent*.

Possibly apocryphal tales are told of Earnest Malenfant, an early Franco mayor of Lewiston, and his malapropisms and misconceptions in English. Asking an audience to applaud his wife, he reputedly exhorted them to "give her the clap." Told by his finance officer the city had experienced a deficit, he was ecstatic. "We will spend the deficit," he declared.

Such stories, true or false, contributed to a negative image of the newcomer from Canada as "a dumb Frenchman." It is a pejorative term now sometimes used sarcastically by Franco-Americans, themselves, to express how far they've come. The prejudice in those days was very real too, when Yankees hurled epithets at them of "Lard-eaters" or "Canucks" or "Frogs."

Hostility from native Yankees wasn't all. They had continual friction with their co-religionists, the Irish. A church hierarchy, dominated by Irish, and bent on resisting efforts to establish French-speaking parishes, added to a conflict inherent in the French-Canadian's "willingness to work harder and longer for less pay." Some newcomers refused to go to *les eglises irlandaises*. Many echoed the complaint of "*Il en coute bien cher pour faire sa religion aux Etats.*" "It costs a great deal to practice your religion in the States."—voicing resentment at how much they were expected to give for offerings. Different philosophies about their relationship to the main American culture also split the two peoples. The Irish were assimilationists; the French sought *la survivance*, the "survival" of their language and customs. "*Qui perd sa langue, perd sa foi*," they said. "Who loses his language, loses his faith." Steady pressure led to an eventual breakdown of Irish resistance. St. Augustine's, a Franco parish in Augusta, was inaugurated in November 1887 with the strong help of an Irish priest, Father Charles Doherty, and French and Irish flags were flown side by side during the ceremonies. Yet this struggle continued into the 20th. century. Paul P. Chassé, writing about the movement for separate French education, states:

265

In Maine, a hostile bishop not only denied French parents the right to open French schools in certain French communities but even closed a school in Skowhegan in 1908, sought to disperse French teaching nuns in Biddeford in 1909 and then closed the French orphanage in that city...

It is perhaps more than symbolic that the Franco-Americans of Augusta named their most important social club the Club Calumet. "Calumet" is an Indian peace pipe and the symbolism allegedly intended was that of wanting peace with the non-French in the city.

That peace, to all extents and purposes, has come. Institutions like the Club Calumet or the Montagnard Snowshoe Club in Lewiston or the Club Richelieu in Biddeford continue to be going concerns, strong pillars of a community that maintains its distinctness, but which is very much an integrated part of the American scene.

Politically, Maine's Franco-Americans, whether Acadians from the north or descendants of the Quebecois elsewhere, have come of age, achieving positions of power and respectability in Maine government. John L. Martin of Eagle Lake has served as Speaker of the Maine House longer than any other person in Maine history. Louis Jalbert of Lewiston at one time was among the top three State legislators nationally in length of service. Armand Dufresne of Lewiston was Chief Justice of the Maine Supreme Court. Another Supreme Court Justice, Elmer Violette of Van Buren and his son Paul have had distinguished careers in Maine government. Dennis Dutremble of Biddeford is presently the Assistant Majority Leader of the Maine Senate. Successful business leaders like Regis Le Page, religious leaders like Bishop Amedée Proulx, education leaders like President Patricia Plante of the University of Southern Maine, noted lawyers such as Severin Beliveau and famous athletes such as Olympic gold medalist Joan Benoit and many others underscore the permanence of the Franco-American contribution to the richness of Maine life.

The Irish

The first non-Anglo Saxon inhabitants of the British Isles to come to Maine were the Scotch—small groups of Highlanders, captured by Oliver Cromwell in the 1650's and sent to the New World as indentured servants. The existence of areas called "Scotland" in certain Maine towns—York is one—commemorate this unwilling exodus. In York, too, the ancestor of a large present-day clan, the McIntires, is fondly remembered, a legendary giant of a man, Micum McIntire, whose bravery when picked to be shot by Cromwell's troops led them to spare him.

On the heels of the Highlanders in the next century were the Scots-Irish, essentially Protestants who had gone from Scotland to northern Ireland and whose "Orangemen" descendants remain a majority in Ulster. They came to America in significant numbers in the early 1700's, many heading for the frontier. In their day, they were called just plain "Irish" and suffered discrimination from the "English." Their compatriot, the King's Surveyor of the Woods, David Dunbar, brought a group from Boston to Pemaquid and the midcoast area was essentially their center in Maine.

The Maine melting pot of different types of Englishmen (West country and East Anglian), Scotch Highlanders, Scots-Irish, Germans and Huguenots had pretty much been completed when those we think of today as "Irish" arrived—a much more alien culture—in some cases Gaelic-speaking and uniformly Roman Catholic in religion, a real break with the past.

James Kavanagh led the way in the Damariscotta area at the end of the 18th. century and by 1820, 500 Irish Catholics lived there. And thanks to Kavanagh's son, Edward, the new state of Maine enshrined religious tolerance in its constitution.

Fourteen years after statehood, another little Irish Catholic island was established in Maine, smack dab in the middle of the wilderness of what is now southern Aroostook County. Benedicta was named to honor the man who had conceived it—the second Catholic bishop of Boston, *Benedict* Fenwick. Bishop Fenwick had bought half of Township 2, Range 5 and offered it at bargain prices "to those industrious Irish families who wish to retire into the country, from the noise and corruption of the cities in order to devote themselves to agriculture." He had a further dream, that in addition to a church, he would build a Catholic college, far from all urban distractions. That institution, Holy Cross, he finally established in a more practical location, Worcester, Massachusetts. But a church did go up in Benedicta and since 1834, there have been 39 priests, almost all with Irish names, Conway, O'Haherty, Brady, O'Connor, Hickey, ministering to a population with monickers just as redolent of the Ould Sod—Dorsey, Qualey, Finnegan, Keegan in the early days and Qualey, McAvoy and Duffy today.

267

MAINE: A NARRATIVE HISTORY

Several years ago, Benedicta attracted statewide attention by "de-organizing"—that is, it ceased to be an organized *town* and instead reverted to a *township*, where the state, in effect, became the local government. Of the 225 people living in Benedicta, 77 voted, and 66 chose to give up their local autonomy for the benefit of a lower tax rate. A good deal of the blame for the higher tax rate was based on the fact the state had pressured Benedicta into giving up its original Catholic school, where the nuns were teachers. Now, the Benedicta school is run directly by the State Department of Education and Cultural Services.

Benedicta has remained remarkably self-contained. "If a Benedicta man married a Catholic, he stayed put. But if he married a Protestant, he left," was one explanation. Most of the farms are gone and the men work at Great Northern in Millinocket yet people rarely sell their land since, as they say, "The land is what brought us here."

The potato famine, commencing a little more than a decade after the founding of Benedicta, was the major cause of Irish emigration to America. Between 1847 and 1854, no less than 1,600,000 Irish left their homeland and most came to the United States. In Maine, they proceeded in relatively heavy concentrations to Bangor and Portland and those two cities remain the heart of Irish settlement in the state, although even Franco-dominated communities like Lewiston and Biddeford have their Irish enclaves.

By the beginning of the 1850's, Bangor was one-quarter Irish and some families had already been there for three or four decades. Many of the lumberjacks were Irish, most of the day laborers were, too, and—a bane of contention with the predominantly "dry" Yankees promoting their *Maine Law*—so were the owners of the Exchange Street grog shops. In 1854, the population of Bangor was *one-third* Irish. The percentage of them in the House of Correction, however, was slightly higher. Out of 60 inmates, 38 were Irish.

The anti-Catholicism of the Know-Nothing period was fueled in part by the perception that the Irish were perpetual lawbreakers. The Maine Temperance Journal claimed the Irish were responsible for 90% of the violations of the Maine Law, plus a good proportion of other crimes. Yet even as the fury of Nativist pogroms was exploding in Bath and Ellsworth and elsewhere in Maine, there were also signs of tolerance and brotherhood. On October 12, 1856, St. John's Catholic Church in Bangor was dedicated, having been built with support from people of all faiths.

Then came the Civil War. Thousands of the Irish fought,

268

some in their own regiments. And afterward, "Paddy became an Irish-American," as one chronicler of Bangor wrote.

An *Irish-American*, to be sure, but still with emotional ties to the old country and its problems, the chief of which was English rule. J. Donald MacWilliams, a present-day Portland City Councilor, illustrates this theme well in his novel, "A Time of Men," about the Irish in Portland in 1866.

It was the time of the Fenians, those forerunners of the Irish rebels of today, the I.R.A. In America, their efforts were focused on an invasion of Canada. Irish-American Civil War veterans joined an expedition led by General John O'Neill, which was eventually thwarted by American troops, but not until it had crossed into Canada and captured Fort Erie.

MacWilliams has his fictional hero, Donald Francis Curran, an agent of the Fenians, stopping in Portland to visit his relative and while he is there, attending a rally and trying to dissuade the hotheaded young men present from supporting a Canadian invasion. Curran's declaration that the Head Centre of the Movement, including James Stephens, the exiled leader, is opposed to the invasion has only a momentary effect.

When a Bostonian named Fitzgerald harangues them in an opposite vein, the crowd goes wild.

"Irish Independence," they cry.

"On to Canada. On to Canada."

In actuality, close to Maine that same year of 1866, there was a projected Fenian Attack on Campobello Island, lying just off Lubec. The interception of a shipload of arms by troops under the command of the Gettysburg hero General George G. Meade put an end to this project.

MacWilliams's book is also a vignette of Irish life in Portland, particularly in that section of the city known as Gorham's Corner. The corner, itself, was the junction of six streets—Fore, York, Pleasant, Danforth, Center and Bank—and even in the pre-Irish era had a reputation for being the liveliest section of town. Its name, contrary to popular belief, came not from an Irishman but a Protestant Englishman who'd arrived there in 1799.

MacWilliams writes that following the enactment of the Maine Law, it became "a rabbit's warren of kitchen saloons" and that "the immigrants coming to Portland, finding the temperance laws in effect, slid easily into bootlegging because of their years of experience circumventing the oppressive restrictions laid on by the English. Anyone looking for a drink or a fight or a lively time could

269

find what he wanted down on Gorham's Corner."

Until fairly recently, Gorham's Corner kept its ethnic identity. The end of World War II marked the beginning of the old neighborhood's decline. Don MacWilliams, one of its products, has attributed this to affluence, the old families moving out when they could afford better.

The Fraternity House on Center Street, a focus for community life, still stands in an area being given over these days to trendy shops. The "Frat House" was a settlement house and in the 1920's and '30's, the domain of a motherly social worker named Hazel Tapley. With the locals around her, she would bang out the "Frat House Anthem" on a beat-up piano.

> Hurrah for the Frat House
> The place we love the best.
> Where every man is a brother,
> And East meets West...

"She was our whole welfare program," reminisced a neighborhood veteran in a newspaper interview many years later.

There were Irish in other parts of Portland, as well. Munjoy Hill, for example. But as this same true Gorham's Cornerite said, "The Irish of Munjoy Hill were a foreign tribe. That was another country."

Less sentimental are the remembrances of a Maine poet, Leo Conellan,[2] in his bitter-sweet work, "The Clear Blue Lobster-Water Country." It is a rags-to-riches-to-rags memoir, that of an Irish immigrant who makes good but whose descendants are unable to match his material success.

> My grandfather, the O'Dock from
> County Clare, Ireland, ordered a house
> to be built of granite in Portland, Maine,
>
> city of sardine stink and Burnham and Morrill
> baked beans, oh it was elegant
> for a self-made man to have his success
>
> in America, what he accomplished from the
> emigration from County Clare, Ireland, gone
> forever from County Clare of his heart...

...The O'Dock, left a granite house behind him in
Portland, Maine, of the clear blue lobster-
water country, not gone to the grave with him

but still standing for me to almost come apart
looking at it because I can't go in it anymore...no.

But, such Celtic gloom apart, Irish success stories abound in
Maine. Joseph E. Brennan, two-term Governor, now in his second
term as the First District Congressman, is a prime example. Of that
"foreign tribe of Irish from Munjoy Hill," the son of a longshore-
man, earning his way through college and grad school, lawyer,
legislator, Attorney General, Joe Brennan exemplified the up side
of the Irish experience in Maine. And so, too, far removed in time
and place, does Peter Charles Keegan.

The scene of his activities was the St. John Valley. His father
had emigrated from Ireland in 1826; his mother, née Parent, was
French. Entering politics as a Democrat in Van Buren, then a
Republican stronghold, he found his election to the Legislature
challenged by a G.O.P.-controlled election board that refused to
certify him. Eventually seated, at the age of 20, he began an
illustrious career, helping to bring the railroad, to establish St.
Mary's College and, above all, to settle the land rights of the
Valley's settlers. Since titles were unclear and the state had given
away some of these rights to private railroads, many local farmers
were summarily ordered to vacate their farms. From 1876 to 1879,
Peter Charles Keegan continually appeared in court to defend
them; and not only that, he made 50 appearances before the
Legislature, arguing cases, and finally was able to obtain a grant of
$30,000 to buy back 60 acres of the disputed land.

His surname graces a suburb of Van Buren, a memorial to the
fusion, now widespread, of Maine's two most populous ethnic
groups, the Irish and French.

The Swedes

Most immigration into Maine from abroad was a hit or miss
affair—individuals who came on their own or, if in groups, on a
private basis, like Waldo's Germans or Bishop Fenwick's settling of
Benedicta. The Swedish migration to Maine differed in that it was

271

planned and executed as a deliberate governmental activity.

Maine's Governors and Legislature had long been concerned about the state's inability to populate its vast wildlands. From 1860 to 1870, Maine actually decreased in population, one of only two states to do so (the other was New Hampshire). While the U.S. as a whole increased its population by 25%, Maine experienced a net loss of 1,364—from 628,279 to 626,915.

William Widgery Thomas, later intimately involved in the Swedish venture, well expressed Maine's frustration in a speech at the time:

> ...Yet what elements of empire do we lack? Fertile lands, exhaustless quarries, noble rivers, colossal water power and harbors countless and unrivaled, all are ours. We lack labor to utilize the resources lying waste around us. Men are the wealth of a State. We lack men.

To Thomas, Maine was like a western state in its need for development and he estimated that each immigrant to the U.S. was worth $100,000.

The idea of seeking Scandinavians had been broached as early as 1861 by Governor Israel Washburn. After the Civil War, Governor Joshua Chamberlain pushed it, too. The 1869 Legislature empowered three Commissioners, including Widgery Thomas, to tour Aroostook County and come back with a plan.

Their proposal had five points:

1. Send a Commissioner to Sweden.
2. Recruit settlers who would pay their own way.
3. Include a Swedish pastor.
4. The Commissioners would lead the effort.
5. They would locate the settlement on Township 15, Range 3, and give each settler 100 acres.

A legislative act on March 23, 1870 created a Board of Immigration and Thomas was appointed its Commissioner. Two months later, he landed in Gothenburg, Sweden, and began his activities in the country's impoverished northern provinces. Thomas had lived three years in Sweden and spoke the language. He soon attracted considerable interest, although some Swedes had only the haziest notions about the United States. One asked if Maine were next to Texas and another if it had wild horses or crocodiles.

By the end of June, Thomas had 22 men, 11 women and 18 children sailing aboard the steamship *Orlando*. All the men were farmers and the land they received had previously been offered in vain to homesteaders. Thus, no one could complain about its being granted to foreigners and the arriving Swedes were warmly welcomed. A crowd of 500 met them in Caribou. On July 23, 1870, a mere four months after the legislative act, the Swedes were in their township of New Sweden.

The State Land Agent, Parker Burleigh, had tried to prepare the area, cutting roads, clearing five acres on each of 25 lots and building 25 log houses. But only six homes were completed by the time the Swedes appeared and only two had windows.

Despite such glitches, the colony was an instant success. News of it brought new recruits, some from Sweden and some from Swedes already in the U.S. The first child was born in August and named William Widgery Thomas Persson and the first harvest was that November. The Swedes had their own Lutheran minister and he supervised communal activities such as the traditional *Midsommers Afton* (Midsummer's Eve) with its maypole dancing. In 1871, a free public school was built, where English was taught. In 1873, when the Swedish population was 600 in New Sweden and 600 in nearby communities, 133 men applied for naturalization.

Ten years after the founding of New Sweden, a massive anniversary celebration was held. More than 3,000 persons attended. Greeted by a bevy of Swedish girls in native dress were such dignitaries as the Governor of Maine, Daniel Davis, and his entire Executive Council, former Vice President Hannibal Hamlin, now a U.S. Senator, the Speaker of the U.S. House Thomas B. Reed, ex-Governor Joshua Chamberlain, Widgery Thomas, and Colonel James M. Stone of Kennebunk, House Chair of the Legislative Committee on Scandinavian Immigration. Also present was a contingent of Swedish naval cadets.

Among the many speeches was one by Colonel Stone that touched upon the original opposition to the Scandinavian Immigration Bill by certain corporations. Over 735,000 acres had been given away to a single railroad without a word if discussion, he complained, yet the immigration question had been hotly debated. As Stone said:

> The great obstacle to the growth of New Sweden is the fact that the State no longer owns our wild lands. In large part, she has squandered them and the private owners into whose hands

273

they have fallen are, for the most part, rigidly opposed to the settlement of their timber townships.

His claim was that if the state had owned the townships north west of New Sweden, there would now be 3,000 Swedes in the region.

As it was, the Swedish colony was hemmed in and ultimately confined to New Sweden and its adjunct communities of Stockholm and Jemtland.

The Germans

Samuel Waldo styled himself "the hereditary Lord of Broad Bay" and a grand and pompous man he was. It was his need to fill up the lands he had wheedled out of the Muscongus Proprietors by his services to them in London that led to a considerable settlement of Germans in Maine. A sidestream of the same effort had sent Huguenots living in Germany to found the town of Dresden, while the main body, the Germans, went to Broad Bay, itself, a name later transmuted to Waldoboro.

From Saxony, Braunschweig, Franconia, Swabia, Wurtemburg, the Palatinate, they came in various waves. The dividing line was set in 1748, the year in which the French and English signed a peace treaty in the small German town of Aachen (or Aix-la-Chapelle) to produce a lull in the French and Indian War. The very first German settlers in Maine had been in the fighting—as attackers, when they had gone with their minister Johannes Ulmer to help Sir William Pepperrell capture Louisbourg—and as defenders, when their community was destroyed by Indians in 1746.

In 1748, 50 new settlers arrived at Broad Bay and congregated around what became known as Schenck's Point. Conditions were still harsh and among those who died of exposure and hunger was Martin Heyer, whose son Conrad grew up to be a living legend, a veteran of Bunker, Hill, not dying until the age of 106.

Peace allowed Waldo to rebuild his colony. Connections at the General Court won him a grant of four townships for the Germans. In 1753, he sent his son Samuel over to Germany to distribute advertising circulars and check with the local recruiting agents. A large group came in September of that year. By 1760, 90-100 German families were at Broad Bay, many bearing names still common today, like Ludwig, Creamer, Hoffses and Winchenbach.

274

They were German Lutherans, pious and industrious, and their main problems, since the war faded, seemed to revolve about religion.

A controversy erupted when a Moravian mission was established by a local carpenter, Hans George Hahn, soon to be superseded by George Soelle. The Moravians found themselves in conflict with the established Lutheran preacher, the Reverend John Martin Shaeffer. After a newspaper article implying Shaeffer had deserted his wife reached Broad Bay, the irate dominie blamed Hahn and Soelle. He had the former arrested for baptizing children, and, in effect, held Soelle prisoner, too, intending to ship both men to Boston. Instead, the Moravians decided to break up their mission, the only one every established in Maine, and in 1769 they left for North Carolina.

Soelle had preached in both German *and* English, and the language question stirred up controversy. The German Protestant Society had kept its church services strictly in the old country vernacular. After the death of Pastor Augustus Ritz in 1811, dissidents pushed for services in *both* languages. But the conservatives managed to choose Reverend Johannes Wilhelm Starman, who arrived from New York in 1812, speaking very little English and unable to preach in it. He lost a goodly number of his flock to a nearby Congregational church until he agreed, eight years later to try to preach in English every third service. Another nine years later, he was forced to preach continuously in English. German continued to be used at funerals and it is said that the funeral of Conrad Heyer in 1856, which was almost a state occasion, marked the end of the old German culture.

An epitaph of sorts has been written for it by the author Joseph Jacob Stahl in his "History of Old Broad Bay and Waldoboro."

> The Germans learned to live like the English and the latter in their turn absorbed some of the more fixed and enduring Teutonic traits, so that this day...(one) can still discern in the present Waldoboro folk an underlay of German culture beneath the overlay of New England Puritanism.

The Russians

An exotic oddity in the Maine ethnic picture is the existence of a colony of Russians in the Kennebec River town of Richmond. Or at least they're generally referred to as "Russians." *Slav* would be a more accurate terminology, for there are essentially two distinct groups, White Russians and Ukrainians. To refine even further, the "White Russians" are not from the geographical section of the Soviet Union known as Bielorussia or White Russia, but derive the name from their political history as "Whites" opposed to the Soviet "Reds" who took over in 1917.

Thousands of political White Russians, defeated in the Civil War by 1920, fled to Bulgaria and Jugoslavia and lived in those countries (and others) between the two World Wars. After 1945, with the dislocations of World War II, they were once more uprooted.[3]

A group of them eventually came to Maine through the activities of one of their compatriots, the Baron Vladimir Kuhn Von Poushental. Despite his German surname, Von Poushental was a bonafide White Russian, one of the first Imperial Russian combat pilots in World War I and a veteran of the White Army, who escaped to Turkey and then went to the United States. In 1951, once he'd moved to Pittston and become involved with a land development group, he learned of the arrival in America of Colonel Anatole Rogoshin and 400-500 surviving members of the White Corps.

Von Poushental offered them 300 acres in Richmond and with the help of the Alexander Nevsky Foundation, some 70 immigrants were brought to Maine. Old and run-down houses in Richmond were purchased, many of the immigrants began farming, particularly raising chickens, and a Russian Orthodox church was built. The first priest was a former Don Cossack officer.

This nucleus of Slavs and the start of a Slavic cultural life drew others of the same heritage.

But now a new group was mixed in, people who had fled the Soviet Union, itself, at the end of World War II, many from the Ukraine. An example was the Krochmalnik family from the Western Ukraine, a part of Poland invaded by the Red Army in 1939. Wasyl Krochmalnik, a newspaper editor, survived this period and the later German invasion, but fled the Soviets' return in 1944.

Soon, enough Ukrainians were in Richmond to form a second church and some tensions developed between the two groups. Ukrainians speak a language that is close to Russian, but still distinct, and they are fiercely nationalistic. A number of Ukrainians, too, are members of their own special Roman Catholic church, the Uniate Church, that owes obedience to the Pope rather than being a branch of the Eastern Orthodox religion. Also among those who came in this second wave were Bielorussians.

Despite the splits, Slavic culture was preserved through the Maine Slavophile Society and the Beriozka Balalaika Orchestra, both active for a time in promoting music and dances. Although one of the most recent ethnic groups to come to Maine, the "Russians," like many others, moved quickly toward assimilation. A number became citizens, including Mrs. Gelina Panko who was elected a Selectman in Richmond. Her odyssey to the town hall was highly unusual. Born in the USSR, she was educated at Leningrad University; her first husband died in a Gulag concentration camp. She fled with the Germans during their retreat from Russia, went to Holland, then to England, where she married a member of the Polish Army-in-Exile. They emigrated to New York, settled finally in Maine and changed their name from Panasienko.

The Richmond experience has also inspired a noted work of Maine literature. Willis Johnson, himself of Hungarian origin but a member of the Balalaika Orchestra, wrote a nationally-published book of short stories, the title one of which was "The Girl Who Would Be Russian."

Johnson's fictional counterpart of Richmond is called Plankton and most of his tales center on Russians who have moved there. But the *girl who would be Russian* is Debbie Brown, described as 110 pounds overweight, a lonely 31 year old college grad living with her very Yankee mother. Debbie takes up the balalaika (her mother calls it a "bellyliker") after attending a performance of the "Andreyev Russian Classical and Folk Music Orchestra of Plankton, Maine." She also takes to spicing her conversation with Russian phrases like *Na zdorovie* or using a put-on Russian accent when speaking English—"Be so good, pliss, as to passing salt."

Using Debbie as a frame for the impact of this exotic Slav community on a typical Maine town, Willis Johnson deftly reveals not only the provinciality of the natives but how the foreignness the Russians represent lures those seeking to escape the limitation of their roots.

When Vernon, a local young man, boasts to Debbie of having been to Boston and that his grandparents went as far as Portsmouth, New Hampshire on their honeymoon, she counters that the Russians have really been somewhere.

"I'm talking about places like Moscow, Vernon, Shanghai, Buenos Aires. That's what I mean by somewhere..."

Yet in the end, Debbie has it brought home to her that she is

277

not part of the Russian community, either. Out of this small and unlikely Slavic patch in the ethnic composition of Maine, a skillful writer has touched an unusual chord in the everchanging experience of life in our state.

The Slovaks

Another Slavic enclave—the Slovak population centered in Lisbon and Lisbon Falls—has been here far longer than the "Russians." The Slovak Catholic Association, still operating to preserve the Slovak heritage, was organized in 1897. It is estimated the first Slovak to reach Maine appeared about ten years earlier and went to work in the Worumbo textile mill.

Slovakia is the eastern region of Czechoslovakia. The Slovaks consider themselves a nationality distinct from the Czechs and at times in their history have enjoyed political independence. Toward the close of the 19th century when most Slovaks came to the U.S., their homeland belonged to the Austro-Hungarian Empire, but specifically was under the rule of the Hungarians. A policy of Magyarization, forcing Slovaks to become Hungarians, contributed to their exodus, as did overpopulation and unemployment.

Prior to World War I, the Worumbo Mill offered almost unlimited job opportunities. Word spread back to Slovakia and young men, seeking to avoid service in the Hapsburg army, left the country illegally while other men, mostly peasant farmers, emigrated with their families. Among the founders of the Slovak Catholic Association were people with names like Borcak, Hruby, Jakubovic and Karkos. Andrew Karkos later became a State Representative and John Karkos coached the Association's baseball team. The Sokols, a world renowned Czechoslovakian gymnastic and athletic movement, had its Androscoggin County counterpart in the Slovak Catholic Sokols, who fielded men and women's track and gymnastic teams.

The large hall built by the Association in 1897 has been remodeled. The 90th anniversary of the group's founding, July 12, 1987, was designated Slovak Heritage Day by the Lisbon Selectmen, in keeping with the Club's work of promoting knowledge of the Slovak nationality, although it now accepts some non-Slovaks.

As with other small ethnic entities in Maine, assimilation has been hard to avoid. Intermarriage with Franco-Americans and German Catholics was facilitated because almost all Slovaks are

278

Roman Catholics. A tiny minority from the Carpathian mountains, known as Ruthenians or Carpatho-Ukrainians, belong to the Uniate Greek Catholic church. In Lisbon, these people built their own Association hall in 1907.

Such clubs, which sometimes were the scene of rowdy fights between Slovak males from different towns in Slovakia, nevertheless served "...as a police force among the Slovak community," to quote their historian. "The aggregation of Slovaks in the name of the club could put effectual pressure on a deviant from Slovak ethics. The club would rule to ostracize the deviant from the club for a certain time..."

Presently, the Slovak Catholic Association has 450 members. Since 1974, it has given out $25,000 in scholarships to local high school graduates. Recently, it presented a video, "Slovak Sunshine," plus a set of Slovak language cassettes, to the Lisbon Falls Community Library. Michael Bohunicky, the Association's secretary, teaches conversational Slovak in the Lisbon Adult Education system.

The Armenians

The tragedy of the Armenian people had not yet reached full flower, which it did with the Turkish massacres during and just after World War I, when the first Armenian came to Maine. His name was Garabed Yeghoian Charles and he was called Charlie Babah and the year was 1896 when a mini-pogrom against Christians in Constantinople forced him to seek refuge in the Russian Embassy and then flee Turkey altogether. He went to Marseilles, France before he and a number of fellow Armenians were helped by an American, Miss Frances Willard, to go to the United States.

Miss Willard was an organizer of the Women's Christian Temperance Union and one of her members was a W.C.T.U. organizer in the Portland area, Mrs. Willard Stevens. With the help of W.C.T.U.'s in Portland, Yarmouth, Cumberland, Casco, Bridgton, etc., she brought these Christian refugees to Maine.

Many found work at the Winslow Pottery Company, making drainpipes, bricks and other building materials out of clay. Eventually, 80 Armenians worked there. Others worked at the Portland Leather Tannery.

The World War I period massacres brought more Armenians to Portland. Among them was Mikael Amergian, a veteran of the makeshift army that had fought back against the Turks. His son, Ralph Amergian, was to become extremely prominent, serving on the Portland City Council and frequently elected as a Cumberland County Commissioner. It was Ralph Amergian who organized the Portland Armenian Club and secured space for an Armenian burial ground.

An Armenian school existed in Portland from 1910 until 1939.

While Portland still retains the core of this particular ethnic group, who hold Armenian dances and celebrations, individual families have now spread to other parts of Maine.

The Lebanese

The slow collapse of the Ottoman Empire brought other refugees to Maine. These, too, like the Armenians, were Christians who had been living under Moslem domination; unlike the Armenians, they did not have an exact ethnic identity. They spoke, not the language of their rulers, Turkish, but Arabic, the tongue of earlier invaders of their land. When they first came to the U.S. in the 1890's, the authorities didn't know what to call them. Legally, they were "Turks" and were often so designated. The part of the Ottoman Empire they came from was called Greater Syria, and a more apropos name seemed to be "Syrian," which they used for many years. *Greater Syria* included today's Syria, Lebanon, Jordan and Israel and since most of these Christian immigrants came from the mountains of Lebanon, in time they viewed themselves as "Lebanese" and continue to do so.

They came from South Lebanon and an area northeast of Beirut, with some from actual present-day Syria, from tobacco-growing Latakia and around Damascus. They were mainly of peasant origin and at least two-thirds were Maronite Christians, owing obedience to the Pope in Rome, 20% were Greek Orthodox and 10% Greek-rite Catholics. There was also a scattering of Protestants and at least one Moslem.

They spread out to many towns in Maine, a family here, a family there, but at one congregating point, a significant community of Lebanese developed. This was Waterville, a booming place at the turn of the century, deep into textiles and site of the repair yards of the Maine Central Railroad.

The Lebanese worked mostly in the mills. The biggest was the Lockwood Cotton Textile Mill; the oldest was the venerable

280

Hathaway Shirt Company, started in 1837. To be close to their
jobs, the Lebanese concentrated in the "Head of Falls' section on
the site of the old Indian village of Taconic. There, amid a much
larger Franco-American population with whom there was sometimes friction, they lived in tenement houses—the census of 1910
reported 27 "Syrians" in one house—until growing prosperity
allowed some to move to other parts of Waterville.

World War I, in which Turkey joined the Central Powers,
put Lebanon and Syria technically on the *enemy* side. Immigration
of Lebanese into the United States stopped. Nor did it pick up
much after the Armistice. America's immigration laws became
highly restrictive. Between 1919 and 1924, only 20 Lebanese
arrived in Maine. No more than 100 a year were allowed in for
the entire country.

Maine's Lebanese followed a pattern set by most other immigrant groups. They formed a social club—the Lebanon Youth
Society, limited to male members—and later, in sports-minded
Waterville, organized the Syrian Athletic Club, which fielded its
own football team. An Arabic-English newspaper was started in the
late 1920's but folded when the owner of the only Arabic language
printing shop in New England died. They also had a school for a
time where children could study Arabic.

Like other groups, they also faced the challenge of establishing
their own church. Originally, the Maronites went to a French-
dominated Roman Catholic church, but antagonisms they encountered led them to switch to an Irish parish. In 1924, they finally
received a Maronite priest and in 1927, established St. Joseph's
Maronite Church.

St. Joseph's rapidly became a community center. The social
event of the year was its *mahrajan*, a three day summer fair, complete with Arab food and sword and belly dancers, attracting
people from all over Maine and New England and from as far away
as New York.

It was one of the early priests at St. Joseph's, the Waterville-
born Reverend Phillip Nagem, who first insisted on using the name
"Lebanese." He had been to school in Beirut. And as the Lebanese
attitude toward themselves changed, so, too, did it change toward
their economic environment. American-born Lebanese became
critical of working conditions that included a $10^{1/2}$ hour day at 35¢
an hour.

Two members of the community, George Jabar and Bernard
Ezhaya, were union leaders who persuaded the local textile workers

281

in 1934 to join a nationwide strike for a 40-hour week and a minimum wage. The violence of this strike caused the Governor to send in the National Guard. During the conflict, Lebanese and Franco-American workers put aside their enmity and joined together in a common cause.

Jabar and Ezhaya are still important names in Waterville's Lebanese community. But even better known is *Mitchell*, thanks to George Mitchell, now Majority Leader of the U.S. Senate, one of the nation's foremost political leaders. Senator Mitchell's family, Lebanese on the side of his mother, an immigrant who worked in the mills, has always been part and parcel of the Lebanese community in Waterville, although half-Irish, too. George Mitchell's rise to national prominence has spotlighted this miniscule yet dynamic ethnic group in Maine.

The Finns

On the rear bumpers of Maine automobiles can occasionally be seen a sticker bearing the cryptic word, "SISU." To most Mainers, it is undoubtedly a total mystery. But to those acquainted with any of Maine's people of Finnish ancestry, the word is a key one. In the unique language that natives of Finland speak, *sisu* means, as a writer has put it, "perseverance, courage, stamina or, more earthly, guts with a touch of stubbornness." It is the perfect adjective to describe denizens of that harsh, forested, northern land next to Russia who came to Maine.

When they started to arrive, not long after our Civil War, most were fleeing desperate economic conditions in their homeland. Or if they were young, they were evading conscription into the Russian Army, for Finland was then a part of the Russian Empire.

The first batch settled in Knox County, congregating at a place called Long Cove between Thomaston and Port Clyde. The reason: they were stonecutters and the quarries at Long Cove and on Vinalhaven and Hurricane Island were in need of workers. Soon, the Finns were 40% of the labor force.

They were paid $9 a day for a 6 day week. But in spite of low wages, these frugal people, who had mostly lived in rural areas, put money aside to buy farms—run-down or abandoned homesteads that they lovingly restored. This pattern was repeated wherever they settled in Maine.

282

The Finns, unlike some other groups, gravitated to more than one center. Even within Knox County, there were those who went into the back hills and were considered "more free-thinkers than the Long-Covers," although on Hurricane Island, the Finns socialized in a building called Anarchist Hall, where unions and cooperatives were often the subject of conversation. Other loci of Finnish settlement were in Oxford County, especially around West Paris, and at Monson in Piscataquis county.

Cooperatives were not only discussed, but put into practice, and called "one of the most significant characteristics of the Finnish enclaves in Maine." The institution was looked upon with suspicion by their Yankee neighbors, who may have feared it was tainted with socialism.

Yet the Finns also exhibited traits of hard work, acquisitiveness and individuality that were at odds with any sense of radicalism.

A spokesman for the Great Northern Paper Company, which used Finns for wood-cutters, had these words of admiration for them:

> They were honest people. Gave you a fair cord of wood...And they were clean! Many of the Yankee woodsmen didn't take off their clothes all winter. The first thing the Finns did was to build a steam bath. They bathed every Sunday, and after the steam they jumped into the lake, even if it meant cutting a hole in the ice.

The *sauna!*—a word now in the American mainstream. Other common Finnish terms have not become as well-known— like *nouris kuuka* (turnip pie), *nissu* (sweet coffee roll) and *pannukakku* (a custard pancake). The tongue-twisting Finnish language was zealously guarded by early generations, but a practical problem was presented by their equally tongue-twisting surnames. When William Honnkonen, a quarry worker at Long Pond, showed up for his pay, the paymaster had trouble with his name. "I'll call you Williamson," the man said and *Williamson* stuck. Mikkonen became McKeen, Komulainen became Cummings and so forth.

Rebecca Cummings, a fine Maine short story writer, specializing in tales about Finnish immigrants in Oxford County, shows a special sensitivity to such name changes. In her story, "Kaisa Kilponen," she writes of the hardworking housewife Kaisa Kilponen and the crisis in her life where her husband Matti, about to receive his citizenship, announces he is planning to change his name to Matt Kilton.

283

"KEEL-TUN!" Kaisa had gasped. "KEEL-TUN". What kind of a name is that? When I married you, I relinquished my own good name, Hannula, and took your name Kilponen...and now you say it's not good enough for this country...

Matti's arguments that Erkki Hiltonen shortened his surname to Hilt and Toivo Pulkinnen changed his to Pike fall on deaf ears.

Kaisa resolves that she will never change her name.

And then it is Matti's turn to soul-search. After a day in town at the courthouse, he returns home, carrying "a beautifully embossed white certificate and a small red, white and blue flag." He is particularly proud that now he can vote for his hero Theodore Roosevelt. Finally, he tells Kaisa that "Teo-dorr Rrroo-se-velte's father didn't change his name." So why should he? Happy ending.

Jaako Mikkonen, the first Finn in the Oxford Hills area, did change his name. He had gone to Canada first, didn't like it, hopped a freight train at Quebec City and was thrown off it at South Paris.

Looking for work, he found an axe in a yard and starting chopping wood, thinking to impress the occupants with his enterprise. They told him to stop because it was Sunday and he was violating the Sabbath. Yet soon he had a job, a house and had sent for relatives from Finland. His son was the first Finn born in Oxford County and later served in the Maine Legislature.

By the year 1939, when Finland was once more in American consciousness due to her gallant fight against a Russian invasion, there were 5,000 Finns in Maine. Throughout the "Winter War" of 1939-40, they raised money for Finnish relief.

Forty years later, this still active community prevailed upon Governor Joseph Brennan to declare March 16 Saint Uhro's Day. Brennan, as one of Irish descent brought up on the legend of St. Patrick driving the snakes out of Ireland, may have been intrigued to know that Saint Uhro was revered in Finland for having driven grasshoppers out of the nation's vineyards.

The Italians

When Maine's James G. Blaine was the U.S. Secretary of State in 1891, he had to deal with an incident in New Orleans that had international repercussions. It was, in effect, the spectacular lynching by a mob of irate citizens of 11 Italians who had been jailed after the unsolved murder of the city's Police Superinten-dent. These three Italian subjects and eight naturalized citizens had just been acquitted of the crime.

Under pressure from the Italian government, Blaine expressed the formal regrets of the United States and telegraphed the gover-nor of Louisiana to protect all Italians and investigate the lynch-ing. When criticized for not being more active, Blaine protested he could do nothing else and added snippily, "It is a matter of indiffer-ence what persons in Italy think of our institutions...I cannot change them, still less violate them."

There were even rumors that the U.S. and Italy would go to war over the "lamentable massacre." Blaine did his best to be con-ciliatory and even dipped into an emergency fund he had to pay an indemnity of $25,000 to the families of the victims.

In Maine, feelings against Italian immigrants never reached these proportions. But tensions there were. The mill town of Rum-ford witnessed one such imbroglio on March 1, 1895 when a gang of local toughs invaded the Italian shanty area on the Flats and a young man named Marco, who knew English and served as an interpreter, had his head smashed with a bottle when he tried to persuade them to leave.

Yet attracted by wages of 5-7¢ an hour for a 10-12 hour day and 6 day week, still they came. The "Rumford Fall Times" of July 21, 1901 reported, "Train Number 6 brought up another carload of Italians, 57 in number..."

An agent for the mill, one James Dellino, was employed in Providence, Rhode Island, to steer incoming Italians to Rumford.

The same "Rumford Fall Times," while not specifically singling out Italians, no doubt had them in minds as the editors expressed their prejudices in the following 1907 editorial:

> The entrance into our political, social and industrial life of such vast masses of peasantry, degraded below our utmost conceptions, is a matter which no intelligent patriot can look upon without the gravest apprehension...We believe that next to the liquor problem, this question of emigration (sic) is the most serious that the American people have to contend with.

Today, Rumford is no longer a major population center for Italians in Maine. That honor belongs indisputably to Portland where, a 1970 study showed over 45% of the state's Italian popula-tion lived. The Italians by then had come a long way from the days

285

of discrimination. The same survey found 34% of Maine Italians above the state's median income, 11-13% college graduates or higher, the largest work category craftsmen and the next largest professionals.

Perhaps the very first Italian in Portland was Charles Nolchini who came to the Forest City in the 1820's as a music and language teacher and became a close friend of the Longfellow family. It was an era when American literati had fanned a great feeling of romance about Italy and when Maine towns were given names like Rome, Palermo, Etna, Naples and Verona.

Immigrants from the poorer strata of Italian society were in Portland as early as 1865, some sheltered by the Bethel Mission, which tried to convert them. In 1873, a Carlo Gabarini opened the first Italian grocery store.

Millinocket's "Little Italy" notwithstanding, Portland's "Little Italy" became the state's largest. Many of the newcomers worked on the railroad at 10¢ a day. They were described as being more like Americans than other immigrants, having "Snap, vigor, push and superactivity." In 1911, they were allowed to build their own Portland church, St. Peters.

Quarrying was another activity in which numbers of Italians participated. Like the Finns, they were on Vinalhaven and Hurricane Islands, and also at Georgetown, Hallowell, North Jay and Stonington. Many others in Portland, became longshoremen and fishermen.

Portland's "Little Italy," despite occasional rough spots like a machine gun battle between rival gangs during the roaring twenties, stayed together as a cohesive neighborhood until the urban renewal of the 1960's. St. Peters saw its congregation drop from 3,000-4,000 to 600-900. With the exception of a few protests, this disruption wasn't fought as Portland changed its face and families moved away from the Peninsula.

But still anchoring a sense of the past is the Italian Heritage Club, which initially opened in 1953 in a former Jewish school on Pearl Street and now counts 1,200 members in its modern building at the Westgate Shopping Center. A limited associate membership is even kept for non-Italians, and Irish, French, Polish and German "Nights" are held for entertainment.

Like the old "Banana Club," started by Dominic Marino, founder of the Roma Restaurant, members gather to play pinochle and other card games.

The Roma, located in the former mansion of the Rines family

286

Italian Social Club, early 1900's

on Congress Street, is one of Portland's oldest continuing fine restaurants, having been started by Marino when he came to Maine from Cleveland after the Depression, escaping a protection racket gang he had defied.

An unusual man, Marino also illustrated a diversity among the Italian population in that, a) he had to learn Italian in America, having come here knowing only his local Apulian dialect; b) he attended the Italian Methodist Church in Portland, not St. Peters.

In 1970, there were 6,083 Italian-Americans in Maine, 3.2% of the foreign-born population and only .6% of all Mainers.

But the community's small size belies its own sense of self worth, expressed by Portland Police Chief Francis Amoroso at a Columbus Day celebration in 1986—the first in half a century. "America, we discovered her, we named her, we built her."

287

The Jews

There is an old joke about a Jewish castaway on a desert island who, when rescued, shows off a building he has erected and proudly announces: "That is the *shul* (synagogue) I go to"; then, he indicates another building he has built and says contemptuously: "And that is the *shul* I don't go to."

This typical Jewish self-deprecating humor illustrates a trait common among adherents of the Jewish religion: a tendency to splinter into different worshipping groups. And since the *shul*, the synagogue, is the center of Jewish life,[4] the vagaries of the various congregations created in Portland, Jewry's population center, speak directly to the history of this people in Maine.

Individual Jews are recorded in Portland before there were enough for a congregation or even a *minyan* (a prayer group). The earliest, no doubt, was the erudite 18th. century itinerant encountered by Parson Thomas Smith who, in his diary, discusses with considerable spleen their theological argument on the divinity of Jesus. Mention has also been made in the city's records of Lieutenant Joseph Israel who died in Commodore Edward Preble's attack on Tripoli in 1804, of Sussman Abrams who died, age 87, in 1830 and a Captain A. Goldman of the 17th. Maine Regiment during the Civil War.

But it was not until the 1870's that a Jewish community began to gel in Portland. By then, (1873), a Jewish baby had been born, Samuel Rosenberg, later to be a City Councillor, and a Jewish cemetery and B'nai B'rith Lodge established (1874). Synagogues were in people's homes and shops. The orthodox gathered at the Judelson house and those of a more modern bent (yet known as *Conservatives*) met over the Aaronson store on Middle Street.

In 1904, 25 Portland Jews took out a bank loan to build the first of the local temples, Shaarey Tphiloh. Since the local bankers wouldn't recognize the community as such, all 25 had to sign individually. A dozen years later, there were several break-away movements. One group, feeling the services weren't modern enough, set up their own worship in the YMHA building; another faction

288

broke off for the exact opposite reason; they wanted a more orthodox synagogue. Then, still another congregation, Etz Chaim, was
formed in a dispute over whether or not the rabbi was being given
proper respect. Still others, strongly secular, put their efforts into
the Jewish Community Center, the Jewish Federation and the
Zionist movement.

A similar diversity now exists statewide. At present, there are
seven Jewish congregations in Maine with full-time rabbis, plus
others, all covering a wide range of religious interests. Maine's current Jewish population is estimated at 10,000, half that number
reside in Portland.

Since Samuel Rosenberg's election to the City Council, Port-
landers of Jewish ancestry have played an important role in public
life. At one point recently, four of the nine City Councillors were
Jewish, including the Mayor, three of the nine School Board members and several of the State Representatives in the 10-member
legislative delegation.

Names like Bernstein, Abromson, Brenerman, Levenson,
Ketover and others less obviously Jewish, like Troubh and Nelson,
have been prominent in recent Portland affairs. Bangor, an even
older Jewish settlement, has had Stern, Trotsky, and Lipsky, and
Augusta, Katz. Yet the most prominent Jewish name in Maine politics, that of U.S. Senator William S. Cohen, is of a person who is
not Jewish, but of a mixed marriage, his father a member of the
Bangor Jewish community and his mother not Jewish, making him,
at least in the eyes of the Orthodox upholders of Hebraic law, not
Jewish.

Jews in Bangor go back to the days before the Revolution.
They came first from Spain and Portugal—Sephardic Jews—of a
population speaking a strange form of Spanish called Ladino.
Then, 1815-1848, German Jews arrived in Bangor, forming the
first congregation, Ahawas Achim, in 1849. Before 1855, there
was a distinct enclave, families with names like Bach, Baer,
Dreyfus, Kurtz, Silber, Stern and Wetzler.

Sephardic Jews from the Middle East also represent a new and
rather unique addition to Maine's Jewish population. This is a
part-time community that exists in Old Orchard Beach, mostly
during the tourist season. The majority are from Egypt, refugees
who fled to the U.S. in 1960 to escape persecution under Nasser.
Others are from Syria and a few from Israel. They run discount
stores, live in New York during the winter and like many Middle
Eastern Jews are extremely devout.

289

For the most part, the Jewish community in Maine has not suffered from anti-semitism and is well accepted in this generally tolerant state. During the 1920's, when the Ku Klux Klan enjoyed a brief popularity in Maine, there were some ugly incidents. Dr. Benjamin Zolov has told how he remembers as a boy when the KKK threatened his father with a tar and feathering and in later years, he helped lead a successful fight against subtler social discrimination by certain exclusive clubs and resorts.

Indeed, the ecumenical nature of life in Maine is aptly illustrated by one of Portland Rabbi Harry Sky's favorite stories. It seems that when Congregation Etz Chaim was opened 60 years ago, the members, wishing to make it a festive occasion, decided to hire Chandler's Band. Thus it was that the sacred five books of the Torah in their scroll were carried into the Temple to the strains of "Onward Christian Soldiers."

The Blacks

There have been Black people—Afro-Americans—in Maine probably since its earliest days. The year 1638 is cited as the first arrival of Blacks in Massachusetts and three years later, the Province's initial laws, "The Body of Liberties," were regulating slavery. Although there may have been slaves in Portland with George Cleeve in the 1630's, the earliest documentary evidence is in a York deed of 1663 wherein one Thomas Bolt gave a "Negro boy named Mingo" to his son-in-law. In the next century, dignitaries such as court justices Charles Frost, Samuel Wheelwright and Francis Hooke all owned slaves and, above all there was Sir William Pepperrell, who would sail on the Piscataqua in an Egyptian-style barge, attended by Black manservants.

In Kittery, too, lived Black Will, who not only obtained his freedom but acquired property and used his land as security so that another slave could be freed by Charles Frost. Black Will apparently fathered a bi-racial child by the notorious Joan Metherell and his son, Will Jr., also cohabitating with a white woman, moved to what later became Bailey's Island.

Slaves who escaped were not unknown. One of the Pepperrell chattels fled, but inexplicably headed south rather than north and ended up in South Carolina where he was captured and returned. Isaac "Hazard" Stockbridge, who belonged to the noted Dr. Sylvester Gardiner, resorted to extreme measures, like sabotage, to persuade his master to let him go. He killed one of Gardiner's horses, set fire to his house and poisoned his family's coffee, before his owner finally banished him to a remote area of his holdings where he remained in semi-independence with his wife and children.

The wars in Maine saw Black participation; an entry of "Ruben, Negro" is on the rolls of Pepperrell's troops who took Louisbourg. London Atus served in the Revolution in the battles at Machias. Connected with the town of Gorham was Prince McLellan who served as a seaman on the frigate *Deane*, which Benjamin Franklin had had built in France. McLellan, noted for his great strength, came back to Gorham after the war and became one of its most respected farmers. Cato Shattuck, Lewis Shephard, Plato McLellan and James Bowes, all buried in Portland, are Black soldiers who fought in some of the Revolution's most noted battles. The first three were at Valley Forge.

Slavery ended in Maine with a Massachusetts Supreme Court decision in 1783. Yet discrimination all too often replaced servitude. About a dozen ex-slaves in Wells were given land on a hill called "Nigger Ridge" and left there is a state of semi-bondage. Those Black veterans of the Revolution were buried in a corner of Portland's old Eastern Cemetery that was carefully segregated from the graves of Whites. Isaac "Hazard" Stockbridge's granddaughter Harriet was denied welfare by the town of Gardiner on the grounds that she was the descendant of a slave.

During the Civil War era, the Reverend Moses Greene, an escaped slave, set up an Abyssinian Church in Portland and the tolerance of Maine people was severely tested later in the 19th. century when a Catholic bishop, given authority over a state with a strong anti-Catholic bias, turned out to be half-Black. Bishop James A. Healey was the son of a slave woman and a plantation owner who, through tact, devotion to his flock, charity and great energy, won over most Maine people. To a young girl who called him "black as the Devil," he gently replied, "You can say I'm as black as coal or black as the Ace of Spades, but please, dear, don't say I'm black as the Devil." In his service to the Diocese of Portland, which lasted until his death in 1900, he added 66 churches, 21 schools, 68 missions and numerous convents. But as inspirational as Healey's example may have been, the shameful episode of Malaga Island showed how far tolerance still had to go.

The island, itself, lay off Phippsburg near the mouth of the New Meadows River. On it, until 1912, lived a racially-mixed colony of fishermen squatters, reputedly descendants of Black slaves who had come there speaking an African language. The earliest known settler, however, was a freed slave, Benjamin Darling. Also involved in populating Malaga was Will Black—"Trader Black"—a frontiersman descendant of Kittery's Black Will.

In the 1890's, stories were run in Maine newspapers of a "degenerate colony" on the coast and the bad publicity so upset the people of Phippsburg that they claimed the place belonged to Harpswell. In 1903, the Legislature placed Malaga under Phippsburg, but two years later repealed its act and had the state take jurisdiction.

Lurid headlines, like one in the "Casco Bay Breeze" in 1905 were typical:

MALAGA, THE HOME OF SOUTHERN NEGRO BLOOD. INCONGRUOUS SCENES ON A SPOT OF NATURAL BEAUTY IN CASCO BAY.

The inhabitants were accused of such malfeasances as *drinking tea, using tobacco* and *being superstitious*, because the screech of an owl was an ominous sign to them.

They had their own "King," James McKenny, who had married into the Darling family, and he was succeeded by his son-in-law, Jerry Murphy.

The state, spending welfare payments of $1,170 on each inhabitant, began placing some of the children in the Maine School for the Feeble-Minded (now Pineland), which had been established in 1908. Some cynics claimed the new institution's purpose was simply to remove such "poor unfortunates" from public view.

If so, that is what happened on a large scale in 1911. The first Democratic Governor in many years, Frederick Plaisted, and his whole Executive Council, led an eviction party that routed 45 persons from the island. Sagadahoc County had decided a family named Perry owned Malaga and the Sheriff served a writ to vacate. All the buildings were torn down and the cemetery even dug up and the bones removed and buried at Pineland, to which many of the unfortunates were forcibly taken. Others were let loose to roam around the mainland and live as paupers. McKenny and Murphy rafted their houses ashore and set them up again. The whole episode was immortalized in a photographic postcard picturing Plaisted and his Council leading the island raid.

Since then, Maine has done somewhat better. A number of Blacks have been elected to local offices and one, Gerald Talbot of

292

Portland, has served in the Maine Legislature. As of this writing, the state's capital, Augusta, has a Black Mayor, William Burney.

Governor Plaisted on Malaga Island

Others

Similar stories to those already told can cover the experiences of many additional ethnic groups in Maine. The Greek experience follows the pattern—an immigration in this case, centering on the Biddeford-Saco area or the Poles, prevalent in Portland and the Lithuanians clustered around Lewiston-Auburn. In the case of the Greeks and the Poles, there are political standouts to boast of—the current 2nd District Congresswoman, Olympia Snowe, nee Bouchles, as one of the numerous Greek-Americans who have been active in Maine public life[5] and, for the Poles, the most renowned of Maine's 20th century political figures, ex-U.S. Senator and Secretary of State, Edmund S. Muskie, whose Presidential campaign in 1972 sported stickers used in Polish sections of the country with his ethnic name of Edziu Sixtus Marciszewski.

These are second and third generation descendants of people who came, as did the illiterate mother of State Representative

293

Frank Drigotas, a Lithuanian, because "she had heard of a wonderful place called America and dreamed of going there."

Nor does it seem the new generations coming over are experiencing problems altogether different from the earlier groups. Thus, the recent public protest by refugees from post-Solidarity Poland, asking for masses in Polish at Portland's St. Louis Church, a parish established by previous Polish immigrants around 1924. The pastor, Father Ronald Sermak, was resisting the demand because he felt the mass would be poorly attended, although he did do a Polish language mass in September 1985 to celebrate the 5th. anniversary of the Solidarity labor union and the 46th. anniversary of the start of World War II.

So it goes among Maine's ethnic communities, new and old. The state continues to absorb newcomers, while it transforms those who have already come, and a memory of roots fuels a movement of cultural discovery found in publications like "Le F-A-R-O-G" and the "Maine Mosaic."

The latter has published statistics like those from the 1980 census showing there are 3,148 Dutch in Maine, 835 Hungarians, 1,948 Norwegians and 1,095 Portuguese, in addition to the numbers of those groups already cited.

Lastly, there are the Native-Americans, the several Indian tribes—Penobscots, Passamaquoddies, Micmacs, Malicetes, Houlton Band, etc.—who complete the ethnic tapestry of Maine. Their story, in detail, would make a chapter by itself and its most modern manifestation—the Indian Land Claims controversy—will be dealt with later in its proper chronology.

CHAPTER Fifteen

Modern Maine Takes Shape

Payrolls or Pickerel?

That question of public policy, quintessentially Maine in its expression—"payrolls or pickerel?" has no specific source. Yet the conundrum Mainers debate to this day—how much development, how much preservation of the environment—was early on in people's minds after the industrial revolution had spread down east. The post-Civil War years had seen the steady growth of mills and factories; the lumbering Thoreau fretted about was turning into the pulp-cutting the giant paper companies needed and tourist hotels were transforming communities on the coast and around the lakes. Theodore Roosevelt, among others on the national level, felt the impending end of America's sense of boundless resources; *conservation* became a new word in the nation's vocabulary and the *National Park* was invented, a first for the world. While a melting post of nationalities was toiling to make the country strong, and in Maine doing the same on a smaller scale, a few far-sighted persons were looking to the future.

Acadia National Park

Eden, Maine had become Bar Harbor, but the sense of a lost paradise had never left those drawn to this unparalleled beauty spot. It may have been inevitable that its first preservationists would be people from "Away." As often happens today, they have

295

the time and money and, perhaps most importantly, a perspective on what has happened other places.

On August 12, 1901, George Bucknam Dorr, a summer resident of Bar Harbor, received a letter from the President of Harvard, Charles W. Eliot, another summer resident, inviting him to a meeting at the Music Room in Seal Harbor to represent the Village Improvement Society of Bar Harbor and, if he wished, to bring others with him. The purpose, according to Eliot, was to establish a committee "to hold reservations at points of interest on this Island for the perpetual use of the public."

Little did Dorr realize as he steamed to the meeting aboard the personal yacht of John S. Kennedy, a New York tycoon, that he was about to embark on his life's work—assembling the land for the first National Park east of the Mississippi, and one of the nation's most popular preserves.

A sense of geographical discrepancy in preservation was high among Dorr's motive forces as he expressed it in a paper written in 1913:

> The question of Public Reservations is of paramount importance in the eastern portion of the country, where we have already got a dense population swiftly created and swiftly growing denser without apparent limit..Magnificent reservations have been created in the west, with wise prevision...

In any event, Dorr was convinced right from the start. But progress was slow. It took almost two years before these "Trustees of Public Reservations" received their charter from the Maine Legislature and, aside from a rod-square site on which to put a placque honoring Champlain's discovery of Mount Desert, no land was given until 1908. That year, Mrs. Charles D. Homans of Boston donated the "Bowl and Beehive" tract on Newport Mountain.

Spurred by her gift, Dorr sought to acquire the summit of Cadillac Mountain and enlisted the help of his friend John S. Kennedy. Another site he wanted had a spring on it and one day he was told that a group of local speculators were ready to buy it for cash. He had fifteen minutes to get downtown or else it would be lost. A messenger he sent arrived with two minutes to spare and the would-be buyers were left sputtering with anger. Dorr named the spring in honor of the Sieur de Monts.

It was as the Sieur de Monts National Monument that Dorr's acquisitions were eventually to enter the public domain. Meanwhile, there were adventures galore as other challenges came and went. John S. Kennedy died, but not before declaring on his death bed to his wife, "Remember...that I promised Mr. Dorr...to help him get that land." His reluctant executors, when prodded by Mrs. Kennedy, finally sent Dorr a check. Then, too, in January 1913, a local opposition group tried to have the Maine Legislature annul the charter of the Trustees of Public Reservations. Dorr rushed to Augusta from his home in Boston and with the help of another friend John Peters of Ellsworth, the Speaker of the House, blocked the move. But Dorr's biggest trial was dealing with a Federal bureaucracy after determining that a safer future for the land he wanted to save would be to place it in the hands of the U.S. Government.

Dorr went to Washington and started his lobbying with the help of Gifford Pinchot, the famed conservationist and founder of the U.S. Forest Service. The Democrats were in power under Woodrow Wilson and although Pinchot was a Republican, he had good ties to the administration. Through him, Dorr met several officials who were to be of help later, like Secretary of the Interior Franklin K. Lane and Secretary of the Treasury William McAdoo, who was also Wilson's son-in-law.

That the area became a National Monument and not a National Park was due to the fact the Park Service did not then exist. It came into being on August 25, 1916, whereas on July 8, 1916, President Wilson issued a proclamation establishing the Sieur de Monts National Monument. The key obstacle to be overcome was the opposition of the Secretary of Agriculture, David F. Houston. Instrumental in changing Houston's mind was President Eliot of Harvard, working at Dorr's request.

The next problem facing Dorr was no appropriation for the facility. In 1917, with the U.S. in World War I, getting money from Congress wasn't easy. The House Appropriations Committee chair, Swagar Sherley, wasn't sympathetic. Dorr got Teddy Roosevelt to intercede and the upshot was a $10,000 grant.

Then, Dorr sought to turn the National Monument into a National Park. U.S. Senator Frederick Hale of Maine submitted a bill at Dorr's behest and it passed. The only point of contention was a new name—Sieur de Monts was considered too obscure and, with American troops in France, Lafayette seemed more appropriate. So it entered the system as Lafayette National Park.

The final name change occurred in 1928. Dorr had a chance to add a magnificent area on the mainland—the Schoodic Peninsula. The problem was that the donor, a woman married to an English Lord, didn't like the name Lafayette. Dorr had been toying with *Acadia* for a long time as far more apropos historically and got Congress to pass a bill to that effect.

And *Acadia* it has remained, a jewel of splendid scenery and a monument to the need for respite in a world crowded far beyond the imaginations of even those who conceived of its preservation.

Water Power

An issue of transcendent importance in Maine, which accelerated as the state industrialized, was control of "water power"—the rivers that could be dammed and their force turned into electricity. Even before electricity existed, mill rights had been a matter of public concern. Governor Joshua Chamberlain in 1867 recommended a commission to study water power and the resultant body included such distinguished Mainers as John A. Poor and Hannibal Hamlin. A man appropriately named Wells made a classic hydrographic survey in 1869. And by 1907, several decades after Thomas A. Edison opened the first electric power plant in New York, a style of controversy familiar in the next few decades erupted when the Union Water Power Company wanted to draw down the Rangeley Lakes and hotelman Edward Ricker defeated the move.

Yet struggles over water power, reaching their peak in the 1920's, were not precisely a matter of "payrolls or pickerel." Much of the furor centered on who would reap the benefits of waters that theoretically belonged to everyone. Would the profits go strictly into private pockets or would the public gain? In this clash of political philosophies, where charges of "socialism" were not infrequent, conservation concerns often were absent.

The Kennebec Reservoir Company controversy of 1923 was an illustration of such a struggle at its most high-fevered pitch.

It began when legislation was introduced to create this company and "Define the Powers thereof." Among the incorporators, all distinguished industrialists, two names stand out through the years, Garret Schenck of the Great Northern Paper Company and Walter S. Wyman of the Central Maine Power Company. The latter was the driving force behind the bill, whose purpose was to authorize the building of "dams and other necessary works" on the Dead River in Township 3, Range 4, a remote corner of Somerset County. As a result, the flow of water in the Kennebec would

298

become more constant, enhancing its use for power and manufacturing, and the log drive down the Dead River would be made easier. Water storage in reservoirs would also be allowed. It seemed like a straightforward and beneficial measure.

The trouble was the State of Maine owned the land to be taken. These were public lots and thus, although there were vague words about "purchase" in the Kennebec Reservoir Bill, it could well seem as if CMP and its partners were grabbing the people's land at no cost to themselves.

This, certainly, was the interpretation of the Governor—that most remarkable figure in Maine political history—Percival Proctor Baxter.

Baxter had become Governor by accident—*unlucky fate*, the bigwigs of the power and paper companies must have moaned. Indeed, there was a certain grand irony in his accession to the chair, since it was said the Republican powers-that-be had "kicked him upstairs" into the office of Senate President to get him out of their hair, only to see him succeed to the Governorship when the elected Chief of State, Frederick Parkhurst, died unexpectedly after less than a month in office.

This was in 1921. In 1923, Baxter had already survived one contentious legislative session, defeated a Democrat opponent handily for re-election and come back to bedevil the G.O.P. establishment for a second term.

Baxter vetoed the Kennebec Reservoir Bill.

But then, again, Baxter vetoed many bills and the Legislature had gotten into the habit of overriding him. It was no problem this time, either. In the House, Baxter was defeated by a crushing margin of 121-25.

Unfazed, he went to the people. He issued a proclamation, calling on all Maine citizens to support an initiated referendum that would effectively repeal the bill. Petitions were circulated and soon flooded back into the Governor's office, filled with signatures. Wyman and his allies began to realize they would have to compromise.

A substitute measure, "An Act To Create the Dead River Reservoir Co." appeared and incorporated Baxter's conditions: the state would not relinquish its rights to the public lots or to the water rights; they would merely lease them for 40 years—for $1 million in all, at $25,000 a year. Payment would begin July 1, 1924, no power would be exported. And after 40 years, the lease could be renegotiated.

299

Helping Baxter deal with the power company reps was State Senator Ralph Owen Brewster of Cumberland County. A final conference was held on the evening of April 4. The company men said they would have the Dead River bill presented to the Legislature the next morning and presented it was, *already engrossed,* that is ready for enactment, and under the name of the Treasurer of the Central Maine Power Company[1]—a most irregular procedure, but aptly illustrating the political clout of the company. Then, two days later, CMP reneged. Walter Wyman sent a letter to Baxter, stating his objection to Baxter's dictum "that there is some right belonging to the state in every storage reservoir..." even when the state might not own the land, as was the case here. Wyman's stretched logic masked the real cause of his pulling out of the Dead River agreement—that the true owners of the company, the great Insull holding company of Chicago, had objected.

In addition, the legislators who had so dutifully lined up in support of CMP and against the Governor were extremely red-faced. "The scene in the Augusta House that evening never will be forgotten and feelings ran high," a contemporary wrote. How could they explain to their constituents why they had voted down Baxter's principles and then accepted them?

So the session ended with no water power bill at all. Four years afterward, when Brewster was Governor, another Kennebec Reservoir Bill was passed, deeding away the same Township 3, Range 4 public lots, but with Baxter's leasing proviso attached and retention of the state's rights. Percival Baxter's monumental stubbornness had prevailed.

Focus

The Baxters

While Governor, Percival Baxter wrote a short biography of his father, James Phinney Baxter, emphasizing in the title that the elder Baxter was an "Historian" and a "Lifelong Opponent of Vivisection." But James Phinney Baxter was a great deal more—a six term Mayor of the city of Portland, a highly successful businessman, a prolific writer of histori-cal tracts, a collector of historical documents about Maine (24 volumes published), President of the Maine Historical Society and the New England Historical-Genealogical Society, and father of 11 children by two wives. Born in 1876, Percival was the child of his second marriage to Mehetable Cummings Proctor, his first wife having died in 1872.

Percival said of his father:

His literary and historical work was his
real life interest. He was devoted to
books and to Art. He loved his State
of Maine and its history was as familiar
to him as is the alphabet to most
people...He wished to be known as an
"Historian" and told me he hoped to
be remembered as one. His political
and business successes were to him as
nothing in comparison with those in
connection with his historical work...

My father believed that our animal
companions deserve fair treatment at
the hand of man, and that man de-
grades and betrays himself when he
practices cruelty upon them...

On the latter score, he inserted a
clause in his will prohibiting any payment
from his estate to persons who practiced
vivisection.

Another not uncharacteristic bequest of his was $50,000 to the city of
Boston to be held until it amounted to $1
million to construct a "New England
Pantheon," or memorial building on the
scale of Westminster Abbey, to honor
New England men and women who had
made significant contributions to the
growth of the United States.

The idea perhaps came to him
because his research at one point took
him to London where he spent two years
(while Percival was sent to an exclusive
English school) tracking down documents
related to the early colonial years in
Maine. Out of this effort came the
"Trelawney Papers," a compendium of
records of the settlements at Richmond's
Island and Spurwink, and works such as
"George Cleaves and his Times," "Sir
Ferdinando Gorges and His Province of

Maine," "The Pioneers of New France in
New England" (for which he learned
French), "The Voyages of Jacques Car-
tier," etc.

As Mayor, he built sewer systems on
the west and north sides of Portland, constructed Baxter Boulevard, financed the
Grand Truck elevators, and pushed
women's suffrage and enforcement of the
liquor laws.

He first ran as a Republican when
the Democrats were in control of the city
and no one else would run. During that
first election, which he lost, several pack-
ages of ballots were found to be missing.
Baxter went to court and successfully
argued for a new election, which he won.
Years later, the missing ballots were
found in a dark corner of an unused
closet in the City Building. After four
years in office, he was finally defeated
because of his insistence on continuing
the roadway that came to be Baxter
Boulevard. Six years later he won again
and served two more one-year terms.

He organized the Associated Char-
ities of Portland and the Walker Manual
Training School (to which he donated
his Mayor's salary), was an overseer of
Bowdoin (although he'd never gone to
college), founded the Portland Society of
Art (he was also an amateur painter) and
donated the Public Library Building.

He died in Portland, age 90, on
May 8, 1921, having lived long enough
to see his youngest son become Governor
of Maine.

On the occasion of Percival's assumption of office in February 1921, his
younger sister Madeleine Tomlinson
alluded to the fatherly hopes of James
Phinney in her letter of congratulations
to her brother:

I knew perfectly well that you would

be something wonderful before long but was afraid papa would not be here to see you fulfill his ambition, (to) be Governor of the State...

Predictions for Percival's bright future were perhaps colored by several subtle indicators: on his mother's side, he was the descendant of seven colonial governors of Massachusetts and, not unrelatedly, of John Proctor, the brave, highly principled martyr of the Salem witchcraft trials. Also, one has to wonder what subliminal influences the young Baxter boy might have received from the fact that the tiles around the hearth of his family's fireplace depicted the story of "Jack and the Beanstalk." Climbing to heights and slaying giants were certainly attributes of his personality.

Economy and an appreciation for the value of money were others. The story was frequently told about the extraordinary trout he caught as a seven year old while fishing on Cupsuptic Lake in the Rangeleys. His father had promised him $10 a pound for every fish he caught over five pounds and Percival, by himself, landed an eight-pounder. That night, at the clubhouse of the Oquossoc Angling Assoc., the little boy was handed eight $10 bills; he promptly banked them and over 80 years the $80 accumulated to $1,000, which he donated to the Department of Inland Fisheries and Game for the purchase of an exhibit to teach children about wildlife.

No incident better illustrates those complementary facets of his character: frugality, sometimes to the point of miserliness (he once vetoed a bill to have the state purchase a single copy of a history of Maine) and generosity, where the money was his.

The crowning achievement in his

life—the buying of a vast amount of wild land in northern Maine and presenting it as a personal gift to the people of the state—has overshadowed the tight-fisted conservative side of the man. For instance, he vetoed a bill to let the state accept Federal aid for maternity and child welfare on the principle that it invaded the privacy of the home and implied Maine could not take care of its own needy mothers and children...this from a man whose opponents labelled him a *Socialist!*

He vetoed the payment of $5,600 to a Warren Prouty for damages caused when a Bangor Mental Hospital patient set fire to the man's property—not because he didn't sympathize but because he was against the notion the state could be held liable. He vetoed an appropriation of $1,000 for the Maine (Potato) Seed Assoc. (and was overridden 125-1), vetoed money for a Maine building at the Eastern States Exposition, vetoed a salary increase for the State Assessor, etc...His vetoes, if not becoming a joke, were definitely a subject for pleasantries. He, himself, could be philosophical about them. He told the assembled lawmakers on the last night of the last session of his last term:

I want to say it is not a pleasant thing for a Governor to indulge in vetoes...It is simply a matter of duty as I look at it. It is your duty to pass these measures if you see fit and my duty to act upon them...and I have absolutely no personal feelings in these matters...

He had just told them, no doubt with his eyes twinkling, that he had brought them "several boxes of vetoes and I want you to enjoy them during the remainder of the session this evening."

The same occasion was used for an exchange of mutual admiration sentiments. The lawmakers presented Baxter with a loving cup and the Speaker lauded him, while he told them: "It will be a lonesome place after you gentlemen have left" and he would be disappointed if they didn't drop in to see him and chat whenever they came back to Augusta.

Percival Baxter was Governor until 1925. He was always controversial, always distinctive. He inspired headlines like this one in 1921: "CLEAVES SAYS BAXTER IS A CALAMITY TO MAINE: IN-FLICTED ON THE STATE BY ACCIDENT OF DEATH" or the editorial comment that "Governor Baxter may as well be paying dues in the Party and become a regular Socialist..." Cleaves, by the way, was Benjamin Cleaves, Executive Director of the Associated Industries of Maine and also at the same time a member of the Public Utilities Commission. When Baxter pressured him to resign, citing the conflict of interest, Cleaves arrogantly bristled that he would only quit if the Governor appointed someone of whom he approved. However, he did finally go.

Yet attacked thought he might be, Baxter had strong defenders, too.

The *Lewiston Journal* stated there was:

> Nothing unusual about him except his zeal, perseverance, power, patriotism and punch. He has wealth, culture and education[2]. He has 'pep'. He will have to be reckoned with.

Holman Day, a popular Maine author, used him as a model for the hero of one of his novels. Entitled "All Wool Morrison," it was the story of a young Mayor, Stuart Morrison, who opposed Governor North, "a ring politician who believes in using the water power as the State's wildlands were used—to parcel out to grabbers who would make millions out of it." The parallels to Baxter and his contemporary situation were a bit stretched, yet unmistakable, and later on, Governor Baxter, himself, played a cameo role in a movie being made from another of Holman Day's books, also loosely based on the political situation in Maine.

The best portrait of Baxter during his years as Governor is contained in a book called "Our American Kings" written by Frederick L. Collins in 1924. The "Kings" were the Governors of the time, most now forgotten but a few still remembered like Al Smith, Gifford Pinchot and Baxter.

Subheaded "Percy Baxter, Bachelor," the piece on Maine's Governor started with his love for dogs. His Irish setter puppy Garry is described, the offspring of another Garry who was the center of a firestorm of protest, nationally as well as in Maine, after Baxter ordered flags flown at half-mast upon his death.

Baxter's relations with the opposite sex were also discussed. "The best I can do for him the way of a love affair," said the author, "is an old Portland tradition that a certain distinguished actress, now playing on Broadway but once the visiting star of a local stock company, played golf with Percy real often."...Their courtship is discussed, but also the news that Percy never proposed to her, possibly because he realized she would never want to live in Maine or, as the author adds coyly, "...perhaps she didn't like dogs."

Percival Baxter remained a bachelor all of his life. Other women were linked by rumor to him, including a beauteous Italian princess whose picture is included among his papers.

On his desk were 23 ivory images—dogs, elephants, rabbits, ducks, lizards, eagles, horses, cats—and the famous loving cup.

Percival Baxter and his Irish setter, "Garry"

That sense of respect if not affection from antagonists was also echoed by a local traffic cop stationed outside the Blaine House, a man reputed to be a member of the Ku Klux Klan, which Baxter openly detested.

Said the Klansman admiringly:

Do I know Percy Baxter? Everybody knows him. He's the most democratic man you ever saw. Walks along with a sack-suit and a dog and a soft hat. You'd never guess he was governor. In fact, everybody calls him Percy.

Summing up the character of his subject, the author makes two final salient points about Percival Baxter.

One is: "He's a rich man's son who has offended every rich man in Maine."

The other is Baxter's motto, translated from Persian, carved in wood and presumably displayed amid the assorted bric-a-brac on his desk:

Who learns and learns
Yet does not what he knows
Is one who plows and plows
Yet never sows.

FOCUS

Baxter Park

Among the "queer things" that Percy Baxter was up to, in addition to lowering flags for dead dogs, was his seeming ob-

session with having the state buy land in and around Mount Katahdin. He'd apparently had this notion since 1905,

304

his first term in the Legislature. He even tried to get the U.S. Congress to do something about it and in 1917, he began putting in bills, himself, for a Mount Katahdin State Park. But even as Governor, he had no luck.

Opponents like Hodgdon C. Buzzell of Belfast (who later ran for U.S. Senator as a Ku Klux Klan candidate) pretty much summed up the argument against it. "I do not feel that I want the State to go into the park business," Buzzell said and added complacently, "...the chances are that the Katahdin Park, or Mount Katahdin, with all its beauties, with all its natural scenery and natural resources ...will be there two years from now. The ravages of the axe will not be very great before that time."

But the real opposition came not so much from Maine conservatism and stand-patism—it was from the Great Northern Paper Company, which owned the land and had no desire to relinquish it.

Having failed in 1917, 1919, 1921 and 1923 to pass a Mount Katahdin State Park bill, Baxter took a new tack after he left the Governor's office. He began buying the land with his own money.

The first purchase in 1930 was of almost 6,000 acres. He had already secured some protection for the mountain by having it included in a 90,000 acre game preserve. But as he later said, buying it was different;

I will never forget the thrill I received the day I met the officials of the Great Northern Paper Company and received from them the deed to the mountain I had purchased. It had taken 28 years to obtain the first 6,000 acres on the mountain, but it was worth it.

Many men might have stopped there. Not Percy. Between 1931 and 1962,

he bought a total of 202,000 acres and all were presented to the State of Maine, the last parcel on the 100th. anniversary of Thoreau's death. "The most majestic State Park in the nation," Interior Secretary Steward Udall called it (and also the largest of its kind).

To govern his magnanimous bequest, Percy had the Legislature create a Baxter Park Authority, composed of the Attorney-General, the State Forester and the commissioner of Inland Fisheries and Game. Percy, himself, foresaw that problems would beset these persons after his death, although perhaps he could not exactly see the shape of some of the disputes, like what to do about snowmobiles and spruce budworm-killed trees and the testing of Navy missiles in the air space over the Park. "While I am living, I fear no encroachments on the Park," he wrote, "but as time passes and new men appear on the scene, there may be a tendency to overlook these restrictions

View of Katahdin

and thus break the spirit of these gifts."

Percival Baxter's largesse to the people of Maine was not exclusively confined to this breathtaking act of selflessness. In 1943, he also donated Mackworth Island, the site of his family's summer home, It is now the location of the Baxter School for the Deaf. His sole personal stipulation was that the state "maintain forever the burial place of my dogs." Fourteen of them are buried on the eastern side of the island.

Eccentricity in a philanthropist is usually always pardoned. In Percy Baxter's case, as he lived on into his nineties, he became a revered, even sainted figure—the harsh battles of his years in politics giving way before the magnificence of his obsession, which private wealth and generous inner vision had turned into a living monument enjoyed to this day by thousands of Mainers and other Americans.

The Ku Klux Klan in Maine

It is a shocking thought that little more than 60 years ago, the Ku Klux Klan was strong enough politically to field a candidate in a Republican U.S. Senate Primary in Maine. Today, the Klan on occasion shows its face in the state, a handful of fanatical haters who are usually met by hundreds of protesters against their intolerance. They vanish as swiftly as they arise. But for a few scary years in the 1920's, open parades of hooded Klansmen were common in numerous down east communities, burning crosses lit up soft Maine nights and politicians were either paying court to the phenomenon or courageously condemning it, as Percival Baxter did.

In 1925, it has been estimated, there were slightly over 150,000 Klan members in Maine—the largest number of any New England state. It was the year in which the 20th century revival of the secret society that had originated in Pulaski, Tennessee in 1866 reached its peak—almost 9 million members nationwide. A year later, an extraordinary shrinkage had set in—only 2 million members nationwide and 61,000 members in Maine. By 1930, there were a laughable 226 of the sheet-wearers left in the Pine Tree State.

F. Eugene Farnsworth was the King Kleagle who in Maine initiated this startling excrescence of feeling on the part of the White Protestant English-origin natives toward foreigners, Catholics, moral turpitude and everything that somehow seemed or could be classed *not American*. This latter category included political parties. As Lawrence Wayne Moores, Jr. wrote in his unpublished thesis about the Klan in Maine, "The Invisible Empire solemnly declared that 'the day of political parties in America is over...the

306

expulsion of the professional political boss from public office' was mandatory. The Klan decreed that 'in the future the sole qualification for election to office will be true Americanism'."

Farnsworth was apparently an eloquent speaker and his emphasis on "Americanism," which he never quite defined, or explicitly admitted was the anti-Catholicism of Know-Nothing days in more modern dress, touched raw nerves among his audiences. He said things like:

> I can show you the tombstones of the murderers of our
> Presidents—and they're not in Protestant cemeteries."
> "This is not an Italian nation, this is not an Irish nation, and
> this is not a Catholic nation, it has always been and always
> will be a Protestant nation.

Those audiences reacted by joining his cause. And he made particular headway among the Protestant clergy. Also, Farnsworth was fond of taking on Percival Baxter directly.

Maine Klansmen

The cheapest thing on sale in New England today is a
politician...and you can tell that to your governor (Baxter).
"I wasn't aware that Governor (Baxter)...owned the State—I
thought the people did.

Frederick L. Collins, Baxter's admirer and mini-biographer,
wrote a satiric article about the Klan in Maine for "Colliers" in
December 1923. He, too, talks about the phenomenon of the
Protestant clergy's alliance with the Klan. Tongue-in-cheek, he
reproduces his interview with a Universalist minister whom he
asks, as he does other Mainers, why everyone in Maine is joining
the Klan. "It is the rising of the Protestant people to take back
what is their own," he is told by the cleric, who turns out to be the
Klan's chaplain.

It is hard to know where Collins is spoofing and where he is is
not. He describes Farnsworth as having been a barber, an oil stock
vendor, a newspaper camera man and a drummer in a Salvation
Army band. Mayor James Michael Curley added that the Maine
Kleagle was from New Brunswick, had been a mesmerist and could
be classified as a "pseudo-patriot and bogus American." The
Boston Herald describes his speaking style, pacing the stage for two
whole minutes in silence before he spoke and toying with the
petals of a flower. Thus, Collins's warning: "He may begin his
speeches with flowers, but he ends them with brickbats."

In early April 1924, Maine people and especially those who
had joined the Klan were stunned to learn that Farnsworth had
been charged with treason by the national organization. A "Captain" Jack Thompson, sent by the Klan from Washington D.C.,
had met with an anti-Farnsworth group in Portland. The charge
against the Kleagle was that he'd created a Klanswomen's organization and kept the dues in Maine. Farnsworth accused Thompson of
ingratitude, claiming he'd originally gotten the "Captain" his job,
and defiantly he swore he would stay in Maine and form a new
organization.

But Farnsworth's departure from the Klan marked the beginning of the end, a precipitous decline aided by bad publicity, such
as a particularly gruesome Klan murder in Louisiana or the death
of two men in a riot between townspeople and Klansmen in
Pennsylvania.

The Maine Klan, despite its scorn for politics, nevertheless
entered the political arena. It strongly and successfully supported a
move to restructure Portland's city government, it ran Hodgdon C.

Buzzell against Baxter and others for a U.S. Senate Republican
nomination and it was able to help Own Brewster win the G.O.P.
gubernatorial nomination by a scant 581 votes and then backed
him against Democrat William G. Pattangall. In later years, Baxter
turned against his former protege Brewster and gained bold headlines by condemning his Klan connections.

For a brief period then, Maine echoed to the tramp of Klansmen marching in holiday parades. In Maine style, their intolerance
was mostly on the benign side. Violence was rare. A fight between
K.K.K. members and militant unionists of the I.W.W. movement in
Greenville led to the jailing of several of the "Wobbly" radicals. A
newsboy in Lewiston, distributing K.K.K. literature, was punched
by an irate passerby. Yet terror on the Southern order of night
riders, whippings and lynchings was distinctly absent.

Still the very inappropriateness of such a strong Klan presence
down east could draw author Frederick L. Collins's sardonic disapproval.

"Thank Heaven that there's nothing in that old one about 'As
goes Maine, so goes the nation.' For Maine's gone mad."

The Volstead Act

During the brief flowering of the Ku Klux Klan in Maine, the
institution overflowed the state's boundaries and took root—also
briefly—in parts of neighboring New Brunswick. A Canadian
K.K.K. appealed to the same type of populace—highly Protestant,
anti-Catholic and bent on imposing moral values, among them a
zeal for temperance.

Actually, at the time, New Brunswick had become a major
center for smuggling liquor into a United States made constitution-
ally dry since 1920.

The key role of Canada and Maine in the bootlegging trade
had been enhanced by several actions attributed to President Calvin Coolidge—namely, in 1924, his extending U.S. jurisdiction 12
miles out to sea and ordering several World War I destroyers de-
mothballed and into coast guard duty. As a result, a "Rum Row," a
line of liquor supply ships resting slightly more than three miles
from ports like New York and Boston, disappeared overnight and a
more circuitous route overland from Canada through Maine had to
be developed.

309

Yet even before 1924, the Maine-New Brunswick border had been a hotbed of liquor smuggling. Not long after Prohibition started, a Van Buren native named J. Candide Dumais was stopped in the woods near Madawaska by a U.S. Customs officer while driving a sledload of booze and when Dumais tried to escape, he was shot and killed. There was also a shootout at Calais in those early years. The authorities had posted a sharpshooter named Harvey Mansfield on the highway leading out of the community. He fired five shots at a pair of daredevils outracing local officials and missed all five times.

Violence, therefore, was not unusual, although northern Maine was hardly gangland Chicago. A teenager from Auburn named Kennedy O'Neil was arrested in New Brunswick for trying to dynamite the homes of two constables, among other escapades, and there was always bad blood between two St. John Valley "mobs," the Joe Walnut gang and the Albert family.

A description of "Joe Walnut" is chilling enough.

> ...Tall and slim, agile as a cat, dark-featured, with thin, cruel lips. His eyes were black as coal, yet slightly protruding, the white bloodshot from constant drinking. He was reported to have a fiendish temper, and few scruples.

His real name wasn't Joe Walnut, but Albenie J. Violette. His wife and 11 children helped him in his bootlegging operations, which were extensive. He owned hotels on both sides of the border, controlled bottling plants and the largest, most modern distillery in New Brunswick, had a fleet of vehicles, paid off inspectors and judges and made his nephew police chief in his own town.

His headquarters was the Brunswick House in St. Leonard on the Canadian side of the St. John River. His contacts were everywhere, as far south as the West Indies and as far north as St. Pierre and Miquelon, those islands off the coast of Canada belonging to France, which were a major supply source for smuggling liquor into the United States.

Car chases and tricks played on the authorities made Joe Walnut a local folk hero and his influence was such that, as his biographer put it, "the name Violette seemed proof against serious interference from the forces of law and order. Even after Albenie's death it appeared that, only when they ventured beyond the Madawaska Kingdom, were they vulnerable."

Corruption was widespread. Southern Aroostook County was

310

shocked in 1924 with the arrest of a number of its prominent citizens, including Houlton's most prestigious lawyer, Charles E. Calvin, the Aroostook County Sheriff Edmund W. Grant and the County Attorney, Herschel Shaw...It turned out that Calvin was the ring-leader of a liquor smuggling band and had been paying Grant $625 a month to allow him to operate...For his crime, the ex-Sheriff spent two years in a Federal penitentiary.

On the coast, not only was there smuggling but there were liquor pirates, as well. A Bangor dealer named Victor Chaisson found that out at Lubec when he was raided by a gang from Campobello who stole $6,000 from him, purloined his liquor and dumped him overboard to drown. Chaisson was saved and his rescuers and other Lubeckers had the good fortune to find 20 cases of whiskey the thieves had overlooked. It made for a monumental celebration in the town.

Of the famous St. Pierre and Miquelon traffic, very little of it was destined for Maine. An exception was the two-masted schooner *Cherie* captained by Henri Ducos, a Frenchman. His *modus operandi* was to lie off the New England coast south of Mount Desert and furnish small boats that came out from shore. A Maine fisherman named Sprague tipped off the authorities one night and a boarding party, led by a future colonel of the State Police Henry Weaver, arrested Ducos who lost his vessel and was fined $1,000. There were rumors that the Frenchman was a disinherited aristocrat, born in a castle and a fighter pilot ace in World War I.

The "roaring twenties," that most colorful era, had its down east counterpart before the "noble experiment" of Prohibition came to an end with the start of the Roosevelt period.

Quoddy

Spanning the twenties and the thirties, as well, in Maine, was a visionary project that tantalized generations of down easters with the dream of harnessing the enormous tides of the Bay of Fundy in the service of humanity. Quoddy was called "the product of one man's imagination," that of an engineer named Dexter P. Cooper, whose extensive practical experience included the building of the Wilson Dam at Muscle Shoals. It is said that he conceived of his tidal power idea while convalescing at his summer home on Campobello Island and he most certainly discussed it with his neighbor Franklin Delano Roosevelt, for the young FDR is known to have spoken of it publicly at Eastport in 1920 when campaigning for the Vice-Presidency.

In 1924, Cooper returned to Campobello to conduct an extended study. His original concept, which would have crossed international boundaries, was grandiose, to say the least. He envisaged two great pools, an upper one in Passamaquoddy Bay (100 square miles on the Canadian side) and a lower one in Cobscook Bay (27 square miles on the American side). The whole thing was to cost $75-100 million, producing several billion kwh at 3/4¢ per kwh. The capital was to be raised from private sources.

But government authorizations were still needed and from the first, Dexter Cooper's dream was controversial. In the Maine Senate, Senator Charles B. Carter condemned it as "a vision and a phantom" and Senator Ralph Owen Brewster raised a far more concrete objection; he claimed it violated Maine's sacrosanct Fernald Law, which forbade the export of Maine-generated power outside of the state.

The Fernald Law had been in place since 1909, when recom-

Low tide in Passamaquoddy Bay

mended by Governor Bert M. Fernald. Its actual sponsor was then
Senator Percival Baxter and its rationale was that by keeping
Maine's power instate, industries would be attracted and out-of-
state speculators, like those who had wanted to draw down the
Rangeley Lakes, discouraged.

Proponents of Dexter Cooper's idea saw the Fernald Law as a
false issue. Senator Fred Hinckley, arguing that Cooper should be
"given a chance," pointed out that the Fernald Law applied only to
rivers and streams and that under it, power could be exported with
legislative permission. The question was finally sent to referendum. Support was overwhelming; 53,000-7,000 statewide and
9,855-119 in Washington County.

On May 28, 1926, Cooper received a preliminary permit from
the Federal Power Commission. Two years later he applied for his
license and also received a New Brunswick charter for the Canadian company he'd formed.

Yet opposition was mounting. Fishermen were against it, as
was the Canadian Pacific Railroad. In April 1929, the Ottawa Parliament refused to allow the renewal of Cooper's charter. The
international aspect of the project was dead.

Undaunted, Cooper scaled back his plans. He opted for a
two-pool, all American proposal, believing that if he could get it
built, the Canadians would later join in.

The advent of the Depression made Quoddy attractive as a
relief measure under Roosevelt's Public Works Administration.
Along with an influential local citizen Moses B. Pike, Cooper
travelled to Washington to see President Roosevelt in July 1933.
Two months afterward, they were applying to the P.W.A. for a $43
million loan. The Maine Legislature helped by extending their
Charter until 1945.

But a year later, the Federal Power Commission declared that
even the reduced Quoddy was unsound financially. It would cost
$40 million while a comparable steam-generated plant would only
cost $16 million. Nor could Quoddy's rates compete and further-
more, no market existed for its power.

Cooper's protests and those of Maine's Congressional delegation went unheeded. On June 7, 1934, the P.W.A. officially rejected the application.

A new wrinkle soon revived it. Quoddy would be built by the
War Department and operated through a State Authority. Governor Louis Brann, the first Democrat to serve two terms since
before the Civil war, was an enthusiastic supporter. FDR professed

313

to be, too. A new study, headed by President Kenneth Sills of Bowdoin, concluded that Quoddy would be a Federal project and Secretary of the Interior Harold J. Ickes went to work, with the President's blessing, to secure Federal funding. By 1935, the P.W.A. was recommending $30 million for a single pool, all-American project and the Maine Legislature was debating a bill to set up a State Authority. The chief opponent, oddly enough, was Chief Justice William Pattangall, the former Democratic war horse turned Republican, and a Washington County native.

Despite the politics, work went ahead. Army engineers started to build Quoddy Village, a housing site for those who would work on the dam. Opponents zeroed in on the "wastefulness" in this construction, particularly aiming at the plush officers' quarters being built on "Snob Hill." At one time, 5,000 workers were employed.

Then, in Congress, opponents succeeded in persuading the House Appropriations Committee to drop Quoddy's funding from their bill. FDR was appealed to but said he wouldn't take the money out of work-relief funds. From then on, it was charged that he had abandoned Quoddy. Dexter Cooper died. And the final blow was dealt by the U.S. Senate, led by Republican Arthur Vandenberg, who defeated its funding by 11 votes.

Some 30 years later, during the administration of John F. Kennedy, a brief attempt was made to revive the idea. A favorable report was delivered by Interior Secretary Stewart Udall for a project that linked Quoddy to a peaking power dam upriver on the St. John at the Dickey-Lincoln School site. Assaults by opponents, some of them environmentalists and others from private utilities opposed to public power, led to the abandonment of Quoddy first, after its initially favorable cost-benefit ratio was shot down, and finally Dickey-Lincoln, too.

As of now, this oft-discussed plan for harnessing tides in Maine, which has been done in Nova Scotia and France, is quiescent and has been for years.

Labor Strife

Organized labor in Maine at the beginning of the 1930's was small in number, spread throughout the state, parochial in outlook and politically ineffective...

314

The words are those of Charles J. O'Leary who, at the present writing (1989) is the President of the Maine AFL-CIO. They are words applicable to the problems of organized labor in Maine throughout much of its history—that it was trying to take root in a culture essentially hostile to unions.

Labor's influence in Maine seemed to rise and fall with the economy—but inversely. When times were hard, they were hard for labor unions, too; people were afraid of losing their jobs. With prosperity, labor organizing picked up considerably.

The pattern had been set even before the first creation of a Maine AFL branch in 1891, but it was especially pronounced around the turn of the century. The 20,000 union members existing in 1891 (some belonged to the Knights of Labor) had dwindled to 6,000 by 1896 as depression struck and then rose after 1900. In 1904, a new state branch of the AFL was organized. Several anomalies to note about those early days were the prominence of ritzy Bar Harbor in the ranks of labor—(it was called "the banner union town in the State of Maine")—and the surprisingly fruitful effort to organize Maine's most rugged individualists, the lobstermen. The "Lobster Fishermen's National Protective Association," with headquarters on Vinalhaven, had 1,055 members in 22 locals in 1907. Organizer Stuart Reid was using the sloop *Marion* to sail the coast and work among these usually contentious harvesters of the sea.

Yet despite such unlikely successes, it was usually rough sledding for organized labor in a state that voted overwhelmingly Republican. The hated "peonage" law, which made it a crime for a workers to leave a place of employment while in debt to the company store, took 10 years to repeal. Strike-breakers, often of Italian or Greek nationality, were frequently brought in to undermine strikes. And even the advent of Franklin D. Roosevelt's New Deal did not improve matters greatly. The G.O.P. was briefly ousted from the Governor's chair by Democrat Louis Brann, but then the Republican tide swept back. The year 1937, a seminal one for organized labor in Maine, saw Republican Lewis Barrows in the executive office and a mere handful of Democrats in either body of the Legislature.

It was a time of extraordinary unrest in industrial America. The national labor movement had been rent by a damaging split the year before when a more aggressive wing, seeking to unionize in whole industries instead of along craft lines, broke from the AFL

315

and became the CIO. In Maine, the break occurred early in 1937 at the State Federation's 33rd Convention. When a representative of the Textile Workers Union, which had been flirting with the CIO, tried to speak, he was refused and the TWU was expelled. It formally joined the CIO in March 1937.

At the end of that same month came the famous Lewiston-Auburn shoe strike. It began with a CIO organizing team attempting to gain representation in the 19 shoe factories in the twin cities. The owners were adamant they would not deal with them. "As long as the walls of my factory stand, I shall never join the CIO," defiantly declared Erwin W. David, head of Maine Shoes Inc., and every weapon of law and legislature and police was brought to bear against the organizers, led by William J. Mackesy of Boston.

Approximately 6,400 workers were employed in the Lewiston-Auburn shoe shops and Mackesy claimed at least 4,500 were out on strike.

Right from the start, the unionists ran afoul of State Supreme Court Justice Harry Manser's injunction that they were to stay 500 feet from the factory entrances. Early on, 40 pickets were arrested for violating the order and soon, Mackesy and five other labor officials were charged with conspiracy to prevent shoe workers from going to their jobs.

The bitterness mounted. Elsewhere in Maine, a major strike, also called because of CIO organizing, was brewing at the Hathaway Shirt Company in Waterville. All through New England, thousands of workers were out. The great Chrysler strike was winding down in the Middle West, but a General Motors strike was in the offing in Canada. Violence between competing unions erupted in Kansas. Even the geisha girls of Osaka, Japan went on strike.

In Lewiston-Auburn, weeks of tension and scattered violence were ignited by a single spark—Justice Manser's injunction against the strike, itself. Outraged, the leaders defied him and called a mass meeting in Lewiston, out of which 1,000 angry workers descended on Auburn. They were met at the bridge by State troopers and Auburn police, flung back and, charging again, met with flailing clubs and tear gas. Flying rocks came from the labor side and a State Police lieutenant, George Fowler, went down, struck in the head and knocked unconscious.

Governor Barrows called out the National Guard. More than 300 steel-helmeted troops with fixed bayonets were soon patrolling in Auburn, enforcing an uneasy peace.

316

Politically, labor was in a weak position. They had a good friend in Democrat State Senator Lawrence Walsh of Lewiston who introduced an order for arbitration, but it only received two votes; one potential voter, another Democrat, Lewiston Senator Charles Fortin, somehow got himself excused from voting. Later in the year, Fortin was to become very controversial when he was appointed as labor's representative on the State Unemployment Compensation Commission. Despite his waffling on the shoe strike, he was considered to be close to the CIO and thus fiercely opposed by the AFL.

An unexpected event on the national scene helped finally bring labor peace to Lewiston-Auburn(and also to Waterville). This was the U.S. Supreme Court's ruling that the National Labor Relations Act (the Wagner Act) was constitutional. The legislation set the stage for union elections and established a National Labor Relations Board to oversee them. Therefore, the biggest sticking point of these 1937 strikes in Maine—union recognition—had a mechanism by which it could be democratically determined.

The year 1937 was also important to labor in Maine in that it witnessed the election of Benjamin J. Dorsky to the presidency of the AFL. A movie picture projectionist in Bangor, Dorsky had already become one of the most effective organizers in the labor movement and, as head of the AFL (and later the AFL-CIO), he presided for many years over labor's growth in Maine, lending it the stability it needed.

Always a pragmatist, Dorsky was even able to get along with labor's chief adversaries. He, himself, tells the story of being summoned by the aged but still redoubtable Benjamin Cleaves, the same feisty executive director for the Associated Industries of Maine whom Governor Baxter removed from the Public Utilities Commission. Dorsky went to Cleaves's home in Portland where the ailing spokesman for industry told him:

...that I had more friends than I thought I had. He further told me that resistance to what I represented was great and it would take years to overcome. He told me that if I would conduct myself in such a manner as to allay fears, I would succeed.

While an effort to pass a "baby Wagner Act" in Maine in 1937 was not successful, labor did become more effective on the

317

legislative front during the following years. By 1941, as Charles O'Leary writes, "It was evident...that labor could wield influence and obtain enactment of legislation."

Then World War II started and Maine, like the rest of America, entered a whole new phase.

A Heritage of the New Deal—the CCC

FDR's legacy of alphabet agencies—WPA, NRA, PWA, NLRB, etc.—passed through Maine, leaving but a few monuments—a book of local history put together by WPA writers, a few murals and paintings, yet little else tangible. However, one of the New Deal Programs—the Civilian Conservation Corps, the CCC—has left lasting memories. Indeed, nostalgia for it even led to a Maine CCC Commemorative Week in 1984, complete with a proclamation by Governor Joseph E. Brennan, and a "first ever state wide reunion" a year later

President Roosevelt had been in office less than a month when Congress passed the Emergency Conservation Work Act on March 31, 1933. Out of this initial set of initials, ECW, came the CCC, under a National Conservation Director, Robert Fechner, funded to the tune of $10 million.

That amount was expanded many times over as Congress extended the program again and again. By the time it was phased out in 1942, the CCC had given employment to 3,190,393 persons in 4,500 camps at an expenditure of $3 billion, plus allotments to dependents of enrollees of $660 million.

Maine handled 20,434 individuals, not all of them from within the state and some $22 million was spent.

The camps ranged from Alfred in York County to Patten and Princeton in the north country. The emphasis was on forestry work, whether for insect control, averting forest fire danger, trail construction, or building roads and bridges in the wilderness. In Maine, the Forestry Department under Commissioner Neil Violette played a key role, although military officers usually ran the camps. The CCC camps in Maine put in 30,000 man days in fire suppression, 2,000 man days in patrolling fire lines, pulled out millions of wild currant and gooseberry bushes (which harbor the white pine blister rust), painted millions of Gypsy Moth egg clusters and tracked infestations of the European sawfly.

Some of the jobless young men enrolled in the programs were

318

veterans of World War I. For a short time, a camp at Seboomook held Negro veterans. Rhode Island, Connecticut and Massachusetts also sent contingents. One Down East supervisor who had to fight a fire with them at Baxter State Park wrote, "This was quite an experience for the boys of East and South Boston...They, however, proved out and received commendation from the old time lumberjacks."

A noted Mainer with CCC experience was the late Bill Clark, a popular author and newspaper columnist. Clark's stint in the Corps did not take place in Maine but in the Adirondacks of New York State where he had gone seeking work after his freshman year at Colby. Without any authorization, he brazenly took the place of a local man who had been hired to teach a bunch of city boys from the Bronx how to use axes. After a month, when pay day came, Clark stepped up to receive the pay of the man he'd replaced and had to admit his name wasn't Joyce but Clark.

The non-plussed CCC officers didn't quite know what to do; to reveal the hoax would cause all kinds of problems and endless paperwork, so they finally decided to cover up for Clark.

The Captain told him, "All right, you stupid jughead, we're going to let you stay. But remember, damn it, if Joyce dies, we'll have to bury you."

A number of CCC projects in Maine were especially noteworthy.

Like building the Evans Notch Road through a remote corner of the White Mountain National Forest—11 miles through the Maine communities of Gilead, Batchelder's Grant and Stow, in an area of wild and magnificent beauty. To do it, the 152nd Company, bivouacked at the Cold River CCC camp and the 156th Company at Hastings, a ghost town once part of Gilead, started at different ends, using mostly simple tools like wheelbarrows, shovels and pickaxes, without the benefit of much heavy equipment. The "height of land," where a bronze plaque now commemorates their meeting is a popular overlook amid breathtaking scenery.

Work on the Appalachian Trail was also accomplished by the CCC, operating out of Bridgton. The last two mile link, finishing the Maine portion, was completed in 1937. When the CCC programs began in 1933, the famous trail hadn't yet reached Maine, ending in Grafton Notch, N.H. Crews established at Rangeley, Flagstaff, Greenville and Millinocket began the work that was eventually to end at Mount Katahdin. Not only trails were built but log shelters, as well. On August 14, 1937, that final link of the

319

2,054 trail from Georgia to Maine was put in place.

The flood of March 1936 was another high point in CCC activity. The town of Bridgton called for help as a small stream flowing out of Highland Lake turned into a raging torrent. The CCC boys from the local camp worked all night piling sandbags and poling off massive ice chunks that could have breached the barriers. They saved the Maine Street business section.

Likewise, in the unexpected and highly damaging Great New England Hurricane of 1938, the CCC went to work, along with the WPA, in salvaging blown down timber and mitigating fire hazards. Some 70 towns in Maine were affected and more than 75 million board feet were saved.

Bill Clark, one of the most conservative columnists Maine has known, nevertheless always kept a soft spot in his heart for the CCC. While "down" on other New Deal programs like WPA or PWA, and consistently unhappy about food stamps, aid to families with dependent children, free school lunches, etc., he saw the CCC differently. As he explained:

> The CCC when it began was a form of workfare. But while other programs eased into publicly scored 'work without results,' the CCC did not. It was guided by men who visualized something besides temporary help, men who visualized development of pride in accomplishment...They got it. The CCC turned boys into men...They paid back then and later the nation's investment in youth...That is also why so many of them feel that programs today put too much emphasis on benefits and too little on responsibilities.

Such thinking also explains the reverence for the past that let the CCC be remembered and celebrated fifty years later in Maine.

CHAPTER **Sixteen**

U P TO THE PRESENT DAY

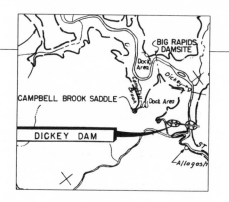

BIG RAPIDS DAMSITE

Dock Area

CAMPBELL BROOK SADDLE

Dock Area

DICKEY DAM

Allagash

World War II

Maine at war has seen various guises: the land a continual battle-
ground as it was for the hundred years of French and Indian conflict; a target for invasion, which happened in the Revolution and
the War of 1812; a source of soldiers and supplies, and subject to
hit-and-run raids, during the Civil War; and then a home front,
whose tranquility seemed disturbed only by an influx of prisoners
to house (the Spanish-American War) or a lone sabotage attempt
(the Vanceboro Bridge, World War I). World War II saw Maine a
home front too, a highly productive cog in the "arsenal of democracy," providing air bases and navy bases and, most important,
building ships and submarines in record-breaking numbers and at
record-breaking speed.

It could be said that World War II inalterably changed
Maine—that the state was never the same afterward. The demands
of war work tended to break down the natural insularity of the
home folk. Women went to work in significant numbers, farmers
left the rural areas for defense jobs, people who had never dreamed
of working in shipbuilding became welders and riveters at the Bath
Iron Works and the Kittery Shipyard. A country fairground in
Aroostook County became a major military airfield at Presque Isle.
Dow Field in Bangor developed into a central transit point for air-
craft flying to the European Theatre. Brunswick Naval Air Station
came into being to patrol for enemy subs off the coast. Even before
America entered the War, President Franklin Roosevelt's "prepar-

321

edness" campaign found Portland's important harbor ringed by anti-aircraft batteries and sealed off with anti-submarine nets, plus enduring if now obsolete installations, like the huge underground fuel depot on Long Island and the brick barracks of Fort McKinley on Great Diamond Island.

A book of reminiscences by Mainer Harold T. Coffin, a cousin of the illustrious Maine poet Robert P. Tristram Coffin, tells of those pre-war years when a still-isolationist America was slowly readying itself for eventual conflict. As an intelligence officer, Coffin had to deal with the threat—real or imagined—of German infiltration, and a prime suspected source was a German-owned quarry at Bickford's Point, South Addison, which a suspicious type named Bruno Lever took charge of in 1940. Apparently unable to rouse up a Fifth Column among the down east denizens of Washington County, Lever disappeared from the scene by 1941. A much more concrete brush Maine had with German espionage occurred in November, 1944. Two spies were landed at Hancock Point by a U-boat that had managed to sneak undetected through Frenchman's Bay. They hid their rubber boat and, carrying suitcases, trudged out to the side road that connected this off-the-beaten-track summer resort community to Route 1. Unfortunately for them, a high school boy named Harvard Hodgkins happened to be driving home from a Saturday night dance and noted the unusual pair. Farther on, he stopped, traced their tracks in the snow to a vacated summer home and reported these findings to his father, a Hancock County Deputy Sheriff. Further tracking found the rubber boat, the FBI was brought in and the German agents were eventually apprehended after they were allowed to reach New York City.

By then, the War had less than a year to run. A far greater number of Germans in Maine at the time were in the prison of war camp at Houlton. There were also a number of them (about 250) who worked as pulp-cutters for the Great Northern Paper Company. These were veterans of the Afrika Korps, some of them of Czech origin, and they were housed in Seboomook Township, working there and around Lobster Lake. A few were also brought from the Houlton camp, which, according to a GNP spokesman, "was full of troublemakers and...a bad scene." Some German P.O.W. camps were known to be controlled by Nazis, where it wasn't safe for Anti-Nazis.

The great Maine war effort contribution of ship and submarine building also began, like Harold Coffin's intelligence work, before the War.

The Bath Iron Works a company incorporated in 1884 by Civil War hero Thomas Worcester Hyde, was already building destroyers under FDR's accelerated pre-war defense programs. With fewer than 2,000 employees in 1939, Bath, under the leadership of William S. "Pete" Newell, more than doubled its payroll to 4,660 by July 1941, six months before America entered the War. This work force was to reach its maximum ever of 12,042 in 1943.

Bath started off building destroyers of 1,630 tons and then graduated to newly-designed ships of the *Fletcher* class, 2,100 tons, 30 feet longer and three feet beamier. The first of this type to be delivered in the United States was the Bath-built *Nicholas*, delivered in June 1942. Observing her full power trial run before she went to Boston to be commissioned was then Commander Hyman G. Rickover, the future "father" of the nuclear navy. After 33 months of combat in the Pacific, the *Nicholas* was among the escort ships that led the battleship *Missouri* into Tokyo Bay for Japan's surrender.

No less distinguished in battle were ships of the next class of destroyers built by Bath—the *Sumner* class of 2,200 tons. These even more powerful vessels from Bath included two that took part in the D-Day invasion, the *Barton* and the *O'Brien*, the latter named for the Revolutionary War hero of the naval battle at Machias, Jeremiah O'Brien.

The final class of destroyer built at Bath was called the *Gearing* class, 2,250 tons, and the first of these ships off the line was the *Frank Knox*, named for Roosevelt's Secretary of the Navy who died during the War.

In all, Bath built 83 destroyers at its yards in Bath, plus four cargo vessels and a private yacht that later became a naval ship.

But it wasn't only in Bath that the company built ships. To help the beleaguered British in 1940, Bath joined with Todd Shipyards of California and established a "basin-type" shipyard at Cushing's Point, South Portland, building *Ocean* class freighters, which eventually evolved into the *Liberty* ships it built for the U.S. government, there, in its East Yard, and at the West Yard it later established next door. In time, both units were incorporated into a single firm, the New England Shipbuilding company.

Their efforts were not without controversy. The West Yard incurred the wrath of the local Congressman, James Oliver, by demolishing 140 homes that it took through eminent domain and its slowness in getting ships built and accusations of profiteering were presented as reasons for actually shutting the facility down.

The War Frauds Unit of the Department of Justice investigated some of the contracts, no indictments were returned and all in all, this yard built 112 Liberty ships by the end of the War, while its counterpart built 132 Liberties plus 30 Ocean class freighters for the British.

Some 10% of all the American Liberty ships were built in South Portland. One of their products, another named after Machias's *Jeremiah O'Brien*, was eventually chosen to be anchored permanently at San Francisco as a memorial.

The submarines built in Maine—85 of them between 1939 and 1945—were all constructed at the Kittery Shipyard. Since the official title of this U.S. Government facility is the Portsmouth Naval Shipyard, New Hampshire partisans might claim these undersea craft for their war effort. But the islands that comprise the shipyard proper—Dennett's, Seavey's and Jamaica—are indisputably on the Maine side of the Piscataqua River. Reputedly, the shipyard received its designation because of a political promise made by President Chester A. Arthur to a group of Republican women in Portsmouth. The famed Treaty of Portsmouth, ending the Russo-Japanese War, was signed in Building 86 on the shipyard's grounds, so it could just as easily have been called the Treaty of Kittery.

At the height of its wartime activities, the Kittery Yard employed more than 20,000 workers. Its Design Division designed half of the American subs built during the War. On one single day, January 27, 1944, four subs were launched there. After the German surrender, a number of U-boats were brought to the Yard and their crews interned in its Naval Prison where, incidentally, 1,000 prisoners from the Spanish fleet that surrendered to the U.S. in Cuba had been held during the Spanish-American War.

In addition to this feverish new construction work, Kittery also overhauled another 74 vessels. The Yard now specializes exclusively in overhauls of nuclear subs.

As civilians did throughout the U.S., Maine people supported the war effort by acting as air raid wardens, conducting scrap drives and raising money for the State War Chest.

V.J. Day and the end of the War brought the same scenes of pandemonium to Maine communities as they did elsewhere. Hundreds of cars, with people on their roofs, drove round and round through the business district of Bangor while church bells chimed and fire sirens wailed. Bonfires were built on Washington Avenue in Portland and soldiers and civilians hoisted a stuffed

324

cloth effigy of Hirohito atop the Soldiers' Monument in Monument Square. Biddeford's main square was filled with dancing people, ships at the South Portland shipyards blasted their whistles, 1,000 State Guardsmen paraded over the State House Grounds in Augusta, on Vinalhaven a dynamite blast set off by celebrators broke 100 windows and in the town of Paris, 96-year-old Percival Parris fired the Revolutionary War musket that some member of his family had fired once a year on July 4 since 1776.

Even as the War was ending, Maine was looking ahead to the challenges of the post-war era. That final week in August 1945, when the headlines were dominated by the new atomic bomb dropped on Hirshima, Governor Horace Hildreth was calling a meeting to discuss what to do about the state's veterans. More than 3,000 of the 15,000 who had come home already were unemployed. There was talk of forming a Maine Council of Veterans' Affairs. The good news was that a delegation from Washington in Maine to discuss the future of aviation let it be known that Bangor's Dow Field would remain active.

Nevertheless, there had to be a sense, with all of the screaming news from Hiroshima, Nagasaki and Tokyo that the world, including out-of-the-way, conservative Maine, would hardly be the same again.

Focus

Two Political Giants

Margaret Chase Smith

Late in October 1938, the former Margaret Chase, wife of first-term Maine Congressman, Clyde H. Smith was scheduled to address the Kennebec County Women's Republican Club on the topic, "The Experiences of a Congressman's Wife in Washington." But Margaret Chase Smith was more than just a Congressman's wife—she was his campaign manager and secretary—and instead of speaking on this safe "woman's" subject, she regaled the G.O.P. ladies with a lecture, unusual in these isolationist times, on the need for a strong Navy.

Two years later, Clyde Smith died and Margaret Chase Smith was nominated to succeed him. Press clippings of her speech on the Navy helped her win the support of Guy P. Gannett, Maine's number one press lord and reigning power in the State's Republican Party. This evidence of her pre-war support for the navy also later swung over a powerful Democrat, Rep. Carl Vinson of Georgia, Chairman of the Naval Affairs Committee, when Mrs. Smith sought a place on that prestigious body (never before accorded to a woman) in late 1942.

325

Cleverly masking her desire to be on the Naval Affairs Committee, she had put it as her second choice after the all-important Appropriations Committee, which she *knew* her crusty Republican leadership would never give her.

The problems Maine's first Congresswoman had with her leadership had already kept her off the Labor Committee, where her late husband had been a leading member. Clyde Smith had been a rarity in the Maine politics of the 1920's and 1930's—a pro-labor Republican. In the Maine Legislature, where he had once served as its youngest member, he had been an ardent if unsuccessful champion of shorter working hours and worker's compensation.

Margaret Chase was his second wife, his first marriage having ended in divorce in 1913, seventeen years before he married the one-time telephone operator and newspaper office bookkeeper from his hometown of Skowhegan. In 1948, when his widow entered a four-person primary for the Republican nomination for U.S. Senate, one of the vicious rumors whispered against her was that she had broken up Clyde Smith's first marriage. Such patently ridiculous tactics helped lead to her overwhelming victory over three males, two of them former governors, Horace Hildreth and Sumner Sewall, and an isolationist minister, Albion Beverage. She gained more votes than the three of them combined.

In the Senate, Margaret Chase Smith became primarily known for three things: she wore a red rose every day, she never missed a roll call vote and, of far more weight, she had the courage to stand up to perhaps the most feared and dangerous demagogue in American history—her fellow Republican Senator, Joseph R. McCarthy of Wisconsin.

Margaret Chase Smith

The late forties and early fifties was a period when the country was gripped by a fierce anti-Communism, fueled by Marxist expansion in Europe and Asia. A "witch-hunt" atmosphere permeated American government. Any public figure who even questioned the junior Senator from Wisconsin would be labelled a Communist sympathizer. From President Dwight D. Eisenhower on down, political figures were afraid to speak out.

Senator Margaret Chase Smith's brave "Declaration of Conscience" speech, delivered in the Senate on June 1, 1950, started to reverse this tide. She was able to convince six other Republican Senators to endorse her sentiments that she did not want the Republican

326

Party to "ride to political victory on the Four Horsemen of Calumny—Fear, Ignorance, Bigotry and Smear."

McCarthy retorted characteristically with snide sarcasm, dismissing this opposition within his own party as that of "Snow White and the Six Dwarfs." But a chink had been opened in his armor. As a member of the Elections Subcommittee of the Rules Committee (McCarthy had gotten her kicked off the Permanent Investigations Subcommittee), Senator Smith continued her pressure, particularly in a report that condemned McCarthy's use of doctored photographs. She defended General George Marshall when McCarthy attacked him and fought his bullying tactics time and time again. When she ran for re-election in 1954, McCarthy found a candidate named Robert L. Jones to run against her in the primary. The Wisconsin Senator came into Maine to campaign against her and he raised money for Jones. The margin, however, by which Mrs. Smith beat Jones was 5-1. That same year, McCarthy's career came to an end with the Army-McCarthy hearings and the Senate's official censure of him.

Margaret Chase Smith, re-elected in 1954, 1960, and 1966, became the first woman in American politics to make a serious run for the Presidential nomination. She entered the 1964 Republican primaries in New Hampshire, Illinois and Oregon, her best showing being in Illinois where she won 30% of the vote. She came to the Republican Convention in San Francisco with 16 pledged delegates and had her named placed in nomination by one of them, Vermont's venerable Senator George Aiken. It was the first time in American history that a woman's name had been placed in nomination by a major political party and she

received 27 votes while Barry Goldwater was winning the nomination.

In 1972, in her bid for a fourth Senate term, Margaret Chase Smith, then in her seventies, was defeated by the Democratic Second District Congressman, William Hathaway. In 1989, she was honored by President George Bush as one of the recipients of the highest civilian award the United States can bestow—the Medal of Freedom. At 92 years of age, spry and alert as ever, Senator Smith pointed out an error in the citation, which listed her as "the Mother of the Waves," the World War II women's naval unit. She hadn't started it, she admitted, a Marine Corps general had, but she had established in legislation that women members would have permanent status and the resulting benefits—yet another breakthrough for which this remarkable Mainer was responsible.

Edmund S. Muskie

In 1954, when Margaret Chase Smith was preparing to run for re-election to the U.S. Senate, an ugly rumor circulated that she had terminal cancer and had stayed in the race so Governor Burton Cross could appoint himself to the post after they were both re-elected and Senator Smith would resign.

That such an unlikely scenario never came to pass was due not only to the fact it was untrue—Senator Smith had no cancer—but also that Governor Cross failed to get himself re-elected. Instead, in a stunning upset, "Uncertain Burton" was forced from office by the House Minority Leader, an obscure legislator from Waterville, Edmund S. Muskie.

The Democrats in those years were at an absolute nadir politically. They held no statewide or congressional offices. The

327

State Legislature elected in 1952 had only 24 House Democrats as opposed to 127 Republicans and 2 State Senators against 33 for the G.O.P. Muskie's run in 1954 was designed to set the stage for 1956. No one thought he could win, least of all the candidate.

Since the Civil War, only five Democrats had served as Governor and none of them had been able to build up party strength. They had been elected, for the most part, due to the splits in the Republican ranks. When Muskie was elected, his party had been in the political wilderness for almost 20 years, going back to the early days of the Depression with Louis Brann. Muskie's election thus drew national attention.

A Republican split again had helped him. Two years before, Burton Cross had won a hard-fought, three-way Republican primary and one of his opponents, a lantern-jawed Stockton Springs farmer named Neal Bishop, then ran as an independent and gained 35,000 votes.[1] In the 1954 race, Republican Bishop openly threw his support to Democrat Muskie.

But it was not only Bishop's defection and Cross's unpopularity that accounted for Muskie's win. Neither was it solely the fact that he was an extremely attractive candidate who, for the first time, now could be seen on television. Maine little by little was changing politically, growing tired to an extent of its total domination by the Republicans, while new blood was entering the Democratic Party, bringing a sense of action to oppose to a sense of existing stagnation.

As Governor, Muskie had to use his wits and charm to build a record of achievement in the face of a Republican Legislature and Republican Executive Council. This latter institution, now no longer in existence, was a carry-over from colonial days, inhibiting the Governor's power to make appointments, often for purely political reasons. Horse-trading was necessary and Muskie all too often was hard pressed to find anything to trade. For example, when he wanted Democrat Thomas Delehanty on the Superior Court, the Council at first turned him down flat. This was at the end of his second term, after he'd been elected to the U.S. Senate. If he resigned the Governorship early, as he'd planned, in order to gain a slight seniority, the Republican President of the Senate Robert Haskell would become Governor, an honor this powerful man coveted although it would only be for five and a half days. Once the Executive Council balked at Delehanty, Muskie let it be know he might stay to the end of his term. Haskell saw to it that Delehanty was confirmed and he proudly bore the title of Governor for the rest of his life.

Haskell had been helpful to Muskie in other ways, too, as the Democratic Governor struggled to get his programs passed. One of Muskie's key victories was to establish a Department of Economic Development—under *state* control—in place of the existing Maine Development Commission, an *independent* body, essentially controlled by the Central Maine Power Company. Haskell, then a vice-president of the rival power company, Bangor Hydro, went to bat for Muskie's idea with Maine business leaders.

Other of Muskie's gubernatorial accomplishments included the classification of Maine's rivers, the imposition of a four-year term for Governor, the passage of highway and education bonds and the creation of a Maine Industrial Building Authority. It was an impressive record for a Governor who did not have enough legislative members of his own party to

328

sustain a veto.

His opponent for the U.S. Senate was former Governor Frederick Payne, a man wounded by several scandals, one involving the State Liquor Commission, the other connected with the then notorious Boston businessman and influence peddler, Bernard Goldfine, who had given Payne a vicuna coat.

Muskie beat Payne by 61,000 votes, helped bring in another Democratic Governor, the Waterville chiropractor Clinton Clausen, and two Democrats in Congressional seats, Frank Coffin, an architect of the Democratic resurgence in Mane and James Oliver, the wartime nemesis of the Bath Iron Works, now switched over from the Republican side. Even in the Legislature, the Democrats didn't fare badly. They now held 12 Senate and 58 House seats.

Ed Muskie's career in Washington moved upward at a steady pace. His interest in conservation, in clean water and clean air, earned him the title of "Mr. Clean" and nationwide attention in an America growing more environmentally conscious. Within 10 years, he had been chosen to run for Vice-President on the same ticket with Hubert Humphrey, a race that was lost by a razor thin-margin. Four years later he was candidate for President, considered the front-runner until he stumbled in an incident where, at Manchester, N.H., answering charges of anti-Franco-American bigotry that later turned out to be a Republican for-

Edmund S. Muskie

gery, he was deemed to have broken down and cried. Ultimately, he lost the Democratic nomination to Senator George McGovern, yet was able to cap his career a number of years later when President Jimmy Carter asked him to become Secretary of State during the Iran hostage crisis.

In all of Maine history, with the possible exception of Governor William King, no more distinguished Democrat has ever served the people of the state than this tall, Lincolnesque son of Polish immigrants who was born in Rumford, lived most of his adult life in Waterville and now resides primarily in Kennebunk.

The Allagash, Dickey-Lincoln and the Prestile Stream

Aroostook County, in the 1960's and beyond, was the site of some of the most contentious environmental battles in Maine history. Here, the decades-old issue of "payroll or pickerel" met in a series of titanic clashes and, in the end, *pickerel* seems to have won the day. The attempt to transform northernmost Maine through massive change met massive resistance and now, after all of the hullabaloo has died down, the areas affected do not seem much different from what they were before.

The Allagash
The Quoddy project, when revived by the Kennedy Administration in the early 1960's, had an Aroostook County component; that is, the notion of a hydroelectric dam on the St. John River to provide peaking power was tied to the original tidal project. In time, as Quoddy proved less and less feasible, the favorable cost-benefit ratio of the St. John project allowed such an idea to take on a life of its own.

A number of these St. John dam proposals were made. The first, apparently, was for a dam at Rankin Rapids and its immediate drawback was that it would flood 98% of the Allagash River area, then already in use as a popular wilderness canoe trip. Later, another proposal in a different location, the Cross Rock dam, purported to create a "Grand Allagash Lake" that would have allowed for at least five canoe trips in the immediate vicinity.

But public alarm over perceived threats to the Allagash led to a Federal study in 1963 for protection of the river, as part of a wider review of proposed flood control and hydroelectric development. The upshot was a proposal to put 150,000 acres around the Allagash into the National Wild Rivers program. Vigorous protests from affected landowners led to pressure for the state, itself, to take action. In 1964, the Maine Legislature created the Allagash River Authority, which presented its plan in 1965 for a Wilderness Waterway.

One argument of opponents was that the Allagash was hardly a bonafide wilderness, having been logged over for more than a hundred years. At least five dams existed in the area and one of the major tourist attractions for canoeists was an abandoned tramway and locomotives left rusting after a particularly heavy lumbering operation in the 1920's. Telos Lake at one end of the Allagash had been the site of the so-called "Telos War" in the early 19th. century between two lumber barons, David Pingree and Rufus Dwinel, and the dams and canals they built had directed the river from its natural northward flow so logs could be diverted into the Penobscot.

But by far the strongest opposition to the Allagash Wilderness Waterway came from proponents of the Cross Rock "Grand

Allagash Lake" proposal, to be constructed by a Maine Power Authority. As it happened, this scheme for "public power" received a sympathetic hearing from the 102nd Legislature, which, because of the Goldwater debacle of 1964, was, surprisingly, overwhelmingly Democratic. The Cross Rock supporters were reluctant to go ahead with the Wilderness Waterway until it had been studied in conjunction with their project. They held up final approval and it was not until the very last session of the 102nd. that the Waterway bill, including a $3 million bond issue that had to go to referendum, was passed. Its chief architect, State Senator Elmer Violette of Van Buren, was invited to be President Pro-Tem of the Senate for the enactment motion. The ultimate protected strip on both sides of the river and chain of lakes, approved by the voters, contained 22,760 acres of land and 30,000 acres of water.

Dickey-Lincoln

With the demise of the Rankin Rapids and Cross Rock dams, yet another alternative means of producing hydroelectric power from the St. John came into focus. Known colloquially as Dickey-Lincoln, the plan actually envisaged two dams—a relatively large

Dickey-Lincoln Dam proposal

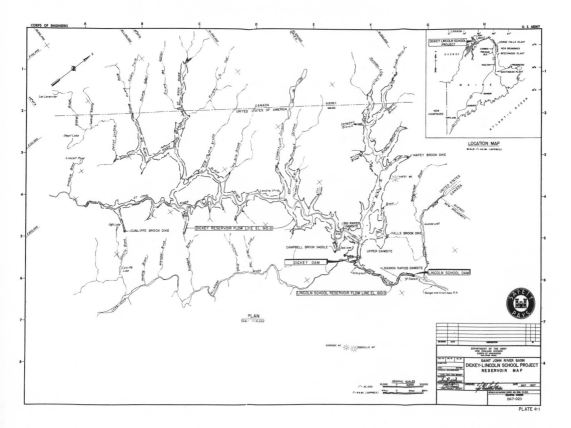

one at Dickey, buttressed by a smaller project at Lincoln School. Both together were to provide mostly peaking power, with some base load power, and were initially tied into Quoddy and then proclaimed able to stand on their own. The initial argument for Dickey-Lincoln was that it was a "conservationists' dam." It was located where it would not flood the Allagash.

Over a period of more than 20 years, Dickey-Lincoln convulsed the public life of Maine, dying a dozen deaths and rising phoenix-like again and again from the political ashes.

A paraphrase of selected newspaper headlines about Dickey-Lincoln tells its own chronological story:

July 28, 1963:	St. John Valley residents eye power project. Dickey area development boosts hope.
January 8, 1965:	Udall pressing for action on St. John dam at Dickey.
July 22, 1965:	Senator Margaret Chase Smith has asked President Johnson for his support in getting quick authorization for the Dickey-Lincoln School power project.
July 27, 1965:	Senator Muskie confident of quick OK on Dickey.
August 4, 1965:	New England private power companies charge...the proposed $300 million Dickey...project...will not bring low cost power to the six state area.
September 23, 1965:	House strikes down Dickey power project 207-185.
October 22, 1965:	House compromise gives Dickey $800,000.
September 21, 1966:	Cut in planning funds to stall Dickey for a year.
November 28, 1967:	Dickey is dead for '67.
January 15, 1969:	Dickey-Lincoln lives!
September 27, 1969:	Dickey suffers worst setback.
January 29, 1971:	Nixon drops Dickey from his budget.
December 1, 1973:	Representative William S. Cohen has appealed to President Nixon to "reconsider the merits" of Dickey-Lincoln and Quoddy.

May 4, 1974:	Senator William D. Hathaway criticized Environmentalists for opposing Dickey-Lincoln.
June 7, 1975:	(Governor) Longley's support of Dickey- Lincoln and (Congressman) Emery's opposition.
October 1, 1976:	L.L. Bean has joined the campaign against Dickey-Lincoln.
November 8, 1976:	A wild snapdragon (the Furbish lousewort) once thought extinct may kill project.
October 27, 1977:	Cohen now opposed.
October 27, 1978:	Longley announces his opposition.
June 6, 1979:	Maine Senate kills state referendum on Dickey.
July 27, 1979:	House Public Works Committee deauthorizes.
June 21, 1980:	Senator Mitchell supports compromise to delay Dickey for 6 years and build Lincoln School now.
October 24, 1980:	Cohen supports Lincoln School if Dickey is deauthorized.
May 11, 1981:	Dickey-Lincoln is finally dead but Lincoln School is alive.
August 4, 1983:	House Public Works Committee votes to deauthorize.
November 15, 1985:	Technically still alive because U.S. Senate has not voted on deauthorization.

So Dickey-Lincoln, like Glooskap or some other mythical figure of the north woods, remains an evanescent presence—yet another Quoddyish dream of super-development receding into memory. At least until 1991—for if a 1984 headline had it right:

October 12, 1984:	Failed to deauthorize, but will be automatically if it gets no appropriation for the next seven years.

The Prestile Stream

"Non-trend development" was a term one often heard in Maine in the 1960's. It meant large-scale projects that were not in line

333

with Maine's traditional industries. The big dams proposed for the St. John or Quoddy Bay were in that category, as were oil refineries and aluminum smelters on the coast. And, in agriculture, the big revolutionary move in the north country was to diversify away from a strict reliance on potatoes into sugar beets.

Here was a whole new crop to which Aroostook farmers, frequently hurt badly by manipulation of the potato futures market, could turn. And here, as well, was a major development project—a sugar refinery that had to be built (at the cost of $14.5 million) bringing what the area needed most—jobs! The County had been losing population steadily; whole communities, it almost seemed, of displaced Mainers from Aroostook had been springing up in Connecticut around Hartford and New Haven.

There was only one catch to this new panacea being dangled before Maine. The promoter of the project, a potato processor from New Jersey by the name of Fred H. Vahlsing, insisted that the water classification of a small river along which he would site the refinery had to be lowered from B, which was suitable for fish life, to D, basically an open sewer.

There were those who argued that the Prestile Stream, even before the sugar refinery was built, represented an open sewer anyway—polluted by an existing Vahlsing plant that processed potatoes. It was argued that the water stank, fish died in what was once a productive trout stream and the Maine Water Improvement Commission had cited 31 violations of the Prestile's B classification.

But Vahlsing had lined up his political ducks. Senators Muskie and Smith had helped gain an allotment out of Congress of 33,000 acres that could be planted to sugar beets. With the support of Republican Governor John H. Reed, himself an Aroostook potato farmer, and the Democratic 102nd Legislature, a bill to lower the stream's classification was passed. The arguments of some conservationists that Vahlsing was merely trying to legitimize the pollution caused by his potato plant fell on deaf ears.

The noble experiment of diversification to sugar beets never worked, however. It was said that Maine farmers were too conservative to change their habits. Closer to the truth was the fact that "Freddie" Vahlsing, after more than 20,000 acres had been planted, stopped paying the farmers. The refinery, built with guaranteed backing by the State and Federal governments, fell into disuse and had to be sold. Political recriminations continued for years.

Perhaps the most dramatic moment of the whole debacle occurred on July 9, 1968. On that date, a placid, middle-aged

334

Canadian electrician the former mayor of Centreville, New Brunswick, Robert Caines, organized a group of his friends to bulldoze an earthen dam across the by-now horrendously smelly Prestile and whilst TV cameras turned, they backed its fetid waters toward the U.S. border.

It was an international incident and was marked afterward by a concrete plaque reading:

> THIS INTERNATIONAL MONUMENT
> symbolizes the beginning of the citizens' war on pollution in
> western New Brunswick and eastern Maine and marks the site
> where aroused citizens built an earthen dam to stem the flow
> of pollution from the Vahlsing Inc. complex in Easton, Maine
> 9 July 1968
> This date marked the beginning of our war on pollution
> The war continues

The makeshift dam didn't last more than a day, but it eventually fulfilled its purpose. The dream of sugar beets had faded from Aroostook like the dream of Dickey-Lincoln and the other dam projects whose ghosts haunt the County. But that is not to say efforts have slackened to find new sources of employment and even new crops. In recent years, broccoli has been profitable for some Aroostook farmers. The Allagash Wilderness Waterway, now firmly established, draws large number of canoeists—too many, it is complained. And small projects—small companies—appear to have become the engine of Maine's present-day economic growth, rather than the grandiose schemes of the past that almost all essentially came to naught.

The Curtis Revolution

In the gubernatorial election of 1966, a slogan used both in the Republican primary and in the general election by the Democrats was a cryptic "7 not 11." Politically-minded Mainers knew that it was an exhortation to reject Governor John H. Reed, the Aroostook potato farmer who had served out three years of the unexpired term of the late Clinton Clausen, then served four years on his own and was seeking another four.

Opposed to Reed was a young, crew-cut graduate of the Maine Maritime Academy, Kenneth M. Curtis, then serving as

335

Secretary of State. Curtis, the son of a farmer in Androscoggin County, was only 35 years old. He was running on a platform of change, advertising that he had a "Maine Action Plan," which, in effect, was a party platform-like wish-list of programs he deemed important for arousing the state from a sense of age-old lethargy.

The people of Maine were impressed enough by Curtis's energy to overlook his youth and he was elected by 18,000 votes. What Maine people perhaps didn't foresee was that a political revolution was quietly in the making.

The Democrats in Maine had been steadily gaining since 1954 with the election of Ed Muskie to the Governor's chair. The post-Civil War pattern that Democrats could only triumph when the Republicans were split was no longer the case. Although Republicans were to dominate the Legislature during all of Curtis's two terms, their grip was weakening.

Governor Kenneth Curtis

Moreover, in terms of accomplishment, Ken Curtis achieved a number of governmental breakthroughs. Two major pieces of environmental legislation—the first of their kind in the United States—were passed. One was the Site Selection Law, which required major development projects to undergo review and receive the approval of a Board of Environmental Protection made up of appointed citizens. The second, the Oil Conveyance Law, put a special tax per barrel on all oil transported through the state (all oil for Montreal goes via Portland) to be used in a special fund to deal with oil spills. Both were initiatives of his office, as was a massive reorganization of the state government, reducing more than 200 governmental bodies that reported directly to the Governor to a more manageable set of some 15 umbrella departments. He also moved to consolidate the separate campuses of the University of Maine into a single system under an overall Chancellor, despite strong parochial opposition. But as notable as these changes were, they paled in importance and controversy beside the startling transformation Curtis wrought in the state's tax structure. Most Governors don't dare even to raise existing taxes. Curtis instituted an entirely new one—the State Income Tax—and survived politically!

He didn't do it easily, winning his 1970 re-election bid by a hairline margin of less than 500 votes. It was not until more than a month after the election that Maine knew who its Governor would be and that Curtis had bested James Erwin, the Attorney General. Next followed a citizen-initiated attempt to repeal the State Income Tax just passed. The conventional wisdom was that voters, if given the chance to vote out a tax, would do so easily. Confounding the experts, Maine people voted almost 3-1 to keep the tax.[2]

Ken Curtis, despite the anger he had engendered by imposing an income tax, finished his eight years as Governor with an extremely high popularity rating. It was generally conceded he had changed Maine government and Maine significantly during his two terms; as his biographer[3] described the theme behind his intent: "the determination to break the hold of obstructive forces that ruled Maine for generations, limiting its options, protecting the interests of the few, driving away the most talented of the young who found no opportunity at home...", it can be said that Ken Curtis and the people he brought into state service acted as a liberating force. Ironically, most of his accomplishments were not in the area dearest to his heart—economic development. Plans for

337

mammoth "non-trend development" projects, which usually attracted his attention and support, like the idea of a major oil port down east, never came to fruition. And Curtis is remembered more for environmental breakthroughs—Site Selection, Oil Conveyance, the single largest bond issue in state history for cleaning up the rivers, zoning the wildlands, coastal zoning, adding land to public access—than for specific economic improvements. He, himself, recognized the limitations that Maine's geographical location and essential nature placed on the direction of its future. As he said:

> I think the next twenty-five years are going to be some of the brightest in the last hundred, but I don't think Maine is going to become a huge area population-wise or development-wise. We're finding out that's not the answer. We're going to have good development. We're going to offer good programs for minority groups, mental health, our hospitals, our prisoners, our educational system. I think we're going to offer good quality which is probably more difficult to offer. I think this is exciting. I think anybody coming up here looking for a blue-print of what's called excitement in other areas is going to be disappointed. They're going to have to take satisfaction in enjoying a good life.

The Indian Land Claims Case

Among the many "firsts" of the Curtis Administration was the Governor's appointment of an Indian to head up the state's Department of Indian Affairs. This had never been done before. In fact, no Native American had even been an executive of that body until Curtis appointed first a Deputy Commissioner, Michael Crawford, a Penobscot, and then a Passamaquoddy, John Stevens, as Commissioner.

Maine Indians were "State" Indians. That is to say, they did not come under Federal jurisdiction, as was the case with most of the tribes in the United States. Ever since 1820, they had been strictly under state tutelage and, for the most part, treated with condescension if not outright hostility and neglect. Once the greater portion of their land had been taken from them by treaty, they were left with only a few small parcels. The Penobscots lived on Indian Island at Old Town and owned some uninhabited islands in the Penobscot River; the Passamaquoddies lived at two sites:

338

Pleasant Point near Eastport and Peter Dana Point in Princeton and owned a township (23,000 acres) of woodland. There were also a few scattered communities elsewhere of Malecites, Micmacs and mixed tribal groupings (like the Houlton Band) who were not officially under state protection.

The treaty, signed in 1794, that had left the Passamaquoddies their township and bits and pieces of other land (including some islands too) had been violated frequently. One hundred and seventy years later, in 1964, the islands had long since passed out of their possession and so had about 6,000 acres of their township. When a white man named William Plaisted began to cut a road through what the Passamaquoddies considered their land, they physically blocked it. A number were arrested and they hired an activist lawyer, new to the area, Don Gellers, to defend them.

It was Gellers' intervention in this affair that led circuitously to the Indian Land Claims case, nothing less than a legitimate demand by Maine's two foremost tribes for essentially two-thirds of the land area of the State of Maine. It was a case that reached to Washington D.C., directly into the White House, involved all of Maine's most prominent politicians and cast a cloud over the land titles of a majority of Mainers. It was, in short, a mammoth challenge.

The involvement of Don Gellers also resulted in the involvement of a young law student from St. Louis, Tom Tureen. When Gellers was arrested in Eastport on a possession of marijuana charge, Tureen succeeded him in supplying legal assistance to the Passamaquoddies. Research on the tribe's status vis a vis State and Federal law led him to examine an early Congressional law—the Indian Non-Intercourse Act of 1790.

This legislation decreed that all treaties signed between states and Indian tribes subsequent to 1790 had to be ratified by Congress. The treaties between Massachusetts and Maine's two major Indian tribes had both been signed after 1790 and neither had been submitted to Congress for ratification. Tureen's conclusion was that the treaties were null and void.

Nor, as it turned out, was he alone in this opinion. A letter from the Passamaquoddies to Louis R. Bruce, Commissioner of the Federal Bureau of Indian Affairs, sent on Washington's Birthday 1972, soon was drawing Federal sympathy for the tribe's request that the U.S. Department of Justice represent them in a lawsuit to recover their lands.

But despite encouragement from Governor Curtis and

Maine's entire Congressional delegation, the Federal government finally balked at assisting the Indians. On June 2, Tureen went into Federal court and obtained an order from Judge Edward T. Gignoux requiring the Justice Department to represent the Indians. That same month, two suits, each for $50 million in damages, were filed on behalf of the Passamaquoddies and Penobscots.

Not until the end of 1975 did a higher court uphold Judge Gignoux's opinion that the Non-Intercourse Act applied to Maine's tribes. By then, the state had a new Governor, James B. Longley, a maverick insurance man from Lewiston who had been elected as an Independent. Tureen tried to negotiate a settlement with him, but Longley refused to concede the claim had merit, as did the new Attorney General, Democrat Joseph Brennan. In September 1976, the gravity of the situation was brought home to Maine people when Ropes and Gray, the prestigious Boston bond counsel, said it would no longer give unqualified approval to municipal bonds issued within the area the Indians claimed. Shortly thereafter, the sale of $27 million in bonds was cancelled or delayed.

In the war of words that followed, Tureen pointed out how the two $150 million damage suits pending represented only the loss of rent the Indians had suffered on their lands. The true cost of indemnifying the Passamaquoddies and Penobscots would be $25 *billion*!

However, the Indians agreed to compromise. They would not press any claim for two million acres of heavily populated land on the Maine coast nor would they pursue claims against any homeowner or small property owner elsewhere in the state.

Attempts by the Maine Congressional delegation to pass legislation to extinguish the Indians' claims met with failure. Then, President Jimmy Carter intervened, naming a Georgia Supreme Court Justice, William Gunter, as his special emissary to adjudicate the dispute.

The compromise proposed by Judge Gunter received mixed review, but included a provision for Federal payment to the Indians. This idea was then included in a settlement proposed by a three person task force next established by President Carter. A memorandum of understanding hammered out between this White House Work Group and a Passamaquoddy-Penobscot Negotiating Committee initially called for payments of $1.7 million a year for 15 years to the tribes, the granting to them of 300,000 acres and options to buy 200,000 more.

The reaction in Maine was explosive, with Governor Longley, Attorney General Brennan and the two Republican Congressmen Cohen and Emery loud in their opposition, while the two Democratic Senators Muskie and Hathaway urged that the proposal be given serious consideration. In the end, the issue was to defeat Hathaway, who offered to broker an out of court settlement, when, up for re-election in 1978, he was challenged by Cohen.

Yet Maine did agree finally to negotiate. The tortured course of these deliberations and the eventual passage of a Maine Indian Land Claims act through the U.S. Congress was to take another two years. An eventual appropriation of $81.5 million was signed by President Carter on December 12, 1980 and the money deposited to the Indians' account in the U.S. Treasury.

Some of the money has been used to buy land. Under the terms of the agreement, the Indians were to acquire up to 300,000 acres. Among the parcels bought by the Passamaquoddies were 4,000 of the 6,000 acres in their own Indian Townships, which had been unfairly taken from them.

The money has also been used for investments. The Passamaquoddies bought the state's only cement manufacturing plant and recently sold it to a Spanish company at a significant profit. They own a major blueberry-producing farm and a radio station. The Penobscots have established a cassette- manufacturing plant on their property, providing jobs for Indians and non-Indians alike. Both tribes also persuaded the Legislature to allow them to run the state's only high-stakes Beano games, which help provide additional funding for community services since the reservations have no property tax base.

The state's Department of Indian Affairs no longer exists. It was felt that with the settlement, the tribes could handle their own affairs. The Passamaquoddies and Penobscots still have their Representatives in the Maine House who advise the lawmakers on Indian matters. In 1975, after a 40 year hiatus, they were allowed to be seated in the chamber following a heated debate.[4] In the intervening years, the change in attitude in Augusta toward Maine Indians has been so marked that it seems inconceivable now that arguments could have been made against including them fully in the governmental process.

In other words, the denouement of the Indian Land Claims case in Maine has been an essentially happy ending. It has brought a measure of prosperity to the tribes and with that prosperity, a modicum of respect. With their enhanced self-image, the Maine

341

Indians are also now actively protecting their cultural identity in such projects as the Museum and Passamaquoddy Language Program established by Joseph Nicholas at Pleasant Point. They are trying equally hard to deal with their social problems, such as a high rate of alcoholism, and to enhance educational opportunities for their people. Their success, according to Tom Tureen, has had an impact on Indian tribes throughout the country.

Longley, the Independent Governor

Toward the close of Ken Curtis's second term in office, he became the first liberal Democratic Governor to institute a Management and Cost Survey Commission—essentially a gimmick dreamed up by a Chicago businessman named Warren King who, for a hefty fee, would set up an organization of businessmen to go over the state government and recommend ways it could save money. Until

Governor James Longley

342

Maine, King's customers had all been conservatives but Curtis's staff argued he needed to balance his image as a big spender, big taxer and promoter of big government with a sense of administrative tightening. To head up the organization, Curtis finally settled upon a former Portland Law School classmate of his, a highly successful Lewiston insurance salesman, James B. Longley.

Longley, although unhappy with the income tax, *had* supported Curtis in his perilous re-election bid. After some prodding, Longley agreed to take the cost survey job. A dispute later raged over whether or not he had ever promised he wouldn't try to use the position for political advancement. Or how he had couched his promise, for he was a master at manipulating words. In any event, at the time, it must have seemed inconceivable that an obscure insurance man, even when brought into the limelight, could do what he eventually did—generate enough heat over a number of cost-cutting proposals, some of them politically preposterous in the eyes of most observers, to become a viable gubernatorial candidate—and moreover, one without a party!

The Longley Report, as it was called when it came out, purported to save millions of dollars. Some of the savings were to come from closing or curtailing institutions—several campuses of the University of Maine, for example,—and in one case, savings of $2.5 million were claimed by the mere shifting to a different budget format. In all, Longley was to state that if he were given free rein, he could save the state $250 million.

But he wasn't given free rein. Strong legislative opposition met many of his recommendations once they were translated into legislation. Out of 92 of them, only 33 survived to become law. The bill containing his plans to trim the University was massacred, 131-4 in the House and 22-4 in the Senate.

Then, he had an issue. The politicians—organized party people—had thwarted the popular good. With his amazing energy, his hypnotic blue eyes and gift of gab, he went out and sold the Maine electorate.

The times, moreover, were propitious. It was the era of Watergate and a searing disillusionment of Americans with government. The party candidates also unwittingly helped. For the Republicans, James Erwin was running again, a conservative of the old school, and many Republicans deserted him because they felt he couldn't win and because Longley's right-wingish message also suited them. The Democratic candidate, George Mitchell, had just been through a bruising primary battle with the Democratic

343

Senate Minority Leader Joseph Brennan, some of whose disillusioned followers rallied to Longley, himself a former Democrat. It also helped that the insurance man came from Lewiston, a Democratic stronghold—and highly conservative.

Running under the "Longley for ME." ticket, the Independent candidate finished 3 percentage points ahead of Democrat Mitchell and 8 percentage points ahead of Republican Erwin.

From the start, his gubernatorial reign was stormy. He frequently clashed with the Legislature. Republicans (who controlled the Senate) and Democrats (who controlled the House) banded together to override his vetoes again and again. On one occasion in the House, the override vote was 135-0. ("Our first shut-out!", one wag cried). In a famous incident, he prompted a shouting match over dinner with the legislative leadership at the Blaine House when he referred to legislators as "pimps." He was also famous for the rambling letters he wrote to those who had offended him and who mostly kept the letters, amused and amazed by their odd syntax, twists of logic and exaggerations. Example: when Democratic Representative Richard Spencer told a party caucus that Longley was being deceitful by claiming his school funding plan carried no tax increase, he received a blistering missive, its last paragraph a masterpiece of Longleyan style:

> At least give me the credit of being more direct and straightforward than you chose to be as your statements and headlines do not injure me or embarrass me personally, but my children and my entire family are entitled to resent you and your statements. very much. Hopefully, they will recognize your character and integrity is best illustrated by the methods and manner of your attacks on another person. With all my faults, they already know that you are not as straight-forward and direct and constructive as I am. Furthermore, I do not think you reflect very well on your constituents, let alone yourself and your family.

Yet for all of the commotion he caused, all of the hand-wringing among those responsible for governmental services, Longley was extremely popular. He undoubtedly could have been re-elected had he chosen to run. But in his campaign, he had promised he would only serve one term. It was all he would need, he boasted, to set the State of Maine straight. And he kept his word. When 1978 approached, he did not offer himself as a candidate.

344

During the 1976 legislative elections, there had been a concerted effort by Longley and his supporters ("Longley's Legions")
to run Independent candidates. Not one of a score of them was
successful, not even the Governor's own sister. Thus, the move to
broaden his constituency, to give him the support he needed to
keep Republicans and Democrats alike from ganging up on him,
had faltered and it might have been thought that his disillusionment had led him to withdraw from the political arena.

But speculation of a different sort claimed he simply had his
eye on bigger game. James B. Longley, this theory held, wanted to
President of the United States and saw a chance to accomplish on
a national scale what he had done in Maine—tarnish both of the
political parties and in their weakened condition, blow past them
on a wave of populism into the White House. His constant contacts with the national press reinforced such an idea. David
Broder, the respected columnist of the Washington Post, came to
Maine and wrote articles speculating on such a possibility.

If so, it was never to be. Shortly after retiring from the Governor's office, Jim Longley was on a ski trip with his family when,
sitting in the lodge, he suddenly suffered a tremendous pain in his
stomach. He later said he felt "as if a horse had kicked me." The
trouble was diagnosed as stomach cancer. All the tremendous
energy and will of this remarkable man were of no avail against a
particularly malignant form of the disease. Within months,
Maine's only Independent Governor, age 50, was dead.

Focus

Samantha Smith

Most of the monuments around the State
House in Augusta are those one would
expect of a governmental entity: portraits
of distinguished-looking men (and one
woman, Senator Margaret Chase Smith),
a bust of Governor Percival Baxter, a
bronze plaque memorializing a particular
war hero. But also on the grounds of the
capitol complex, hard by the Cultural
building, is the full-length statue of a
young girl, holding a dove in her hands.

It is a tribute to Samantha Reed
Smith of nearby Manchester who died at
the age of 13 in a plane crash at the Lewiston-Auburn airport. By then, she had
become world-famous for her visit to the
Soviet Union two years earlier at the
invitation of Yuri Andropov, the
General Secretary of the Communist
Party of the USSR.

Samantha's odyssey had begun
quite inadvertently. As an intelligent, in-

quiring ten year old, she had been troubled by the threat of nuclear war she had heard discussed on a television program and at her mother's suggestion, she wrote to the Soviet leader. Point-blank, she asked him: "...Are you going to vote to have a war or not? If you aren't, please tell me how you are going to help to not have a war..." With even more ingenuous bluntness, she demanded, "...I would like to know why you want to conquer the world or at least our country. God made the world for us to live together in peace and not to fight."

The first inkling, after a silence of four or five months, that Andropov might show any interest was an article in *Pravda* about the Maine schoolgirl's letter. Then came word from the Soviet embassy in Washington that Andropov would reply to her.

Likening Samantha as "a coura-geous and honest girl" to Becky Thatcher, the heroine of Mark Twain's "Tom Sawyer," Andropov emphasized the Soviet Union's desire for peace and then invited Samantha to visit his country, preferably in the summer, one of the objects being for her to go to the "Artek" international children's camp in the Crimea.

Andropov's gesture made Samantha Smith an instant celebrity, interviewed by dozens of reporters and invited to be on national television talk shows. Even a Soviet TV crew came to Manchester to interview her.

Then, her journey took place, amid the same frenzy of publicity. Although Samantha never did get to meet with Andropov, she did travel extensively in the Soviet Union and climaxed her trip with a stay at the Artek camp.

On exhibit in the State House in Augusta have been artifacts of her

Statue of Samantha Smith

historic voyage—the many gifts she received, including a magnificent samovar, the "Pioneer" uniform she wore as an Artek camper, posters of cultural events, costumes, dolls, scrapbooks, etc.

That she received such VIP attention from the Soviet authorities also caused some dissenting views on what she was doing. Russian emigres in Richmond complained that she was being used for propaganda purposes. An ex-U.S. Ambassador to Moscow, Mal-colm Toon, sounded a familiar theme.

Through this whirl, Samantha, a remarkably poised and photogenic

346

youngster, handled herself in a manner that not only won high praise but later drew her into other public activities. She narrated a series of television ads for the Maine Department of Inland Fisheries and Game, instructing children lost in the woods what to do. She went on NBC's "Today Show" and asked questions about the arms race of Kenneth Adelman, the head of the U.S. Arms Control Agency. She and her family went to Japan to help promote an international science and technology exposition. She did coverage of the 1984 presidential campaign for the Disney Channel. And all of her exposure on television led eventually to an invitation to try out for a role in a television series. She won the part on a show called "Lime Street," cast as actor Robert Wagner's teen-age daughter. It was while returning from the filming of an episode that she and her father died on the last leg of the flight back to Augusta.

Jane Smith, her mother, has since created the Samantha Smith Foundation, dedicated to perpetuating her daughter's achievements on behalf of international understanding. A key feature of the Foundation's activity is the exchange of young people, particularly between the U.S. and the U.S.S.R. In the summer of 1989, the Samantha Smith World Peace Camp opened in Mane in Poland Springs, with 20 Soviet teenagers mingling with 150 Americans. Also, 32 additional Soviet youth were at other Maine camps, sponsored by the Samantha Smith Foundation.

Maine, heavily wooded, dotted by lakes, struck a familiar chord with some of the Soviet youngsters—perhaps too familiar. "I thought the United States was skyscrapers, Pepsi, cowboys and jeans," said one with a touch of disappointment. But clearing up misconceptions could be deemed what Samantha Smith was all about.

Recent Times

Not too long ago, a Maine schoolgirl's foray from her hometown to places as exciting as Bangor or Portland or as distantly exotic as Boston would have been considered something extraordinary. That Samantha Smith went to the Soviet Union and Japan, as she did, betokens Maine's escape from a parochialism that hung on until perhaps the last twenty years.

It has been pointed out that Maine in the 1830's, 40's and 50's, with its seafaring background, was far more cosmopolitan than Maine in the 1930's, 40's and 50's. The breakthrough of modernization, once it began in the late 1960's and early 1970's, never has been interrupted. People have flocked to Maine from "Away," settling here, helping to change the state's demographic balance from a negative outflow to a positive inflow and bringing new ideas and energy. Samantha Smith was actually an example.

347

Her father, Arthur Smith, came from West Virginia to teach at Ricker College in Houlton, where she was born. The family later moved to the Augusta area where her mother, also from "Away," worked for the State Department of Human Services.

And yet with such growth, pushing Maine over the one million mark in population, has come a determination, often fueled by these very same immigrants from other states, to preserve a sense of the quietude and distinct charm that attracted them. Environmental protests have flared against virtually every major development proposal presented in recent times, whether a still-pending cargo port at Searsport, a power-line from Canada through Franklin County, an incinerator ash dump in Washington County, and most especially, the Federal government's consideration of nuclear waste sites in western Cumberland County and Piscataquis County. Three times, also, in the past few decades, Maine voters have faced initiated referenda, seeking to shut down the Maine Yankee nuclear power plan in Wiscasset. Three times, the vote has been remarkably close, although in favor of keeping the facility open.

The huge economic development projects of the past—Dickey-Lincoln, Quoddy, Machiasport, etc.—seem to have faded from the Maine scene. Small flareups have occurred, like the Great Northern Paper Company's proposed "Big A" dam on the West Branch of the Penobscot, but in this case faced with determined opposition, the company rather quickly withdrew from the fray.

The crises of these latter years thus may be viewed as "normal crises." Strikes, like those in the 1980's at International Paper in Jay and Boise-Cascade in Rumford, were bitter and prolonged, but somehow lacked the drama of earlier labor-management collisions like the Lewiston-Auburn strike of 1937. And despite these occasional disputes, new industries came to Maine n record numbers and most of them small outfits, earning the fashionable title of "entrepreneurial." Parts of Maine, Portland and surroundings in particular, became "yuppified," another favorite word of the '80's, and the revitalized city gained what it boasted of as a "world-class" art museum. Sugarloaf developed into a major ski resort and condominium area. Hallowell, playing on its picturesqueness became a somewhat bohemian antiques capital. Kittery and Freeport blossomed as discount outlet havens.

If nothing else, the transformation of L.L. Bean, the venerable mail-order merchandising company, epitomized the melding of an old Maine institution into a new entity. It was a company formed almost by accident when a young Maine devotee of hunting, Leon

348

Leonwood Bean, invented a new type of part-leather, part-rubber boot to keep his feet dry in the woods. He marketed it through the mails, offered other sporting goods, plus a total guarantee of his product, kept his store open seven days a week, 24 hours a day and built a modestly successful retail operation. Now, with hundreds of computers and more than 30,000 orders to fill a day, (a growing number from overseas), L.L. Bean is a giant in the mail order and sporting goods trade, also drawing thousands of visitors, while retaining its Maine philosophy of pleasant service and backed-up quality.

Politically, these latter years have seen the state on a generally level keel. The Republican hegemony of the post-Civil War era has been broken in Augusta by several Democratic governors and a series of Democratic Legislatures. Democrat Joseph Brennan followed Independent James Longley in the Governor's chair and served two terms in which he managed to restore state services diminished by Longley, but without raising taxes. He was succeeded by the first Republican Governor in more than 20 years, John R. McKernan of Bangor.

George Mitchell, the unsuccessful Democratic gubernatorial candidate in 1972, has had a meteoric career since then. Appointed a Federal Attorney and then a Federal Judge, he left the latter lifetime sinecure when Governor Brennan appointed him to the U.S. Senate in 1982 to fill the unexpired term of Ed Muskie. Less than seven years later, George Mitchell was elected by his peers to be the Majority Leader of the U.S. Senate. He is currently one of the most powerful political figures in the United States.

And the most powerful, the President, also has Maine connections. George Bush, although a Texas voter, spends most of his spare time, it seems, in Kennebunkport where his magnificent family home at Walker's Point has become a national tourist attraction. This has also become a local problem as the town, the county, the state and the Federal government all quibble over who is going to pay the added cost of protecting he nation's chief while on vacation. Kennebunkport, exercising down east spunk, has refused any longer to absorb the cost.

In any event, the Bush residency and the Mitchell position of leadership in Washington have once more cast Maine into the national limelight. They have brought back echoes of the days of Blaine and Speaker Reed. Today, Maine no longer is spoken about as "a finished piece," a sort of quaint, pretty doodad tucked on a shelf up in the north east corner of the country. It is still a land of

349

unsurpassed beauty, diamond-bright in its attractiveness, human in its dimensions, rich in its history, and now, about to enter the 21st century, adapting rapidly, not without strain, to a global world that once seemed remote. The land that emerged from under the glacier of 14,000 years ago has been shaped by its people and shapes their values, in turn. Maine! The image seems sharper than ever before.

A FINAL WORD

It has become fashionable within the state at present to speak of
"the two Maines"—a phenomenon attributed to an aura of prosperity seemingly lending a gilt edge to certain sections. Some call
it a "north-south" split, with the traditional underdevelopment
and poverty bemoaned statewide in the past now assigned to the
north, alone. This notion, perhaps, misses the point that the most
notable exposition of Maine poverty as a way of life, told with ex-
cruciating reality in the novel "The Beans of Egypt, Maine," had
York County in the south as its setting. Or at least that was the
home of its author, Carolyn Chute.

"The other Maine" is a term also used for the seamier side of
life in the picturesque Pine Tree State. Crystallizing around the
Chute novel has been a proliferation of literary works, identifying
in fiction and non-fiction alike a "real Maine," far from the sugar-
coated images of earlier literature and of glossy magazines like
Downeast. The *Maine Times* pioneered as a muck-raking publication and now has imitators. Counter-culture exists and the state's
most famous native-born author, Stephen King, makes millions
out of horror stories straight from an unconscious that seems tied
to some sublime gothic quality in the Maine air and landscape.

What all this talk of "two Maines" is doing is reinforcing the
sense of a changing Maine. Once, not very long ago, all of Maine
could have been termed poor and economically undeveloped.
Now, true or not, the southern counties particularly are perceived

as having experienced a genuine boom.

But the idea of "two Maines" or even a "single" Maine is too simplistic for at least one important group that has recently examined the state of the state. The Commission on Maine's Future, the second of its kind established by the Legislature, this one in 1987, commissioned a poll to study the contemporary values of Maine people and whole new set of population break-downs emerged from this "psychographic" survey. Thus, Mainers are no longer divided *north or south*, or *east or west*, but fall into categories of *Suburbanites, Yankees, Bystanders, Milltowners, Post-Hippies, Young Urbanites, Activists* and *Expatriates*. Of the conclusions drawn from what was termed the first use of these "psychographic" groups in a poll done in Mane and "possibly the first ever conducted in the United States by a state-sponsored public body," the following stood out:

- Maine people are conservative in their religious, social and family values. But the growing up of the baby boomers and the influx of newcomers (now 8% of the population) portends a shift to less conservative ideas, particularly more active government intervention in social issues.
- Maine people are also tolerant of different beliefs, backgrounds and even lifestyles, despite their natural conservatism.
- Maine people give high priority to preservation of the state's natural beauty and access to it—an even higher priority than to the creation of economic development opportunities.
- Maine people are still wary of government, 40% feeling the state bureaucracy is unresponsive to their needs.
- Maine people support education, but see it primarily as a means to further career opportunities.

Finally, a distinction was made by the respondents to the survey between "quality of life" and "way of life." In this regard, "quality of life" is seen as economic growth and betterment; "way of life' the simple Mane lifestyle, rooted in the natural beauty of the state and people's access to the outdoors.

No one has quite yet exactly defined the Maine "way of life." Perhaps the closest to come to it are Maine's humorists, a group, essentially, of storytellers who are achieving significant popularity. The often hilarious performances of humorists such as Tim

Sample, Kendall Morse, Joe Perham, Robert Skoglund, etc., drive home the point that there is a quintessential Maine culture and these extended jokes are its contribution to the nation. On the drawing boards at the moment is even a proposal for a Museum of Maine Humor to be established as a tourist attraction in Freeport, that burgeoning center of retail trade inspired by L.L. Bean.

"Maine Humor," therefore, has reached a plateau of recognition. "New Hampshire Humor" doesn't have the same ring, nor does talk of "North Dakota Humor" or "Ohio Humor." It is done in its own inimitable dialect and accent, as well, which its progenitors admit has a resemblance to English. It is "dry," yet ineffably flavored, so that it is identified at once and is usually played out against the foibles of people from "Away," who, in turn bring out a perverse quality of wit in the natives that all of the audience, whichever "psychographic" cast they fit can appreciate.

Maine began forming under glacier ice a mile thick fourteen thousand years ago. Maine humorists might quip that some people from "Away" think the same frigid condition prevails to this day. Those who live in this extraordinary state know it 'taint so—that the warm, kindly, level-headed people of Maine have forged out of the vicissitudes of history a lasting and unique civilization, which they'd just as soon keep hidden from the rest of the world but are extremely proud of, nonetheless.

END NOTES

CHAPTER TWO

[1] Luring them overseas were stories of stupendous fishery resources. Sebastian Cabot, John's son, even claimed his ship's progress had been held up by unimaginably thick schools of cod.

[2] Norumbega traditionally has been located in Maine. It is said that Verrazano gave a name like Oranbega to a place on Penobscot Bay which was transmuted into Norumbega. A large, palisaded Indian Village at Penobscot Falls may have been another source.

[3] The one town there is named Gosnold.

[4] Shortly after arriving in England, Biard and the other French captives were freed and sent home to France.

CHAPTER THREE

[1] Wells included Kennebunk until 1820 and Ogunquit until 1819.

[2] He left an estate of £290, whereas under Winter he earned £5 a year.

[3] Lygonia comes from Lygon, the maiden name of Sir Ferdinando Gorges's mother. It was also called the Plough Patent from the ship *Plough*, which carried the initial Patentees to America.

[4] Francis Jennings in "The Invasion of America"

CHAPTER FOUR

[1] The mission had an ill-starred finish. Dutch Privateers seized the ship carrying all of their papers and their spokesman, Sir Robert Carr, died as soon as they landed.

CHAPTER FIVE

[1] His majesty's ire was communicated to Massachusetts in the following words: "We were much surprised, while listening to the complaints of Mr. Gorges, that you should presume without asking our royal permission to purchase his interest in the Province of Maine, acquainted, as you know we are, with some of the effects of the severe hand you have holden over our subjects there."

[2] Ironically, the same date of Concord and Lexington.

[3] Phips was uncommonly big. "Thick as well as tall and strong as well as Thick," wrote Cotton Mather.

[4] A replica can be seen on the same site today.

CHAPTER SIX

[1] There is the town of Pepperell in Massachusetts, named for Sir William, but misspelled with only one r.

CHAPTER SEVEN

[1] The deed is attributed to Calvin Lombard of Gorham, a minister's son.

[2] Also often spelled Pier Thoma

[3] A kindly American settler was given 500 *lashes* for feeding an English deserter.

CHAPTER EIGHT

[1] In 1778, when the Continental Congress divided the country up into admiralty districts, Maine officially became the *District* of Maine.

[2] During the activist years of the 1960's, a Penobscot civil rights leader who called herself Sipsis sardonically demanded that the Maine government, which long ago had converted these items to cash equivalents, provide the actual goods enumerated in the treaties.

[3] The same William Widgery of New Gloucester who had been such a foe of the U.S. Constitution.

[4] Another rejected suggestion was "Ligonia."

CHAPTER NINE

[1] The Whig, Edward Kent, both preceded and succeeded Fairfield.

[2] John Forsyth was Secretary of State under both Jackson and Van Buren.

[3] Kent didn't run for re-election in 1842 and Fairfield easily defeated Edward Robinson, Whig and James Appleton of the Liberty Party.

CHAPTER TEN

[1] Ancestral home of President John F. Kennedy.

[2] The State's main Democratic newspaper, the

Eastern Argus, fumed that they were "temperance men know-nothings, know-somethings, Free-Soilers, Abolitionists, Whigs who had forgotten their names. Democrats who had forgotten their principles...all lying down in the same political trundle bed."
[3] She was the daughter of his first wife. His second wife was the niece of Governor William King.
[4] Changed to "Pink Chimneys" in a recent novel about the era by Ardeana Hamlin Knowles of Hampden.
[5] Now preserved at South Portland.

CHAPTER ELEVEN

[1] "The Civil War" by Ralph Newman & E.B. Long, Grosset & Dunlap, Inc., New York, 1956, Volume II.
[2] Like Berry, Burnham was killed in action.
[3] A guilt-ridden Charles Sumner helped him get the appointment.

CHAPTER TWELVE

[1] "A bastard, scrub aristocracy," he called the clique around Jefferson Davis.
[2] Under the Freedmen's Bureau Legislation, the South was divided into 10 districts, each headed by an Assistant Commissioner.
[3] Charles Edward Russell "Blaine of Maine His Life and Times" New York, 1931
[4] Chase was no illiterate; he edited a newspaper in his hometown of Turner, but later candidly admitted that if he'd said "those steers," he would have lost his audience.
[5] Frederick Hale, son of U.S. Senator Eugene Hale, also became a G.O.P. U. S. Senator from Maine.

CHAPTER THIRTEEN

[1] International Paper, a conglomerate of 20 mills, was formed in Maine around 1897.
[2] Based on the distance between the wheels of ancient Roman chariots.

CHAPTER FOURTEEN

[1] When the Acadians were exiled in 1755, they were scattered from Maine to Louisiana. In 1761, 21 of these unfortunates lived in York as paupers, supported by welfare payments from the Province of Massachusetts.
[2] With a national reputation, and touted as a future winner of the Pulitzer Prize.
[3] The author was in Belgrade, Jugoslavia in 1951 and met a U.N. official who was searching for the several hundred thousand White Russians who had disappeared since Tito's assumption of power.
[4] The very word *Shul* means "School" in Yiddish, indicating that a synagogue, more than a place of worship, is a place for study and education.
[5] Others: Congressman Peter Kynos, Democratic Party Chairman Harold Pachios, State Senator Peter Danton.

CHAPTER FIFTEEN

[1] Another version has it that it was Wyman's name on the bill.
[2] Bowdoin and Harvard Law School.

CHAPTER SIXTEEN

[1] Election laws have since been changed in Maine to prevent this type of "sorehead" candidate; today, an independent has to announce as an independent prior to the Primary.
[2] An oddly coincidental aspect of this fight was the names of the two leading proponents for and against the tax: *Scott Fox* versus *Scott Lamb!*
[3] Kermit Lipez, a one-time staffer, now a superior court judge.
[4] The author, as Majority Leader in the Maine House at the time, had to lead the fight for the order that seated the Indian Reps.

BIBLIOGRAPHY

Allen, Charles E.: *Huguenot Settlers in Dresden, Maine*; Maine Historical Society Paper, March 17, 1892.

Allen, James P.: *Franco-Americans in Maine, A Geographical Perspective*; University of New Brunswick.

American Revolution Bicentennial Administration, Region I: *The Underground Railroad in Maine*.

Bagley, Marion M.: *Maine History Can Be Fun*; J. Weston Walch, Portland, 1956.

Bakeless, John: *The Eyes of Discovery*; Dover Publications, Inc., New York, 1961.

Baker, Emerson: *John Howland's Howling Wilderness*; The Kennebec Proprietor, Vol. 3, No. 2, Spring 1986.

Banks, Charles Edward: *History of York, Maine*; Regional Publishing Co., Baltimore, 1967.

Banks, Ronald (Ed): *A History of Maine*; Kendall Hunt Publishing Co., Dubuque, Iowa, 1969.

Barry, William David: *The Shameful Story of Malaga Island*; Down East, Nov. 1980.

Baxter, James Phinney: *The Pioneers of New France in New England*; Joel Munsell's Sons, Albany, N.Y., 1894.

Baxter, Percival P.: Mount Katahdin State Park Speech given January 27, 1921.

Beals, Carleton: *Brass-Knuckle Crusade*; Hastings House, New York, 1960.

Beck, Horace P.: *The Folklore of Maine*; J.B. Lippincott Co., Philadelphia & New York, 1957. *Gluskap The Liar*.

Bellarmin, Antonio Dragon: *L'Arcadie et ses 40 Robes Noirs*; Les Editions Bellarmin, Montreal, 1973.

Bonfanti, Leo: *Biographies and Legends of New England Indians*, Vols. 1 & 2; Pride Publications, Wakefield, Mass., 1970. *The Massachusetts Bay Colony*, Vols. 1 & 2; 1974 & 1980.

Bradley, Robert: *Maine's First Buildings*; Maine Historic Preservation Commission, Augusta, 1978.

Burrage, Henry S.: *The Beginnings of Colonial Maine*; Marks Printing House, Portland, 1914.

Byrne, Frank L.: *Prophet of Prohibition, Neal Dow and his Crusade*; Peter Smith Publications, Gloucester, Mass., 1969.

Campeau, Lucien: *La Premiere Mission des Jesuites en Nouvelle France, 1611-13*; Les Editions Bellarmin, Montreal, 1972.

Chadbourne, Ava Harriet: *Maine Place Names and the Peopling of Its*

Towns; Bond-Wheelwright, Freeport, Maine, 1957 (series).

Chase, Edward E.: *Maine Railroads*; A.J. Huston, Portland, 1926.

Churchill, E. A.: *A Most Ordinary Lot of Men*; New England Quarterly, June 1984.

Clark, Calvin Montague: *American Slavery and Maine Congregationalists*; Published by the Author, Bangor, 1940.

Coffin, Harold: *Assignment in Military Intelligence*; Privately published.

Collins, Federick: *Way Down East With The K.K.K.*; Colliers, Dec. 15, 1923.

Conellan, Leo: *The Clear Blue Lobster Water Country*; (poem).

Conquest, Edward J.: *William R. Pattangall of Maine*; Published 1954.

Curran, Mary H.: *Maine Anti-Catholic Riots of 1833*; a compliation of articles.

Davis, Albert H.: *History of Ellsworth, Maine*; Lewiston Journal Printshop, Lewiston, 1927.

Dibner, Martin (ed.): *Portland*; Publication of Greater Portland Landmarks, Inc. , Portland, 1972.

Dietz, Lew: Man on the Maine Frontier, the Maine Finn; *Down East*, Jan. 1973.

Dorr, George B.: *The Story of Acadia National Park*; Acadia Publishing Co., Bar Harbor, 1942.

Dow, Joseph; *An Historical Address at Hampton, New Hampshire*; Asa M. McFarland, Concord, N.H., 1839.

Doyle, J.A.: *English Colonies in America*, Vol. III; Henry Holt & Co., New York, 1889.

Dunn, John C. (ed.): *The Revolution Remembered*; University of Chicago Press, Chicago, 1980.

Earley, Sharon: *Walter Wyman and Five Maine Mills, 1925-33*; Thesis, Bates College, Lewiston, 1973.

Eastman, Ralph M.: *Some Famous Privateers of New England*; State Street Trust, Boston, 1928.

Faulkner, Alaric: Archaeology of the Cod Fishery, Damariscove Island; *Historical Archaeology*, Vol. 19, No. 2, 1985.

Faust, Albert Bernhardt: *The German Element in the United States*, Vol. 1; Houghton-Mifflin Co., Boston, 1909.

Fay, Bernard: *Une Colonie Rhenane en Nouvelle Angletere au XVIII Siecle*.

Fecteau, Albert C.: *The French-Canadian Community of Waterville, Maine*; Thesis, University of Maine, Orono, June, 1952.

Folsom, George: *History of Saco & Biddeford*; Alex C. Putnam, Saco, 1830.

Gauvin, Marie Anne: *Linguistics and Cultural Heritage of the Acadians in Maine and New Brunswick*; Thesis, Madawaska, 1969.

Giguere, Madeleine: *A Franco-American Overview*, Vol. 3; New England Center for Bilingual and Bicultural Education, Cambridge, MA., 1981.

Godfrey, John Edwards: Claude de la Tour; *Maine Historical Society*, 1st. Series, Vol. 9, November 15, 1879.

Grant, B.J.: *When Rum Was King*; Fiddlehead Poetry Books, Fredericton, N.B.

Grant, W.L. (ed.): *Voyages of Samuel de Champlain*; Charles Scribner & Sons, New York, 1907.

Griffin, Carl R. and Faulkner, Alaric: *Coming of Age on Damariscove Island.*

Hale, Richard Jr.: *The Forgotten Maine Boundary Commission*; Massachusetts Historical Society, Vol. LXXI, December, 1954. Story of Bar Harbor; Washburn, Inc., New York, 1949.

Hamlin, Charlesm Eugene: *The Life and Times of Hannibal Hamlin*; The Riverside Press, Cambridge, MA., 1899.

Hasenfus, Nathaniel J.: The Popham Colony; *Down East*, August, 1969.

Hatch, Louis Clinton: *Maine, A History*; American Historical Society, New York, 1919.

Haugen, Einar: *Voyages to Vinland, The First American Saga*; Alfred A. Knopf, New York, 1942.

Hirshson, Stanley P.: *Farewell To The Bloody Shirt*; Indiana University Press, Bloomington, Ind., 1962.

Holbrook, Stewart: *Yankee Logger*; International Paper Co., New York, 1961.

Holmes, Herbert Edgar: *The Makers of Maine*; The Haswell Press, Lewiston, 1912.

Hooglund, Eric J.: *Crossing the Waters*; Smithsonian Institution Press, Washington, D.C. & London, 1987.

Hyde School Franco-American Studies Class: *Immigrants From The North*; Bath, 1981.

Ingstad, Helge: *Westward to Vinland*; St. Martins Press, New York, 1969.

Isaacson, Doris (ed.): *Maine, A Guide Down East*; Courier-Gazette, Inc., Rockland, 1970.

Jellison, Charles A.: *Fessenden of Maine, Civil War Senator*; Syracuse University Press, Syracuse, 1962.

The Jesuit Relations and Allied Documents, Vol. II; The Burrows Brothers Co., Cleveland, 1896.

Johnston, Edward F.: *A History of Potatoes in Maine.*

Jones, Herbert G.: *The King's Highway from Portland to Kittery*; Bond-Wheelwright, Freeport, 1953.

The Journals of each Provincial Congress in 1774 and 1775; Dutton and Wentworth, Boston, 1838.

Journals of the Massachusetts House, Vol. I, 1715-17.

Kidder, Frederick: *Military Operations in Eastern Maine and Nova Scotia During the Revolution*; Joel Munsell, Albany, 1867.

LaPomarda, Vincent A.: *The Jesuit Heritage in New England*; College of the Holy Cross, Worcester, Mass., 1977.

Laverty, Dorothy Sowler: *Millinocket, Magic City of Maine's Wilderness*; Bond-Wheelwright, Freeport, 1973.

Lawler, Jeanne: *The Russians in Richmond*; Randolph, Maine, 1954.

Leamon, James: *Historic Lewiston, A Textile CIty in Transition*; CMVTI, Auburn, Maine, 1976.

Lenentine, Charlotte: *Madawaska, A Chapter in Maine-New Brunswick Relations*; St. John Valley Publ. Co., Madawaska, 1966.

359

Libbey, Dorothy Shaw: *Scarborough Becomes a Town*; Bond-Wheelwright, Freeport, 1955.

Longfellow, Henry Wadsworth: *The Baron of St. Castine*; Kavanagh.

Lucey, William L.: The Irish Merchants of New England; *The New England Quarterly*, Vol. XIV, No. 4, December 1941.

McBeath, George (ed.): *Champlain and the St. John, 1604-1954*; New Brunswick Historical Society, St. Johns, N. B., 1954.

Maine State Federation of Labor, 1904-1954; Souvenir Program, Augusta, 1954.

Martin, Kenneth R. and Lipfert, Nathan R.: *Lobstering and the Maine Coast*; Maine Maritime Museum, Bath, 1985.

Massachusetts House of Representatives: Journals, Vol. XXXII, Part 1, 1755.

McPherson, Edward: *The Political History of the United States of America During the Period of Reconstruction*; Da Capo Press, New York, 1972.

McLeod, John: *The Great Northern Paper Co.*

Mezoin, Anthony P.: *The Armenian People of Portland, Maine*; University of New Hampshire Press, Durham, N.H. 1985.

Michaud, Charlotte: *Historic Lewiston, Franco-American Origins*; CMVTI, 1974.

Miller, Samuel: *History of the Town of Waldoboro, Maine*; Emerson Printer, Wiscasset, Maine, 1910.

Molloy, Anne: *Five Kidnapped Indians*; Hastings House, New York, 1968.

Morrison, Samuel Eliot: *Samuel de Champlain, Father of New France*.

Murchie, Guy: *St. Croix, the Sentinel River*; Duell, Sloan & Pierce, New York, 1947.

Neagle, Marjorie Spiller: The Longest Day; *Galaxy Magazine*, Spring 1975.

Nelson, William H.: *The American Tory*; Clarendon Press, Oxford, England, 1961.

O'Leary, Charles J.: *A History of Organized Labor in Maine During the New Deal*; Thesis, University of Maine, Orono, 1970.

Olsson, Andrew Werenils: *Celebration of the Decennial Anniversary of the Founding of New Sweden*; B. Thurston & Co., Portland, 1881.

Parker, Arlita Dodge: *A History of Pemaquid*; MacDonald & Evans, Boston, 1925.

Parkman, Francis: *A Half Century of War*; Pioneers of France in the New World.

Pattangall, William R.: *The Maine Democrat*; Waterville, July 16, 1909.

Pearson, Heskell: *Henry of Navarre*; Harper & Row, New York, 1963.

Perkins, Esselyn Gilman: *Wells, the Frontier Town of Maine*; Ogunquit, 1970.

Phillips, David Graham: *The Treason of the Senate*; Quadrangle Press, Chicago, 1964 (originally published, 1906).

Preston, Richard Arthur: *Gorges of Plymouth Fort*; University of Toronto Press, Toronto, 1953.

Prins, Harald: The Most Convenient Place for Trade; *The Kennebec Proprietor*, Vol 3, No. 1, Winter 1986.

Proper, Ida Sedgwick: *Monhegan, the Cradle of New England*; The Southworth Press, Portland, 1930.

Reid, John G.: *Acadia, Maine and New Scotland*; University of Toronto Press, Toronto, 1976.

Richardson, H. W.: *The Pemaquid Country Under the Stuarts*; Maine Historical Society, Vol. VIII, March 14, 1878.

Rolde, Neil: *Sir William Pepperrell of Colonial New England*; Harpswell Press, Brunswick, Maine, 1982.

Russell, Charles Edward: *Blaine of Maine*; Cosmopolitan Book Corp., New York, 1931.

Scontras, Charles A.: *Organized Labor in Maine, 20th Century*; University of Maine, Orono, 1985; *Organized Labor and Politics in Maine, 1880-1890*; University of Maine Press, Orono, 1966.

Sevigny, Father Andre: *Les Abenaquis, Habitat et Migrations*; Les Editions Bellarmin, Montreal, 1976.

Shapleigh, Maine, A History; Shapleigh, Maine, 1985.

Sherman, Sylvia J. (Ed.): *Dubros Times*; Maine State Archives, Augusta, 1975.

Skelton, William B.: *Walter S. Wyman, 1874-1942, One of Maine's Great Pioneers*; Newcomen Society, Princeton University Press, 1949.

Smith, Lincoln: *The Power Policy of Maine*; University of California Press, Berkeley & Los Angeles, 1951.

Snow, Edward Rowe: *The Romance of Casco Bay*; Dodd, Mead & Co., New York, 1975.

Snow, Ralph Linwood: *Bath Iron Works, the First Hundred Years*; Maine Maritime Museum, Bath, 1987.

Spencer, Wilbur D.: *Pioneers on Maine Rivers*; Lakeside Printing Co., Portland, 1930.

Stahl, Jasper Jacob: *History of Old Broad Bay and Waldoboro*; Bond-Wheelwright, Freeport, Portland, 1956.

Stakeman, Randolph: Slavery in Colonial Maine; *Maine Historical Society Quarterly*, Fall 1987.

Taylor, Linda Maule: *Limerick - Historical Notes*; Limerick, Maine, 1975.

Tepaske, John J. (ed.): *Three American Empires*; Harper & Row, New York, 1967.

Trelease, Allen W.: *White Terror, the KKK Conspiracy and Southern Reconstruction*; Harper & Row, New York, 1971.

Tuttle, Charles Wesley: *The Dutch Conquest of Acadia*; John Wilson & Son, Boston, 1889.

Violette, Maurice: *The Franco-Americans*; Vantage Press, New York, 1976.

Wade, Mason: *The French Parish and "Survivance" in 19th Century New England*.

Ward, Henry M.: *The United Colonies of New England*; Vantage Press, New York, 1961.

Webster, John Clarence: *Acadia at the End of the 17th Century*; New Brunswick Museum, St. Johns, 1934.

Wheeler, George Augustus: *Fort Pentagoet and the French Occupation of Castine*; Maine Historical Society, December 9, 1892.

Wheeler, George Augustus and Wheeler, Henry Warren: *History of Brunswick, Topsham and Harpswell*; Reprint, New Hampshire Publishing Co., Somersworth, N. H., 1974.

Willis, William: *The History of Portland*; Maine Historical Society, 1831.

Wing, Henry A.: *Maine's War Upon the Liquor Traffic*; Portland Evening Express, 1910.

Wood, Richard G.: *A History of Lumbering in Maine, 1820-1861*; University of Maine Press, Orono, 1935.

Index